WITHDRAWN

FOR REFERENCE

NOT TO BE TAKEN FROM THE ROOM

HISTORICAL DICTIONARIES OF
INTERNATIONAL ORGANIZATIONS SERIES
Edited by Jon Woronoff

Historical Dictionary
of the
International Monetary Fund

Second Edition

Norman K. Humphreys

Historical Dictionaries
of International Organizations, No. 17

The Scarecrow Press, Inc.
Lanham, Maryland, and London
1999

SCARECROW PRESS, INC.

Published in the United States of America
by Scarecrow Press, Inc.
4720 Boston Way, Lanham, Maryland 20706
http://www.scarecrowpress.com

4 Pleydell Gardens, Folkestone
Kent CT20 2DN, England

British Library Cataloguing in Publication Information Available

Library of Congress Cataloging-in-Publication Data

Humphreys, Norman K., 1924–
    Historical dictionary of the International Monetary Fund / Norman
K. Humphreys. -- 2nd ed.
        p. cm. (Historical dictionaries of international
organizations ; no. 17)
    Includes bibliographical references (p.)
    ISBN 0-8108-3659-9 (cloth : alk. paper)
    1. International Monetary Fund--History Dictionaries.
    2. International finance dictionaries. 3. International Monetary
Fund--History. I. Title. II. Series : Historical dictionaries of
international organizations series : no. 17.
HG3881.I58H86   1999
332.1'52--dc21   99-24226
                                                                          CIP

⊖™ The paper used in this publication meets the minimum requirements of
American National Standard for Information Sciences—Permanence of
Paper for Printed Library Materials, ANSI/NISO Z39.48–1992.
Manufactured in the United States of America.

To our grandchildren
—Angela, Carissa, Gavin, Jessica, Nathan, and Robin—
wishing them well for their future.

Contents

Editor's Foreword

Once a relatively obscure organization, known mainly to bankers and academics, over the past decade or two the International Monetary Fund, more commonly called the IMF, has become better known that it would perhaps wish. It is talked up by some as a "central bank's central bank" and main savior in the event of serious financial crises. By others it is decried as a villain imposing its will on developing countries and maybe actually being the cause of some of the crises. This debate is far from resolved; if anything it has been fueled by recent events. But what is actually more important than whether the praise and criticism, the hopes and fears are justified today is whether the IMF will be better tomorrow. In studying its history, since it was founded in 1945, the growth and changes are unmistakable. And it is clear that the IMF does learn from its mistakes and is improved and reinforced by crises.

One can see this in the second edition of the *Historical Dictionary of the International Monetary Fund*, remarkably different from the first edition less than a decade ago. While not strictly a history, it does present the IMF as it is today and also shows what it was like at earlier stages in its evolution while mentioning proposals for the future. It considers the IMF's constituent bodies, its policies, programs and rules, its action in crucial member countries, those who have played an important part in managing it, and many of the problems and crises it has gone through. The dictionary entries are supplemented by a handy chronology, a list of abbreviations and acronyms, an explanatory introduction, and a substantial bibliography. The result is a bigger and better volume on an organization that is itself bigger and better . . . although still far from ideal.

This second edition was written by the author of the first edition, who has been following events very carefully during his years with the

IMF and since his retirement. Norman K. Humphreys, a member of the staff for nearly 23 years, was its chief editor for more than a decade, during which time the IMF experienced a dramatic enhancement of its role. A graduate of the London School of Economics and Political Science, he was a banker and freelance contributor to various financial journals in the City of London for a dozen years, served as resident economist and financial correspondent in Brazil for two years, and joined the staff of the IMF in 1964. This career has provided exceptional insight into the IMF and its workings and contributed to making this volume particularly enlightening.

Jon Woronoff
Series Editor

Acknowledgments

In updating and preparing the manuscript of this second edition of the *Historical Dictionary of the International Monetary Fund*, I have again drawn extensively on the published work of others, particularly on the publications of the Fund. Much of the basic material that appeared in the first edition was drawn from the published histories of the Fund prepared by its historians J. Keith Horsefield and, subsequently, Margaret Garritsen de Vries. I have also been able to draw on the works of Sir Joseph Gold, the former general counsel of the Fund, who has written comprehensively on the legal aspects of the Fund and international monetary law.

Several of my former colleagues have been kind enough to read the manuscript and to make helpful comments on and improvements to the text. These include James Boughton, the current Fund historian, and Joseph Keyes, former assistant director in the African Department. I am also grateful to Ian McDonald, the current Fund's chief editor, and his colleagues in the Editorial Division for the generous assistance that they gave to me at various critical points in the formulaion of the manuscript. My thanks also go to my wife, Dorothy, for a patient and thoughtful reading of the manuscript in its various stages of gestation and for catching numerous errors and discrepancies.

It remains to be noted that although the factual material for this volume has been drawn mainly from "official" sources, responsibility for its accuracy and interpretation rests solely with the author.

Norman K. Humphreys

Abbreviations and Acronyms

It is the convention to refer to institutions and organizations, particularly international bodies, by their abbreviations and acronyms. This volume has tried to avoid the resultant "alphabet soup," but the abbreviations and acronyms in common use for many of these organizations, as well as the facilities, accounts, and organs of the Fund, are listed below.

ADB	Asian Development Bank
AREAER	Annual Report on Exchange Arrangements and Exchange Restrictions
ASEAN	Association of South-east Asian Nations
BCEAO	Banque Centrale des Etats de l'Afrique de l'Ouest
BEAC	Banque des Etats de l'Afrique Centrale
BIS	Bank for International Settlements
BRSA	Borrowed Resources Suspense Account
BSFF	Buffer stock financing facility
CCFF	Compensatory and contingency financing facility
CRU	Collective reserve unit
DC	Development Committee
DSBB	Data Standards Bulletin Board
EAP	Enlarged access facility
EBRD	European Bank for Reconstruction and Development
EC	European Community
ECB	European Central Bank
ECOFIN	Council of Economic and Finance Ministers
ECU	European currency unit
EFF	Enhanced structural adjustment facility
EMS	European Monetary System

EMU	Economic and Monetary Union
ESAF	Enhanced structural adjustment facility
EU	European Union
GAB	General Arrangements to Borrow
GATT	General Agreement on Tariffs and Trade
GDDS	General Data Dissemination System
GDP	Gross domestic product
GNP	Gross national product
GRA	General Resources Account
HIPC	Heavily indebted poor countries
IBRD	International Bank for Reconstruction and Development (World Bank)
IC	Interim Committee
ICSID	International Center for the Settlement of Investment Disputes
IDA	International Development Association
IDB	Inter-American Development Bank
IFC	International Finance Corporation
IMF	International Monetary Fund
ITO	International Trade Organization
MERM	Multilateral exchange rate model
NAB	New Arrangements to Borrow
NGA	Nongovernmental agencies
ODA	Official development assistance
OECD	Organization for Economic Cooperation and Development
OPEC	Organization of Petroleum Exporting Countries
PIN	Press/Public Information Notices
RAP	Rights accumulation program
SAF	Structural adjustment facility
SCA	Special Contingent Account
SDA	Special Disbursement Account
SDDS	Special Data Dissemination Standard
SDR	Special Drawing Right
SFF	Supplementary financing facility
SRF	Supplemental reserve facility
SRP	Staff Retirement Plan
SSNs	Social safety nets
STF	Systemic transformation facility
UN	United Nations
UNCTAD	United Nations Commission on Trade and Development

UNDP	United Nations Development Program
UNEP	United Nations Environmental Program
VAT	Value-added tax
WAEMU	West African Economic and Monetary Union
WEO	World Economic Outlook
WTO	World Trade Organization

Chronology

1944

July 1-22   The International Monetary and Financial Conference was held at Bretton Woods, New Hampshire, attended by representatives from 44 countries. The Articles of Agreement of the IMF and the World Bank were put in final form.

1945

December 27   The Fund's Articles of Agreement entered into force with the signatures of 29 governments, accounting for 80 percent of the original quotas.

1946

March 8-18   The inaugural meeting of the Board of Governors was held in Savannah, Georgia. It was decided that the Fund's headquarters would be in Washington, D.C., the By-laws were adopted, and the first Executive Directors were elected.

May 6   The Executive Board held its inaugural meeting, consisting of 12 Executive Directors, five appointed by each of the five members having the largest quotas in the Fund, and seven elected by groups of members. Camille Gutt, of Belgium, became the first Managing Director of the Fund.

September 27   The first Annual Meetings of the Boards of Governors of the Fund and the World Bank opened in Washington, D.C.

December 18   Initial par values were agreed upon for most members and their nonmetropolitan areas.

1947

March 1   The Fund opened its doors for financial operations.

May 8   The first drawing on the Fund was made by France, for $25 million.

December 18   The Fund circulated a letter to all members, setting out its policies on multiple currency practices.

1948

January 25   The Fund first exercised its authority over members' exchange rates by objecting to a proposed change in the par value of the French franc on the grounds that it involved the introduction of a multiple currency practice.

September 19   The pound sterling was devalued, a move that was followed in the next few days by similar devaluations by a number of other members.

1950

March 1   The first issue of the *Annual Report on Exchange Restrictions* was published (renamed the *Annual Report on Exchange Arrangement and Exchange Restrictions* after the par value system collapsed in the 1970s).

1951

August 3   Ivar Rooth, of Sweden, became the second Managing Director of the Fund.

1952

February 13   The Fund codified its policies on the use of its resources, establishing the tranche policies. Members were allowed virtually automatic use of their gold tranche. A period of three to five years was established for repayments to the Fund. In addition, a general framework was agreed upon for use of the Fund's resources under what later came to be known as "stand-by arrangements."

March 1   In accordance with its Articles, the Fund began annual consultations with members who were maintaining exchange restrictions under Article XIV five years after the Fund began financial operations.

June 19   The Fund entered into its first stand-by arrangement, with Belgium.

1956

September 7   Per Jacobsson, of Sweden, became the third Managing Director of the Fund.

October 17   The Fund approved drawings and stand-by arrangements for France and the United Kingdom, prompted in part by the loss of revenue from the closing of the Suez Canal. These drawings were the first major use made of the Fund's resources by advanced industrial countries and served to signal that the Fund would be a significant player in the international financial community.

1958

December 29   Fourteen Western European countries made their currencies externally convertible for current transactions. Nonresidents were able to freely transfer holdings of one currency into any other currency. It was the first major step toward the multilateral trading system envisioned in the Articles of Agreement.

1959

September 9   The first general increase in Fund quotas became effective, raising total quotas from $9.2 billion to $14 billion.

1961

February 15   Nine Western European countries accepted the obligations of Article VIII, thereby making all major currencies convertible.

1962

October 24   The General Arrangements to Borrow went into effect, whereby the 10 largest industrial members agreed to be on call to lend the Fund the equivalent of $6 billion if needed to prevent a disruption of the international payments system. The participants were Belgium, Canada, France, Germany, Italy, Japan, the Netherlands, Sweden, the United Kingdom, and the United States. The arrangements were the beginning of the so-called Group of Ten.

1963

February 27   The compensatory financing facility was established. Under the facility, members experiencing temporary shortfalls in their export earnings could draw on the Fund. It was the first of the facilities established to finance a particular element in a country's balance of payments, rather than dealing with the balance of payments as a whole. Other later facilities were the oil facilities, the buffer stock financing facility, the emergency assistance facility, the structural adjustment facility, and the systemic transformation facility.

May 5 Per Jacobsson, the Fund's Managing Director, died in office.

September 1 Pierre-Paul Schweitzer, of France, became the fourth Managing Director.

September 27 The Managing Director announced in his opening address to the Annual Meetings that the question of international liquidity was the business of the Fund and that the Fund would be intensifying its studies on the problem. The announcement was a contradiction of the Group of Ten's efforts to make international liquidity a matter of concern only to the industrial countries and to limit any scheme for reserve creation to those countries.

1965

October 15 The Executive Board agreed to a four-year renewal of the General Arrangements to Borrow, as from October 24, 1966. The terms of the arrangements were left unchanged, providing for the Fund to borrow up to the equivalent of $6 billion from 10 members.

1966

February 23 A second general increase of 25 percent in quotas was agreed to, along with special increases for 16 members. Total quotas in the Fund rose, as a result, from $16 billion to $21 billion.

March 3 The Managing Director proposed to the Executive Board, and then to the Group of Ten, an approach to reserve creation through the Fund that would include distribution of any new reserve assets to all members. It was an approach that would culminate in the Special Drawing Rights (SDRs) scheme three years later.

September 20 The compensatory financing facility, introduced in 1963, was extended and liberalized.

November 23 It was agreed that Executive Directors of the Fund, representing all Fund members, would hold a series of meetings with Deputies of the Group of Ten to discuss reserve creation schemes. These meetings, in effect, brought representatives of Third World countries face-to-face with their counterparts from the industrial countries for the first time in discussing problems of international liquidity.

November 28-30 The first joint meeting of the Executive Directors and Deputies of the Group of Ten, held in Washington, D.C., was a further step toward a universal reserve creation scheme.

1967

January 25-26 A second meeting of the Executive Directors and the Deputies of the Group of Ten, held in London, began to consider seriously a plan based on SDRs.

April 25-26 The Executive Directors and Deputies of the Group of Ten met for a third time, in Washington, D.C.

June 19-21 The Executive Directors and Deputies of the Group of Ten met for the fourth time, in London. The SDR scheme began to take final shape.

August 26 The ministers and governors of the Group of Ten met in London and agreed on voting majorities and reconstitution provisions for an SDR facility.

September 29 At the Annual Meetings held in Rio de Janeiro the Board of Governors adopted a resolution, to which was attached an *Outline of a Facility Based on Special Drawing Rights in the Fund*, requesting the Executive Board to begin drafting appropriate amendments to the Articles of Agreement, incorporating the new facility and other, mostly minor, reforms into the Articles.

November 19-29 The United Kingdom devalued the pound sterling from $2.80 to $2.40 per pound. The Fund approved a stand-by arrangement for the United Kingdom in the amount of $1.4 billion.

1968

March 16 A two-tier market for gold was established as a result of a decision by the central banks from seven industrial member countries to buy and sell gold at the official price of $35 an ounce only in transactions with monetary authorities. The price at which private transactions in gold were transacted was thus left to be determined by supply and demand.

March 29-30 The ministers and governors of the Group of Ten met in Stockholm, Sweden, to resolve several issues in the proposed first amendment to the Articles of

	Agreement that were being drafted by the Executive Directors.
April 16	The Executive Board completed its work on the amendment to the Articles and submitted its report to the Board of Governors.
May 31	The Board of Governors approved the proposed first amendment, which was then submitted to members for acceptance and ratification.
June 4-19	Heavy use was made of the Fund's financial resources when France drew $645 million and the United Kingdom drew $1.4 billion under stand-by arrangements approved in November 1967.
September 20	Prompted by what they considered to be the favorable terms of the stand-by arrangement approved for the United Kingdom in 1967, Executive Directors representing the developing countries successfully pressed for the adoption of guidelines that would ensure uniform and equitable treatment for all members in the use of the Fund's financial resources.

1969

June 20	A new stand-by arrangement, in the amount of $1 billion, was approved for the United Kingdom.
June 25	The buffer stock financing facility was established.
June 28	The first amendment to the Articles of Agreement entered into force, authorizing the establishment of the SDR facility and introducing a number of minor operational reforms.
August 6	The Special Drawing Account was established, setting the stage for a distribution of SDRs in the years 1970-72.
August 10	France devalued the franc by 11.1 percent.
September 19	A stand-by arrangement, for $985 million, was approved for France.
September 29	In the face of persistent surpluses in its balance of payments, the Federal Republic of Germany allowed the rate for the deutsche mark to float.
October 3	The Board of Governors approved the Managing Director's proposal to make an allocation of SDRs, amounting to SDR 9.3 billion over a basic period of three years, beginning January 1, 1970. This was the first allocation of SDRs.
October 17	The Executive Board approved a second renewal of the General Arrangements to Borrow, under which the

Fund could borrow up to the equivalent of $6 billion from its 10 largest industrial members. The renewal was for five years, to begin October 24, 1970.

October 28   The Federal Republic of Germany ended the floating of its currency by revaluing the deutsche mark by 8.39 percent.

1970

January 1   The first allocation of SDRs was made, for SDR 3.5 billion, distributed among 104 participants, with the largest participant, the United States, receiving SDR 867 million and the participant with the smallest quota, Botswana, receiving SDR 504,000.

February 9   A third general increase in Fund quotas was approved by the Board of Governors, raising total quotas from $21.3 billion to $28.9 billion, an increase of 36 percent.

November 25   The International Tin Agreement became the first commodity agreement for which use of the buffer stock financing facility was authorized.

1971

January 1   The second allocation of SDRs was for SDR 2.9 billion, distributed among 109 participants.

May 9-11   In the face of heavy capital movements, the Federal Republic of Germany and the Netherlands allowed the rates for their currencies to float. Austria revalued its currency, and Belgium-Luxembourg enlarged their free market for capital transactions.

July 16   The first purchases under the buffer stock financing facility were made by Bolivia and Indonesia.

August 15   The United States announced that it would no longer freely buy and sell gold for the settlement of international transactions, thus suspending the convertibility of the dollar held by official institutions. The announcement, in effect, brought to an end the Bretton Woods system, although there was an attempt to maintain a fixed-rate (i.e., central rate) exchange rate system for another 18 months, before the Bretton Woods system finally collapsed and generalized floating became the norm.

August 16   For the next four months exchange rates were in total disarray, with Fund members introducing various exchange rate arrangements, including floating currencies by some members.

December 17-18   The Group of Ten concluded the Smithsonian agreement, providing for the realignment of the major currencies and an increase in the official price of gold from $35 to $38 an ounce. It was the first time that exchange rates had been negotiated in a multinational conference.

December 18   The Fund formally established a temporary regime of central rates and wider margins, set at 2.25 percent either side of an established central rate, thereby providing for an overall margin of 4.5 percent.

1972

January 1   The third and final allocation of SDRs, amounting to SDR 2.95 billion, was made for the first basic period.

March 20   The Board of Governors authorized the Fund to express its accounts in terms of the SDR instead of U.S. dollars.

April 24   The European Community's (EC's) narrow margins agreement went into effect for six currencies, limiting margins to 2.25 percent, half the margin established under the Fund's temporary regime of central rates.

May 8   A new par value for the U.S. dollar was established, based on the new price of gold of $38 an ounce agreed at the Smithsonian Institution in December 1971.

June 23   The British authorities announced that the pound sterling would float. This action was the first break in the pattern of rates established by the Smithsonian agreement.

July 26   The Committee of Twenty (formally known as the Committee of the Board of Governors on Reform of the International Monetary System and Related Issues) was established to negotiate a reformed international monetary system.

September 6   The Executive Board published a report, *Reform of the International Monetary System,* establishing a base for further study and discussion.

September 28   The Committee of Twenty held its inaugural meeting, setting a target of two years to complete its work.

1973

January 1   A second basic period began, in which no SDRs were allocated.

January 22-23   Italy introduced a free market for capital transactions and Switzerland floated the Swiss franc, further undermining the Smithsonian agreement.

March 19   The EC countries introduced a joint float for their currencies against the U.S. dollar. This marked the beginning of generalized floating and the end of the attempt to maintain an international system of fixed rates.

March 22-27   In view of the final breakdown of a regulated system, the Deputies of the Committee of Twenty embarked with urgency on the drafting of an outline of a reformed system. The Committee, reflecting the desire of the international financial community, reiterated its preference for a new exchange rate regime based on "stable but adjustable par values."

May 21-July 31   The Deputies of the Committee of Twenty drafted an *Outline of Reform*, and the Committee of Twenty held its third meeting.

September 1   H. Johannes Witteveen, of the Netherlands, became the fifth Managing Director of the Fund.

September 5-24   The Deputies of the Committee of Twenty met in Paris and failed to agree on arrangements for a reformed international monetary system. Later, at a meeting of the Committee of Twenty, held in Nairobi in conjunction with the Annual Meeting of the Board of Governors, it became clear that there would be no early agreement on reforming the system.

October 10-17   Six members of the Organization of Petroleum Exporting Countries (OPEC), meeting alone, increased prices for crude oil by about 70 percent. The meeting was a forerunner of future crude oil price increases that would disrupt the world economy throughout the 1970s.

December 23   Six oil exporting countries again announced increases in the prices of crude oil, thus nearly quadrupling prices that had come into effect three months earlier.

1974

January 3   The Managing Director of the Fund proposed the establishment of a temporary facility in the Fund to finance members' balance of payments deficits caused by the additional costs of oil imports.

January 17-18   The Committee of Twenty, meeting in Rome, suspended efforts for a full-scale reform of the international monetary system. The Fund staff presented the Committee with its estimate that in 1974 the aggregate balance of payments deficit of developing countries would be of an unprecedented magnitude.

May 7-9   The Deputies of the Committee of Twenty completed a draft of a revised *Outline of Reform* and discussed the immediate steps required to move existing arrangements forward.

June 10-11   The Deputies of the Committee of Twenty held a final meeting and completed their recommendations.

June 12-13   At its final meeting, the Committee of Twenty agreed on a number of immediate steps to help the international monetary system evolve and on an *Outline of Reform* that the international monetary authorities should endeavor to work out and implement in the future. The immediate steps included the establishment of an Interim Committee, with advisory powers; the adoption of a method of valuing the SDR based on a basket of 16 currencies; establishment of guidelines for the management of floating exchange rates; establishment of an oil facility in the Fund; provision for members to pledge, on a voluntary basis, not to intensify restrictions; early adoption of an extended facility in the Fund, whereby developing countries could use Fund financing on terms of up to 10 years to address structural changes in their economies; and the establishment of a committee to study the question of the transfer of real resources to developing countries.

July 1   The Fund introduced a new method of valuing the SDR, based on a basket of the 16 currencies most used in world trade instead of gold.

August 22   First use was made of the oil facility.

September 13 An extended facility was established in the Fund to give medium-term assistance to developing member countries.

September 30 The Managing Director proposed that another larger oil facility be established for 1975.

October 2   The Interim Committee of the Fund's Board of Governors on the International Monetary System was established, as was the Joint Ministerial Committee of the Boards of Governors of the Bank and Fund on the Transfer of Real Resources to Developing Countries (the Development Committee).

October 23   The General Arrangements to Borrow were renewed
                  for the third time, until October 1980.

1975

January 15-16   The Interim Committee recommended the establish-
                  ment of an oil facility for 1975 and a Subsidy Ac-
                  count to help the most seriously affected developing
                  countries defray the interest cost of using the facility.
                  It was also agreed that under the sixth general review
                  total quotas should be increased from SDR 29.2 bil-
                  lion to SDR 39 billion, with the quotas of oil export-
                  ing members as a group being doubled.
March 14   An oil facility for 1975 was established.
August 1   A Subsidy Account was established to assist the
                  Fund's most seriously affected members to meet the
                  cost of using the 1975 oil facility.
August 31   The Interim Committee agreed upon the sale of one-
                  sixth of the Fund's gold (25 million ounces) for the
                  benefit of developing members, the establishment of
                  a Trust Fund, and the restitution of one-sixth of the
                  Fund's gold to all members.
November 15-17   The first economic summit meeting was held by six
                  industrial nations in Rambouillet, France. The U.S.
                  and French monetary authorities settled their differ-
                  ences on the exchange rate system that was to be in-
                  corporated in the amended Articles of Agreement of
                  the Fund.
December 24   The compensatory financing facility, which had been
                  established in 1963 and liberalized in 1966, was fur-
                  ther liberalized. The changes included a technical
                  change in the method of calculating export shortfalls
                  so that the shortfalls could be larger than under the
                  previous procedure, and that drawings under the facil-
                  ity would be allowed up to a larger proportion of a
                  member's quota.
December 31   The United Kingdom drew SDR 1 billion under the
                  1975 oil facility and the Fund approved a one-year
                  stand-by arrangement for SDR 700 million, in the
                  first credit tranche.

1976

January 7-8   Meeting in Jamaica, the Interim Committee agreed on
                  an interim reform of the international monetary sys-
                  tem, to be legalized in a second amendment to the Ar-

ticles of Agreement. The Committee's conclusions included agreement on exchange arrangements, the treatment of gold, establishment of the Trust Fund for developing countries, and the distribution of quota increases among individual members. The quota increases were subject to the second amendment coming into effect, but until that time the Committee agreed to a temporary enlargement of members' access to the Fund's resources under existing quotas.

January 19 Following the recommendation by the Interim Committee, the Executive Board extended the size of each credit tranche by 45 percent, enabling members to increase their potential for drawing on the Fund's regular resources by that amount, pending the coming into effect of the sixth general review of quotas.

April 30 The Board of Governors approved the proposed second amendment to the Articles of Agreement, which was then submitted to member governments for acceptance and ratification.

May 5 The Fund announced a program to dispose of one-third of its gold holdings, one-sixth to be sold by auction over a two-year period and one-sixth to be restituted to members. The Trust Fund was established.

November 3 Participants in the General Arrangements to Borrow agreed that Japan should almost quadruple its commitment under the arrangements, thereby raising the total amount available to about SDR 6.2 billion.

1977

January 3 The Executive Board approved a two-year stand-by arrangement for the United Kingdom for SDR 3.36 billion, the largest amount ever approved.

January 25 The Fund made the first loans to 12 members from the Trust Fund.

February 23 The Fund completed the first of four annual restitutions of gold to its members, amounting to six million ounces, sold at the official price of SDR 35 an ounce to 112 members in proportion to their quotas.

April 29 The Executive Board took its first decision on how "firm surveillance" of members' exchange rate policies would be implemented after the second amendment became effective. It agreed on three broad principles: (1) members should avoid manipulating exchange rates to gain unfair advantage; (2) members

	should intervene in exchange markets to counter disorderly conditions; and (3) members should take into account in their intervention policies the interests of other members.
August 6	The Managing Director invited 14 potential lenders to the Fund to meet in Paris to discuss the amounts and terms on which they would lend to the Fund to establish a supplementary financing facility in the Fund. The borrowed resources would be used to supplement the Fund's regular resources, enabling members to draw resources from the Fund in excess of their credit tranches, with longer repayment terms.
August 29	The supplementary financing facility was established, to become effective when loan commitments totaling not less than SDR 7.75 billion were in effect.

1978

March 13	The quota increases resulting from the sixth general review went into effect.
April 1	The second amendment to the Articles of Agreement went into effect, after three-fifths of the membership representing four-fifths of total voting power had accepted the increases. The relevant resolution had been submitted to the membership on April 30, 1976, and its acceptance by the requisite number of members and votes had taken nearly two years.
April 29-30	The Interim Committee, meeting in Mexico City, agreed on a coordinated strategy to regenerate growth in a stagnant world economy.
June 16-17	Jacques de Larosière, of France, succeeded Witteveen as the sixth Managing Director of the Fund.
September 24	The Interim Committee recommended an increase of 50 percent in the overall size of members' quotas under the seventh general review, raising total quotas from SDR 39 billion to SDR 59.5 billion. The Committee also agreed on an allocation of SDRs of SDR 4 billion in each of the three years 1979, 1980, and 1981, the third basic period.
December 4-5	The European Council agreed to introduce the European Monetary System on January 1, 1979.

1979

January 1	SDR 4 billion were allocated to 137 Fund members as the first of three annual allocations in the basic pe-

	riod 1979-81.
February 23	The supplementary financing facility became operative after lending commitments had reached SDR 7.5 billion.
March 2	The Executive Board completed a comprehensive review of conditionality attached to the use of the Fund's financial resources, the first such review since 1968. The review codified and clarified existing guidelines on the use of the Fund's general resources (i.e., resources not borrowed or held by the Trust Fund).
March 7	The Interim Committee, meeting in Washington, D.C., asked the Executive Board to set up a substitution account that would accept deposits in foreign exchange from members on a voluntary basis in exchange for an equivalent amount of SDR-denominated claims. Such an account had been discussed extensively by the Committee of Twenty and other bodies as part of the reform of the international monetary system. The Interim Committee's proposal did not come to fruition.
March 13	The European Monetary System came into existence.
April 12	The Tokyo Round of Multilateral Trade Negotiations was concluded.
June 28	The OPEC announced an increase of 24 percent in the price of crude oil. This large increase, which followed smaller increases announced a few months earlier, raised the "marker" price of oil by 42 percent over its 1978 level (i.e., from $12.70 to $18.00 a barrel).
August 2	The compensatory financing facility was further liberalized by, among other things, permitting receipts from travel and from workers' remittances to be taken into account in calculating shortfalls.
August 24	The General Arrangements to Borrow were renewed, for the fourth time, for another five years, until October 23, 1985.
December 3	The maximum repayment period under the extended facility was increased from eight to 10 years.

1980

January 1	The Fund allocated SDR 4 billion to 139 members, the second of three annual allocations to be made in the third basic period.
April 17	The People's Republic of China was recognized as a member of the Fund.

April 25   The Interim Committee, meeting in Hamburg, agreed that the Fund should play a growing role in the adjustment and financing of payments imbalances and the recycling of funds of surplus balance of payments countries to members in balance of payments deficit. It was recognized that further Fund borrowing and longer terms of repayment for members in balance of payments deficit were needed. The Committee, reversing a position that it had taken earlier, concluded that agreement on a substitution account was unlikely in the foreseeable future.

May 7   The gold sales program agreed in August 1975 was completed. Under the program, 25 million ounces of gold had been sold (restituted) to countries that were members of the Fund on August 31, 1975, at the official price of SDR 35 an ounce. In addition, 25 million ounces of gold had been auctioned over a four-year period, raising a total of SDR 4.6 billion, of which $1.3 billion had been distributed directly to 104 developing members and the balance, together with income from investments, had been made available for concessional loans by the Trust Fund to 62 eligible members.

September 8   China's quota in the Fund, which had remained at SDR 550 million set in the original Articles, was increased to SDR 1.2 billion.

September 17   The Executive Board took a number of decisions to enhance the attractiveness of the SDR, the most important of which were reducing the basket from 16 to five currencies (U.S. dollar, deutsche mark, French franc, pound sterling, and Japanese yen) and raising the rate of interest on the SDR to the market rate.

September 27   The Interim Committee, meeting in Washington, D.C., recommended that potential Fund assistance to members be enlarged to 200 percent of quota over a three-year period, up to a total of 600 percent, excluding use of the compensatory financing facility and the buffer stock financing facility.

November 29   The increase in quotas under the seventh general review became effective, raising the Fund's general resources from SDR 39.8 billion to SDR 60.0 billion.

December 17   A subsidy account for the supplementary financing facility was established.

1981

January 1   The third and final allocation of SDRs, amounting to SDR 4.0 billion, was made to 141 members for the third basic period.

March 11   In accordance with the Interim Committee's earlier recommendation, the Executive Board introduced a policy of "enlarged access." Under the new policy, the Fund could approve stand-by or extended arrangements for up to 150 percent of a member's new quota each year, for a period of three years, with a cumulative limit of 600 percent of quota.

March 31   The final loan disbursement from the Trust Fund, which was established in May 1976, brought total disbursements from the Trust to SDR 3 billion.

May 6-7   After the Executive Board had authorized the Managing Director to borrow from the Saudi Arabian Monetary Agency, the Fund concluded an agreement under which the Agency would lend the Fund SDR 4 billion in the first year of the commitment period and up to SDR 8 billion in the second year of a six-year commitment period. These commitments enabled the enlarged access policy to become operative.

May 13   The compensatory financing facility was again amended to cover financing to members that encountered balance of payments difficulties caused by an excessive rise in the cost of cereal imports that were largely beyond the control of the member. The amendment was expected to be of particular benefit to low-income countries.

May 21   The Interim Committee, meeting in Gabon, emphasized the need for effective adjustment policies among members and urged the Executive Board to work on the eighth general review of quotas.

May 31   The quota for Saudi Arabia was increased from SDR 1 billion to SDR 2.1 billion, in view of its enlarged role in the world economy resulting from the oil price increases in the 1970s.

June 9   As required under the Articles, the Managing Director consulted with participants in the SDR facility and found no consensus in favor of allocations for the fourth basic period, to begin on January 1, 1982.

August 4   The Fund reached agreement with the Bank for International Settlements and with the central banks or monetary agencies of 16 industrial countries to lend the Fund the equivalent of SDR 1.3 billion over a period of two years.

September 27   The Interim Committee, after a two-day meeting in Washington, D.C., again urged industrial countries to reduce inflation and noted concern about the problems of adjustment and financing in non-oil developing countries. While agreeing that the Fund should continue its borrowing efforts, the Committee stressed that the Fund should rely on quota increases as the basic source for its funds and urged that the eighth general review of quotas be expedited.

1982

January 13   The Executive Board established guidelines for borrowing by the Fund stipulating that total outstanding borrowing, plus unused credit lines, should not exceed 50 to 60 percent of total quotas.

May 12-13   The Interim Committee, meeting in Helsinki, called for quotas to be the primary source of the Fund's resources, a commitment to complete the eighth general review of quotas, and effective surveillance of exchange rates for all members.

August 13   Mexico closed its foreign exchange market in the face of serious difficulty in servicing its foreign debt. This marked the onset of the debt crisis that was to affect many developing countries in the ensuing years.

December 23   The Fund approved a three-year extended arrangement for Mexico of SDR 3.6 billion to support a medium-term adjustment program.

1983

January 1   The year opened with a general recognition by the world's monetary authorities that a major and widespread debt crisis among developing countries was at hand. The Chairman of the Interim Committee called for an early meeting of the Interim Committee.

January 18   The Group of Ten agreed to a major enlargement of the General Arrangements to Borrow, from SDR 6.4 billion to SDR 17 billion, with additional lenders and revisions in its terms to allow the arrangements to be used for drawings from the Fund by all members.

January 24   The Fund approved a stand-by arrangement and compensatory financing drawing for Argentina totaling SDR 2 billion.

February 10-11   The Interim Committee, meeting in Washington, D.C., recommended an increase in quotas under the eighth general review that would enlarge total quotas from SDR 61 billion to SDR 90 billion.

February 28   The Fund approved an extended arrangement for Brazil for SDR 5 billion.

May 20   A borrowing arrangement with Saudi Arabia, associated with the General Arrangements to Borrow, was approved by the Executive Board in the maximum amount of the equivalent of SDR 1.5 billion.

September 25   The Interim Committee, meeting in Washington, D.C., endorsed the Managing Director's strategy of adjustment and financing for dealing with the debt problems of developing countries and agreed that the temporary enlarged access policy on Fund resources should be continued and that there should be new access limits under that policy.

November 30   The increased quotas under the eighth general review went into effect.

1984

January 6   The policy on enlarged access was extended until the end of the year, but access limits were set in terms of the new quotas established under the eighth general review. Thus, annual limits were set at 102 or 125 percent of quota, three-year limits at 306 or 375 percent, and cumulative limits at 408 or 500 percent, depending on the seriousness of the member's balance of payments need and the strength of its adjustment efforts. Similarly, the limits under the compensatory financing facility were reduced, as were those set for the buffer stock financing facility.

April 24   The Fund concluded four new short-term borrowing agreements, totaling SDR 6 billion, with the Saudi Arabian Monetary Agency, the Bank for International Settlements, Japan, and the National Bank of Belgium.

November 16   The policy of enlarged access was extended to the end of 1985 and access limits were reduced in accordance with the request of the Interim Committee. The new annual limits were set at 95 or 115 percent of quota (instead of 102 or 125 percent), three-year limits at 280 or 345 percent (instead of 306 or 375 percent), and cumulative limits at 408 or 450 percent (instead of 408 or 500 percent), depending on the severity of the member's balance of payments difficulties and the strength of the adjustment effort.

December 28   The Fund approved a drawing of SDR 1.7 billion for Argentina under a stand-by arrangement and the compensatory financing facility.

1985

March 25   In its review of surveillance procedures, the Executive Board stressed the need for "evenhandedness" of surveillance of all members and put forward suggestions for improving the surveillance procedures by the Fund.

April 17-19   The Interim Committee, meeting in Washington, D.C., reiterated that adjustment in economic policies of members was essential and unavoidable to correct external imbalances and called for improvements in the effectiveness of surveillance over policies of members.

May 3   The Executive Board extended for four years, until May 1989, the coverage of the compensatory financing facility to cereal imports.

September 25   Members of the Group of Five met in New York and agreed to pursue a policy of coordinated intervention in the foreign exchange markets to reduce the value of the dollar.

October 6-7   The Interim Committee, meeting in Seoul, stressed the need for noninflationary growth policies for industrial countries, for renewed growth in developing countries, and for adequate financing support of developing countries in their adjustment efforts.

1986

March 26   The structural adjustment facility was established with funds that accumulated in the Special Disbursement Account, and the low-income countries eligible to use the facility were listed.

July 25   The Fund established the principle of "burden sharing," whereby the rate of charge was increased on the use of the Fund's resources and the rate of remuneration was reduced on creditor positions in order to strengthen the Fund's reserve position. A special contingency account was established to supplement the Fund's general reserve.

1987

January 16   Michel Camdessus, of France, became the seventh Managing Director of the Fund.

November 23   The General Arrangements to Borrow were renewed for a period of five years from December 26, 1988.

December 18   The enhanced structural adjustment facility was established.

1988

April 20   The initial maximum limit on access of each eligible member to the enhanced facility was set at 250 percent of quota, with a provision that this limit could be increased to 350 percent of quota in exceptional cases. The interest rate on loans was set at 0.5 percent.

June 6   The mix of ordinary and borrowed resources for purchases under the enlarged access policy was set at the ratio of two to one in the first credit tranche and one to two in the next three credit tranches. Thereafter, purchases were to be made with borrowed resources. Purchases under extended arrangements were to be made with ordinary resources up to 140 percent of quota, and thereafter with borrowed funds.

1989

May 19   The compensatory and contingency financing facility was established, extending the Fund's financing to members in balance of payments difficulties for: (1) temporary export shortfalls; (2) adverse external contingencies; (3) excess cost of cereal imports; and (4) temporarily, for excess cost of oil imports.

1990

March 16   The Managing Director outlined the timetable for dealing with members having overdue obligations to the Fund, leading to compulsory withdrawal from the Fund up to two years after the emergence of arrears.

June 20   The Executive Board adopted the "rights" approach to overdue obligations. A member in arrears to the Fund would be able to earn rights, conditioned on a satisfactory performance under an adjustment program monitored by the Fund, toward a disbursement by the Fund once the member's overdue obligations had been cleared and upon approval of a successor arrangement by the Fund.

June 28   The Board of Governors adopted a resolution that increased by 50 percent the quotas of members under the ninth general review of quotas; no increase was to become effective until members having not less than either 85 percent or 70 percent (depending on whether the determination was made before or after December 30, 1991) of total quotas had consented to the increase and not before the effective date of the third amendment of the Articles. The proposed third amendment to the Articles of Agreement was also adopted by the Board of Governors on this date.

October 5   The Executive Board reviewed the currencies and their weights making up the SDR basket and determined that the list of currencies and their weights should be as follows: the U.S. dollar (with a weight of 40), the deutsche mark (21), Japanese yen (17), French franc (11), and pound sterling (11).

December 5   In view of the Middle East crisis, the Executive Board took a number of decisions to help members face unexpected economic difficulties. The measures included (1) suspending, until the end of 1991, the lower annual, three-year, and cumulative borrowing limits under the enlarged access policy; (2) increasing the financing under the enhanced structural adjustment policies at the time of midyear reviews for such arrangements and, where necessary, adding a fourth year to those programs due to be completed before November 1992; (3) adding an oil import element to the compensatory and contingency financing facility; and (4) providing for a contingency mechanism to be attached to current Fund arrangements at the time that they come up for review.

1991

March 1   The Fund published a joint study of the Soviet economy by the Fund, World Bank, Organization for Economic Cooperation and Development, and European Bank for Reconstruction and Development.

October 14   Michel Camdessus, of France, was reappointed Managing Director of the Fund for a term of five years.

1992

May 4   The Board of Governors approved membership resolu-

	tions for Russia and 14 other states of the former Soviet Union.
November 9	The Executive Board announced new access limits on the amounts of financing available to members that would apply once the 50 percent increase in quotas under the ninth general review of quotas went into effect. It terminated the enlarged access policy in effect since 1981, under which the Fund supplemented its quota resources with borrowed funds. The new limits, expressed in terms of the new quotas, were intended to maintain members' access to the Fund's resources.
November 11	The quota increases under the ninth general review of quotas entered into force, providing for an increase in a member's quota of nearly 50 percent and for total quotas in the Fund to rise from SDR 97.4 billion to about SDR 145 billion ($200 billion). At the same time, the third amendment to the Articles of Agreement became effective, providing for the removal of voting and other rights of "ineligible" members.

1993

April 16	The Executive Board approved the creation of the systemic transformation facility—to assist countries facing balance of payments difficulties arising from transformation from a planned to a market economy—to be in place through 1994.
April 27	Tajikistan was the fifteenth and the last of the countries of the former Soviet Union to join the Fund.
June 30	The Fund approved a drawing by Russia amounting to SDR 1.1 billion ($1.5 billion) under the systemic transformation facility.

1994

January 12	The CFA franc was devalued. The CFA franc zone consisted of seven members of the West African Economic and Monetary Union, six members of the Banque des états de l'Afrique Centrale, and the Comoros. The devaluations were followed in the ensuing weeks by Fund arrangements for 13 of the countries.
February 23	The Executive Board initiated operations under the renewed and enlarged enhanced structural adjustment facility.
June 6	The Fund announced the creation of three Deputy Managing Director posts.

October 2   The Interim Committee adopted the Madrid Declaration calling industrial countries to sustain growth, reduce unemployment, and prevent a resurgence of inflation; developing countries to extend growth; and transition economies to pursue bold stabilization and reform efforts.

1995

February 1   The Executive Board approved a stand-by arrangement of SDR 12.1 billion for Mexico, the largest financial commitment in the Fund's history.

September 12   Emergency financing mechanism approved by the Executive Board.

1996

March 26   The Executive Board approved an SDR 6.9 billion extended Fund facility (EFF) for Russia—the largest EFF in the Fund's history.

April 16   The Fund established a voluntary special data dissemination standard for member countries having, or seeking, access to international capital markets. A general data dissemination system would be implemented later.

September   The Interim and Development Committees endorsed a joint initiative for heavily indebted poor countries.

1997

January 27   The Executive Board approved New Arrangements to Borrow as the first and principal recourse in the event of a need to provide supplementary resources to the Fund.

April 25   The Executive Board approved the issuance of Press/Public Information Notices (PINs) following the conclusion of members' Article IV consultations with the Fund—at the request of members—to make the Fund's views known to the public.

May   The Fund reclassified, for statistical purposes, several newly industrialized economies in Asia (Hong Kong SAR, Singapore, and Taiwan Province of China), as well as Israel, in the group of countries classified as industrial countries and renamed this expanded group of countries "advanced economies." The reclassification reflected the advanced stage of development in

	these economies and the characteristics that they now shared with the industrial countries.
May 19	The Fund issued its first PIN after concluding its Article IV consultation with the Kingdom of the Netherlands: Aruba. Two additional PINs followed on June 5 for Belize and Tunisia.
July 2	Thailand introduced a managed float for its currency, the baht, followed by a prompt depreciation of the currency of about 20 percent.
July 11	Following increased pressure on its reserves, accentuated by the float of the baht a few days earlier, the Philippine authorities allowed the peso to float.
August 4	The Executive Board adopted guidelines covering the role of the Fund on the issue of governance.
September 1	The Fund opened its Regional Office for Asia and the Pacific in Tokyo.
September 25	The Board of Governors adopted a Resolution approving a special, one-time SDR equity allocation of SDR 21.4 billion that would equalize all members' ratio of SDRs to quotas at 29.3 percent, and it also agreed on a 45 percent increase in members' quotas.
October 11	Indonesia adopted the first of its economic programs to cope with the Asian economic and financial crisis.
November 5	The Fund approved an SDR 10 billion three-year stand-by arrangement for Indonesia.
December 4	The Executive Board approved an SDR 21 billion stand-by credit for Korea. Fund assistance was requested by Korea on November 21, and negotiation of the arrangement was concluded with unprecedented speed.
December 17	The Executive Board approved the establishment of the supplemental reserve facility to provide financial assistance to a member country experiencing balance of payments difficulties due to a short-term financing need resulting from a sudden and disruptive loss of market confidence reflected in capital flight.

1998

January 15	Indonesia adopted a reinforced Fund-supported reform program after Indonesian financial markets had declined sharply, as investors expressed doubts over the country's commitment to reform.
February 6	The Board of Governors adopted a Resolution proposing an increase of 45 percent in the total Fund quotas

to approximately SDR 212 billion (about $288 billion). The increase would only become effective when members having not less than 85 percent of total quotas have consented to the increase in their quotas.

February 19 — The Fund and Russia agreed to extend the current SDR 10 billion extended Fund facility credit for an additional year and to augment the Fund's financial assistance under the program.

March 24 — Malaysia introduced a package of measures to strengthen its financial sector and rebalance its macroeconomic policies.

April 27 — The Interim Committee adopted a Code of Good Practices on fiscal transparency.

May 4 — The Fund-Singapore Regional Training Institute was opened.

June 24 — The Indonesian government and the Fund signed a new agreement aimed at halting the deterioration in the Indonesian economy and paving the way for a resumption of international trade.

June 25 — The Executive Board completed the seventh review of Russia's economic and financial program and added a further $670 million to the financial package, bringing the total disbursement under the program to $5.8 billion, out of a total credit of $10.1 billion.

July 13 — The Managing Director of the Fund and Russian authorities agreed on a major strengthening of Russia's economic program with additional financial support from the Fund amounting to SDR 8.5 billion (about $11.2 billion) in 1998, bringing total Fund financing available for Russia in the year to SDR 9.5 billion ($12.5 billion). The new financing was subject to the Russian legislature enacting required reforms and to the approval of the Executive Board.

July 20 — The General Arrangements to Borrow were activated for the first time for a nonparticipant and for the first time for 20 years to finance the SDR 6.3 billion augmentation of the extended arrangement for Russia.

September 30 — The Fund announced that after the launch of the Economic and Monetary Union (EMU) in Europe on January 1, 1999, the euro will replace the current currency amounts of the deutsche mark and the French 13franc in the SDR valuation basket.

October 30 — The Fund announced in Moscow that after a 10-day meeting with the Russian authorities a number of points in the formulation of Russia's new economic program had been clarified, but necessary measures in important areas needed to be agreed upon, particularly the budget for 1999, before the financial program agreed to in July could be resumed.

December 2   The Executive Board approved a three-year stand-by arrangement for Brazil, with a total financial package from the Fund, other international financial organizations, and bilateral lenders amounting to about $41 billion. The New Arrangements to Borrow was activated for the first time.

December 22   The Fund announced that effective January 1, 1999, the euro will replace the deutsche mark and the French franc in the basket of currencies making up the value of the SDR.

Introduction

In its more than fifty years of existence, the International Monetary Fund has evolved from a small, obscure international agency, with new and uncertain responsibilities, into a powerful institution that today has assumed center stage in the international monetary system. This evolution has occurred even though twenty-five years ago, when the Bretton Woods system had collapsed, the Fund would seem to have lost the central purpose of its existence. It is a remarkable story of how an institution has developed and adapted itself to an evolving world and a changing membership in a way that perhaps no other international agency has been forced or able to do. And, moreover, this transformation has taken place despite bouts of criticism from industrial and developing countries alike, frequent exploitation by national politicians as a convenient way of deflecting criticism from their own disastrous national policies, serious controversy and criticism in the academic community, general suspicion in the trade union movement, antagonism from nongovernmental organizations (i.e., charity, church, and relief organizations), and a widespread lack of interest on the part of the general public in an institution that has such a remote and technical role.

Along the way, the Fund has developed new financing facilities; extended and enlarged the financial assistance available to its members; taken on new and wide-ranging responsibilities in the area of international surveillance of member countries' economic and financial policies; developed programs of reform in the areas of fiscal, monetary, structural (i.e., aspects of banking, corporations, and contract law), governance, and social policy; and broadened and intensified its technical assistance and training programs. At the same time, from an inward-looking and rather secretive bureaucracy, the Fund has become an institution anxious to explain itself to the public, although still mindful of its confidential relations with its members. It now has a very large publications program, covering country economic reports, comprehensive and authoritative reports on the world economy, international capital markets, economic and financial statistics, and, with the agreement of the member involved, a web site (www.imf.org) that reproduces the results of the Fund's Article IV consultations with member countries, as well as letters of intent and memoranda on the programs that it is supporting in those countries. In urging greater transparency on its members, the Fund in its own operations has now gone a long way in putting into practice what it preaches.

Growing through crises

Several developments and international crises have given the Fund the opportunity to be an important international player. Its first significant appearance on the international stage was in 1956, when all four combatants in the Suez Canal military adventure sought the Fund's financial assistance, for an amount that far exceeded the total amount of funds disbursed in the preceding nine years. In 1974 and 1975, when the par value system had crumbled, the Fund created the oil facilities, which played an important role in acting as a conduit for recycling petrodollars from the suddenly rich oil-producing countries, caused by the action of the Organization of Petroleum Exporting Countries (OPEC) in tripling international oil prices, to the poorer, hard-hit oil-consuming countries. In 1982, when Mexico abruptly announced that it could no longer service its loans and was on the brink of default, the Fund took a major role in persuading the international banking community not to run for cover but to reschedule old loans and provide new money in support of Mexico, predicating the Fund's own financial assistance on the condition that the banks come up with a sufficient financial package to give Mexico time to implement corrective policies. Concerted lending, as it was called, was the pattern of the financial packages that was used for the rest of the decade in providing assistance to heavily indebted countries. During the 1980s, when many countries were strapped with high indebtedness, the Fund also introduced the structural adjustment facility (SAF) and the enhanced structural adjustment facility (ESAF) to provide expanded and concessional assistance to poorer countries, as well as the enlarged access policy (EAP) for other countries.

The Fund's role as crisis manager emerged fully in 1994, when Mexico was struck by a resurgence of investors' fears and the country again turned to the Fund for assistance. When the U.S. Congress refused the Administration's request for $40 billion in loan guarantees, the Fund stepped in (with the support of the U.S. Administration) and increased its financing package from an initial $7.8 billion to $17.8 billion. In addition, the U.S. Administration provided $20 billion from the Exchange Stabilization Fund (a resource that did not require congressional approval). Investors' confidence was thereby very shortly restored, Mexico was able to repay its credits ahead of schedule, and a wider conflagration was avoided. All told, as many as 20 countries were involved in a crisis, which up to that point was considered one of the most serious in the postwar world.

It was in the 1990s, also, that the Fund received an influx of over 30 new members, including all the countries of the former Soviet Union, as well as those from the Soviet bloc in Eastern Europe. For this new group of members a special temporary facility, the systemic transformation facility, was established to help the economies of these countries make a transition from a command to a free-market economy. In this endeavor, in addition to substantial financial assistance, the Fund provided intensive and widespread technical assistance and training in spearheading the effort to establish the basic infrastructure, legal environment, and social policies necessary to bring about market economies. In this period, Switzerland also became a member and by the mid-1990s, the Fund had finally become a universal organization, with only North Korea, Cuba, and a few ministates outside its orbit.

In 1997-1998, the Fund's role as crisis manager, as demonstrated in 1982 and 1994, was put to a severe test as the Asian economic and financial crisis broke. Using the emergency financing facility that it had introduced after the 1992 Mexican crisis, the Fund put together massive financing packages, including multilateral and bilateral financing, in support of macroeconomic and structural reform programs in the countries involved—mainly Korea, Indonesia, the Philippines, and Thailand—and counseled other countries to which the contagion had spread, such as the Hong Kong Special Administrative Region (SAR), Malaysia, and Singapore. Outside the Asian area, other countries, principally Russia but also several countries in Latin America, also suffered from the resurgence of investors' fears, requiring many billions of dollars in emergency financing. The result was the emergence of a severe pressure on the Fund's resources, both in terms of manpower and finances.

Although a general increase of 45 percent in quotas had been approved by the Board of Governors early in 1998, the reluctance of the U.S. Congress to authorize payment of its subscription brought about a general slowdown in the payment of all subscriptions, thereby delaying through the following 12 months a much needed reinforcement of the Fund's financial resources. Similarly, the New Arrangements to Borrow (NAB), which were approved by the Executive Board in January 1997, became linked to the quota increase and suffered a corresponding delay in becoming effective. Neither the quota increase nor the NAB could become effective without payment of the subscription by the United States, since it alone holds 18 percent of the total voting power and for the quota increase and the NAB to become effective both measures require members totaling 85 percent of the Fund's total voting strength to enact all necessary legislation and make the relevant payments to the Fund. In August 1998, therefore, with the Fund's liquidity at a historically low level, it became necessary to activate the General Arrangements to Borrow (GAB) to replenish the Fund's resources—the first time that the GAB had been activated since 1978. Subsequently, the NAB became effective in November 1998 and the quota increase shortly thereafter.

It is visionary to see the International Monetary Fund progressing to become the world's central bank, but the movement to a "one world" is not to be denied. The establishment toward the end of 1998 of a powerful regional central bank, the European Central Bank (ECB), serving 11 advanced industrial countries, is an interesting precursor of wider international developments. The Fund has already clearly become the world's lender of last resort—an important attribute of a central bank. It has also demonstrated that it has the experience, expertise, and staff to take the lead in a crisis. Its attempt to create the Special Drawing Right (SDR) in the late 1960s, in order to be able to regulate the level of international liquidity in accordance with the world's need (i.e., a role parallel to a national central bank's role in controlling the domestic money supply), has been swamped by the integration of the international capital markets and the unhindered flow of capital across borders. The attempt, therefore, to make the SDR the principal international reserve asset—as set out in the Fund's current Articles of Agreement— has failed, and the role of the SDR has been reduced to that of mainly facilitating transactions within the Fund itself.

On the broader question of coordinating national economic and financial policies, the Fund has worked diligently and with increasing sophistication in carrying out and expanding its responsibilities of surveillance over members' economic and financial policies, and its analysis carries great weight in international financial organizations, summit meetings of the industrial countries, regional gatherings, and other fora, but so far it has had less impact in national capitals. It has, therefore, yet to realize its goal of being able to coordinate the policies of its member countries and thus to place the world economy on a secure and stable basis. This is the test that it now faces, and it is the test that its members also face in becoming fully cooperative participants in the international monetary system, and thereby furthering the goals of the Fund's founders.

The gold and gold exchange standards

The International Monetary Fund was born out of the experience of the interwar years. During the last half of the nineteenth century and up to the outbreak of World War I, the world's monetary and exchange rate system was based on gold, as was the domestic money supply in most countries. The gold standard system was, in theory, self-regulating; a deficit in a country's balance of payments would result in an outflow of gold, followed by a reduction of money in circulation, deflation, and thus a correction in the external balance. The gold standard was accepted as the natural order of things, and although it may not have been ordained by God, it was a religion that central bankers could believe in. While industrial countries competed on an equal footing and the rules of the game were adhered to, the system worked well. The center of the monetary universe was London, and the Bank of England was the fulcrum on which the system was balanced. The London bank rate was the signal for monetary retrenchment or expansion, as the case might be, and the rest of the trading world watched and acted accordingly. Adjustments tended to be made in unison, with each economy in lockstep with the others. The exchange rate, that is, the value of a currency in terms of gold, was "a given," and was immutable. There were signs, however, even before World War I that cracks were appearing in the edifice. Reserve currencies were becoming a growing part of countries' reserves, and the impact of gold movements was being neutralized. World War I brought the system temporarily to an end.

The outbreak of World War I led to currency inconvertibility, blocked balances, and the imposition of exchange controls. After the war ended, repair of the system was neither easy nor immediately possible. Exchange controls persisted, currencies remained inconvertible, and central banks intervened in exchange markets to manipulate the rates. The war and its aftermath had been accompanied by a vastly uneven increase in the general price levels among countries and a profound redistribution of gold, away from London. Nevertheless, sentiment for a return to the gold standard remained strong, and the pound sterling returned to gold in 1925 at its prewar parity. At that rate, the pound was substantially overvalued, and the cost at home was severe unemployment. The move to gold, moreover, did not restore stability to the world's exchange rate system; the pound began to lose its primacy to the U.S. dollar, and reserve currencies were increasingly being held as major components of international reserves alongside gold. The world, in fact, had moved to a gold exchange standard, a system in which gold bullion was the only ultimate means of settlement among nations, and one in which gold specie rarely circulated. The link between the balance of payments and domestic money supply had been broken, and national economic policies began to be set mainly to achieve domestic objectives rather than to uphold the gold content of currencies. Confidence in the system was severely weakened, and it became subject to increasing speculative attacks.

The pound sterling was forced off gold in 1931, followed two years later by the U.S. dollar and the currencies of most other industrial countries. The collapse of the gold exchange standard ushered in a period of near chaos in international financial relations. Discriminatory currency blocs, bilateral trade and exchange agreements, multiple currency practices, trade quotas, and any other stratagem to gain national advantage were pursued at the expense of the common good. It was the "beggar-thy-neighbor" decade. The Great Depression, the breakdown of the international financial system, and the growth of economic nationalism all fed on each other, resulting in a startling contraction in international trade. The Tripartite Agreement of 1936, between France, the United Kingdom, and the United States, was an early and notable attempt to bring some measure of stability among exchange rates. Of more importance, perhaps, it indicated to future policymakers a way to go forward.

Establishment of the Fund

World War II saw a repeat of the economic disruption that had accompanied World War I—exchange controls, blocked balances, and bilateral arrangements in external dealings, and physical controls and suppressed inflation at home. The lessons of the interwar years, however, were there for all to see. Men on both sides of the Atlantic, with vision and expertise—notably John Maynard Keynes in Great Britain and Harry Dexter White in the United States—almost simultaneously, and independently of each other, began to assemble a blueprint for the international monetary system of the postwar world. Each produced a plan for a new international organization, the one called an International Currency (or Clearing) Union and the other a Stabilization Fund, and though each came to the task from a different perspective and with somewhat different national interests in mind, there was a remarkable overlap in their proposals. These two plans, drawn up late in 1942 in the midst of war, were joined over the following two years by other plans and proposals from several other countries, officials (including those of governments in exile), economists, and other individuals. The final texts of two international agreements—the Articles of Agreement of the International Monetary Fund and the Articles of Agreement of the International Bank for Reconstruction and Development (IBRD)—were hammered out at the International Monetary and Financial Conference held at Bretton Woods, New Hampshire, during July 1-22, 1944. Delegates from 44 countries, plus a representative from Denmark, were present, as well as observers from several international organizations.

The aim in setting up the International Monetary Fund was clear and simple. It was to establish a new world order based on an open exchange and trading system that would operate under international scrutiny and control. In particular, exchange rates were recognized as being matters of international concern. Currencies would have internationally approved par values in an exchange rate system that aimed at stability without rigidity; discriminatory and unfair practices would be outlawed; and a new spirit of enlightened self-interest would be fostered. The establishment and maintenance of such a system would be the responsibility of the International Monetary Fund, an organization whose membership, open to all countries, would entail both obligations and privileges. The Fund would enunciate a code of conduct to be observed by all its members. Members would subscribe to and have available to them a pool of currencies that they could draw upon in times of external payments difficulties. Within this unique framework, which included regulatory functions, financial operations, multilateral consultations, and technical assistance, the Fund would bring into existence a new comity of nations. The Fund was to be firefighter, policeman, and counselor simultaneously.

Par values and exchange restrictions

The inaugural meeting of the Board of Governors was held in Savannah, Georgia, in May 1946, and the Fund opened its doors for business in Washington, D.C., in March 1947. Its first order of business was to invite its members to propose par values for their currencies, to be established in terms of gold as a common denominator or in terms of the U.S. dollar of the weight and fineness in effect on July 1, 1944. Apart from a cumulative initial change of 10 percent, par values could be changed only on a proposal by the member and subject to a finding by the Fund that the member's balance of payments was in fundamental disequilibrium. Among a number of general obligations included in the Articles of Agreement, each member was to avoid restrictions on current payments, abstain from discriminatory currency practices, and establish convertibility for foreign-held currency balances (Article VIII). Recognizing the uncertain conditions brought about by the war, however, the Articles also provided (Article XIV) for a transitional period, in which members could maintain and adapt to changing circumstances the restrictions on payments and transfers for current transactions.

In the event, all but a handful of members availed themselves of the transitional arrangements under Article XIV, and it was not until 1961 that most industrial countries had formally established convertibility for their currencies and had undertaken to perform the obligations of Article VIII. Informal convertibility had, in fact, been established two or three years earlier, and by 1960 the preponderance of international trade and payments was being conducted on an open, nondiscriminatory basis. One of the major goals of the Bretton Woods system had thus largely been attained. Despite the disruption of the Bretton Woods exchange rate system in the early 1970s, the drive to an open trading system has been maintained, and the number of members accepting the obligations of Article VIII has increased steadily over the years. By the end of April 1998, 144 members, including all the major trading countries, had accepted the obligations of Article VIII; with 38 other countries, all developing countries or new members (such as the successor states of the former Soviet Union), still availing themselves of the transitional arrangements.

The rise and fall of the Bretton Woods systems

The 1960s proved to be an expansive decade. The value of world trade increased by about 135 percent, world economic growth averaged nearly 6 percent a year, and inflation, though increasing, remained moderate until the end of the decade, especially compared with developments that were to occur in the 1970s. The revolution in communications and transportation, together with open exchange and trade arrangements over much of the world, unleashed capital movements, encouraged the formation of multinational and transnational corporations, and began the transformation of the world economy into what was later to be called "the global village."

But disquieting trends began to surface. Economic growth was uneven among countries, as were rates of inflation, and the system began to lose its center as Europe started competing with the United States, both economically and politically. The system came under stress. The United States, increasingly involved in the Vietnam war, found it politically difficult to adopt corrective domestic economic policies and continued to run balance of payments deficits. Externally, the U.S. authorities felt that their hands were tied. On the one hand, they believed that the United States was unable to change the value of the dollar against other currencies by raising the price of gold, because they were convinced that devaluation would have prompted offsetting moves by other countries. On the other hand, they were unwilling to raise the price of gold, partly because of the political implications of benefiting South Africa and the U.S.S.R., the world's main gold producers. Other countries, too, were unable or unwilling to devalue or appreciate their currencies against the dollar, resulting in a general stickiness in the exchange rate system. The continued growth of foreign-held dollar balances intensified the pressure on the dollar, and the almost riskless cost of speculating against a fixed-rate currency invited periodic bouts of speculation against the weaker currencies. The Bretton Woods par value system came to an end on August 15, 1971, when the United States suspended the convertibility of official holdings of dollar balances into gold.

A brief attempt to restore the fixed-rate system was made in December 1971, when finance ministers of the Group of Ten countries held a meeting, the first of its kind, at the Smithsonian Institution in

Washington, D.C., to negotiate a new pattern of rates for their currencies, including a devalued rate for the dollar and the creation of central rates, with wider margins and a less formal procedure for exchange rate changes. One by one, however, the major industrial countries abandoned fixed rates for their currencies and let them float. By March 1973, all the major currencies were floating against each other, marking the end of the exchange rate system established at Bretton Woods.

After the breakdown of the Bretton Woods system, several difficult years for the Fund followed. The main currencies floated against each other, either as a managed float or floating freely according to demand and supply (referred to at the time as "dirty" or "clean" floating), depending on the degree or absence of official intervention. Other members adopted a variety of exchange arrangements. Some preferred to let their currencies float, some opted to peg the value of their currencies to one of the major currencies, some to a trade-weighted composite of currencies, and a few to the Special Drawing Right (SDR), the new reserve asset created in the Fund in 1968. In 1974, the SDR itself was revalued by the Fund in terms of a basket of 16 currencies, reduced to a basket of five currencies seven years later. The link between gold and currency values having been broken, national monetary authorities were no longer able to maintain an official price for gold. Nonmonetary gold transactions (i.e., private sales and purchases) took place at three or four times the nominal official price. All these developments were, of course, contrary to the legal obligations that members had assumed under the Articles of Agreement.

Despite its loss of control over the value of its members' exchange rates, the Fund continued to exercise what authority remained to it. It requested members to provide the Fund with full details of their exchange arrangements, continued to hold members bound by their undertakings on exchange restrictions, lent heavily on the obligation that each member had undertaken to "collaborate with the Fund to promote exchange stability, to maintain orderly exchange arrangements with other members, and to avoid competitive exchange alterations," and promulgated a set of guidelines to be observed by members engaged in managed floating. Further, following a recommendation by the Committee of Twenty, the Fund circulated a declaration on trade to all members, asking them to voluntarily pledge that they would not introduce or intensify trade or other current account measures without a finding by the Fund that there was a balance of payments justification for such measures.

Reform of the international monetary system

While these attempts were being made by the Fund to continue exercising some control over international monetary relations, it was also focusing intensively on a reform of the system. Early in 1972, the Executive Directors had submitted a report to the Board of Governors, entitled *Reform of the International Monetary System*, which, among other things, suggested further study on a number of issues on which the Executive Directors had not been able to agree. Publication of the report was followed by the establishment of the Committee of Twenty and its Deputies, charged with the task of putting together a draft of a reformed system. The Committee worked for two years, produced many interesting and useful technical studies, but, citing the highly uncertain economic conditions then prevailing in the world economy, admitted that it had been unable to reach agreement on a comprehensive reform. It settled instead on an *Outline of Reform*, indicating the general direction in which the Committee believed the international monetary system could evolve, and proposing a list of immediate measures that could assist in the evolution of the system. Among these immediate measures was a recommendation to establish an Interim Committee to advise the Board of Governors on the supervision, management, and adaptation of the monetary system.

The task of negotiating a reformed system had thus reverted to the Fund. After two years of intensive work within the Fund, along with several referrals to the Interim Committee and bilateral negotiations on a number of key points, agreement was reached on a full-scale reform of the international monetary system in 1976. The new system came into effect in April 1978. Its main themes, spelled out in the second amendment to the Articles of Agreement, were: (1) each member could adopt the exchange arrangement of its choice; a system of par values could be introduced if 85 percent of the total voting power of the membership agreed; exchange arrangements would be subject at all times to firm surveillance by the Fund; (2) the role of gold would be reduced, including the disposition of the Fund's own gold holdings, to be effected by the elimination of gold as a common denominator of the par value system, the abolition of its official price, the abrogation of obligatory gold payments to the Fund, and a requirement that the Fund complete the disposition of 50 million ounces of its gold holdings, as well as authorization to dispose of the remainder of its holdings; (3) the introduction of changes in the characteristics of the SDR, so as to assist it to become the principal reserve asset of the international monetary system; (4) simplification and expansion of the types of the Fund's financial operations and transactions; (5) provisions to establish a Council as a new organ of the Fund, its establishment to be subject to an 85 percent majority of the total voting power; (6) certain improvements in the organizational aspects of the Fund, principally involving the composition of the Executive Board and the election of Executive Directors; and (7) a reduction in the categories of special majorities to

70 percent and 85 percent, but with a considerable expansion in the number of decisions of the Executive Board or the Board of Governors subject to these special majorities; all other decisions would be taken by a majority of the votes cast.

Surveillance over exchange rate policies

Although the second amendment to the Articles was comprehensive, with ramifications throughout the operations of the Fund, the fundamental change that overshadowed all others related to the exchange rate system, under which a member could adopt the exchange arrangement of its choice and no longer had to declare the value of its currency to the Fund or gain approval for a change in its value. Instead of having the responsibility of approving currency values and their changes, the Fund was charged with a less specific but broader, and more important, responsibility of exercising firm surveillance over members' exchange rate policies. Firm surveillance was a new, crucial provision of the reformed system, and in order for it to become effective the Fund needed the continuous cooperation of its members, particularly the major industrial countries, in areas of national policy that had not hitherto been under compelling continuous scrutiny. To be effective, surveillance would have to apply not only to exchange rate policies, as such, but also to the broader national monetary and financial policies that were being pursued by national monetary authorities, whether they used the Fund's resources or not. The major industrial countries had always sought to maintain their independence of the Fund under the Bretton Woods system, and even when they had altered the par values of their currencies they had notified the Fund of the change at the last minute, rather than following the impractical procedure of seeking its approval, thereby complying with the obligations of the Articles in form rather than in substance. It was unlikely, therefore, that an important advance in policy coordination could be developed suddenly, particularly in the light of the difficult economic circumstances of the 1980s.

Surveillance did, indeed, become gradually more sophisticated and effective over the ensuing decades, but, nonetheless, it proved to be a difficult area for the Fund and for the major industrial countries, which were loath to cede any of their sovereignty over economic policy to an international forum. The analysis conducted in the Fund, the probing of national economic policies, and the regular examination by the Fund of exchange rate movements and their underlying causes gradually gained weight and influence, particularly in the more restricted fora outside the Fund, such as in the economic summit meetings of the leaders of the Group of Seven industrial countries and other multinational fora. These meetings proved to be a more intimate forum in which the major powers could be open with each other. Since the Plaza Hotel meeting in

New York in September 1985, the major industrial countries have sought, still with only partial success, to bring some measure of harmony to their national economic policies and to cooperate—sometimes with success—in exchange rate management.

In 1977, the Executive Board established three broad principles for the guidance of members' exchange rate policies. These were: (1) a member should avoid manipulating exchange rates or the international monetary system in order to prevent balance of payments adjustment or to gain an unfair competitive advantage; (2) a member should intervene in the exchange markets to counter disorderly conditions; and (3) members should take into account in their intervention policies the interests of other members. The Board also established a number of other criteria that would be taken into account in judging the application of these principles, such as protracted large-scale intervention in one direction, an unsustainable level of borrowing for balance of payments purposes, the pursuit for balance of payments purposes of monetary and financial policies that provide abnormal encouragement or discouragement to capital flows, and the behavior of the exchange rate in a manner that would appear to be unrelated to the underlying economic and financial conditions.

The Fund's surveillance procedures include analyzing the economic and financial conditions in member countries and focusing on the international issues that are of concern to all members. Regular consultations are held, normally each year, with each member country to assess the appropriateness of its domestic macroeconomic and structural policies and the impact of these policies on exchange rates. The Fund also conducts a multilateral surveillance procedure twice a year through the Executive Board, aimed at assessing the world economic outlook, the interaction of members' economic policies, and the presentation of alternative policy options, together with related projections of various international scenarios. These reviews by the Executive Board are supplemented by periodic discussions on exchange rate developments and on the conditions of the financial markets in the major industrial countries. The Managing Director's attendance at the meetings of the Group of Seven industrial countries brings to those meetings a broad and knowledgeable international perspective, based on the Fund's surveillance procedures.

International liquidity

In the 1960s, a new and major problem began to emerge, that of international liquidity, a subject that had been discussed but not actively engaged at the Bretton Woods Conference of 1944. The dilemma was that as world trade and other international transactions expanded, and the potential magnitude of external imbalances increased, the need for international liquidity would rise. Unconditional liquidity (i.e., owned reserves) consisted of gold, reserve currencies (mainly U.S. dollars), and reserve positions in the Fund (the reserve tranche). Of these three components, only U.S. dollar reserves were capable of expansion, since both the world's stock of monetary gold and reserve positions in the Fund were fixed, at least in the short and medium term. The continued growth of the U.S. dollar in international reserves itself involved a paradox. On the one hand, dollar holdings by foreign national monetary authorities could expand only if the United States continued to run a balance of payments deficit, thereby expanding claims by foreigners on the United States, and on its stock of gold. On the other hand, the viability of the U.S. dollar required that foreign national authorities (and private foreigners) continue to have confidence in it as a stable unit of value and in its convertibility into gold. These were two contradictory lines of development that, at some point in time, were bound to bring the system into crisis.

The discussions involved issues of whether the need was for better adjustment policies or increased international liquidity; whether the potential need should be met through increased conditional liquidity (such as drawings on the Fund) or through increased unconditional liquidity (i.e., owned reserves); whether a scheme for reserve creation should be confined to a group of industrial countries or be a universal one; and whether such a scheme should be linked to the needs of developing countries by establishing a mechanism for promoting the growth of development finance, the so-called link. An overriding issue was to what extent any new provisions should be mandated or be left to voluntary compliance. Many proposals were put forward, including special reserve balances in the Fund, multicurrency reserve schemes, various forms of a substitution account, and several schemes for the creation of reserve units. The debate ended in a compromise, with the establishment of the SDR facility in the Fund, brought into effect by the first amendment of the Articles of Agreement (1969).

The SDR facility and gold

The chief characteristics of the SDR facility were: (1) it was a universal scheme open to all members of the Fund, although participation in it was voluntary; (2) allocations and cancellations of SDRs would seek to meet long-term global needs as a supplement to existing reserve assets; (3) allocations and cancellations would be made to all participants in the facility as a percentage of each member's quota; (4) SDRs would be created on the books of the Fund, backed by an international agreement (the Fund's Articles of Agreement); (5) use of the SDR would rest on two legal foundations: the obligation of the Fund to designate a transferee of SDRs if requested by a participant, and the obligation of the designated transferee to provide freely usable currency in exchange for SDRs; (6) SDRs would be for use through the Fund by national monetary authorities and a limited number of other official holders, and would not be available for use in private markets; (7) decisions on allocations and cancellations of SDRs would be made for basic periods of five years (although the Fund was authorized to vary the length of the period) and be subject to a cautionary procedure that subjected the final decision to an 85 percent majority vote of the Fund's Board of Governors; and (8) the value of the SDR, originally defined in terms of gold, was to be determined by a basket of currencies.

The international community, eager to test its fledgling reserve-creating mechanism, authorized allocations of SDRs during the first basic period of three years (1970-72) amounting to SDR 9.3 billion. Thereafter, however, the new system of floating exchange rates and the availability of petrodollars for recycling purposes fundamentally changed the world's liquidity position. No further allocations of SDRs were made until the third basic period (1978-81), when SDR 12.1 billion was allocated, partly, one can surmise, to be in accord with the second amendment to the Articles (1978), which called for the SDR to be the principal reserve asset of the international monetary system. The assumption then was presumably that a virtually nonexistent reserve asset could hardly be a principal asset, but even so, no further allocations have been made since 1981, and the total of SDRs in circulation has remained at SDR 21.4 billion.

In mid-1998, however, the Executive Board drew up a proposed amendment to the Articles of Agreement that would provide for a one-time allocation of SDRs. The amendment was aimed at correcting a perceived inequity, insofar as members that had joined the Fund since 1981 had not received any allocations of SDRs, and many that had joined before that year had received only partial allocations.

Despite the fact that measures have been taken to make the SDR more attractive (e.g., its valuation in terms of a basket of five currencies, its market related interest rate, and a broadening of its uses), the SDR has remained very far from being a principal reserve asset. Indeed, measured by the extent of its use, the SDR is declining sharply in relative importance. Whereas world transfers in currencies amount to many billions a day, total transfers of SDRs reached a record level of only SDR 27.4 billion in the year ended April 30, 1996, and have declined since then. Similarly, since the last allocation in 1981, SDRs have been a declining and insignificant proportion of international reserves, accounting in 1998 for about 1.2 percent of nongold reserves and, with gold valued at London market prices, about 1.5 percent of total reserves (*see* Chart 1).

Chart. 1. International Reserves-All Countries
(Billions of SDRs)

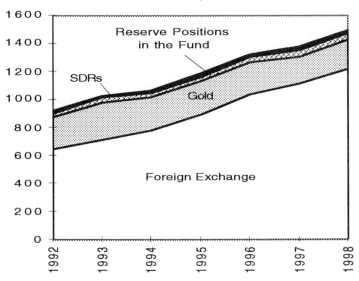

Nevertheless, from the early 1970s, international liquidity ceased to be a current widespread problem, although the increasing diversification and uncontrolled growth of reserve currency holdings, and the potential for switching from one reserve currency to another, remain potential concerns for the future. A more immediate concern in the 1990s, however, was that the integration of the world's capital markets, although bringing undoubted long-term benefits, posed short-term problems in view of the volatile character of capital movements that moved in and out of immature and vulnerable private banking sectors in developing, and even some advanced, economies.

The second amendment to the Articles of Agreement eliminated gold from the operations of the Fund and required the Fund to sell 50 million ounces of its gold holdings. Accordingly, in the period from 1976 to 1980, the Fund sold (restituted) half of this amount (25 million ounces) to its members at the official price of SDR 35 an ounce and sold by auction a further 25 million ounces at prices several times higher than the official price of gold, placing the profits on these sales in a Trust Fund for the benefit of low-income countries.

Conditionality

One of the purposes of the Fund is to "give confidence to members by making the general resources of the Fund temporarily available to them under adequate safeguards," as stated in Article I of its charter. Before a member can use the Fund's financial resources it must represent that it has a need to make the purchase "because of its balance of payments or its reserve position or developments in its reserves." It is these conditions—the requirement of a balance of payments need, temporary use, and adequate safeguards—that have distinguished the Fund's financial operations from its sister institution, the World Bank, facing it across the street in Washington, D.C. Whereas the World Bank primarily deals in long-term finance for development purposes, such as agricultural, irrigation, and transport projects or for sectoral development, and is concerned, among other matters, with the viability of the particular project being financed and the credit status of its loan recipients, the Fund provides short- to medium-term finance for general balance of payments support and is concerned primarily with a member's macroeconomic policies (i.e., monetary and fiscal policies, and related structural improvements) and the ability of the member to repay the Fund within a specified time period. It should be noted, however, that the character of the Bank's lending is also changing, with project financing accounting for a declining proportion of the total, while sectoral lending is increasing.

In the very early days of its operations, the Fund settled on a pragmatic and flexible set of policies and procedures, known as "conditionality," which established the terms that would govern the use of the Fund's financing.

First, members' drawing (purchasing) privileges were divided into tranches, each amounting to 25 percent of a member's quota. The first 25 percent of quota, known as the reserve tranche (formerly the gold tranche), could be drawn (purchased) without challenge. Requests for drawings in the second 25 percent of quota, known as the first credit tranche, could be made subject only to moderate conditionality. Use of a member's second, third, and fourth credit tranches, known as the upper credit tranches, required substantial justification and agreement by the Fund on a sound corrective program. Second, it was determined that "temporary" use of resources should mean that repayments (repurchases) should be made in three to five years. Third, use of the Fund's resources in the upper credit tranches would be made available under what was then a new instrument of international finance, the stand-by arrangement. With the introduction of the stand-by arrangement, which was normally for a period of one year (although members often entered into successive one-year arrangements), came two other precautionary measures—the quarterly phasing of members' drawings under the arrangement and the setting of performance criteria to assess the progress of programs.

Conditionality in Fund-supported programs is based on the basic and incontrovertible proposition that a deficit in a country's external payments, as long as it is not transitory or reversible, will have to be corrected eventually, whether or not there is policy action. The issues are whether the adjustments will be effected in good time, be carried out efficiently, and be successful in balancing a country's external accounts without unnecessary disruption of national or international economic activity. The financing obtained from the Fund, along with the conditionality attached to it, enables the period of adjustment to be extended, allows the corrective measures to be less severe than they would otherwise be, and eases the pain of adjustment.

A balance of payments deficit normally springs from excessive aggregate demand and expenditure. The objective of an adjustment program is to keep the level and growth of aggregate demand in line with the level and the rate of growth of a country's productive capacity. For this purpose, adjustment needs to concentrate on the fiscal balance—government revenues and expenditures—and on monetary policies that will subdue the expansion of bank credit and control monetary flows. In addition, adjustment programs may contain provisions for the implementation of appropriate price incentives, including the exchange rate, interest rates, and other prices, as well as policies on external debt management.

The character, range, severity, and efficacy of the conditionality required by the Fund have been much discussed for many years, both inside and outside the organization. The Fund's guidelines on conditionality have evolved over four decades and are reviewed periodically by the Executive Board. They were last codified in 1979 and have been reviewed several times since then, but have undergone little change. One guideline to which developing countries attach importance is the directive that the Fund will pay "due regard to the domestic social and political objectives, the economic priorities, and the circumstances of members." Another states that "performance criteria will normally be confined to (i) macroeconomic variables, and (ii) those necessary to implement specific provisions of the Articles or policies adopted under them." In the past few years, the Fund has given greater attention to the impact that adjustment programs may have on the poor and on the environment.

From time to time, Fund conditionality has been criticized as being too harsh, too insensitive to social conditions, and heedless of programs of economic growth. In fact, Fund-supported adjustment programs have had mixed success, with failures coming mainly as the result of internal political will and exogenous and unforeseen factors.

More rarely, the fault has lain with an ill-designed program. Certainly, the Fund must be assured that in accordance with its Articles, a Fund-supported program will consist of policies that will result in a sustained balance in a country's external payments and provide the basis for further economic growth, but in the last analysis the elements of the program and the timing of their implementation must rest with the national authorities of the country in question.

Resources of the Fund

The resources of the Fund consist of its ordinary resources and its borrowed resources. Ordinary resources consist of gold, SDRs, and currencies of members' paid to the Fund in accordance with their quota subscriptions, and the undistributed net income from the use of those resources. The value of these resources is maintained in terms of SDRs, the Fund's unit of account.

A member's quota establishes its basic relationship with the Fund. First, it determines a member's voting power. Second, it determines a member's maximum potential access to the Fund's financial resources. Third, it determines a participant's share in the allocation of SDRs. After the second amendment of the Articles (1978), gold was eliminated from the Fund's operations, and that part of the quota subscription that used to be paid in gold (up to a maximum of 25 percent of quota) is now paid in SDRs or a usable currency, and this amount establishes the reserve tranche.

A quota is established in accordance with a member's relative economic strength in the international community of nations. For this purpose, the original formula used at Bretton Woods (1944) included a range of basic economic variables, such as the value of annual average imports and exports, gold holdings and dollar balances, and national income. Since then, beginning in the early 1960s, that formula has been supplemented by four other formulas containing the same basic variables but with different weights. These five formulas were run with alternative sets of data, roughly measuring the same economic characteristics but using somewhat different concepts. The resulting 10 formulas were used, in the period up to 1980, to determine the initial quotas of new members and to adjust existing members' quotas under the periodic general quota reviews. Subsequently, the number of formulas was reduced to five, but further changes were made to the weights and in the data. The proliferation of formulas and the conceptual changes made in the data suggest correctly that a member's calculated quota is not a definitive determination of its final quota. In the last analysis, a member's quota is determined by the Executive Board's recommendation to the Board of Governors, guided by the use of formulas.

The Fund is required by its Articles of Agreement to conduct a general review of quotas at intervals of not more than five years, and the last such general review was completed in 1997, raising total quotas to SDR 212 billion ($288 billion). In view of the length of time that it can take for the Fund to increase its ordinary resources through a quota increase, whereas payments imbalances may appear suddenly and may be the result of temporary factors, such as occurred in the 1970s through the oil shocks, the Fund has resorted to borrowing to tide it over periods in which members have an enlarged need for its financing. From 1962, the Fund entered into the GAB with members of the Group of Ten for the purpose of having available access to borrowed funds in the event of a major disruption to the world balance of payments. These arrangements were enlarged in the 1980s and have been renewed through 2003.

In January 1997, the Executive Board further strengthened the Fund's financial resources by approving new borrowing arrangements (NAB). Under these arrangements, 25 participating countries and institutions stand ready to lend the Fund additional resources when needed, on terms similar to the GAB, in a total amount of SDR 34 billion (about $47 billion). The NAB, which were still awaiting ratification by member countries at the end of 1998, do not replace the GAB, but they will be the facility of first recourse.

Other borrowing arrangements have been entered into over the years, such as those in 1974 and 1975 with the OPEC to finance the oil facilities (a total of SDR 5.7 billion); in 1979 for the supplementary financing facility (SDR 7.8 billion); and in 1981-84 for the EAP (SDR 18.3 billion).

The Fund also receives income from investments and from charges levied on its financing operations. From such income, the Fund covers its administrative budget and pays remuneration to members with creditor positions in the Fund. Net income is placed to the general and special reserve accounts.

Special facilities

Most of the Fund's financing is provided on condition that corrective policy actions will be taken to bring about an appropriate adjustment to a member's domestic economy, thus ensuring that the Fund will be repaid. However, the Fund also provides financing for members' balance of payments difficulties that are transitory or reversible, where no corrective policies may be required. The first of such facilities established the compensatory financing facility, under which members could draw on the Fund to offset export shortfalls caused by factors largely beyond their control. Use of this facility is based on the assumption that the shortfall is temporary (such as a crop failure) and that export earnings will recover over the short- to medium-term. Drawings on the facility are not only subject to a low level of conditionality (such as merely an obligation to collaborate with the Fund), but the facility also floats, allowing members to draw on it independently of, and in addition to, drawings under the regular tranche policies.

The Fund also established a special facility to help members finance international buffer stocks and subsequently expanded the compensatory financing facility to include variations in expatriate workers' remittances and cereal import costs, renaming the facility the compensatory and contingency financing facility (CCFF).

Enlarged use of the Fund's resources

The decade of the 1970s experienced the oil price shocks, worldwide recession, and persistent high levels of inflation. The quadrupling of international oil prices led the Fund to establish in 1974, and again in 1975, the so-called oil facilities to help countries meet the higher cost of their oil imports. Drawings under the facilities, which were financed by borrowings from members of the OPEC, were repayable over seven years (an extension over the three to five years that had normally been in force up to then), carried light conditionality, and were additional to the availability of normal tranche drawing.

The reasoning behind the extended repayment terms was that whereas the balance of payments deficits were spread among nearly all developing countries, many with relatively large economies and sizable populations, the balance of payments surpluses were concentrated among a few oil-producing countries, mostly undeveloped economies with sparse populations. In these circumstances, it was clear that the oil- producing countries would not be able to absorb quickly their new wealth through increased imports, while attempts by non-oil-producing countries to correct their external imbalances would mainly impact each other, and thus run the risk of causing a further general contraction in international trade and world economic growth. Accordingly, the facility was designed to finance the deficits rather than to promote adjustment. Drawings under the facility did not affect the amount that members could purchase under the credit tranche policies.

Nevertheless, despite the evident rationale behind the Fund's approach to the worldwide oil-price difficulties of the 1970s some critics have maintained that the failure of the developing countries to adjust to the new circumstances sowed the seeds for the debt problems of the 1980s. Certainly, the payments problems experienced by many member countries in the late 1970s and early 1980s called for a different approach from that adopted for the oil facilities. For one thing, the balance of payments for a number of countries had not only worsened, but had been superimposed on long-standing imbalances. For another, the causes of the imbalances had become deep-seated and of a structural character that would take longer to correct and require larger resources than those available under the Fund's normal financing facilities.

To meet these new conditions, a new facility, providing for extended arrangements over a three-year period, was introduced in 1974 to focus on structural adjustments and provide members with access to the Fund's financing in amounts larger and with longer repayment terms than had hitherto been available under the Fund's regular tranche policies. In 1979, the extended facility was complemented by the supplementary financing facility, again established with borrowed funds, to provide further enlarged access to the Fund's financing, up to 300 percent of a member's quota in exceptional cases.

Within two years, the resources of the supplementary facility were exhausted and the facility was replaced by the EAP, involving similar high levels of conditionality and access to Fund resources, and financed by another round of borrowing.

Facilities for low-income countries

The mounting difficulties of developing countries, particularly the low-income countries, during the 1970s and 1980s made these countries increasingly restive against what they considered to be the Fund's traditional approach to balance of payments problems, contending that the adjustment policies and the extent and duration of the financing available from the Fund did not take into account the special character of their problems. In response to these needs, the Fund introduced financing programs specifically for low-income countries. As noted above, the Fund had been authorized to sell at auction 25 million ounces of its gold holdings, which yielded a profit (over the former official price of SDR 35 an ounce) of $4.6 billion. Of this amount, $1.3 billion was distributed directly to 104 developing countries in proportion to their quotas, and the remainder, after meeting expenses, was placed in a Trust Fund. The resources of the Trust Fund, established in May 1976, were to be used exclusively for the specific purpose of providing loans to poorer developing countries. The conditions governing use of the Fund's ordinary resources did not apply to the Trust Fund, which made loans, as distinct from providing financing through purchasing operations. The loans were subject to very light conditionality, carried a highly concessional rate of interest of 0.5 percent per annum, and had a maturity of 10 years. The Trust Fund made its final disbursement in March 1981, when its business was terminated and the interest payments and loan repayments were transferred to the Special Disbursement Account (i.e., an account within the main body of the Fund). These interest payments and loan repayments that began to accumulate in the Special Disbursement Account (SDA) provided the resources for the establishment of another, similar facility, the SAF.

The SAF, established in 1986 to replicate the aims of the preceding Trust Fund, provided assistance on concessional terms to low-income member countries facing protracted balance of payments problems. Conditionality under the new facility was tightened and, in view of the modest resources available in the facility, it was hoped that its loans would act as a catalyst in encouraging the provision of additional resources to members from other international organizations and member countries. Programs supported by the loans were to be explicitly directed toward the elimination of structural imbalances and rigidities. Annual programs were to be put forward within the context of a three-year policy framework paper, prepared in collaboration with the staffs of the Fund and the World Bank, setting out the objectives, the priorities, and the broad thrust of macroeconomic and structural adjustment policies, and referencing the likely requirements and sources of the external financing envisaged under the program. Loan disbursements were made in three annual installments, bore an interest rate of 0.5 percent per annum, and were repayable in five-and-one-half years to 10 years.

To supplement the funds available under the SAF, the ESAF was established as a trust fund in the following year, to operate concurrently with the SAF. Finance for the ESAF was to be derived in part from the SDA and in part from contributions in the form of loans and grants from aid agencies of member countries. Members eligible to use the ESAF and the terms of its loan were similar to those of the SAF. In 1996, the Fund and the World Bank jointly initiated a new facility for heavily indebted poor countries (HIPCs) that, linked to the ESAF, was aimed at bringing a country's debt burden down to sustainable levels through a combination of internal economic policy reforms and the renegotiation of external debts in an orderly and comprehensive program through the Paris Club and other multinational groupings.

The combination of the EAP and the establishment of the SAF and ESAF brought a dramatic rise in the use of the Fund's resources by low-income countries. Total loans and credits outstanding from the Fund rose to over SDR 37 billion by the end of 1984 and climbed again in the 1990s to a record SDR 56 billion ($75.4 billion) on April 30, 1998, reflecting in large part the extraordinary drawings made as a result of the Asian crisis (see Chart 2). By December 31, 1998, the Fund had programs in effect with 62 countries, and the total amount approved under its various facilities had reached $83.2 billion.

The debt crisis

In August 1982, at the Fund-World Bank annual meetings in Toronto, Mexico announced it was unable to service its debts, thereby initiating a debt crisis that would persist for the next decade or so. The origins of the debt crisis sparked by the deep world recession of 1982-83

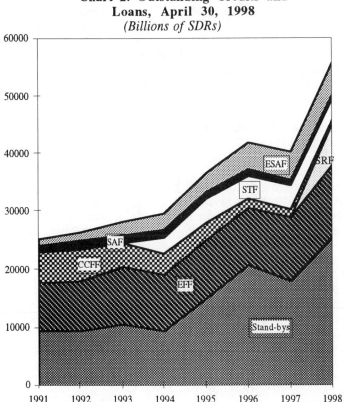

Chart 2. Outstanding Credits and
Loans, April 30, 1998
(Billions of SDRs)

lay in the two oil shocks of the 1970s, the resurgence of inflation toward the end of the decade, the easy availability of credit from the commercial banks at low or even negative rates of real interest that had persisted since the early 1970s, and the failure of many developing countries to adjust to evolving economic conditions. By 1982, the aggregate debt of non-oil-developing countries amounted to about $600 billion, of which about half was from commercial sources and one-fifth was of a short-term character.

In response to the Mexican announcement, the Fund took the initiative and drew up an adjustment program in conjunction with the Mexican government that embraced spending and pricing policies, investment priorities, monetary policy, and flexible exchange rates over a three-year period, and approved SDR 3.6 billion of its resources in support of the program. Even with the Fund's financial support, however, there was still a financing gap of about $7 billion, of which about $2 billion was to be sought from official institutions and the remainder from the commercial banks. The Managing Director took the initiative and instead of waiting for other potential creditors to come forward in their own time after the Fund had committed its resources, he insisted that they reach agreement on rescheduling existing loans, adjusting interest rates, and extending new loans to fill the financing gap before the Fund itself committed resources. In the end, financing of $5 billion was arranged with as many as 530 commercial banks. The Fund's response to the Mexican crisis was to set the pattern for a number of similar "rescue" operations, such as for Argentina, Brazil, and the Philippines, in the years to follow.

The Fund, however, was beginning to feel the effects of the debt crisis on its own operations. More and more developing countries ran into debt-servicing difficulties and began to default on their obligations to the Fund. From 1985 onward, a growing number of members that had overdue obligations to the Fund of six months or more were declared ineligible to use the Fund's resources. Ineligibility is the initial step in a procedure in which the Fund endeavors to enlist the member in a cooperative program, without further Fund financing, aimed at restoring the member to good standing. In the event that the member is judged not to be cooperating with the Fund, and not paying off, or even freezing, its arrears, a series of further steps can eventually lead to the compulsory withdrawal of the member from the organization. On April 30, 1992, overdue obligations had risen to a peak of SDR 3.5 billion, and eight members remained ineligible to use the Fund's resources. By April 30, 1998, however, total overdue obligations had fallen to SDR 2.3 billion, and the number of members that were ineligible to use the Fund's resources had declined to four.

In dealing with the problem of overdue obligations, the Fund adopted a three-prong strategy—prevention, deterrence, and intensified collaboration. Prevention consisted of designing adjustment programs that would analyze and take special account of risks attached to the program, thereby ensuring that any member using the Fund's resources would be able to meet its obligation to the Fund. Deterrence comprised a procedure that would lead, successively, to a declaration of ineligibility, a declaration of noncooperation, suspension of the member's voting rights and representation in the Fund, and, ultimately, the member's compulsory withdrawal from the Fund. In a related move, the Fund proposed a third amendment to its Articles of Agreement, which became effective in November 1992, under which the Executive Board could, by a 70 percent voting majority, suspend the voting and related rights of those members in arrears in their repayments to the Fund. The third aspect gave ineligible members an opportunity to implement, in conjunction with consultants or major creditors, a Fund-monitored "shadow" program, allowing a member to accumulate "rights" to future drawings on the Fund under a successor program, once the member had paid off its arrears. The Fund also adopted guidelines providing for a proportion of the resources committed under a stand-by or extended arrangement to be set aside to finance operations involving a reduction in the stock of debt (through buybacks, debt conversion, and other debt-reducing mechanisms), as well as providing for additional access to its resources to be made available to a member to facilitate debt and debt-service reduction and to catalyze other financial resources. Of the 11 members eligible to participate in the "rights" program since its establishment in 1990, eight had cleared their arrears with the Fund by April 30, 1998, and had remained current.

To place its financing on a sound footing, the Fund also adopted a burden-sharing strategy, setting up two special contingency accounts, one to cover outstanding overdue charges and repurchases, and the other to safeguard purchases made by members under a successor arrangement after a "rights" accumulation program has been successfully completed. The reserve accounts were funded in accordance with a burden-sharing formula, which increased the charges on the use of the Fund's resources and reduced the rate of remuneration on creditor positions in the Fund.

Services

The Fund has provided its members, and particularly developing member countries, with a growing array of training and technical assistance, in accordance with the provisions of Article V, Section 2(b) of its Articles of Agreement. Indeed, in recent years the needs of many new developing member countries and of new members in Eastern Europe and the former Soviet Union have required a major expansion in the Fund's technical assistance and training services. The IMF Institute, founded in 1964, provides courses in macroeconomics, fiscal affairs, statistics, and balance of payments at the Fund's headquarters in Washington, D.C., for officials of member countries. The Institute also provides lecturers for overseas seminars and courses related to the work of the Fund. Several other technical assistance programs have increased their reach in recent years. The Fiscal Affairs Department specializes in taxation, theory and practice; the Monetary and Exchange Affairs Department focuses on central banking, commercial bank supervision, and other aspects dealing with instruments of monetary policy; and the Statistics Department assists in the establishment of statistical bulletins and the compilation of data over a wide range of economic and financial activity. Technical assistance is provided in a variety of forms, through technical assistance missions, resident advisors, or secondment of outside experts to key positions in institutions of member countries.

Beginning at the end of the 1980s, membership of the former communist countries in Eastern Europe and the Soviet Union, with their desperate need to reshape their economic systems, added a new dimension and urgency to the provision of Fund technical assistance. In addition to expanding its training in Washington, D.C., the Fund opened, in conjunction with five other international organizations, an institute in Vienna to present courses in macroeconomics and statistics to officials of the former Soviet Union and countries in Eastern Europe. In May 1998, the Fund inaugurated the IMF-Singapore Regional Training Institute, which was established in cooperation with the Singapore authorities to hold seminars and training courses for officials in the Asia and Pacific areas.

The Fund issues a variety of periodicals dealing with the work of the Fund and related matters. These include the *World Economic Outlook* and related studies (twice a year); *International Capital Markets: Developments, Prospects, and Policy Issues;* the *IMF Survey* (twice a month); *Finance & Development* (quarterly); *International Financial Statistics* (monthly); *Staff Papers* and the *Direction of Trade* (both quarterly); *Government Financial Statistics* and the *Balance of Payments Yearbook,* as well as the *Annual Report of the Executive Board,* the *Annual Report on Exchange Restrictions and Exchange Arrangements,* and *Summary Proceedings* of the Annual Meetings (all annuals). In addition, the Fund has an extensive publishing program, which includes pamphlets, *Occasional Papers,* working papers, books, country reports, as well as videos and press material *(see* the bibliography).

Membership

Representatives from 45 countries attended the International Monetary and Financial Conference of the United and Associated Nations at Bretton Woods in July 1944, and the Fund came into existence when 29 of those countries had completed ratification of the agreement and their representatives had attended a formal signing ceremony on December 27, 1945. All the other members, except one, that had attended the Bretton Woods Conference joined the Fund in the following years, although New Zealand did not do so until 1961 and Liberia not until 1962. The U.S.S.R., the one exception, had been an active participant at the conference and had been given a quota of $1.2 billion (then the third largest quota in the Fund, after the United States and the United Kingdom), but it did not take up the ratification procedure. It was not until the communist system collapsed and the Soviet Union broke up into 15 sovereign countries that all of its former members joined the Fund, completing the relevant membership procedures in the period from June 1992 to April 1993.

Three founding members withdrew from the Fund: Poland in 1950, alleging that the Fund had failed to fulfill the expectations of its founders; Czechoslovakia in 1955, in a dispute as to whether it was required to provide data to the Fund; and Cuba in 1964, after protracted negotiations on overdue payments to the Fund. Both Poland and Czechoslovakia rejoined in 1986 and 1990, respectively. Germany and Japan joined the Fund in 1952; mainland China's request for the ouster of the Chinese National Government was rejected in 1950, but accepted 30 years later. Switzerland, after maintaining a long association with the Fund as a nonmember, became a member in 1992. By April 30, 1998, membership in the Fund had climbed to 182 members, and only Cuba, North Korea, and a few scattered ministates remained outside the Fund.

Structure of the Fund

The highest authority of the Fund is the Board of Governors, which consists of a Governor and an Alternate appointed by each member country. The Governors are usually ministers of finance, central bank governors, or officials of comparable rank. Under the Articles of Agreement, the Board of Governors has a number of specific powers, as well as all powers under the Articles not expressly conferred on the Executive Board or the Managing Director. The specific powers, which cover such matters as the admission of new members, the determination of quotas, and the allocation of SDRs, can be exercised only by the Board of Governors. All other powers can be, and have been, delegated by the Board of Governors to the Executive Board.

The Executive Board consists of 24 Executive Directors, in addition to the Managing Director, who is Chairman. Each Executive Director appoints an Alternate, who can participate in meetings but can vote only when the Executive Director is absent. Members having the five largest quotas in the Fund (the United States, Germany, Japan, France, and the United Kingdom) each appoint one member to serve until his or her successor is appointed. Of the remaining Executive Directors, 18 are elected for two-year terms, in elections that take place every even-numbered year at the time of the Annual Meetings. One (Saudi Arabia) is appointed under a provision in the Articles stipulating that if the members with the five largest quotas do not include the two members whose currencies have been most used in outstanding transactions of the Fund in the preceding two years, one or both of these members, as the case may be, can appoint a Director.

Of the 18 elected Directors, three countries (China, Russia, and Switzerland) have each chosen to elect their own Director, and have large enough quotas and sufficient votes to do so. The remaining 15 Directors are elected by groups of countries, with some Directors having over 20 countries in their constituencies. In order to cope with the business of so many countries, it has become the practice for an Executive Director representing a large constituency to appoint one or more Advisors to help in the day-to-day business and to take a seat at Executive Board meetings when the Executive Director and the Alternate are both absent.

The size and composition of the Executive Board have changed radically since the Board was first formed in 1946. Originally, it consisted of 12 members, but as the Fund's membership increased, so too was the Board enlarged, although not proportionately to the growth in membership. Thus, whereas the 45 countries participating in the Bretton Woods Conference in 1944 were to be represented by 12 Executive Directors, by 1998 the number of members had quadrupled, but the number of Executive Directors had only doubled, to 24. There have also been important changes in the rankings of the five members with the largest quotas; Germany replaced China (Taiwan) in 1960 and Japan took the place of India in 1972. Within the group of members having the five largest quotas, Germany and Japan with equal quotas have moved up to second and third places, while France and the United Kingdom, also with equal quotas, have moved into fourth and fifth places.

The personalities on the Board have also undergone a marked change. At the Bretton Woods Conference, Lord Keynes and several other delegates had argued for an Executive Board composed of high-level officials who would meet only periodically to settle substantive policy matters. Although that proposal was overruled in favor of having the Board in "continuous session," in the early years a number of the Directors were high-level officials and did not stay in Washington, D.C., to attend all Board meetings. Inevitably, the evangelical spirit and determination of the pioneers to make the organization a success have faded over the years. Executive Directors tend to be younger, from less senior positions in their home governments, and Board meetings have become more frequent, longer, and more demanding in time and effort.

The trend to less senior representation has, in part, been encouraged by the introduction of the Interim Committee, which succeeded the Committee of Twenty and, since 1976, has met at least twice a year to discuss and advise on major policy issues. The structure of the Interim Committee replicates that of the Executive Board, but its members are ministers of finance, central bank governors, or officials of comparable rank. Its terms of reference are (i) to supervise the management and adaptation of the international monetary system, including the operation of the adjustment process; (ii) to consider proposals by the Executive Board to amend the Articles of Agreement; and (iii) to deal with sudden disturbances that pose a threat to the international monetary system. The Committee is an advisory body and does not possess the authority to take decisions. It was called Interim because the second amendment to the Articles of Agreement provided for the establishment of a Council, as an organ of the Fund, that would have decision-making power. The Council, to be structured along the same lines as the Interim Committee, would require an 85 percent majority vote by the Board of Governors for it to come into existence. So far, there have been no signs that such a Council would be established in the near future, although the Managing Director at the time of the Fund-Bank Annual Meetings in 1998 suggested that it was time for the Council to come into existence.

Along with the Interim Committee, the Development Committee was also established, a joint committee made up of Governors of the World Bank, Governors of the Fund, ministers, or others of comparable rank. The Committee was set up to continue the work of the Committee of Twenty to study the question of, and to make recommendations on, the transfer of real resources to developing countries. The Interim Committee and the Development Committee normally meet twice a year (in May and September) and in the same place, with sessions of the Interim Committee being followed by those of the Development Committee, or vice versa.

The Articles of Agreement specify that the principal office of the Fund shall be located in the territory of the member having the largest quota. Accordingly, the headquarters of the Fund is located in the United States, in Washington, D.C., where its staff is stationed, apart from three small liaison offices outside the United States, one in Paris, another in Geneva, and a third in Tokyo. The organization consists of six area departments, seven functional and special services departments, and three departments, two bureaus, and four offices providing support and information services (*see* Chart 3).

The Managing Director, selected by the Executive Board, is Chairman of the Board and chief of the operating staff. The Articles of Agreement specify that he or she shall not be a Governor or Executive Director. In June 1994, the number of Deputy Managing Directors was increased from one to three, the first major structural change in management since the Fund's inception. The Managing Director and the staff owe their duty entirely to the Fund, and to no other authority. Unlike the United Nations, the Fund is not bound by a national quota system for recruiting staff members. The Fund's Articles of Agreement states that "In appointing staff the Managing Director shall, subject to the paramount importance of securing the highest standards of efficiency and of technical competence, pay due regard to the importance of recruiting personnel on as wide a geographical basis as possible." This language has enabled the Fund, in recruiting staff, to avoid purely political nominations from member countries.

Chart 3. Organization of the Fund

Board of Governors
|
Executive Board
|
Managing Director
Deputy Managing Directors
|

Area Departments	Functional & Special Services Departments	Information & Liaison	Support Services
African Department	Fiscal Affairs Department	External Relations Department	Administration Department
Asia & Pacific Department	IMF Institute	Office in Europe	Secretary's Department
European I Department	Legal Department	Office in Geneva	Bureau of Computing Services
European II Department	Monetary & Exchange Affairs Department	Regional Office for Asia & the Pacific	Bureau of Language Services
Middle Eastern Department	Policy Development & Review Department	Fund Office United Nations	Office of Internal Audit & Inspection
Western Hemisphere Department	Research Department		Investment Office-SRP
	Statistics Department		Office of Budget & Planning
	Treasurer's Department		Technical Assistance Secretariat

On April 30, 1998, the number of full-time staff totaled 2,181, recruited from 122 countries. On that date there were also 480 "other authorized staff," consisting of experts, consultants, and other nonregular resources.

Voting

The Fund has a system of weighted voting power. Each member has a basic allotment of 250 votes and, in addition, has one vote for each portion of its quota equivalent to SDR 100,000. This formula has not changed over the years (except SDRs have replaced U.S. dollars). Consequently, in 1944, at the Bretton Woods Conference, basic votes of the 44 prospective members amounted to 11.3 percent of total votes, whereas in 1998 the basic votes for the 182 members accounted for just over 2 percent of total votes. As quotas are based on a number of economic variables, the relative size of a member's quota can be adjusted over time, reflecting changes in its economic position among members. Moreover, as the Fund's overall membership has grown, each individual member has suffered a corresponding reduction in its proportionate voting strength.

Thus, when the eleventh general review of quotas has been completed and becomes effective, the U.S. voting strength (the largest in the Fund) will fall from 29.6 percent of the total under the 1944 Bretton Woods schedule to 17.5 percent, the United Kingdom from 14.25 percent to 5.1 percent, the Netherlands from 3.2 percent to 2.4 percent, and Panama from 0.27 percent to 0.097 percent. Major policy decisions taken by the Board of Governors, such as approval of a quota increase, provisions for general exchange arrangements, or establishment of the Council, require a high majority vote of 85 percent of the total. The United States alone, or the members of the European Union or the developing countries when voting together, can veto proposals subject to a high majority. The high majority requirement applies to 22 types of decisions, but they pertain to important structural and operational aspects of the Fund that rarely come up for decision. In addition to these issues, another 21 types of decisions require a voting majority of 70 percent. All other decisions, and these are by far the majority of those taken, require only a simple majority vote.

The Board of Governors meets once a year at the annual meeting, but apart from the votes that may be taken on those occasions, all votes are normally conducted by mail. The Executive Board rarely votes, but tries to reach a decision by a sense of the meeting. A consensus decision, however, usually reflects the voting power of Executive Directors for or against a proposed decision.

In retrospect, the last two decades of the twentieth century will be seen as a period of tremendous economic change and progress toward a truly international economy. It encompassed a revolution in the means of communication, the breakdown of major barriers to trade, the integration of capital markets and the flow of capital across borders on an unprecedented scale, and the emergence of developing countries in a new world economic order. The gains everywhere were impressive; the integration of Europe, the incorporation into the world economy of the former communist countries, the transformation of the "tiger economies" of Asia, the reinvigoration of economic growth in Latin America, the startling economic progress made by China, and even by India, and, finally, the emerging signs in Africa that many countries in that continent were on the threshold of belatedly setting out on the path to sustained economic development.

Problems, of course, abounded—famine, civil wars, ethnic violence, political dissension, and corruption in governments, all developments that were mostly beyond the control of the international financial institutions, such as the Fund, the World Bank, and other regional and multinational organizations. Other problems, however, that were well within their scope were only addressed half-heartedly, not the least of these being the relatively small amount of resources required to lift the tremendous weight of debt borne by the poorer developing countries, while in other parts of the world the almost reckless and uncurbed pursuit of short-term profits by investment firms, banks, and brokerage houses led eventually to the squandering of billions of dollars in wasted enterprises.

The warning signs emerged first with the economic and financial crises that overwhelmed Mexico in 1982 and 1994. Subsequently, the Fund attempted to apply the lessons of these experiences. It intensified its surveillance over members' economic and financial policies, established standards for the timely and accurate dissemination of economic data, urged a strengthening of members' financial and banking sectors, advocated greater transparency in government, potentially strengthened its own resources by authorizing a substantial increase in members' quotas and entering into new borrowing arrangements, and introduced changes in its lending policies to enable it to meet sudden demands on its resources.

These measures, however, proved to be too late in their effect to head off the profound crises that began in Thailand in June 1997 and that, by the end of 1998, had spread to half the world economy. At that point, no matter that the economic fundamentals did not justify the almost universal loss of investors' confidence, capital movements into the new industrial economies and emerging developing countries were brought almost to a standstill, and the very stability of the international monetary system was under threat.

In tackling the Asian crisis, the Fund first concentrated on restoring confidence to the economies under stress by putting together for the three countries initially most affected by the economic crisis—Indonesia, Korea, and Thailand—a financing package from the international financial community amounting to total commitments of $117.7 billion and at the same time devised economic reform programs for these countries that concentrated on the strengthening of the structure of their economies. Indonesia proved to be the weak link in these operations, and from Indonesia the contagion spread to the Philippines, Hong Kong SAR, and Malaysia, and then to Latin America and Russia. For Russia, the Fund raised a massive financial assistance package, requiring activation of the GAB, only to have the reform program agreed upon with the authorities destroyed by internal political developments. At the end of 1998, the immediate challenge for the Fund was to strengthen its financial resources through the implementation of its quota increase, which after being stalled in the U.S. Congress for almost a year was finally enacted by the United States and other member countries following the 1998 Annual Meetings. Similarly, the NAB, which were approved by the Executive Board in January 1997, were also receiving approval from members. Beyond that, it was recognized by the Fund and by the leading industrial countries that there was an urgent need for the architecture of the international monetary system to be further strengthened.

Proposals broadly embraced by the Interim Committee at its meeting in April 1998 included the following: (1) Strengthening of the international and domestic financial systems through sound and stable macroeconomic policies; (2) Development of a supervisory and regulatory framework for bank and nonbank financial institutions, the strengthening of Fund surveillance, with a focus on financial sector issues and capital flows through new forms of collaboration, supported by a "tiered" response to countries that are seriously off course in their policies; (3) Establishment of greater availability and transparency of economic data and policies, including continued progress in the implementation of the Special and General Data Dissemination initiatives, further openness by the Fund in its policy recommendations, and the release by members of Public Information Notices on the conclusion of their Article IV consultations with the Fund; (4) Affirmation of the central role that the Fund plays in crisis management, particularly its role in catalyzing financial support from the international financial community and assembling adequate resources of its own through the quota increase approved by the Board of Governors in January 1998 and the NAB; (5) Development of more effective procedures to involve the private sector in forestalling and resolving financial crises.

The Committee stressed that in times of crisis it was important that all creditors, including short-term creditors, more fully bear the consequences of their actions. The private sector should be involved at an early stage in a crisis so as to achieve an equitable sharing of the burden and limit moral hazard (the so-called "bailing-in" provisions). It said excessive reliance on short-term credit should be discouraged, and that investors should be encouraged to make better use of the economic and financial information available so as to improve risk analysis. The Committee recommended that the Fund examine a number of measures that would provide for closer contacts with creditors, including the possibility of introducing provisions in bond contracts for bondholders to be represented, in case of nonpayment, in negotiations on bond contract restructuring. It was in favor of extending the Fund's policy of providing financing to members in arrears on their debt payments to some private creditors under appropriate safeguards. It urged the adoption of strong bankruptcy systems. And it advised members to exercise caution with respect to public guarantees in order to reduce the risk of a private debt problem turning into a sovereign debt problem.

Turning to the role of capital movements, the Committee stated that the effects of the crisis in Asia had not negated the contribution that capital movements had made to economic progress in the region. "Rather, the crisis has underscored the importance of orderly and properly sequenced liberalization of capital movements, the need for appropriate macroeconomic and exchange rate policies, the critical role of sound financial sectors, and effective prudential and supervisory systems." The Committee reiterated its earlier view that it was now time to add a new chapter to the Bretton Woods Agreement by making the liberalization of capital movements one of the purposes of the Fund and extending, as needed, the Fund's jurisdiction for this purpose.

However, these measured proposals, put forward by the Interim Committee at a time when the crisis was deepening and spreading, did not subdue the increasing criticism of the Fund's policies, and in the subsequent weeks an array of new proposals from all points of the spectrum were put forward by politicians, academicians, and private financiers covering a wide range of policy and institutional changes. These included proposals to abolish the Fund and rely on free-market forces, the creation of a new institution to provide insurance for international capital movements, and a U.S. government proposal to establish a new facility within the IMF that could be drawn on promptly by members to head off potential crises that may strike fundamentally healthy emerging economies impacted by a sudden and unjustified lack of confidence by investors.

Neither did the 1998 Annual Meetings of the International Monetary Fund and the World Bank, held in Washington, D.C., in October at a critical moment in the spreading crisis, lack proposals and criticisms. "Managed development," the too close a link among banks, corporations, and the state, was identified as a major weakness in many countries. But by the end of the meetings, it was generally conceded that there would be no quick fix for the crisis. One suggestion was to convert the ministerial-level Interim Committee into a Council, with formal decision-making powers, thereby enabling ministers and Governors to have a direct involvement in strategic decisions. The consensus of the meeting, however, focused on the broader and more fundamental reforms encompassed in the five lines of approach advocated by the Interim Committee—transparency, sound financial systems, involvement of the private sector, orderly liberalization, and internationally accepted standards and codes of good practice.

On these matters, the three working groups of the Group of Twenty-Two had already submitted reports to the Fund and other international institutions outlining how they could see the system evolve. In his closing remarks to the meeting, Michel Camdessus, the Fund's Managing Director, acknowledged that there had been a systemic failure and that it would take some time to accomplish all that needed to be done.

Dictionary

-A-

Access Limits. A member's access limits to the Fund's financial resources is set as a percentage of a member's quota (q.v.). These limits are subject to periodic review, usually annually, by the Executive Board (q.v.), taking into account the Fund's liquidity (q.v.), and the demand for its resources (q.v.) by members. The following access limits, which may be exceeded in exceptional cases, were in effect at the end of September 1998 (as a percent of a member's quota):

Stand-by and Extended Arrangement

Annual	100
Cumulative	300

Special Facilities

Supplemental reserve facility (q.v.)	none
Compensatory and contingency financing facility (q.v.)	
Export earnings shortfall	30
Excess cereal import costs	15
Contingency financing	30
Optional tranche	*20*
Buffer stock financing facility (q.v.)	35

Enhanced structural adjustment facility (q.v.)

Three-year access	
Regular	190
Exceptional	255

Accounting Unit. The Fund's unit of account in which its books and financial records are maintained is the Special Drawing Right (SDR) (q.v.), an international reserve (q.v.) asset created by the Fund in 1968. Since 1981, the SDR's currency value has been determined daily by the Fund by summing the values, in terms of U.S. dollars, of a basket of five currencies (q.v.), based on market exchange rates. The currencies making up the basket are the currencies of the five members having the largest exports of goods and services. The composition of the basket, and the weight of each currency in the basket, are reviewed every five years. Last reviewed in September 1995, the Executive Board (q.v.) decided that with effect from January 1, 1996, the list of currencies in the SDR valuation basket (q.v.) should remain the same, and the weight of each currency in the basket for the following five years should be as follows: U.S. dollar (with a weight of 39 percent), deutsche mark (21 percent), Japanese yen (18 percent), French franc (11 percent), and pound sterling (11 percent). On January 1, 1999, the SDR was valued at 1.41089 U.S. dollars.

Gold (q.v.) deposits held by the Fund and by its members continue to be valued by the Fund on the basis of SDR 35 per fine ounce, a rate that has remained unchanged for over 30 years in terms of the SDR.

Accounts of the Fund. The Fund's accounts fall into three categories: the General Department, the Special Drawing Rights (SDRs) Department (qq.v.), and the Administered Accounts. All three accounts are operated and maintained in the Treasurer's Department, and the account names refer to accounting entities, rather than structural departments.

The General Department is the main source of finance available to members. It consists of: (1) the General Resources Account (q.v.), which is the basic account of the Fund, consisting of ordinary resources made up chiefly of quota subscriptions (q.v.) paid to the Fund by members and borrowed resources; (2) the Special Disbursement Account (q.v.), whose resources come from the profits on past gold sales by the Fund (q.v.), interest on loans made by the Trust Fund (q.v.), income from investments by the Fund (q.v.), and other transfers and interest payments; (3) the Investment Account, which has not been activated; and (4) the Borrowed Resources Suspense Account (q.v.), which authorized the Fund to invest in SDR-denominated deposits and borrowings made under agreements for the enlarged access policy (EAP) (q.v.).

The SDR Department records all transactions and operations in SDRs (q.v.). SDRs are an interest-bearing asset allocated by the Fund to each member that is a participant in the SDR Department. SDRs may be used by participating members to settle accounts between themselves and in transactions (q.v.) with the Fund.

Administered Accounts include various accounts administered

by the Fund, principally the enhanced structural adjustment facility (q.v.) trust, the Trust Fund, and the supplementary financing facility subsidy account (q.v.), as well as accounts holding grants, concessional loans, and other loans contributed by members to provide technical and other assistance to members.

Adjustment Program. *See* Balance of Payments Adjustment; Credit Controls; Financial Programming; Stabilization Programs.

Administrative and Capital Budgets of the Fund. The budget is prepared annually by the staff of the Office of Budget and Planning, which in 1992 was transferred from the Administration Department to the Office of the Managing Director. The budget is subject to the approval of the Executive Board (q.v.). Unlike the United Nations, which requires annual budgetary subscriptions from its members, the Fund is self-financing, deriving income from its financial operations with members. In setting its budgetary target, the Fund aims to cover its administrative expenses and to be able to allocate prudent amounts to its reserve after meeting remuneration and interest payments to members. The Fund's financial year begins on May 1 and ends on April 30.

The Administrative Budget for the financial year ended April 30, 1999, provided for total expenses of $519.5 million, an increase of 3.1 percent over the budget approved for the previous year. The small increase reflects the efforts by the Executive Board and management to restrain expenditures, despite an increase in the Fund's surveillance (q.v.) activities, a rise in the provision of technical assistance (q.v.), and a small increase in the number of staff (q.v.) necessitated by the Asian crisis (q.v.). An estimated breakdown of the costs in 1998 shows that Surveillance accounted for 28.8 percent of total expenditures; Administrative Support for 15.6 percent; Use of Fund resources (q.v.) for 24.3 percent; Technical Assistance for 15.5 percent; the Executive Board for 7.3 percent; External Relations for 3.6 percent; and the Board of Governors (q.v.) for 4.0 percent.

The capital budget in the year ended April 30, 1999, was set at $14.4 million for capital project budgets and $46.4 million for disbursements of capital projects during the year. The capital budget represents a continuation of plans for completing major building projects, replacing older facilities and electronic data-processing equipment, and other medium-term programs.

In the late 1960s, the Fund adopted a long-term strategy for housing its staff in one location in the Washington, D.C., central business district and designed a headquarters building that could be expanded over time. The first phase of the headquarters building was completed in the early 1970s, the second phase in the early 1980s, and the third phase in 1997. To accommodate the Fund's growth brought about by the increase in Fund membership (q.v.) and increased activities over the past decade or so, a fourth phase was initiated, which consisted of purchasing a building adjacent to the Fund. When the fourth phase has been completed, all of the Fund staff will be accommodated in two adjacent buildings, owned by the Fund, with a resultant reduction in overall occupancy costs.

African Franc Zone. On January 12, 1994, the CFA franc and the Comorian franc (CF) were devalued, the CFA franc to 100 per French franc and the CF to 75 per French franc. These devaluations were accompanied by major fiscal, monetary, wage, and structural policy measures and were followed by Fund stand-by or enhanced structural adjustment facility (ESAF) programs in seven of the CFA franc countries. The CFA franc zone had experienced some 30 years of strong growth and low inflation compared with other sub-Saharan African countries, but in the years 1986-1993 growth had begun to weaken in the face of a sharp deterioration in the zone's terms of trade. At the same time, fiscal imbalances and the external public debt had increased substantially and had been accompanied by the emergence of sizable domestic and external payments arrears and a major weakening of the soundness and financial position of the banking systems in the CFA franc zone.

The 14 countries of the franc zone consist of two separate groups of sub-Saharan countries and the Islamic Federal Republic of the Comoros. One group includes the seven members of the West African Monetary Union (WAMU)—Benin, Burkina Faso, Côte d'Ivoire, Mali, Niger, Senegal, and Togo—which have assigned responsibility for conducting monetary policy to a common central bank, the Banque Centrale des Etats de l'Afrique de l'Ouest (BCEAO). The other group includes six members of another common central bank, the Banque des Etats de l'Afrique Centrale (BEAC)—Cameroon, the Central African Republic, Chad, the Republic of the Congo, Equatorial Guinea, and Gabon.

Each of the two groups and the Comoros maintain separate currencies, commonly referred to as the CFAF. For 45 years prior to January 12, 1994, the CFAF was pegged (q.v.) to the French franc at the rate of CFAF 50 = F 1. The peg for the Comorian franc was last changed in 1988.

The coming into existence of the European Economic and Monetary Union (EMU) (q.v.) and the creation of a single currency, the euro (q.v.), on January 1, 1999, raises a number of issues for the CFA franc zone. The CFA franc was pegged to the French franc, and after France became a participant in the new single currency on January 1, 1999, the CFA franc was pegged to the euro, with a parity of CFAF 655.957 per euro. Although the change is likely to leave the operating arrangement and operating features of the zone essentially unchanged, a number of other questions arise.

Allocations of SDRs. Allocations of Special Drawing Rights (SDRs) (q.v.) are made by the Fund to those members that have agreed to become participants in the SDR Department (q.v.) and are made annually in proportion to participants' quotas (q.v.) in the Fund. In considering a decision to allocate SDRs, the Fund is obligated under its Articles (q.v.) to "seek to meet the long-term global need, as and when it arises, to supplement existing reserve assets (q.v.) in such a manner as will promote the attainment of its purposes and will avoid economic stagnation and deflation as well as excess demand and inflation in the world." Because the decision to allocate SDRs gives the Fund a unique power to create unconditional international liquidity (q.v.), the procedure to be followed is hedged around with precautionary features, designed to ensure that the Fund will exercise due care and caution in using its power.

First, the Managing Director (q.v.) is required to make a proposal for an SDR allocation, consistent with the criteria established in the Fund's Articles, at least six months before a basic period begins or within six months of a request for a proposal from the Executive Board or Board of Governors (qq.v.). In making such a proposal, the Managing Director must ascertain that it has widespread support among SDR participants. Second, the Executive Board must concur in the proposal. Third, the Board of Governors has the power to approve or modify the proposal by a majority of not less than 85 percent of its total voting power. If the Managing Director, after consulting with participants, concludes that broad support for an SDR allocation does not exist or that he cannot make a proposal that he considers to be consistent with the terms of the Articles, he is required to submit a report on his finding to the Executive Board and the Board of Governors.

Decisions on allocations of SDRs are made for successive basic periods of up to five years, although the Fund can alter the duration of the basic period. The first basic period was for three years (1970-72), when a total of SDR 9.3 billion was allocated. In the following basic period (1973-77), no allocations were made, but in the third basic period (1978-81), SDR 12.1 billion was allocated. No allocations of SDRs have been made since 1981 so that at the end of 1998, total SDRs in circulation remained at SDR 21.4 billion.

At the 1997 meetings of the Board of Governors, the Governors adopted a Resolution approving a special one-time allocation of SDRs, amounting to SDR 21.4 billion, that would equalize the ratio of SDRs to quotas for all members at 29.3 percent and allow the 38 members that have never received SDRs to participate in the SDR system. This special allocation required an amendment to the Articles of Agreement, which was before the Board of Governors at the end of 1998.

Alternate Executive Director. Each Executive Director (q.v.) appoints an Alternate, with full power to act in his or her absence. When Executive Directors who appointed them are present, Alternates may participate in Executive Board (q.v.) meetings but may not vote.

Annual Meetings. Annual Meetings of the Board of Governors (q.v.) are held jointly with the Governors of the World Bank (q.v.) Group. The inaugural meeting was held in Savannah, Georgia, in March 1946. The first meeting of the Board was held in Washington, D.C., in September/October 1946; the second meeting, in London, England, in September 1947; the third, fourth, fifth, and sixth annual meetings were held in Washington, D.C., in September 1948, 1949, 1950, and 1951, respectively. The seventh meeting was held in Mexico City in September 1952, and thereafter it became the convention to hold consecutive meetings in Washington, D.C., and every third meeting in a member country other than the United States. Insofar as it is physically feasible, it is the practice to rotate the meetings held outside the United States among the world's geographical regions. Thus, the meeting was held in Istanbul, Turkey, in 1955; Delhi, India, in 1958; Vienna, Austria, in 1961; Tokyo, Japan, in 1964; Rio de Janeiro, Brazil, in 1967; Copenhagen, Denmark, in 1970; Nairobi, Kenya, in 1973; Manila, the Philippines, in 1976; Belgrade, Yugoslavia, in 1979; Toronto, Canada, in 1982; Seoul, Korea, in 1985; Berlin, Germany, in 1988; Bangkok, Thailand, in 1991; Madrid, Spain, in 1994; and Hong Kong SAR, China, in 1997.

Although traditionally little official business is accomplished, the Annual Meetings provide an important and rare opportunity for a face-to-face exchange of views by members. The meetings have assumed increasingly informal importance over the years as the largest international conference at which the world's financial officials, private financiers, and economists, journalists, and special guests are present. The Joint Fund-World Bank meetings are regularly preceded by meetings of the Group of Ten, the Group of Twenty-Four, the Interim Committee, and the Development Committee (qq.v.). All told, the meetings are attended by several thousand participants, observers, and journalists, forming a unique confluence of official and private interests in the world of finance.

Annual Report of the Executive Board. Prepared for the financial year by the Executive Directors (q.v.) and submitted by the Chairman of the Executive Board (q.v.) to the Chairman of the Board of Governors (q.v.). The *Report* briefly reviews international financial and economic developments during the previous financial year, reports on the Fund's operations during that period, and discusses and explains the policies adopted or applied during the year. The *Report* is the major item for discussion on the agenda of the Annual Meetings (q.v.) and is usually submitted to the Governors approximately one month before the date of the meetings.

During the 1950s and 1960s, the *Annual Report* was the primary source of information on the Fund's activities and policies; it was in the *Report* that the Fund's assessment of the world economy first appeared and where its major policy decisions, such as its reserve and credit tranche policies (qq.v.) and its views on conditionality and international liquidity (qq.v.), were given publicity. In the 1970s, however, the *Report* lost its primacy, partly because of the publication of the staff's *World Economic Outlook* (q.v.) and other publications such as the *IMF Survey* and *Finance & Development,* which were able to give more timely attention to the world economic situation, and partly due to the establishment of the Interim Committee (q.v.), which raised and discussed most major policy questions in advance of the publication of the *Report.* The *Annual Report* continues to be an important document of record and chronicles the activities and policies of the Fund, together with an account of the evolution of the world economy, over the past 50 years.

Annual Report on Exchange Arrangements and Exchange Restrictions (AREAER). Provides an overview of the foreign exchange (q.v.) restrictions prevailing in the international monetary system (q.v.), and describes the exchange rate system in effect in each member country.

The authority for publishing the *Report* is derived from the Fund's original Articles of Agreement (q.v.), which envisioned the establishment of a multilateral system of payments, free of restrictions on current transactions. The Articles recognized, however, that in the exceptional conditions of the postwar years, it would not be possible to establish a freely operating system immediately, and thus provided for a transitional period in which members would be able to maintain restrictions and adapt them to changing circumstances. But after a transitional period of three years, the Fund was required to report on any restrictions remaining in force, and after five years, and each year thereafter, members retaining such restrictions had to consult with the Fund to determine whether retention of the restrictions was inconsistent with members' obligations under the Articles. The transitional provisions in the Articles have been maintained through all subsequent amendments to the Articles.

The *Report* fulfills the Fund's obligation to report on the restrictions in effect in each country and includes a detailed description of each country's exchange arrangements.

Archives of Fund Opened. For nearly 50 years, since its inception, the Fund maintained that its archives should not be made available to the public and was one of the few international or national institutions to keep its records private. In January 1996, however, the Executive Board (q.v.) decided that outside persons would be allowed access to archived material in the Fund that is over 30 years old, provided that access to Fund documents originally classified as "Secret" or "Strictly Confidential" would be granted only upon the Managing Director's (q.v.) consent to their declassification. The Board added that it was understood that this consent would be granted in all instances except those in which, despite the passage of time, the material remained highly confidential or sensitive.

It was agreed that access to the following would not be granted: (1) legal documents and records maintained by the Legal Department that are protected by attorney-client privilege; (2) documentary material furnished to the Fund by external parties, including member countries, their instrumentalities and agencies and central banks, that bear confidential markings, unless such external parties consent to their declassification; (3) personnel files and medical and other records pertaining to individuals; and (4) documents and proceedings of the Grievance Committee

Argentina. Argentina has made frequent use of the Fund's financial resources (q.v.) since it became a member in 1956. For several decades after the end of World War II, however, economic policies were heavily interventionist, with high tariffs to protect local industry, government boards to regulate all aspects of commerce, and political decisions taking precedence over the marketplace.

The transformation of the economy began at the end of the 1980s under President Carlos Menem, when a start was made on privatization, a reduction in government expenditures, a drastic reduction in import tariffs, and a transformation of the central bank into a currency board arrangement, with the peso backed by gold or foreign exchange (qq.v.).

The transformation was assisted first by a 17-month stand-by arrangement (q.v.) in November 1989, amounting to SDR 1,104 million (about $1,500 million), and by a nine-month stand-by arrangement in July 1991, amounting to SDR 780 million (about $1,120 million), which was replaced in March 1992 by an extended Fund facility (EFF) (q.v.) authorizing drawings (q.v.) up to SDR 2,483 million (about $3.6 billion). During this period Argentina also benefited by drawings under the compensatory financing facility (q.v.) and by the use of Fund financing in support of a reduction in its debt- and debt-service-support operations, covering an estimated total of $29.2 million of debt and debt servicing and reducing its obligations by about $980 million a year for the rest of the decade. All told, the financial assistance available to Argentina at this time amounted to about $3.8 billion.

During 1991-93, the authorities reinforced fiscal adjustment and structural reforms. A key feature of the reform program was the Convertibility Law, enacted in March 1991, providing for the convertibility of the peso at a fixed parity to the U.S. dollar. It established the backing of the monetary base with the central bank's gross international reserves (q.v.) and prohibited the indexation of domestic-currency contracts. In the area of public finance, the authorities eliminated the fiscal deficit, streamlined the tax system, rationalized government spending, expanded privatization, and restored Argentina's creditworthiness. Other measures included structural reforms, such as deregulation and trade liberalization, and a start on reforming the financial markets, the social security system, and provincial government finance.

This bold economic program produced remarkable results. Real investment recovered strongly and real consumption expanded rapidly, with real average GDP growth averaging 7 percent a year in 1991-93. Consumer price inflation fell abruptly to 80 percent during 1991 (down from 1,300 percent the year before) and then moved down to industrial-country levels in 1993 and thereafter. A tripling of imports (led by capital goods) moved the external current account into deficits, averaging more than $8 billion a year in 1992-93 (3.5 percent of GDP) from a surplus of $2 billion in 1990. Capital inflows, however, more than covered the current account deficit, thereby raising the central bank's gross international reserves to over $15 billion (about 10 months of imports).

The contagion (dubbed *Tequila*) affect of the Mexican (q.v.) financial crisis at the end of 1994 triggered a slump in investor confidence, and Argentina experienced a large outflow of capital. By April 1995 reserves had fallen by one third. Argentina, introduced a strong package of fiscal measures to stabilize the financial situation, including a temporary increase in the value-added tax (VAT), increases in import duties, a broadening of the tax base, reform of the wealth tax, and improvements in the tax administration, aimed at restoring liquidity to the financial sector, raising domestic saving, and reestablishing confidence in the government's ability to defend the fixed exchange rate that is at the heart of the Convertibility Plan. Structural policies included further steps toward privatization, labor market reform, and a bankruptcy law. The program was supported by an extension of the extended facility for a further year and an increase of SDR 1,537 million (about $2 billion) in the available financing. As confidence gradually strengthened, deposits reflowed into the country, interest rates declined, and access to foreign borrowing was restored. While real GDP contracted by 4.4 percent, inflation declined to 1.6 percent in 1995, the lowest level in 50 years. The external current account deficit was halved in 1995, mainly due to an increase in exports.

In April 1996, the Fund approved a stand-by arrangement (q.v.) authorizing drawings up to the equivalent of SDR 720 million (about $1.0 billion) over the following 21 months in support of an economic program for 1996-97. Its aim was to restore economic growth under conditions of low inflation and external viability, based on the strategy of maintaining fiscal and monetary discipline in the context of the Convertibility Law. Structural reforms were centered on the restructuring of the federal and provincial governments, as well as merging or eliminating a number of public institutions. At the end of the program period, real GDP had risen from 4.2 percent in 1996 to 8.1 percent in 1998, consumer prices remained flat, the overall fiscal balance declined from a deficit of 2.2 percent of GDP to a deficit of 1.4 percent, and although the external current account balance had increased from 1.9 percent to 3.8 percent, the authorities had no difficulty in financing the deficit through favorable capital movements, despite the turbulence that affected international capital markets in the latter part of the year.

In February 1998, the Fund approved another three-year credit for Argentina, equivalent to SDR 2.08 billion (about $2.8 billion) under its extended Fund facility, to support the government's medium-term economic program for 1998-2000. In requesting the credit, it was the government's intention to regard the credit as precautionary and to draw on it only if adverse external circumstances made it necessary.

The medium-term program for 1988-2000 basically envisaged more of the same that had been implemented in the previous six or seven years. It included further reforms in the labor market, in the tax system, and in budgetary procedures, the conclusion of the privatization process, and reforms in the health and judicial systems, thus completing a decade of economic, financial, and social reform. Although buffeted during the year by the effects of the Asian crisis (q.v.) in September 1998 the Fund announced at the conclusion of its first review of the extended arrangement that all applicable performance criteria had been met and that substantial progress had been made in the implementation of structural reforms.

Arrears in Payments. Payment arrears were defined by the Fund in the early 1970s as undue delay in making foreign exchange (q.v.) available for international transactions, and were regarded as a payments restriction. The emergence of payment arrears was, of course, also a symptom of balance of payments (q.v.) difficulties, and the Fund was, therefore, often involved with members in payment arrears. Adjustment programs (q.v.) supported by the Fund have always given high priority to setting macroeconomic targets that would allow accumulated arrears to be cleared.

Article VIII. *See* Obligations Under Article VIII.

Article XIV. *See* Transitional Arrangements.

Articles of Agreement. The original Articles of Agreement of the International Monetary Fund were agreed upon at the International Monetary and Financial Conference of the United and Associated Nations that was convened at Bretton Woods (q.v.), New Hampshire, on July 1, 1944. The Conference was attended by delegates from 44 members of the United and Associated Nations and by a representative of Denmark, as well as delegates from several international organizations. The Final Act, embodying the Articles of Agreement of the International Monetary Fund and of the International Bank for Reconstruction and Development (World Bank) (q.v.), was signed by all delegates on July 22, 1944.

The original Articles were based on the concept of a multilateral trade and payments system, operating with convertible currencies and free of payment restrictions on transfers relating to current transactions. They envisaged an exchange rate system that, contrary to the rigidity of the old gold exchange standard, would be stable, but flexible. The Fund was given authority to approve initial par values (q.v.) (i.e., to accept an exchange rate value declared by a member), and members could change these initial exchange rates (beyond an accumulated 10 percent) only with the concurrence of the Fund. Members were to subscribe to a pool of gold and currencies (q.v.) that could be drawn upon temporarily by members to help them finance their balance of payments disequilibria.

The first amendment to the Articles became effective on July 28, 1969. Its main purpose was to establish the SDR Department (q.v.) and to provide for the creation of special drawing rights (SDRs) (q.v.), a new international reserve (q.v.) asset to be issued by the Fund to supplement existing international reserve assets.

The second amendment to the Articles of Agreement became effective on April 1, 1978. This was a comprehensive reform of the Articles, recognizing that the old Bretton Woods par value system (q.v.) had collapsed. In the place of par values, the new Articles allowed a member to establish the exchange arrangement of its choice, although the Articles continued to require members to foster orderly economic growth with reasonable price stability, promote stability through orderly underlying economic and financial conditions, and avoid the manipulation of exchange rates or the international monetary system (q.v.) to gain unfair competitive advantage over other members. The second amendment also introduced the concept of firm surveillance (q.v.) over the exchange rate policies of members by the Fund and required the cooperation of members in this endeavor. Thus, the Fund had lost the authority given to it under the original Articles to approve members' initial par values and subsequent changes in them, but had gained a wider, although perhaps a more nebulous, authority, that of firm surveillance over members' exchange arrangements. The effective exercise of this new authority proved to be a critical but difficult challenge for international monetary cooperation in succeeding years.

A third amendment to the Articles of Agreement was approved by the Board of Governors (q.v.) in 1990 and became effective in November 1992. This amendment, whose principal feature was the suspension of voting and related rights of those members in arrears in their repayments to the Fund, was also linked to an increase in members' quotas (q.v.) in the Fund, in accordance with the ninth general review of quotas.

A fourth amendment to the Articles was being prepared by the Executive Board (q.v.) in 1998 to give the Fund jurisdiction over capital account movements and to provide for a one-time equity allocation (q.v.) of SDRs, as requested by the Interim Committee (q.v.) at its meeting in Hong Kong SAR in September 1997.

In order to become a member, the Fund's Articles of Agreement must be ratified under the legislative procedure mandated for an international agreement in the member country, and membership (q.v.) does not become effective until the country has paid its subscription (q.v.) to the Fund and deposited with the designated depository, which is currently the government of the United States, an instrument setting forth that it has accepted the agreement in accordance with its law and has taken all the steps necessary to enable it to carry out all of its obligations under the agreement. *See also* Obligations Under Article VIII; Transitional Arrangements.

Asian Financial Crisis.   One of the most serious postwar international economic and financial crises erupted in 1997 when the financial and exchange markets in Thailand (q.v.), after a decade of rapid economic development, came under acute pressure. The erosion of Thailand's international competitiveness and a dramatic fall in the value of the baht following the attempt by authorities to adopt a managed float for the currency led to an abrupt loss of confidence by domestic and international investors alike. The crisis in Thailand quickly spread to other Asian economies, involving Indonesia and Korea (qq.v.), as well as other economies in the region, such as Hong Kong SAR, Malaysia, the Philippines (qq.v.), and Singapore. Precipitous declines in currency values and stock markets were widespread throughout the region.

The crisis in Asia occurred after several decades of outstanding and unprecedented economic performance. Annual GDP growth in five countries of the Association of South-East Asian Nations (ASEAN)—Indonesia, Malaysia, the Philippines, Singapore, and Thailand—averaged close to 8 percent over the previous decade, and during the 30 years preceding the crisis per capita income levels had increased tenfold in Korea, fivefold in Thailand, and fourfold in Malaysia. Per capita income levels in Hong Kong SAR and Singapore had climbed to be in excess of those in some industrial countries. Until the crisis, Asia had attracted almost half of total capital flows to developing countries—nearly $100 billion in 1996. In the past decade, the share of developing countries and emerging market economies of Asia in world exports nearly doubled, to almost one fifth of the total. They were the "tiger" economies of the age.

The very success of these economies ironically also contributed to their undoing. Intoxicated by the success of their growth policies, the authorities in several of the countries brushed off warnings from the Fund and other organizations that their economies were overheating and had serious structural weaknesses, particularly in the financial sectors. Hong Kong SAR, Malaysia, and Singapore, after the initial impact of the crisis, quickly took corrective action in raising interest rates and undertaking fiscal reforms to stabilize their currencies and stock prices without resorting to Fund resources, while Thailand, Korea, and Indonesia appealed for and received very large amounts of assistance from the Fund and other international institutions.

In pursuit of its immediate goal of restoring confidence in the region, the Fund responded quickly by using the recently established emergency financing mechanism (q.v.) to enter into adjustment programs (q.v.) with Indonesia, Korea, and Thailand and extended and augmented its existing program with the Philippines. All told, about $36 billion of the Fund's resources were committed to the countries under speculative attack, and the Fund took the lead in helping to mobilize additional commitments of $81 billion from other multilateral and bilateral sources (although as the crisis widened and deepened, a number of these bilateral lenders themselves required assistance).

The Asian countries affected by the crises had different degrees of financial and structural problems, notably in current account positions and fiscal situations, but they also had a number of fundamental structural weaknesses in common. The Fund's first priority was to restore confidence in the region through massive injections of financial resources and the correction of excessively low interest rates. Beyond that, however, the Fund's challenge was not so much to devise corrective macroeconomic policies, but to lay out a series of structural reforms. To this end, the IMF-supported adjustment programs had many of the following common features:

- the introduction of flexibility to exchange rates where it did not exist already;
- a temporary tightening of monetary policy (q.v.) to stem pressures on the balance of payments (q.v.) and staunch the outflow of reserves;
- immediate action to correct obvious weaknesses in the financial system;
- structural reforms to remove features of the economy that had become impediments to growth, such as monopolies, trade barriers, and preferential practices among corporations;
- assistance in reopening or maintaining lines of external financing; and
- the maintenance of a sound fiscal policy, taking into account the budgetary cost of restructuring the financial sector and the need to protect social spending.

The heart of all the programs was structural reform, in contrast to many of the Fund-supported programs of the past, where the focus had most often been on macroeconomic policies to rectify monetary, fiscal, and external imbalances. Moreover, because financial sector problems were the major cause of the crises, the centerpiece of the Asian programs was a comprehensive reform of the financial systems. Such reforms included closure of financial institutions that were not viable, with an associated write-down of shareholders' capital; the recapitalization of undercapitalized institutions; close supervision of weak institutions; and increased foreign participation in the domestic financial system.

Greater transparency and efficiency in government was addressed through measures designed to improve the effectiveness of markets, break the close links between business and governments, and prudently liberalize capital markets. Improvements in data collection and dissemination were also addressed, not only for the economy (particularly for external reserves and liabilities), but also for the fiscal, corporate, and banking sectors. These efforts were coordinated with the World Bank (q.v.), with its focus on structural and sectoral issues, and with the Asian Development Bank, with its regional specialization.

An underlying early concern was that the market overreaction to the crises, which had brought about sharp currency devaluations that were not justified by the "fundamentals" of the countries involved, would be regarded by others in the region as competitive devaluations that would provoke them to devalue their own currencies. In this respect China was a major concern, and the Fund management gave high marks to the Chinese authorities in making it clear that they had had no intention to devalue the renminbi. A second concern was that some of the weaker Japanese banks would buckle under the strain and initiate a major world banking crisis. The Japanese economy had been essentially flat for six years and entered into what was officially designated as a recession in the first quarter of 1998. Under heavy international pressure, the Japanese authorities were urged to implement a program to stimulate the economy through tax cuts and government expenditures, along with structural reforms, including the closure or consolidation of nonviable banking institutions. But, in the event, national elections and a change in the administration in mid-1998 weakened the internal political situation and nullified any effective legislative action. As a result, the Japanese economy remained a drag on the world economy throughout the year.

Although the overall situation remained volatile, a financial turnaround in most of the Asian crisis countries began in the first quarter of 1988, with both the Thai baht and the Korean won strengthening by about 18 percent and ending the quarter worth about 38 percent less in terms of U.S. dollars than they were before the crises. Similar gains were made in the stock markets of both countries. More moderate gains, but still positive ones, were made in the markets of Malaysia and the Philippines.

The course of recovery suffered a severe setback, however, when Indonesia failed to follow through on its program with the Fund. Ironically, Indonesia had called for Fund assistance at a far earlier stage of the crisis than others in the region, but had delayed the implementation of corrective measures, particularly those requiring the closure of nonviable banks and government enterprises (some of which were owned or operated by members of the President's family). It was not until April 1998 that a further renegotiation of the Indonesia program was completed and full support for it had been pledged by President Suharto. By that time, however, the Indonesia rupiah had lost 70 percent of its value since the middle of 1997 and 35 percent since the beginning of 1998. The delay in implementing corrective measures proved extremely costly; the austerity program, seen against a political regime that was perceived to be corrupt and marked by cronyism and nepotism, aroused widespread opposition from vulnerable groups of the population. On May 20, in the face of mounting pressure, violence in the streets, and demands for his resignation, President Suharto announced his withdrawal from the presidency. The Vice President, B. J. Habibie, was immediately sworn in as head of state and the Fund began the negotiations for a new recovery program. But it was not until July 1998 that a far tougher program was completed—12 months after the first signs of the crisis had appeared.

Additional measures taken by the Fund during this period included the appointment of the former Deputy Managing Director (q.v.) of the Fund, Prabhakar Narvekar (q.v.), as special advisor to the President of Indonesia, and the establishment of Fund resident representatives (q.v.) in Korea and Thailand. As part of its new approach in explaining its programs to the public, the Fund also conducted extensive dialogues with a variety of constituencies in the program countries, including consultations with labor groups, the press, and the public.

The mounting stress in Indonesia was enough to disrupt an already extremely fragile situation in the rest of Asia, and progress of the recovery slowed and was even reversed in some countries. Malaysia, setting out on a course of its own, imposed capital controls in a physical attempt to stop the hemorrhaging, raising fears that this would start a wider movement toward restrictions, akin to what had occurred in the 1930s. Subsequently, when Prime Minister Mahathir had taken over the post of Finance Minister, the government embarked on a huge spending program in an attempt to restore growth to the economy.

With the confidence of international investors shattered, the crisis rapidly spread to other parts of the world economy, notably Russia and countries in Latin America. For Russia, which in 1997 had finally produced a small but positive growth of GDP and appeared to be set for continued progress, the Fund entered into a massive multinational financial aid program, linked to a broad range of macroeconomic policies and structural reforms. However, political instability inside Russia and the continuing incapacity of its President severely damaged the government's ability to carry through the program. In September 1998, with the recovery program already a nonstarter, a new government took office containing cabinet members leaning against further free-market experiments. With crucial elements of the reform program inoperative, disbursements from the Fund were halted. The government announced a default on its foreign debts and floated the ruble, which fell from 6 to 15 to the U.S. dollar by the end of the month.

From Russia, which, although of strategic importance, was not of major economic significance, the battle line moved to Latin America, where both Argentina (q.v.) and Brazil (q.v.) were suffering stress. Argentina had entered into a three-year arrangement with the Fund in 1997 and, despite some loss of reserves and rising interest rates, succeeded in riding out the storm. At its first annual review of the arrangement in September 1998, the Fund found that Argentina had met all the performance criteria under the program and was making satisfactory progress in implementing structural reforms. In Brazil, where a presidential election was due early in October, international reserves (q.v.), the exchange rate, and the stock market were all under pressure, but the government was reluctant to enter into an arrangement with the Fund until after the elections. Both the U.S. authorities and the Fund indicated that they were prepared to extend financing to Brazil, should the request be made, and the Fund agreed with the Brazilian authorities on the initial parameters of a program.

On November 13, 1998, the Fund and Brazil were able to announce a major economic adjustment program, supported by a financing package totaling $41 billion over the following three years, in which the Fund, the World Bank (q.v.), the Inter-American Development Bank (IDB), and the Bank for International Settlements (BIS) (q.v.), as well as many industrial countries, were all participants. As much as $37 billion of the package could become available almost immediately, if needed, through drawings (q.v.) on the supplemental reserve facility (SRF) in the Fund, from proportionate drawings on the loans from the bilateral lenders through the BIS, and from World Bank and IDB resources. The strong front-loading of the financing program was designed to allow Brazil to be able to approach its creditors in the private sector and to voluntarily negotiate a restructuring of its external credits. The financing program was accompanied by a three-year economic program, under which the Brazilian authorities undertook to implement a comprehensive set of revenue-raising and expenditure-saving measures achieve a major fiscal adjustment by the year 2001.

Toward the end of 1998, the crisis seemed to have reached rock bottom, and was beginning to recover. The volatility of the Asian financial markets had eased, and many currencies had stabilized, and even strengthened. Interest rates in the crisis countries had come down and foreign exchange reserves were rising. Even in Indonesia, there were also first signs of improvement. In Japan, the Diet passed long-awaited legislation providing $500 billion in public funds to accelerate the task of restructuring the Japanese banking industry, and the authorities renewed their commitments to bring about tax cuts and increased public spending. The yen strengthened, and fear of a Chinese devaluation of the renminbi receded. At the end of 1998, therefore, the world economy was not yet out of the woods, but there were grounds for cautious optimism.

The efforts of the Fund to cope with the Asian crisis were greeted on all sides by criticism. The programs were too tough, they were too soft, they addressed the wrong problems, the measures proposed were inappropriate, they rewarded bad behavior, and even that the Fund had caused the whole crisis by its intervention in the first place. At one extreme were those who wanted to abolish the Fund and leave events to the free market. At the other were those who wanted to erect a new institution to operate alongside the Fund to control international financial movements. In between these two extremes were the Fund's management and probably most officials and professionals advocating a steady further evolution of the existing system.

Throughout the entire period of the crisis, the Fund strenuously refuted the main charges, but did admit that its initial insistence on retrenchment was probably too tough in view of the depth and weaknesses of the economies in question—an underestimate shared by others and promptly rectified when the depth of the crisis became apparent. It launched an unusually large-scale media effort to combat criticism. The Managing Director and the Deputy Managing Directors (qq.v.) spoke in numerous fora explaining the

Fund's programs; its mission chiefs appeared on television and before the press in the countries involved to answer questions; the programs themselves were published (with the permission of the countries concerned); and a mass of information was made available on the Fund's web site, including letters of intent, news briefs, country studies, and economic data. The crisis provoked a new scrutiny of the efficacy of the international monetary system and produced what Deputy Managing Director Stanley Fisher referred to as a "blizzard of metaphors" for improving its architecture. *See also* Moral Hazard.

Asset Settlement. A proposal made by the staff (q.v.) of the Fund in connection with discussions on the reform of the international monetary system (q.v.) after the breakdown of the par value system (q.v.) early in the 1970s. The idea was to replace the currency convertibility (q.v.) provisions of the original Articles of Agreement (q.v.) and eliminate or reduce the role of reserve currencies (q.v.) by requiring the issuers of such currencies to prevent the further buildup of liabilities in their currencies and to reduce existing holdings by using reserve assets—gold, SDRs, or reserve positions in the Fund (qq.v.). Thus, the proposal would have required reserve currency (q.v.) centers, such as the United States, to move toward settling their balance of payments (q.v.) deficit on a current basis and would have eliminated the privileges that accrue to a currency issuer.

Asset settlement was one of the proposals examined by the Committee of Twenty (q.v.) in an attempt to reach agreement on a comprehensive reform of the international monetary system. The serious disagreement over the various issues, together with the sharp increase in world oil prices toward the end of 1973, led the Committee of Twenty to abandon its efforts to reach agreement on a comprehensive and immediate reform, including the asset settlement proposal.

Assets of the Fund. *See* Resources of the Fund; Subscriptions to the Fund.

-B-

Balance of Payments. The concept of a country's balance of payments and the ability to determine to what extent a country is under pressure on its external payments account is of critical importance in the operations of the Fund, since a member may not use the Fund's financial resources unless it has a balance of payments need. Under the Bretton Woods system (q.v.), indeed, a member could, in general, change its par value (q.v.) only when its balance of payments was in "fundamental disequilibrium" (q.v.). The term itself was never defined by the Fund, but was identified and applied on a case-by-case basis.

In an accounting sense, the balance of payments must always balance, since it is a systematic record of all economic transactions between residents of one country and residents of other countries, presented in the form of double-entry bookkeeping. Debit and credit entries in such a statement must show an overall balance, since net differences in any one item in the statement—merchandise trade, services, and capital flows—must be offset by other entries, including monetary movements (i.e., changes in assets and liabilities). Similarly, since exports by one country correspond to the imports of other countries, and payments by one country must be received by others, globally the sums of all payments and receipts should balance. Unfortunately, this is not so, because all kinds of discrepancies arise from errors, omissions, timing, and asymmetries in reported payments data, primarily on trade in services and on portfolio investment. These discrepancies on a global basis can be substantial, involving many billions of dollars a year, and can fluctuate unpredictably as the pattern of international payments changes.

The framework of the overall balance of payments comprises the current account (merchandise trade, services, and official transfers), and the capital account (long-term and short-term capital movements) (q.v.); any net difference in these accounts will be reflected in the movement in monetary assets and liabilities. Within the overall balance of payments statement, it can be useful to examine particular components, or a combination of particular components, to analyze the position of countries, groups of countries, or worldwide trends in payments. The decision on where to draw the line in a balance of payments statement reflects a judgment as to which set of transactions best indicates the need for balance of payments adjustment (q.v.). No unambiguous criteria exist for making such a judgment and the ultimate decision rests on a subjective assessment of the situation. It is not surprising, therefore, that several balance of payments concepts have developed.

The narrowest definition of payments imbalance relates to the trade balance—the difference between exports and imports. A somewhat broader and more informative representation of a country's transactions is the current account. It covers transactions in goods, services, and income, and may or may not include private or all unrequited transfers, again depending on the judgment of the classifier. The basic balance attempts to indicate a longer run balance of payments position by including long-term capital flows in addition to the current account items. A variant of the basic balance is the liquidity balance, which includes short-term domestically held claims on nonresidents among the components making up the balance. Finally, there is the overall balance, which includes in the balance everything except the reserve assets (q.v.) and liabilities that automatically change to accommodate the payments imbalance of the rest of the items.

For most developing countries, the current account captures the essential picture of their external accounts, although as these countries develop and benefit from capital inflows, the overall balance and reserve movements assume greater importance. In addition, for countries such as the United States that act as a reserve currency (q.v.) center and whose currency is widely used in international transactions, the traditional concept of a balance may not be appropriate and may send a wrong signal in terms of balance of payments adjustment. Reserve centers perform the role of financial intermediaries, such as a commercial bank, by lending on a long-term basis and providing short-term investments to foreign monetary authorities. Partly for this reason, the United States ceased publishing official balances on the grounds that they might be positively misleading, although it does show balances as memorandum items in the accounts.

The choice of a balance of payments measurement depends, therefore, on the purpose of the exercise and the structure of a country's overseas payments, as well as the very practical consideration of the reliability of the statistical records in question. Use of the Fund's financial resources (q.v.) by a member is dependent, in the first instance, on a requirement that the financing is needed for balance of payments purposes, or, as stated in Article I, "to give confidence to members by making the general resources of the Fund temporarily available to them under adequate safeguards, thus providing them with opportunity to correct maladjustments in their balance of payments without resorting to measures destructive of national or international prosperity." Under the current Articles (q.v.), in order to use the Fund's financial resources, a member must represent "that it has a need to make the purchase because of its balance of payments or its reserve position or developments in its reserves." In practice, developments in a country's reserve position (q.v.) become a critical factor and one that can be more easily identified and verified.

Balance of Payments Adjustment. Adjustment of a country's balance of payments (q.v.) is at the center of the use of the Fund's financial resources (q.v.) by its members. Those resources can be availed of by a member only when there is a balance of payments need (i.e., an adverse disequilibrium in a country's external accounts, reflected in a pressure on reserves). Moreover, use of the resources must be only temporary, and thus the member is required to repay the Fund—under a normal stand-by arrangement (q.v.) within three to five years and under other arrangements up to 10 years. The borrowing member, therefore, is under an obligation to introduce corrective economic and financial policies to improve the productivity of the economy and bring about a sustainable balance in its foreign trade and capital flows. In making its financial resources temporarily available to a member, the Fund cooperates with it in working out and agreeing on an adjustment program that will strengthen the economy and enable the member to repay the Fund. The severity of the adjustment program and the terms of the repayment to the Fund will depend on the nature and the extent of the disequilibria to be remedied.

An adjustment program must be tailored to the particular requirements of the country in question, but in general it is aimed at restraining domestic absorption (i.e., domestic consumption, investment, and imports), raising national savings to allow higher productive investment, and using resources more effectively. Such a program will require supporting macroeconomic policies, such as fiscal and monetary measures to correct underlying imbalances, exchange rate policies to improve competitiveness and strengthen the supply side of the economy, and interest rate and pricing policies to increase domestic savings and promote efficient resource allocation and investment. In addition, adjustment programs require adequate financing, not only of the type available from the Fund, but also, if possible, other financial resources from international banks, governments, and in the form of direct private investment. Finally, experience shows that, internally, there must be a political will and cohesion to carry the program through and, externally, a favorable environment of positive terms of trade, buoyant and open markets, and favorable interest rates.

Balance of Payments Manual. First issued in 1948, this manual has been updated several times since, taking into account changes in the international financial situation as new financial instruments and markets have been developed. It contains an internationally agreed-to exposition of balance of payments (q.v.) methodology, along with detailed instructions as to how members should report their balance of payments data to the Fund.

Balance of Payments Yearbook. First issued in 1949, the *Yearbook* provides annual and, when available, quarterly balance of payments (q.v.) statements for member countries, as well as presentations by regions and by category of payments. The statements, drawn up in a uniform and internationally comparable format, are comprehensive, covering trade and invisibles, as well as short-term and long-term capital movements (q.v.).

Bancor. Under the Keynes Plan (q.v.), first put forward by Lord Keynes (q.v.) in 1941, it was proposed to establish a currency union, designated as an International Clearing Union, based on international bank money, which Keynes called Bancor, with a fixed (but not unalterable) value in terms of gold (q.v.) and to be accepted as the equivalent of gold by all members of the Clearing Union for the purpose of settling international balances. Each member would subscribe a quota (q.v.) in gold and currency (q.v.), the amount to be adjusted annually, and would be allowed to draw 25 percent of its quota from the Union annually, in the form of an overdraft. A key feature of the plan envisaged that the burden of balance of payments adjustment (q.v.) should be shouldered by both surplus and deficit countries. Exchange rates could only be changed with permission of the governing body, and growing balances, either debit or credit, would require the adoption of specific economic and financial policies, including changes in exchange rates. The plan also foresaw a transitional period after the end of World War II in which members would be able to adjust their exchange and trading systems to their evolving situations.

The Keynes Plan and other plans, principally that proposed by Harry Dexter White (q.v.) in the United States, became the basis for drawing up the Articles of Agreement (q.v.) of the Fund at the Bretton Woods Conference (q.v.) in 1944. The idea of deliberately creating a new form of international reserve money did not then survive, but 25 years later a conceptually very different form of international money came into being with the birth of Special Drawing Rights (SDRs) (q.v.).

Bank for International Settlements (BIS). The BIS was established in Basle, Switzerland, in 1930 to handle the payment of reparations by Germany after World War I and to promote cooperation among the central banks of the principal industrial countries. It developed into a center for economic and monetary research and consultation, and became responsible for the execution of certain specific multicountry agreements. Although liquidation of the Bank was recommended at the Bretton Woods Conference (q.v.) following the establishment of the Fund and the World Bank (q.v.), it continued in existence and has played an active role in facilitating cooperation among central banks in Europe, North America, and Japan.

It holds regular monthly meetings attended by the central bank governors of member countries and the Fund's Managing Director (q.v.), or his representative. In addition, the staffs of the BIS and the Fund maintain continuous informal contacts. The BIS was the agent for the Organization for European Economic Cooperation, serving the European Monetary Union. In 1973, it became the agent of the European Monetary Cooperation Fund, set up by the European Community.

The Bank tends to be regarded by the developing countries as an exclusive club for rich countries, but it has a prestigious reputation among central bankers. It has proven to be a convenient institution to take on various ad hoc arrangements and responsibilities in areas that, although not genuinely international in character, are of concern to its multinational membership.

Basle Agreement. Following the approval of a stand-by arrangement (q.v.) for the United Kingdom in January 1977, agreement was reached in Basle by the United Kingdom and the other nine countries in the Group of Ten (q.v.) and Switzerland, meeting under the auspices of the Bank for International Settlements (q.v.), affecting the future role of the pound sterling as a reserve currency (q.v.). Under the agreement, $3 billion was made available by several participating central banks and the Bank for International Settlements in support of the pound sterling. The resources, available over a two-year period, were furnished on the understanding that there would be an orderly reduction in the use of the pound sterling as a reserve currency. The Managing Director (q.v.) of the Fund was offered, and accepted, the central role of monitoring the implementation of the agreement.

Basle Committee on Banking Supervision. Set up in 1974 by the Governors of the Group of Ten (q.v.) industrial countries, the purpose of the Committee was to coordinate the supervisory efforts of individual countries at the international level over banks and other financial institutions that were increasingly engaging in banking activities. Originally seen as confining its activities to the industrial countries, it soon became apparent that as the financial sectors of emerging and transitional economies assumed greater importance, with expanding cross-border operations, the Basle Committee's standards for capitalization and broad guidelines for sound banking had a wider application. In its adjustment programs (q.v.), the Fund is guided by the Committee's standards in its recommendations on the restructuring that may be required in the financial sectors of its member countries. In furthering this work, the Fund has cosponsored workshops and held seminars on banking supervision, seeking to provide operational guidance on bank licensing; off-site supervision, of banks; loan portfolio analysis, classification, and provisioning; and supervisory responses and procedures for intervening with problem banks.

Berne Union. The popular name for the *Union d'Assureurs des Crédits Internationaux*, comprising a large group of government and related public agencies that guarantee or insure export credits, including short-term trade credits. Members of the group exchange information on their operations, with particular emphasis on countries that might be overextended in their external credit position.

Bernstein, Edward (1910-1996). Deputy to Harry Dexter White (q.v.) when the latter was Assistant Secretary in the U.S. Treasury, Edward Bernstein played a leading role in the early negotiations with British officials on the conception of the Fund and in the detailed negotiations on the Articles of Agreement (q.v.) at the 1944 Bretton Woods Conference (q.v.). He was the first Director of the Fund's Research Department, from 1948-58, and in that position was responsible for developing much of the policy and operational approaches adopted by the Fund in those important and formative years. After he left the Fund, he established a private consultancy and remained active in speaking on the Fund and on developments in the international monetary system (q.v.) until his death.

Board of Governors. The senior decision-making body in the Fund, it consists of one Governor and Alternate Governor appointed by each member of the Fund. The Governor is chosen by the member and is usually the minister of finance, the governor of the central bank, or an official of similar rank.

Under the Articles of Agreement, the Board of Governors (qq.v.) has a number of specific powers, as well as all powers under the Articles not expressly conferred on the Executive Board or the Managing Director (qq.v.). These specific powers, which cover such matters as the admission of new members, the determination of quotas (q.v.), and the allocation of special drawing rights (SDRs) (qq.v.), can be exercised only by the Board of Governors. All other powers can be—and, in fact, have been—delegated by the Board of

Governors to the Executive Board. Of the specific powers conferred on the Board of Governors, 45 types of decisions require special voting (q.v.) majorities of 70 percent or 85 percent, but these relate to membership (q.v.) and quota resolutions or to issues that only rarely arise, and most decisions taken by the Board require a simple majority. In accordance with the Articles, weighted voting is in effect, with each Governor able to cast the number of votes held by the member that appointed him (see Voting Provisions).

The Board of Governors is required to meet whenever called upon to do so by at least 15 members or by members having at least one fourth of the Board's total voting power. A quorum for a meeting exists when a majority of the Governors having at least two-thirds of the total voting power of the Fund's membership are present. The Board normally meets only at the Annual Meetings (q.v.), which are held jointly with the World Bank (q.v.). The governing boards of these two institutions have established the convention of holding the Annual Meetings in consecutive years in Washington, D.C., and every third year in a member country other than the United States. The Board may vote on a specific question without meeting, and most votes taken by the Board of Governors are, in fact, taken by mail.

The second amendment to the Articles provides for the establishment of a Council, to come into being only when a decision to do so has been approved by 85 percent of the total voting power of the Board of Governors. The Council has never been voted into existence, but the Board established an Interim Committee (q.v.), which has advisory functions.

Borrowed Resources Suspense Account (BRSA). Established in 1981, the Borrowed Resources Suspense Account was set up in the General Department (q.v.) to hold and invest borrowed funds pending their use by members. Investment (q.v.) of borrowed funds is made in short-term SDR-denominated deposits with an official national institution of those members whose currencies (q.v.) are freely usable or with the Bank for International Settlements (q.v.).

Borrowing by the Fund. Although quota subscriptions (qq.v.) by its members are the basic source of resources for financing the Fund's operations, under its Articles of Agreement (q.v.) the Fund is authorized to borrow currencies (q.v.) from its members and others in order to accommodate the financing of a large and temporary payments imbalance. Although the authority to borrow does not preclude borrowing from private sources, so far the Fund has borrowed only from official institutions. From time to time such borrowing has provided an important supplement to the Fund's subscribed resources.

The first borrowing arrangements entered into by the Fund were the General Arrangements to Borrow (GAB) (q.v.), which became effective in 1962. Under these arrangements the Fund may borrow, in certain circumstances, specified amounts from 11 industrial countries, including 10 members (the Group of Ten [q.v.]) or their central banks (Belgium, Canada, France, Germany, Italy, Japan, Netherlands, Sweden, United Kingdom, United States) and Switzerland (which became a member in 1992). The arrangements call upon the main industrial countries to stand ready to lend the Fund up to specified amounts of their currencies when such resources are needed to forestall or cope with an impairment of the international monetary system (q.v.). Originally the arrangements provided for credit lines amounting to a total of the equivalent of $6 billion, but in 1983 the total lines of credit were raised to SDR 17 billion, with an additional arrangement with Saudi Arabia amounting to SDR 1.5 billion. The arrangements have been activated 10 times since their establishment, their most recent use in July 1998 to help finance a three-year arrangement with Russia. Before that, the GAB had not been activated since 1977. They have been renewed successively for five-year periods, and are due to expire on December 25, 2003.

In addition to the GAB, Fund borrowings have included: (1) a total of SDR 5.7 billion from several oil-producing countries to provide resources for the Fund's temporary oil facilities (q.v.) established in 1974 and 1975; (2) SDR 7.8 billion under the supplementary financing facility (q.v.) established in 1979; (3) a series of borrowings, mainly short-term, amounting to SDR 15.3 billion under the policy of enlarged access (q.v.) established in 1981; and (4) SDR 3 billion from Japan in 1984 under that same policy.

Under guidelines adopted in 1982, the Fund's total outstanding borrowing plus unused credit is not allowed to exceed the range of 40 to 50 percent of total Fund quotas (q.v.). Throughout the 1980s total borrowing was well below this level, amounting in 1990 to about 17.5 percent of total quotas in the Fund. As the quota increase under the ninth general quota review (q.v.), completed in November 1992, enabled the Fund to make credit available to its members without borrowing, the Fund terminated the enlarged access policy.

To further enhance the Fund's ability to safeguard the international monetary system (q.v.), the Fund entered into New Arrangements to Borrow (NAB) (q.v.) in January 1997. Under these new arrangements, 25 participant countries and institutions stand ready to lend the Fund additional resources—up to SDR 34 billion (about $47 billion)—to supplement its regular quota resources when needed to forestall or cope with an impairment of the international monetary system or deal with an exceptional situation that threatens the stability of the system. The NAB do not replace the credit lines available under the GAB, but the NAB will be the facility of first recourse.

The NAB was first activated in December 1998, when 21 participants lent the Fund about $12.5 billion to help finance the arrangement approved for Brazil.

Brazil. For nearly 40 years in the post-World War II era, the Brazilian authorities, like most others in the region, relied on government intervention to promote economic growth, such as price controls, subsidies, import substitution, trade barriers, and forced industrialization through state ownership of many of the basic industries and services, such as steel, oil, aviation, banks, communications, utilities, and other services. Although Brazil went further than any other country in the region in establishing the basic infrastructure of a developing industrial economy, the result was an array of state enterprises kept afloat by the Government at the expense of continued high inflation and even hyperinflation.

In 1994, under President Cardoso, the country changed course and embarked on the *Real* Plan, a program whose central theme was stabilization, deregulation and an open economy based on market forces, both to those at home and to those from abroad. With the introduction of the Plan, the Brazilian economy achieved a remarkable and sustained reduction in inflation, from an annual rate in excess of 2,500 percent in 1993 to under three percent by September 1998—a rate that Brazil had not experienced for over 50 years. This low inflation was achieved without significant loss in economic activity or income. Real GDP grew at an average annual rate of 4.1 percent and real GDP per capita at an annual rate of 2.7 percent, in sharp contrast to the stagnation of real income and high inflation of the 1980s and early 1990s.

This progress in financial stability was accompanied by substantial structural reform, which included the continued opening of the economy through the liberalization of trade and capital flows, a large privatization program, demonopolization and deregulation of key sectors of the economy, and a fundamental strengthening of the banking system (including state banks). Investment rose from 15 percent of GDP in 1994 to 18 percent of GDP in 1998, and foreign direct investment from $2 billion to $23 billion over the same period.

Despite the *Real* Plan's successes in macroeconomic stabilization and structural reform, and despite the federal government's efforts to restrain federal spending, modernize the tax system, strengthen its administration, and promote fiscal discipline at the state level, it has not been able to stabilize the financing of the nonfinancial public sector. This weakness resulted in a significant deterioration in public finances, persistent, substantial overall deficits in the public sector, in the range of 5 to 7 percent of GDP, and a steady climb in the ratio of public debt to GDP.

This imbalance in the finances of the public sector led to a growing resort to external savings in order to finance the rise in domestic investment, with the result that the deficit in the current account of the balance of payments rose to over 4 percent of GDP in 1997. Foreign direct investment covered nearly 50 percent of this deficit, but by mid-1998 gross external debt had risen to $228 billion, or over 28 percent of GDP. With the dramatic worsening of the Asian crisis (q.v.) in the last quarter of 1997, the exchange rate came under substantial pressure. The central bank responded promptly, however, doubling its basic lending rate to 43 percent and raising revenue by about two percent of GDP. These timely measures succeeded in rebuilding confidence and allowing a gradual return of interest rates to their precrisis levels, but not without cost in terms of lower economic activity and higher unemployment.

In February 1998, at the time of Brazil's Article VI (q.v.) consultations with the Fund, the Executive Directors (q.v.) commended the authorities on their quick and decisive policy response to the pressure on the *real* in the foreign exchange (q.v.) market, adding that the higher interest rates and the strong fiscal package had played an important role in limiting the impact of the Asian turmoil on Brazil and the rest of Latin America. Executive Directors at that time, however, also noted a number of vulnerabilities in the debt structure, and the federal and state fiscal situations, but commended the authorities on their actions in many other areas, such as privatization, the proposed constitutional reforms concerning social security and public administration, the strengthening of bank supervision, and the restructuring that had taken place in the banking sector. They urged the authorities to remove the remaining exchange restrictions (q.v.) and move quickly to accept the obligations of Article IV, Sections 2, 3, and 4. They encouraged the Brazilian authorities to take further steps to improve the comprehensiveness of the financial sector and external debt statistics and also to take steps to increase their transparency by subscribing to the Fund's Special Data Dissemination Standards (SDDS) (q.v.).

In August 1998, the capital account again came under serious pressure in the wake of the crisis in Russia. A tightening of fiscal policy by further cuts in public expenditures and cuts in investment expenditures of federal enterprises, together with successive increases in interest rates (with overnight interest rates reaching 42 percent in late October), succeeded in moderating the outflow of reserves (q.v.) but did not halt it. International reserves, which had amounted to $70.2 billion at the end of July 1998, declined to $45.8 billion at the end of September and to $42.6 billion at the end of October. It became clear that a speeding up of the pace of change in policy and reforms was needed. President Cardoso, 11 days before the presidential elections, stressed in an important campaign speech that a major fiscal adjustment and reform effort would be the cornerstone of a second mandate for his government.

By the third quarter of 1998, it was not at all clear what course the contagion from the Asian crisis would take. The Russian situation had deteriorated and financial markets in North America and Europe were in a nervous state. In this context, the management of the Fund felt that it was crucial to stop the contagion from spreading to Brazil, fearing that otherwise the whole of Latin America would be affected, and eventually the U.S. economy too, thus creating the real possibility of a worldwide recession. In the ensuing weeks the Fund worked with the Brazilian authorities to put together the parameters of a comprehensive reform plan. On November 13, 1998, the Fund and Brazil were able to announce a major economic adjustment program, supported by a financing package totaling $41 billion over the following three years, in which the Fund, the World Bank (q.v.), the Inter-American Development Bank, and the Bank for International Settlements (BIS) (q.v.), as well as many industrial countries, were all participants.

Drawings (q.v.) on the Fund are specified in SDRs (q.v.), so actual U.S. dollar amounts may vary somewhat, depending on the conversion rate for the U.S. dollar. Bearing this qualification in mind, of the total package of $41 billion, about $18 billion (or 600 percent of quota [q.v.]) would come from the Fund, of which $5.5 billion (180 percent of quota) would be under a three-year stand-by arrangement (q.v.) and $12.5 billion (420 percent of quota) from the supplementary reserve facility (SRF) (q.v.). The World Bank and the Inter-American Development Bank each committed

$4.5 billion, and the BIS a further $14.5 billion, which included contributions from a large number of industrial countries.

Innovations in the financing program included precautionary elements, including an effort to round up more financing than was thought to be necessary and provisions under which a large part of financing package would become available almost immediately in the form of a first tranche and a second tranche drawings, if needed. Drawings from the Fund would bring about a proportionate use of the bilateral loans from the industrial countries through the BIS, thereby making part of this financing also available immediately. This strong front-loading of the program would have enabled Brazil, in certain circumstances, to draw up to $37 billion in the first year of the program. Furthermore, it was hoped that the design of the program would enable Brazil to approach its creditors in the private sector and negotiate a voluntary restructuring of its external credits (i.e., to "bail in" the private sector).

Under its three-year economic program, the Brazilian authorities undertook to bring about a comprehensive set of revenue-raising and expenditure-saving measures in order to achieve a major fiscal adjustment by the year 2001. These measures included reform of social security, public administration, and public expenditure management; a thorough-going reform of the tax system, both direct and indirect, as well as a series of increased taxation in a number of areas, such as financial transactions and corporate turnovers; and, of some importance, stricter control over bond offerings and bank loans to finance state expenditures.

The Brazilian authorities were also committed to opening up the economy and to ensuring firm monetary discipline and macroeconomic stability. The current exchange rate regime was to be maintained, with an annual slide or crawl of about 7.5 percent, together with a gradual broadening of the band around the central rate. On privatization, the government's program had already encompassed industries as diverse as telecommunications, energy, ports, railways, mining, steel, urban transport, and financial institutions under what has been called one of the largest privatization programs in the world. In the next three years the continuing privatization program would focus on utilities, most of which were state owned, such as power generation and distribution, a few remaining state banks, and a number of water, gas, and sewerage public utilities.

The financial and economic program was approved by the Executive Board early in December 1998, and a first disbursement, amounting to $5.3 billion, was immediately made available under the stand-by arrangement. Further drawings from the Fund were subject to key provisions of the program being enacted by the Brazilian Congress. To assist in the financing of the package, the New Arrangements to Borrow (q.v.), which had come into effect only a week or two earlier, were activated for the first time.

However, congressional delay in implementing fiscal reform measures, together with the announced opposition of some States to a readjustment of their financial situation, led to a weakening of confidence in the exchange rate and to increased pressure on Brazil's foreign exchange reserves. On January 15, 1999, the announcement by the Brazilian authorities that henceforth the exchange rate would be determined by market forces was followed by a rapid depreciation of the *real*, which by early February had fallen 40 percent below its predevaluation level.

Agreement on a new Brazilian economic program was announced on March 8, based on the financial package negotiated in November 1998 by the Fund, other international financial organizations, and the Bank for International Settlements (BIS). The new program was basically a recommitment to the original reform program, but with stricter financial discipline and tighter monetary policy to counter the deterioration in the fiscal situation brought about by the devaluation of the *real*. It envisaged a decline in GDP of 3-4 percent in 1999, a decline in the rate of inflation to 5-7 percent by the end of the year, and, as a result of the new competitiveness brought about by the devaluation of the *real*, a favorable trade balance of $11 billion in 1999, compared with a deficit of $6.4 billion in the previous year.

The new program was submitted to and approved by the Fund's Executive Board in March 1999.

Bretton Woods Agreement. *See* Articles of Agreement.

Bretton Woods Conference. The International Monetary and Financial Conference of the United and Associated Nations (known more generally as the Bretton Woods Conference) was convened at the Mount Washington Hotel, Bretton Woods, New Hampshire, on July 1, 1944. The Conference was attended by delegates from 44 members of the United and Associated Nations, by a representative from Denmark, and by delegations from the International Labour Office, the United Nations Relief and Rehabilitation Administration, the Economic Section of the League of Nations, and the United Nations Interim Commission on Food and Agriculture. The Conference lasted longer than was expected, but closed on July 22, 1944, having negotiated, often with some difficulty, an agreement on a Final Act, signed by all delegations, embodying the Articles of Agreement (q.v.) of the Fund and of the World Bank (q.v.).

Bretton Woods System. Envisioned the establishment of a multilateral world trade and payments system that was free of restrictions and a stable system of exchange rates that could not be unfairly manipulated by one country to achieve advantage over others. Discriminatory exchange practices and multiple exchange rates were outlawed. The value of each member's currency (q.v.) was to be fixed by declaring to the Fund an initial par value in terms of gold (qq.v.). Thereafter, apart from initial adjustments up to a cumulative total of 10 percent, the Fund had to concur in any change in the par value proposed by the member. Changes in the value of a currency could be justified only for balance of payments (q.v.) reasons; more specifically, the Fund had to find that there was a "fundamental disequilibrium" (q.v.) in the member's balance of payments position. Thus, the Bretton Woods system sought to reestablish the stability of the gold standard, but with a degree of flexibility that allowed needed changes in exchange rates to be made under international supervision.

It was the first time that sovereign countries voluntarily agreed to give up part of their sovereignty by recognizing that exchange rates, the single most important price for any economy, were matters of international concern and should be brought under some degree of international control. This fixed, but adjustable, system of exchange rates arose directly from the experiences of the interwar years. The rigidity of the gold exchange standard was believed to have contributed to the onset of the Great Depression, and, after it had broken down, much of the subsequent chaos in international financial relations was attributable to the absence of a worldwide system to bring order and discipline to international trade and payments.

Buffer Stock Financing Facility (BSFF). This facility, established in June 1969, provides resources to help finance members' contributions to buffer stocks established under approved international commodity (q.v.) price stabilization arrangements. Since its inception, the Fund has authorized the use of its resources (q.v.) under the facility in connection with buffer stocks established under international agreements for tin, sugar, and natural rubber. Access limits under the buffer stock financing facility were set in November 1992 at 35 percent of a member's quota (q.v.). No drawings (q.v.) have been made under this facility since 1984 and its merits are under review in the Fund.

Burden Sharing. As the number of Fund members with overdue obligations (q.v.) to the Fund grew in the late 1980s and early 1990s, the Fund adopted a series of policies designed to share the burden of financing these overdue obligations among all members. These policies included a buildup in the Fund's reserves (q.v.) through the establishment of special contingency accounts (q.v.). Contributions to the accounts would be made in accordance with an agreed-to formula that shared the cost of the overdue obligations among both debtor and creditor countries by reducing the rate of remuneration (q.v.) paid on credit balances and raising charges (q.v.) on the use of the Fund's financial resources (q.v.).

Burkina Faso. Burkina Faso, located in Western Africa, is one of the world's poorest countries, landlocked, with a population and a per capita income estimated in 1996 at 10.8 million and $740, respectively. It has a high population density, a high birth rate, few natural resources, and a fragile soil, subject to a highly variable rainfall. It is estimated that 80 percent of the population is engaged in subsistence agriculture.

The country's sustained adjustment effort has been supported by the Fund under successive programs since 1991. The first of these programs was under the structural adjustment facility (SAF) (q.v.), followed in March 1993 by a three-year enhanced structural adjustment facility (ESAF) (q.v.). A second ESAF arrangement was approved in June 1996. Under programs supported by these arrangements, Burkina Faso has implemented a broad range of macroeconomic and structural reforms, which have succeeded in redirecting the economy away from a centralized economy to one with market orientation. These programs have brought results in a number of areas, notably in rising per capita GDP and a reduction in the country's internal and external balances. In September/October 1997, the Fund and the World Bank (q.v.) approved the country's eligibility under the highly indebted poor country's initiative (HIPC) (q.v.), under which external debt will be reduced by April 2000 to the equivalent of 205 percent of exports in net present value terms.

In 1997, economic and financial performance continued to be encouraging, with GDP growth estimated to have reached 5.5 percent, slightly below the 6.0 percent level in the previous year, reflecting erratic rainfall that affected cereal production, but well above the performances of earlier years of 1.2 percent in 1994 and 4.0 percent in 1995. At the same time, inflation has been brought down from 29 percent in 1994 to a negligible figure in 1997. Although the deficit on current account in terms of GDP remains high, at 13 percent, the capital account improved sharply in 1997, mitigating the fall in gross external reserves, which remained sufficient for over six months' imports.

In 1997 and early 1998, the Burkinabé authorities implemented structural reforms in a number of areas, completing the first phase of the program to restructure and privatize public enterprises— involving 20 out of the 80 existing public enterprises—and made significant progress in implementing the second phase, involving 19 companies. Actions were also taken to strengthen the banking system, including the liquidation of the development bank, the privatization of a commercial bank, and the licensing of two new private banks. In the area of civil service, legislation was enacted in April 1998 to introduce enhanced flexibility into personnel policies.

By-laws of the Fund. The By-laws complement the Articles of Agreement (q.v.) and are subordinate to them. They are drawn up by the Executive Directors (q.v.) and approved by the Board of Governors (q.v.). The Rules and Regulations (q.v.) are intended to supplement the Articles of Agreement and the By-laws and are subordinate to both. They are drawn up and amended by the Executive Board (q.v.), but are subject to review by the Board of Governors.

Both the By-laws and the Rules and Regulations have been amended many times since their original formulation in 1946. The

By-laws, to the extent consistent with the Articles of Agreement, address the organization of the Fund and policy matters falling within the sphere of the Executive Board. The Rules and Regulations deal with the more day-to-day business of the Fund, including its operating rules, procedures, regulations, and interpretations.

-C-

Camdessus, Michel (1936-). Michel Camdessus, a French national, is the seventh and current Managing Director (q.v.) of the Fund. Appointed in January 1987, he was reappointed for a second five-year term from January 1992 and for a third term, beginning January 16, 1997. He is the only Managing Director to have served three successive terms

Before his appointment as Managing Director, Michel Camdessus had been Governor of the Bank of France (1984-87), Director of the French Treasury (1982-84), Chairman of the Paris Club (1978-84), Chairman of the Monetary Committee of the European Community (1982-84) and named Governor of the Fund for France in 1984. He was educated at the University of Paris and earned postgraduate degrees in economics at the Institute of Political Studies of Paris and at France's National School of Administration.

Capital Budget. *See* Administrative and Capital Budgets of the Fund.

Capital Movements. The Fund's original Articles of Agreement (q.v.) and those in force through subsequent amendments drew a distinction between current and capital transactions. The Articles stipulated that a member may not use the Fund's general resources (q.v.) to meet a large and sustained outflow of capital, and authorized the Fund to request a member to exercise controls to prevent such use of its resources. Contrary to the code of conduct prevailing for current transactions, the Articles expressly permitted members to regulate international capital movements (q.v.), even going so far as to state that a member failing to exercise appropriate controls could be declared ineligible to use the Fund's resources. The actual wording of Article VI, Section 1(a) of the Fund's Articles of Agreement, as drafted at Bretton Woods (q.v.) and left substantially unchanged until a projected change in them was formulated in

1998, stated that "a member may not use the Fund's resources to meet a large or sustained outflow of capital as provided in Section 2 of this Article, and the Fund may request a member to exercise controls to prevent such use of the resources of the Fund. If, after receiving such a request, a member fails to exercise appropriate controls, the Fund may declare the member ineligible to use the resources of the Fund."

The Articles attempted to refine the distinctions between the two kinds of transactions, however, by stating that members may use the Fund's resources for capital transactions of reasonable amount required for the expansion of exports or in the ordinary course of trade, banking, or other business. In practice, the terms "large, sustained, and reasonable" were never defined for operational purposes, nor was it easy to ascertain when capital movements were not connected to exports or to the ordinary course of trade, banking, or other business. In the past, a number of members had imposed forms of capital controls while still fulfilling their obligations to maintain current transactions free of restrictions, but the obvious existence of capital flows, and their role in aggravating the balance of payments (q.v.) position of a member, were never found to be an impediment to the use of the Fund's resources, or to have been seriously considered as such.

Thus, no country was ever declared ineligible to use the Fund's resources on grounds of its failure to control capital movements. Nevertheless, the distinction between capital and trade flows became increasingly difficult to maintain, particularly as capital markets became open and international capital flows underwent a sea change. For many countries, capital movements became a key factor in the balance of payments. Average annual net capital flows to developing countries, for example, exceeded $150 billion in 1990-96, and although the Mexican crisis (q.v.) provoked a slowdown in 1995, in the following year the pace quickened again, to a net total of $235 billion. The Asian crisis (q.v.) produced a similar slowdown in 1997, but there seemed to be no reason to believe that in a global economy the pace of the inflow would not recover once the crisis had been contained.

In these circumstances, Article VI of the Fund's Articles of Agreement was seen to be increasingly anachronistic, particularly as the Fund was being called on to assist in the financing of balance of payments imbalances in which capital movements, both inward and outward, were playing a significant role. The belief spread that it was, indeed, time for capital movements to be subject to international oversight, similar to the treatment afforded current account transactions under the original Articles of Agreement.

At the Fund-Bank Annual Meetings in Hong Kong SAR in 1997, the Interim Committee (q.v.) of the Fund's Board of Governors (q.v.) agreed that it was "time to write a new chapter to the Bretton Woods agreement," and invited the Executive Board (q.v.) to work on a proposed amendment of the Fund's Articles of Agreement to make the liberalization of capital movements one of the purposes of the Fund and extend its jurisdiction over capital movements.

At its meeting in Washington, D.C., in April 1998, the Interim Committee's communiqué issued after the meeting reaffirmed the view expressed at its Hong Kong SAR meeting, stating that the crisis in Asia had given heightened attention to the role of capital flows in economic development. It noted the work that the Executive Board had already completed on that part of the amendment dealing with the Fund's purposes and requested the Board to pursue with "determination" its work on other aspects, with the aim of submitting an appropriate amendment of the Articles for the Committee's consideration as soon as possible.

Central Rates. The concept of central rates came into being after the United States suspended the convertibility (q.v.) of U.S. dollars into gold (q.v.), signaling the end of the par value system (q.v.) agreed upon at the Bretton Woods Conference (q.v.) in 1944. Members of the Group of Ten (q.v.), meeting in Washington, D.C., in December 1971, agreed on a realignment of exchange rates (the so-called Smithsonian agreement [q.v.]). Following that agreement, the Fund adopted a decision authorizing the establishment of central rates (q.v.).

Central rates were defined in terms of gold, but they were not to be subject to the formal procedure for their establishment and change pertaining to par values under the Articles of Agreement (q.v.). The margins within which central rates were allowed to fluctuate were widened from 1 percent under the par value system to 4.5 percent under the central rate system. The measures were intended to install an interim system with the object of promoting stability in the international exchange rate system, pending the negotiation of amendments to the Articles of Agreement bringing about a fundamental reform of that system.

Charges on the Use of the Fund's Resources. The Fund aims to be self-financing, and thus the objective is to cover expenses from revenue, mainly from charges on the use of the Fund's resources (q.v.) by members. Despite the rise in the scale of charges through the 1970s and 1980s, the Fund adheres to the view that there should be a concessional element in the cost of using the Fund's resources, reflecting the cooperative character of the organization. The basic rate of charge applied to the use of the Fund's resources is set at the beginning of each financial year as a proportion of the weekly SDR (q.v.) rate of interest, so as to achieve a predetermined net income target. The mechanism is designed to ensure that the Fund's operational income closely reflects its operational costs, which depend largely on the SDR interest rate since the rate of remuneration (q.v.) (i.e., the interest rate paid on members' credit balances) is linked to the SDR rate.

To strengthen its financial position against consequences of overdue obligations (q.v.), the Fund has adopted "burden-sharing" (q.v.) measures to accumulate additional precautionary balances and to distribute the financial burden of overdue obligations between debtor and creditor members. As part of this mechanism, adjustments are made to the rate of charge and the rate of remuneration. The resources so generated are intended to protect the Fund against risk associated with arrears and to provide additional liquidity (q.v.).

For 1997-98, the proportion of the rate of charge to the SDR interest rate was set at 109.6 percent at the beginning of the financial year to meet a net income target of 5 percent of the Fund's reserves (q.v.). At the end of the year, the actual net income in excess of the target was refunded to members paying charges during the year, effectively reducing the proportion of the rate of charge to the SDR interest rate to 105.6 percent. At the beginning of 1998-99, the proportion of the rate of charge to the SDR interest rate was set at 107.0 percent. The SDR interest rate, which is adjusted weekly, is a weighted average of the yields on specified short-term instruments in the domestic money markets of the five countries whose currencies are included in the SDR valuation basket (q.v.). For 1997-98, the average rate of charge was 4.65 percent and the average rate of remuneration was 3.97 percent.

The Fund also charges a uniform service charge of 0.5 percent on amounts purchased from the ordinary resources of the Fund (except for purchases in the reserve tranche [q.v.], for which there is no charge). It also charges a commitment fee of 0.25 percent on undrawn balances under stand-by (q.v.) and similar arrangements.

China—Hong Kong SAR. *See* Hong Kong SAR.

Classification of Countries. The Fund operates on the principle of uniformity of treatment for all members, and it was not until the second amendment to the Articles (q.v.) (1978) that mention was made of developing countries (q.v.). For analytical purposes, however, the Fund has established a comprehensive classification, grouping countries according to their key economic and financial characteristics. The classification must necessarily change to reflect world economic developments, and beginning in May 1997, the group of countries traditionally known as industrial countries was expanded to include the newly industrialized economies in Asia (Hong Kong SAR [q.v.]; Korea [q.v.]; Taiwan Province of China; and Singapore, as well as Israel), and the category was renamed "advanced economies," in recognition of the declining share of employment in manufacturing common to all the countries in the group. All other countries were classified as developing countries, with subgroups of "countries in transition" (*see* Transitional Economies [q.v.]) (i.e., countries in Central and Eastern Europe and members of the former Soviet Union) and other subgroups as needed for analytical purposes. These groupings, which have no relevance for the operations of the Fund, are primarily used by the Fund in its surveys and analysis of world economic developments, published twice a year in *World Economic Outlook* (q.v.).

Cochran, Merle H. (1892-1973). A U.S. national, Merle Cochran was Deputy Managing Director (q.v.) of the Fund in 1953–62. Before joining the Fund, he had been serving in the U.S. Foreign Service and resigned as Ambassador to Indonesia to take up his post in the Fund.

Collective Reserve Unit (CRU). Early in the 1960s, the adequacy of the level of international liquidity (q.v.), and the role that the U.S. balance of payments (q.v.) deficit played in the creation of international liquidity, began to be recognized as a growing problem. Several proposals, centered around the creation of a collective or composite reserve asset (q.v.), were formulated with the aim of being able to control the growth of international reserves (q.v.). The proposals had several basic features in common: the assets would be backed by gold or currencies (qq.v.) in defined amounts; they would be exchangeable for currencies among the participants; they would not be available for direct intervention in exchange markets (q.v.); they would be deliberately created by agreement among a defined group of countries; their creation, allocation, and withdrawal would be determined by the overall need for international liquidity and not based on the situation of any one country; the countries participating in and controlling the scheme would be limited to advanced industrial and trading countries; and reserve units would not be issued to developing countries (q.v.) or be used for development finance.

Many of these features were later included in the scheme for creating SDRs (q.v.), authorized by the first amendment to the Articles of Agreement (q.v.), which became effective on July 28, 1969. The value of the SDR was first fixed in terms of gold and then later in terms of a basket of currencies; it was an asset for use only by national monetary authorities (q.v.) and other prescribed official holders; and it was to be created, and withdrawn, with reference to the world's need for international liquidity. The SDR, however, was conceived as a universal asset and not confined to an exclusive group of countries; it was established as a supplement to existing reserve assets and designed to have a hybrid appearance of part credit and part reserve unit; although its value was at first fixed in terms of gold, it had no tangible backing; and it was an asset created by international law, which established the rules for its transfer and acceptance.

Committee of Twenty. Formally, the Committee of the Board of Governors on Reform of the International Monetary System and Related Issues, this committee was established in 1972 to negotiate the draft of a reformed international monetary system (q.v.) after the United States had announced, in August 1971, that the convertibility of the dollar into gold (q.v.) was suspended, thus bringing the Bretton Woods system (q.v.) to an end. The Committee consisted of 20 members of the Board of Governors (q.v.) of the Fund, modeled on the representation of the same countries and constituencies forming the Executive Board (q.v.). The inaugural meeting of the Committee was held in September 1972 and elected Ali Wardhana, the Governor for Indonesia, as its Chairman, and established a Committee of Deputies under the chairmanship of Sir C. Jeremy Morse, Alternate Governor for the United Kingdom and, at that time, a Director of the Bank of England. The Committee met at the ministerial level six times and the Deputies met 12 times during the next two years. During the course of its work, the Committee established seven technical groups to examine certain aspects of reform of the international monetary system in greater detail.

The Committee began its work on the presumption that some form of the par value system (q.v.) would eventually be restored. The confusion and stress of the 1970s, however, was not a background that lent itself to calm and orderly planning for the future. After two years of effort, the Committee was not able to reach agreement on a fully reformed international monetary system, admitted defeat, and in June 1974 submitted its final report to the Board of Governors, to which was attached an *Outline of Reform.* The report explained that the Committee had not been able to reach agreement on a full-fledged reform because of the uncertainties affecting the world economic outlook caused by gathering inflation, the repercussions of the sharp increase in international oil prices, and other unsettled conditions. It urged that immediate steps be taken to begin an evolutionary process of reform. In Part I of the *Outline of Reform,* the Committee indicated the general direction in which the international monetary system could evolve in the future. Part II of the *Outline* set forth the immediate steps that could be taken before final agreement could be reached on a comprehensive reformed system.

Part I of the *Outline of Reform* was based on the idea of retaining as much of the Bretton Woods system as possible, although the Committee foresaw the need for some additional flexibility in applying the reformed system. In discussing the future exchange rate (q.v.) mechanism, the Committee envisioned that exchange rates would continue to be a matter of international concern, competitive depreciation (q.v.) and undervaluation of currencies would be avoided, the exchange rate system would continue to be based on stable but adjustable par values (q.v.), and changes in them would still be subject to approval by the Fund. Countries could, however, adopt floating exchange rates (q.v.) in particular situations, subject to authorization, surveillance (q.v.), and review by the Fund. On other aspects of the reformed system, the Committee was able to point to weaknesses in the Bretton Woods system, and to discuss possible remedies without reaching agreement on them. Thus, it recognized the need, among others, for improvements in the adjustment process, the management of international liquidity and currency reserves (qq.v.), and the need for special provisions for developing countries (q.v.) in the new system. A series of 10 annexes examined in detail possible approaches to a number of important aspects of the international monetary system. Prepared by the Chairman and Vice Chairman of the Committee of Deputies, the annexes were not endorsed by the full committee.

Part II of the *Outline* recognized that there would be an interim period before full reform came into existence. During this period, the Committee proposed that the Fund tighten its surveillance and consultative procedures, experiment with some aspects of reform, and begin drafting reformed Articles of Agreement (q.v.). Many, but not all, of the ideas in the *Outline* eventually found their way into the second amendment to the Articles of Agreement, which became effective in April 1978.

Commodities. During the postwar era, the instability of export earnings from primary products had had a severe impact on developing countries (q.v.), a number of which were, and still are, heavily dependent on the export of just a few commodities for their receipts of foreign currency (q.v.). The consequences were injurious "stop and go" policies as economies underwent boom and bust cycles, leading to inflation at home, a lack of confidence in the exchange rate (q.v.) abroad, and the disruption of long-term development plans. National monetary authorities (q.v.) and international organizations have attempted to ameliorate these adverse developments by adopting three complementary approaches—export diversification, stabilization of commodity prices through international action, and compensatory financing. Export diversification is a long-term approach, addressed in the Fund's annual consultations with members and taken into account in Fund-supported adjustment programs (q.v.). Stabilization of commodity prices through international agreements is, technically speaking, outside the Fund's jurisdiction, but, nevertheless, it is an endeavor that the Fund has been able to support by making finance available to members under the buffer stock financing facility (q.v.) established in 1969. As regards compensatory financing, the Fund's facility to offset shortfalls in export earnings was established as early as 1963 and has been liberalized several times since. Over the years it has been used extensively by developing countries.

Compensatory Financing Facility. *See* Compensatory and Contingency Financing Facility.

Compensatory and Contingency Financing Facility (CCFF). As originally conceived, the Fund's financial resources (q.v.) were to be available to finance general balance of payments (q.v.) needs and, apart from drawings (q.v.) in the reserve tranche (q.v.) (previously gold tranche [q.v.]), countries using the resources would need to adopt corrective adjustment policies in order to be able to repay the Fund. No attempt was made to distinguish various elements in the balance of payments, and no allowance was made that some of these elements might be self-adjusting. In the 1950s, however, experience suggested that some balance of payments difficulties were caused by factors largely beyond the control of the country in question, such as a crop failure, a temporary decline in international commodity (q.v.) prices, or a natural disaster, and that these difficulties would be largely self-correcting over time, without the need to adopt an adjustment program (q.v.). Special facilities (q.v.) were established, therefore, to meet such adverse developments, allowing a member to use the Fund's financial resources as a floating facility (i.e., over and above the use of other facilities) free of conditionality (q.v.), subject to the proviso that the member was willing to cooperate with the Fund.

The first of the special facilities to be introduced was the compensatory financing facility, which was established in 1963 and covered export shortfalls. In 1979 the facility was widened to include receipts from tourism and workers' remittances, and in 1981 to cover excess cereal import costs. In 1988, a contingency financing element was added and all the elements were amalgamated into a single facility, the contingency and compensatory financing facility. The elements of this amalgamated facility are explained below. The special facility for buffer stock financing (q.v.) and the provisions for emergency assistance (q.v.) are dealt with in separate entries. The compensatory financing facility was established to provide additional assistance to member countries experiencing balance of payments difficulties arising from export shortfalls, provided the shortfalls were temporary and largely attributable to circumstances beyond the member's control. In theory, it is a contra-cyclical facility, enabling the member to borrow from the Fund when its export earnings and financial reserves are low and to repay the Fund when they are high. In this way, fluctuations in a country's export earnings can be neutralized over the longer-term, enabling it to maintain its import capacity, and thus reduce potential disruption of its domestic economy.

Established in 1963, the facility was little used in its first 13 years. In 1975, however, when commodity prices were at their trough, the rules governing the use of the facility were substantially liberalized, and financing made available under it increased sharply. Part of that liberalization was achieved by modifying the method used to calculate the shortfall, which was calculated as the amount by which export earnings in the shortfall year were below the geometric average of export earnings for the five-year period centered on the shortfall year (i.e., the latest 12-month period for which data were available). Exports for the two post-shortfall years were based on projections worked out between the staff and the authorities in the member country.

In 1981, the facility was further widened to include coverage for balance of payments difficulties caused by excessive costs in cereal imports. An excess in cereal import costs was calculated as the amount by which the cost of cereal imports in a given year exceeded the arithmetic average of the cost of cereal imports for the five years centered on that year.

The distinguishing feature of the compensatory financing facility is that drawings (q.v.) under the facility are to compensate for a shortfall in export earnings or the rise in cereal import costs caused by temporary factors largely beyond the member's control, and thus the situation is self-regulating and may not require corrective adjustment policies. However, although drawings under the facility may not necessarily be linked to corrective policies to restore balance of payments equilibrium, a fall in export receipts or a rise in cereal import costs may be associated with wider domestic economic problems that need to be, or already are being, addressed under a Fund-supported program.

Compensatory financing is available to all member countries, but its beneficiaries tend to be exporters of primary products, particularly developing countries (q.v.) relying on just one or two export products. Primary product exports are especially prone to temporary cyclical fluctuations in price and earnings that arise from changes in demand in industrial countries, as well as from changes in output owing to weather and other natural causes. In the past 25 years, the compensatory financing facility has become a major source of financial assistance to members, amounting to about 15 to 20 percent of total outstanding credit from the Fund in the early 1990s, but has since fallen to much lower levels, amounting to only 3 percent of outstanding Fund credit in 1997.

Contingency financing was added to the facility in 1988. The aim was to provide additional financing to a member country following a Fund-supported adjustment that has been blown off course by external developments. Contingency features attached to such programs are aimed at providing part of the additional financing required to keep the program on track in the face of adverse external developments. The external variables covered depend on the economic circumstance of the country in question, but include export earnings, import prices, and interest rates, as well as others, such as workers' remittances and tourist receipts, if they are important elements in a country's current balance of payments account.

Maximum access limits (q.v.) under the compensatory and contingency financing facility—export shortfalls, excess cereal costs, and contingency financing—were set after the ninth general quota review (q.v.) came into effect in November 1992 at 95 percent of a member's quota (q.v.), with sublimits of 30 percent for compensatory financing, 30 percent for contingency financing, 15 percent for cereal import financing, and an optional tranche of 20 percent of quota to supplement any one of the three elements. Drawings beyond these levels incur conditionality—a willingness to cooperate with the Fund and adherence to an adjustment program—but amounts up to 30 percent of quota would be available immediately, pending the implementation of appropriate adjustment policies.

Purchases (q.v.) under the contingency and compensatory financing facility, as well as those under the buffer stock financing facility, are additional to purchases under credit tranche (q.v.) policies. A member, therefore, may use the Fund's resources beyond the limit set for cumulative use under credit tranche policies and under the enlarged access policy (q.v.). Repurchases under the facility are made in equal quarterly installments, beginning three years, and ending five years, after purchase.

Competitive Exchange Depreciation. Identified as one of the destructive elements of the world's trade and payments system of the 1930s, competitive depreciation was a practice that the establishment of the Fund was designed to prevent. Manipulation of exchange rates for national advantage was to be prevented by the authority conferred on the Fund to accept or reject initial par values (q.v.) proposed by member countries, and by the requirement that the Fund approve any subsequent changes to initial par values. In fact, the term "competitive depreciation," like its associated term "fundamental disequilibrium" (q.v.), was never defined by the Fund, although a number of exchange rate changes (q.v.) proposed by members aroused some concern and resistance on the part of the Executive Board (q.v.).

By March 1973, the par value system (q.v.) had collapsed and all the major currencies (q.v.) were floating against each other. Nevertheless, the code of conduct established in the preceding 20 years survived largely intact. The main concern was that those countries that had adopted floating exchange rate (q.v.) systems should practice "clean" floating (as distinct from "dirty" floating) and that they should not resort to manipulating the system. Until the reform of the Articles (q.v.) in 1978, very little international control could be exercised over exchange rates, since the provisions governing par values and currency convertibility (q.v.) had been abandoned. The Fund stressed, however, that members were still under their obligations regarding exchange stability set out in Article IV, Section 4, which stipulated that "each member undertakes to collaborate with the Fund to promote exchange stability, to maintain orderly exchange arrangements with other members, and to avoid competitive exchange alterations." It was a moral authority, and perhaps the only authority, that the Fund was able to use in the interim period between the breakdown of the Bretton Woods system (q.v.) and the second amendment to the Articles in 1978.

In the reformed international monetary system (q.v.) ushered in by the second amendment, stress was again laid on the need to avoid competitive alterations of exchange rates. Thus, in Article IV of the amended Articles, members are enjoined "to seek to promote stability by fostering orderly underlying economic and financial conditions" and "to avoid manipulating exchange rates or the international monetary system in order to prevent effective balance of payments adjustment or to gain an unfair competitive advantage over other members." Whereas the original Articles establishing the par value system could be said to have given the Fund direct power to control exchange rates, insofar as it had to approve changes in a member's par value, the reformed Articles of 1978 ceded to the Fund a broader, but a more indirect, power, that of "firm surveillance" (q.v.) over the exchange rate policies of its members. This implied that the economic and financial policies of members would also be of international concern, but experience has shown that, in practice, it has not been easy to exercise these broader powers effectively, particularly over powerful industrial countries that in recent years have not needed to use the Fund's resources (q.v.). Nevertheless, the increasingly volatile nature of international financial markets in the 1990s has concentrated attention on the urgent need to improve the surveillance functions exercised by the Fund.

Conditionality. The term "conditionality" is the body of policies and procedures governing a member's use of the Fund's resources (q.v.) in support of adjustment (q.v.) policies that will enable the member to overcome its balance of payments (q.v.) problem in a manner that is not unnecessarily destructive of national or international prosperity and also enable the member to repay the Fund over the medium term. The rationale of the approach is that in the absence of unlimited outside resources a country's external payments imbalance will not be able to endure forever, and that sooner or later adjustment will take place, either precipitately with widespread disruption, or deliberately with corrective policy actions, supported by financing, to bring about a smooth adjustment over time. Fund conditionality in earlier years concentrated primarily on macroeconomic policies involving monetary, fiscal, exchange rate, and pricing policies, and only to a lesser extent on more deep seated, longer term structural measures. With the growth in membership (q.v.) of developing countries (q.v.) and countries in transition after the collapse of the communist command economies, attention to the economic infrastructure, privatization, and institution-building has been an important and growing complement to the Fund's macroeconomic adjustment programs. Furthermore, the need for such programs was demonstrated anew in 1997, with the unexpected emergence of the Asian crisis (q.v.). *See also* the Introduction; Use of Fund Resources.

Consultations by the Fund. Regular consultations between the Fund and each member are required under Article IV of the Fund Agreement and are central to the Fund's mandate under its Articles of Agreement (q.v.) to "exercise firm surveillance over the exchange rate policies of members." These consultations comprehend those required under Article XIV—members that are maintaining exchange restrictions under the transitional arrangements (q.v.) set out in the Articles—and place on a formal basis the consultations that prior to the second amendment of the Articles (1978) were held on a voluntary basis with members that had accepted the obligations of Article VIII (q.v.). The consultations under Article IV provide the data the Fund needs to exercise surveillance over the economic policies of member countries. They allow the Fund to analyze economic developments and policies in member countries; to examine members' fiscal, monetary, and balance of payments (q.v.) accounts; and to assess how policies influence their exchange rates and external accounts.

Article IV consultations may be held annually, or at intervals of up to 24 months, depending on the member country. The focus of Article IV consultation depends on the characteristics of the member country. In recent years, given the large payments imbalances among industrial countries and debt-servicing problems of many developing countries (q.v.), the Fund has devoted greater attention to the medium-term objectives of sustaining economic growth and a viable balance of payments, restoring external creditworthiness, and improving structural policies. During the consultations, the Fund's staff analyze economic developments and policies; examine fiscal, exchange rate, and monetary policies; review balance of payments and external debt developments; and assess the impact of policies—including trade and exchange restrictions (q.v.)—on a member's external accounts. The basic procedure for these consultations is as follows: first, the staff carries out at headquarters a preliminary assessment of the country's economic and financial situation, assembling and making a preliminary analysis of all the economic data available on the economy; second, a mission visits the country in question and carries out discussions with the relevant authorities in the country; third, the staff prepares a detailed background report on the country's economic and financial situation, together with an assessment by the staff; fourth, the Executive Board (q.v.) discusses the staff report; fifth, the comments of the Executive Board are transmitted to the country in question; and sixth, subject to the approval of the country, the comments by the Executive Directors are published on the Fund's web site. In 1994, the Fund made available to the public the staff's background economic reports prepared under Article IV consultations.

In addition to Article IV consultations, some members are on a periodic schedule of consultations for other reasons, such as having stand-by (q.v.) and other arrangements with the Fund. Special consultative procedures have also been introduced for selected countries in connection with the preparation of the Fund's report on world economic developments, published twice a year under the title *World Economic Outlook* (q.v.).

Convertibility of Currencies. Convertibility is basic to the functioning of a freely operating multilateral payments system, as envisaged at the Bretton Woods Conference (q.v.). The Articles of Agreement (q.v.), in Article VIII, Sections 2, 3, and 4, spelled out the obligations of members to avoid restrictions on current payments and discriminatory currency practices, and to maintain convertibility of their currency (q.v.).

The original Articles defined a convertible currency in Article XIX *(d)* as a currency of a member not availing itself of the transitional arrangements (q.v.) set out in Article XIV and the acceptance by the member of the obligations of Article VIII (q.v.). By 1961, in fact, all the major trading countries had formally accepted the convertibility obligations prescribed in the Articles. The obligation of members to avoid restrictions on, and to maintain the convertibility of, their currency for current transfers and payments has been continued in the first, second, and third amendments to the Articles. By 1998, only 42 member countries—all developing countries or transitional economies (qq.v.)—were still availing themselves of the transitional arrangements. Thus, the international monetary system (q.v.) by and large was operating in a manner envisaged by the Fund's founders, largely free of restrictions on current payments and transfers.

One aspect of convertibility, that of official convertibility of currency holdings into gold (q.v.), was eliminated from the Articles by the second amendment in 1978. Only the United States had agreed to such conversions on demand, but it was the linchpin of the Bretton Woods system (q.v.). When the United States announced in 1971 that it would no longer convert officially held U.S. dollar balances into gold, the Bretton Woods system collapsed.

Council of the Board of Governors. Originally this Council was to have succeeded the Interim Committee (q.v.), set up in 1974. Establishment of the Council requires an 85 percent majority vote of the Board of Governors (q.v.) and in the 25 years that the Interim Committee had been in existence little interest has been shown in implementing the original intention, mainly because of political opposition by developing countries. In 1998, however, in the aftermath of the Asian crisis (q.v.), and as one of a number of proposals to strengthen the architecture of the international monetary system, the replacement of the Interim Committee by the Council was mooted.

Crawling Pegs. Sliding par values (q.v.), or crawling pegs, gained some favor, particularly in academic circles, late into the Bretton Woods system (q.v.), and especially after that system collapsed in the 1970s. Its advocates sought to remove what they perceived had become rigidities in the par value system (q.v.). Countries had found it difficult, for political or other reasons, to devalue their currencies. The crawling peg system seemed to offer the advantages of stability and of small, periodic adjustment, without the traumatic disruption caused by an announced devaluation (q.v.). The proposal was thought of as an adjunct to the par value system, to be adopted optionally by individual members, with the aim of improving the working of the par value system.

In the event, the Committee of Twenty (q.v.) and national monetary authorities (q.v.) could not agree on a continuation of the par value system in any form, and the crawling peg, as a codified system, became irrelevant in the situation of generalized floating (q.v.) that came into effect after 1973. Nevertheless, some countries have adopted a variation of the crawling peg system and allow their currencies (q.v.) to appreciate or depreciate under controlled circumstances, in accordance with the implementation of their economic and financial policies.

Credit Controls. Credit controls play a major role in the monetary approach to the balance of payments (q.v.), an approach initiated and developed by the Fund through research and pragmatic experience. The approach recognizes that there is a defined relationship between domestic monetary policy (q.v.) and a country's external balance and that the curtailment of domestic absorption (i.e., cutting back on consumption, investment, and imports) will bring about an improvement on external account. The relationship among all the economic variables, however, may not be stable over time or uniform for all countries. Credit controls have proved to be the most direct, immediate, and effective instrument for applying monetary policy.

The Fund has nearly 50 years' experience in applying credit controls, and their implementation has become both more selective and precise. In addition to overall limits on the expansion of bank credit and the money supply, ceilings are applied to selected activities of the economy, such as central bank credit to the government and ease of access to it by the commercial banks, and commercial bank lending to the private sector. These ceilings, which are arrived at in detailed discussions with the monetary authority (q.v.) in question and from the Fund's own macro-modeling, also serve as performance criteria to measure the progress of an adjustment program (q.v.). Stand-by arrangements (q.v.) regularly include quarterly credit ceilings on selected sectors of the economy. Disbursements under stand-by arrangements may be phased and made subject to the member meeting performance criteria. Credit limits will normally be an important element in those criteria.

Credit Tranches. Credit tranche policies determine the level of conditionality (q.v.) attached to the use of the Fund's resources (q.v.). A member can make use of the general resources of the Fund in four credit tranches, each equivalent to 25 percent of a member's quota (q.v.). Use of Fund resources up to the limit of the first credit tranche (i.e., 25 percent of a member's quota) can be made on liberal conditions, provided that the member is making reasonable ef-

forts to solve its balance of payments (q.v.) problems. Use of resources beyond the first credit tranche requires a convincing presentation on the part of the member that its balance of payments difficulties will be resolved within a reasonable period. Use of the
Fund's resources in these upper credit tranches is usually made under a stand-by arrangement (q.v.) or an extended arrangement. Phasing of purchases, performance criteria, and reviews of progress
made under the program apply to the use of the Fund's resources in
the upper credit tranches. A member may use its reserve tranche
(q.v.) without challenge.

Currencies. A currency is issued by a single issuer—a central bank,
government, or currency board—and may circulate as legal tender
(1) only in the country of issuance; (2) independently, in other
countries as well as the country of issuance (e.g., the U.S. dollar is
legal tender in Panama, and the Panamanian balboa, which is
pegged to the U.S. dollar, is limited to small denominations); and
(3) in several countries belonging to a currency union, with a central currency board responsible for the issuance of the currency (i.e.,
the seven countries belonging to the West African Monetary Union
or the six member countries of the Central African Monetary Union, each of which has a common currency area with a fixed exchange rate pegged to the French franc). The important provision
from the Fund's point of view is that each member country should
be able to control effectively its own monetary conditions.

Internationally, a currency can (1) be used as an intervention
currency in the world's exchange markets (q.v.), i.e., a central bank
or a central monetary authority (q.v.) may buy or sell a currency
(such as the U.S. dollar) to influence the value of its own currency
in the market; (2) be a vehicle currency, or one that is extensively
used in world trade and payments; and (3) be a reserve currency
(q.v.), or one that countries use in which to hold their international
reserves (q.v.). The U.S. dollar is the principal currency that fulfills
all these roles, but other currencies, such as the pound sterling, the
French franc, the deutsche mark, and the Japanese yen, also have
significant international functions. All five currencies make up the
SDR valuation basket (q.v.).

The Fund also employs a concept of "freely usable" currency
in its operations. When a member uses the Fund's resources, it
buys with its own currency other members' currencies that are be-

ing held by the Fund. If these other currencies are not recognized as being freely usable (and up to now, the Fund has recognized only the U.S. dollar, the pound sterling, the French franc, the deutsche mark, and the Japanese yen as being freely usable in the principal foreign exchange markets), then the member whose currency is being purchased must itself convert its currency into one of the freely convertible currencies, as requested by the purchasing member, at the official exchange rate notified to the Fund. Similar conversion procedures apply in respect to repayments (repurchases [q.v.]) to the Fund.

As distinct from "freely usable," not all currencies held by the Fund are usable, because they are currencies of members that have weak balance of payments (q.v.) positions or are using the credit facilities of the Fund. In projecting future operations, therefore, the Fund draws up each quarter an operational budget (q.v.), setting out currencies to be used in drawings (q.v.) (purchases [q.v.]) and repayments (repurchases).

Currency Convertible in Fact. A concept employed under the first amendment of the Articles (q.v.) to ensure that members wishing to transfer their SDRs (q.v.) in return for a desired currency (q.v.) could do so at a rate that was not at variance with its market value. The concept, designed solely for transactions in SDRs, ensured that those members using SDRs would receive "equal value" (i.e., equal to its market value). Under the second amendment, the concept of a currency convertible in fact was eliminated, and members using SDRs were assured of equal value by the creation of a new concept, that of a "freely usable" currency.

Currency Stabilization Fund. Several member countries of the Fund have established currency board arrangements, including Argentina (q.v.), Djibouti, Estonia, and Lithuania.

A currency board is a monetary arrangement that commits the authorities to issue domestic currency (q.v.) only in exchange for a specified foreign currency at a fixed rate, thus sharply limiting or eliminating the authorities' discretion to create money by extending credits. The chief advantages of a currency board is the simplicity of operation, the strengthened capability it provides in the conduct of monetary and fiscal policy, and the usefulness of this rule-based arrangement in enhancing transparency and encouraging financial discipline.

In 1995, the Fund's Executive Board (q.v.) discussed the conditions and modalities of possible Fund support for currency stabilization funds. In the light of experience, it recognized that, in certain circumstances, a nominal exchange rate anchor can be a powerful instrument when used in the context of strong macroeconomic stabilization policies, in bringing about a rapid decline in inflation. In the framework of an upper credit tranche stand-by or extended arrangement (qq.v.), Fund financial support for the specific purpose of establishing a currency stabilization fund could provide, for a transitional period, additional confidence in support of an exchange-rate-based strategy. Access could be up to 100 percent of quota (q.v.), but would be subject to the limits applicable to stand-by and extended arrangements.

The most appropriate arrangement to be supported by a currency stabilization fund would be an exchange rate peg with relatively narrow margins, or a preannounced crawl (*see* Crawling Pegs). The policy condition required would include fiscal adjustment and credit creation consistent with targeted inflation; appropriate measures to deal with backward-looking automatic wage and other indexation schemes; establishment of current account convertibility and an open trade regime; contingency plans to deal with large capital account inflows or outflows; integrated management of foreign exchange reserves and intervention policy; and other structural and institutional elements designed to reduce inflation sharply.

A staff study in 1996 found that currency board arrangements were especially attractive to three groups of countries: small open economies with limited central bank expertise and incipient financial markets; countries that wished to belong to a broader trade or currency area; and countries that wished to enhance the credibility of exchange-rate-based disinflation policies.

On the other hand, the study warned that currency board arrangements were not appropriate for every country. The inflexible commitment to a fixed exchange rate parity, for example, might deprive a government of a major tool in addressing real exchange rate misalignments. Similarly, the restrictions that such arrangements bring with them could seriously limit the freedom of the monetary authorities (q.v.) to take action in a financial crisis or in addressing the effect of destabilizing capital flows. The forgoing of important central bank functions in this way could have severe costs and frequently require a level of fiscal consolidation that would be difficult to attain or sustain.

The study also warned that doubt about the soundness of the banking sector is among the greatest threats to the credibility of a currency board arrangement. Countries experiencing banking sector problems require additional measures before initiating a currency board, including a restructuring or closing of banks that do not comply with established prudential standards.

Currency Swap Arrangement. Bilateral swap arrangements among central banks of the industrial countries have been used extensively over the past three decades. Their use to influence movements in exchange markets has become increasingly problematic as the world has become a global economy. Even in the 1960s, when a network of reciprocal lines of credit was established among the main central banks to relieve pressure on the U.S. dollar in the exchange markets (q.v.) and ensure the smooth functioning of the international monetary system (q.v.), the mechanism was ultimately not successful in easing the strains on the international monetary system and saving it from collapse. The growing swap arrangements, however, were symbolic of the "one world" character of the international monetary system and the responsible attitude assumed by nations to sustain it. Since the breakdown of the Bretton Woods system (q.v.), the network of swap arrangements has from time to time continued to be activated in selected conditions to facilitate coordinated central bank intervention in international exchange markets.

-D-

Dale, William B. (1924-). William Dale, a U.S. national, was the fourth Deputy Managing Director (q.v.) from 1974 until 1984. Prior to becoming Deputy Managing Director, he was Executive Director (q.v.) appointed by the United States from 1962 to 1974, and before that he had served with the U.S. Government in the Department of Commerce and in the Department of the Treasury.

Debt Reduction Mechanisms. Since the latter part of the 1980s,

Fund-supported adjustment programs (q.v.) have included, where appropriate, specified amounts of financing earmarked for debt reduction purposes, particularly if the country in question is making a strong effort under an adjustment program. Some of these programs have been accompanied by the adoption of a number of devices to reduce the indebtedness of individual developing countries (q.v.). One such device is the buyback mechanism, whereby countries are permitted to repurchase their debt at a discount for cash. Either the country's international reserves or foreign exchange (qq.v.) donated or borrowed from official or private sources may be used for such operations. Another such device is the use of swaps (q.v.), whereby foreign banks may swap their loans for an equity investment, while foreign nonbanks may purchase loan claims at a discount in the secondary market to finance direct investment or purchase domestic financial assets. Importers have also used swaps in this manner, buying bank debt in the secondary market and redeeming it at the central bank for local currency in order to pay the exporter. A third mechanism for debt reduction involves debt exchange, whereby old debt is exchanged for new debt, usually at a discount on the face value or at a lower rate of interest. Fourth, exit bonds have been introduced in a number of restructuring agreements, whereby a commercial bank that does not wish to remain part of a concerted restructuring package takes up an exit bond. Such a bond usually bears a rate of interest that is lower than the current market rate, and this discount is viewed as the cost of withdrawing from the concerted lending operation.

The Fund's strategy to the debt problem was based on a case-by-case approach with three basic elements: the pursuit of growth-oriented adjustment and structural reform in debtor countries; the provision of adequate financial support by official, multilateral, and private sources; and the maintenance of a favorable global economic environment. In May 1989, the Executive Board (q.v.) agreed that a certain portion of Fund resources (q.v.) committed under an extended or stand-by arrangement (q.v.) could be set aside to reduce the stock of debt through buybacks or exchanges. The Board stressed that this percentage would be determined on a case-by-case basis, but that it would normally be around 25 percent. The Board also agreed to consider additional access—up to 30 percent of a member's quota (q.v.)—to the Fund's resources (q.v.) for debt-service reduction in certain cases, providing that such support would be decisive in promoting further cost-effective operations and in catalyzing other financial resources.

Since the May 1989 guidelines were established, the Fund has approved stand-by and extended arrangements for several members (such as Argentina [q.v.], Costa Rica, Ecuador, Mexico, Philippines [q.v.], Uruguay, Venezuela) that have set aside 25 percent of the total financing provided under the arrangement for debt reduction, with the possibility of additional amounts for debt-service reduction. In November 1992, when a new quota increases became effective, the Fund announced that the limit on the augmentation of arrangements to reduce the stock of debt and the service on debt would be 30 percent of quota, where such support would facilitate further cost-effective operations and catalyze other resources.

In September 1996, the Interim Committee (q.v.) authorized the Fund, in coordination with the World Bank (q.v.), to introduce a new initiative for heavily indebted poor countries (HIPCs) (q.v.), aimed at assisting them, both through adjustment programming and financing, to meet their debt problems. *See also* Paris Club.

De Larosière, Jacques (1929-). Jacques de Larosière, of France, became the sixth Managing Director (q.v.) and Chairman of the Executive Board (q.v.) in June 1978. He came to the Fund after a distinguished career in the French civil service: Director of the French Treasury, and for a time Personal Assistant and Director of the Cabinet Office of Valéry Giscard d'Estaing when he was Minister of Economy and Finance. He was well known among financial officials and had participated in meetings of the Committee of Twenty, the Interim Committee, and the Development Committee (qq.v.) and had served on the Economic Policy Committee and the Development Assistance Committee of the Organization for Economic Cooperation and Development (OECD). At the time he became Managing Director, de Larosière was serving as Chairman of the Deputies of the Group of Ten (q.v.). He was the Fund's Managing Director for eight-and-a-half years and was succeeded by Michel Camdessus (q.v.), also of France, in 1987.

Deputy Managing Director. The appointment of the Deputy Managing Director is approved by the Executive Board (q.v.) and is customarily for a term of five years. By convention, the position has always been filled by a U.S. national, while the Managing Director (q.v.), also by convention, has always been a European.

On June 6, 1994, the Fund announced that it would increase the number of Deputy Managing Directors from one to three, and it named Stanley Fischer (U.S.A.), Alassane D. Ouattara (Côte d'Ivoire), and Prabhakar R. Narvekar (India) (qq.v.) to the positions. The three Deputies succeeded Richard Erb (q.v.), the fifth Deputy Managing Director, who had been appointed in 1984 and had served two five-years terms in the position. To preserve the convention that the Deputy Managing Director should be a U.S. national, Stanley Fischer was designated as First Deputy Managing Director. When Prabhakar Narvekar retired in 1997, he was succeeded by Shigemitsu Sugisaki (Japan) (q.v.).

Working under the direction of the Managing Director, each Deputy Managing Director has the authority to chair Executive Board meetings and to maintain contacts with officials of member governments, Executive Directors, and other institutions.

The role of a Deputy Managing Director has never been defined. It is not a position that is enumerated in the Articles of Agreement or dealt with in any substance in the By-laws or Rules and Regulations of the Fund (qq.v.). In the absence of the Managing Director, a Deputy Managing Director serves as Acting Chairman and assumes in that role the power of the Managing Director. Like the Managing Director, a Deputy cannot vote, except in the event of an equal vote by Executive Directors, when the Acting Chairman may cast a deciding vote.

Deputy Managing Directors also assist in the administration of the staff. They are active in shaping the Fund's administrative budget (q.v.), in the assignment of staff to missions to member countries, and in overseeing the day-to-day working of the Fund. They are integral members of the policymaking group, attend the Managing Director's meetings with staff and Executive Directors, and are the central links among various departments, divisions, and sectors of the Fund's staff. The precise role and the extent of a Deputy Managing Director's influence on the affairs of the Fund depend very much on the personal characteristics of the occupant.

Prior to Richard Erb, the position of Deputy Managing Director had been held by Andrew Overby (1949-52), Merle Cochran (1953-62), Frank Southard (1962-74), and William Dale (1974-84) (qq.v.). *See also* Fund Management Structure Change.

Devaluation. Under the Bretton Woods system (q.v.) the value of a currency (q.v.) was defined in terms of gold (q.v.), and changes in a par value (q.v.) required the approval of the Fund. One of the perceived causes of the failure of the Bretton Woods system was that countries, particularly industrial and major trading countries, were reluctant to devalue their currencies for fear of political repercussions. Maintenance of the value of a country's currency in exchange markets (q.v.) became a prestige factor in domestic politics, and any lowering of that value tended to be associated with a failure of policy. After the collapse of the Bretton Woods system early in the 1970s, the Fund ceased to exercise direct authority over exchange rate changes (q.v.), although it continued to have responsibility for the orderly and smooth functioning of the international monetary system (q.v.).

Since the second amendment of the Fund's Articles of Agreement (q.v.) in 1978, member countries have opted for a variety of exchange arrangements—pegging (q.v.) to a single currency or to a trade-weighted group of currencies or to the SDR (q.v.), maintaining a fixed rate under the European Monetary System (q.v.), or allowing a freely floating (q.v.) rate. The new freedom to adopt exchange arrangements of choice has made it easier to adjust exchange rates or to let them find their market levels. Under these new arrangements, in fact, volatility, not rigidity, has been of concern as exchange rates of the major currencies have sometimes tended to gyrate against each other, with little or no change in the underlying economic and financial conditions.

Developing Countries. The term *developing countries* was not mentioned in the original Articles (q.v.), even though there was some pressure on the part of developing countries at the Bretton Woods Conference (q.v.) to include a reference to the special position of developing countries. The term was included in the second amendment to the Articles, but only in connection with setting up a Council (q.v.), which has never come into existence, and with the sale of the Fund's gold (q.v.) holdings and the distribution of their proceeds. An implicit principle embedded in the Articles is that all members should receive uniform treatment.

The term *developing countries* has itself evolved from what was considered pejorative terminology, first from backward countries and then from underdeveloped countries. Like most labels, it is understood as a term of art, rather than a depiction of reality, since all countries are developing, in one sense or another. In the Fund's classification, countries that are not classified as "advanced economies," a group which is comprised of the Group of Seven (q.v.) and 15 other advanced economies, are classified broadly as "developing countries," although this large group of about 160 countries is broken down into subgroups for analytical purposes.

Over the years the Fund has established a number of facilities, such as the compensatory financing facility, the buffer stock financing facility, and the structural adj.ustment facility (qq.v.), that are particularly beneficial to developing countries. The Trust Fund, which was funded largely by proceeds from the sales of the Fund's gold (q.v.) holdings, was specifically established for the benefit of the least developed or low-income countries. However, although some of its facilities are particularly beneficial to developing countries, and, indeed, have been designed to be so, its financial resources are open to all members on the same terms and on an even-handed basis.

Development Committee. The Joint Ministerial Committee of the Boards of Governors of the Bank and the Fund on the Transfer of Real Resources to Developing Countries (known as the Development Committee) was established on October 2, 1974, under a parallel composite resolution adopted by the Boards of Governors of the World Bank (qq.v.) and the Fund. It was one of two successor committees (the Interim Committee [q.v.] was the other) to the Committee of Twenty (q.v.).

Members of the Committee are Governors of the World Bank, Governors of the Fund, ministers, or others of comparable rank, appointed for successive terms of two years by members of the World Bank and members of the Fund. There can be up to seven associates for each member of the committee. The composition of the Committee parallels the constituencies making up the Executive Boards (q.v.) of the World Bank and the Fund. The President of the World Bank and the Managing Director (q.v.) of the Fund participate in the meetings of the Committee, which are held at the time of the Joint Fund and Bank Annual Meetings (q.v.) and, in addition, at any other times deemed appropriate.

The Committee was founded mainly at the urging of the developing countries (q.v.), which were disappointed that they had not been able to achieve a "link" between SDR allocations and development finance (qq.v.). It was established at a time when a sharp increase in the world price of crude oil, together with a slowdown in the growth of the world economy, was causing severe balance of payments (q.v.) difficulties for many developing countries. The Committee's terms of reference are: (1) to maintain an overview of the development process and advise and report to the Boards of Governors of the World Bank and the Fund on all aspects of the question of the transfer of real resources to developing countries (2) to prepare a program of work to implement the proposals concerning developing countries made in the final report by the Committee of Twenty; and (3) to give urgent attention to the problems of the least developed countries and to developing countries most seriously affected by the current situation, which as mentioned earlier was dominated by the oil crisis at that time. By the end of 1998, the Committee had held 48 meetings, the proceedings of which were made available to the public in a communiqué issued at the end of each meeting.

Development Finance. The Fund does not provide development finance, which is the function of its sister institution—the World Bank (q.v.). Development finance is long-term financing, often in grant form or on concessional terms, directed to a specific project or sector of the economy. The Fund provides short-term to medium-term balance of payments (q.v.) financing in support of macroeconomic and structural adjustment programs (q.v.). All its financing, however, is in support of adjustment programs that are designed to bring about conditions for sustained economic growth.

Discrimination. Both the Fund and its members are obligated to deal with all of its members on the principle of uniformity. All members are able to use the Fund's resources (q.v.) on the same terms and all members must receive symmetrical treatment from the Fund. Similarly, no member can discriminate against any other member in the context of its exchange rate arrangements (q.v.).

Documents and Information. For almost the first four decades of its operations, the discussions and negotiations that the Fund held with member countries, its staff reports on countries, and the adjustment programs (q.v.) supported by the Fund were all held to be confidential. The Fund attached great importance to preserving its confidentiality on these matters, since it believed that only under conditions of absolute trust and confidentiality would it be possible to have full and frank discussions with member governments on sensitive national issues. Thus, a vast amount of documentation on country-specific matters was never made public, even though the Fund was, and still is, charged under its Articles (q.v.) to "act as a center for the collection and exchange of information on monetary and financial problems." It was judged that publication of the Fund's economic journal, *Staff Papers,* and its statistical data base, *International Financial Statistics,* as well as one or two official reports, met this charge. Moreover, unlike many of its member governments and other international organizations, the Fund set no time period for breaking this confidentiality, and only in January 1996 was it decided to open material in the Fund's archives (q.v.) when it was 30 years old.

In the 1980s, however, the Fund went through a gradual transformation in its attitude to public relations and information services. Once content to be the "scapegoat" for public officials in member countries that were adopting unpopular adjustment policies, the Fund came to see that that such criticisms, particularly when they were indulged in by high authorities who were themselves responsible for steering the country into desperate situations, were counterproductive and seriously impeded its work. As a result, the Fund took a new approach to information services and over the following decade or so fundamentally changed the way the Fund operated in the public arena. It established an External Relations Department, to replace an office that had been staffed by only two or three press officers, and became much more aggressive in its press and information activities. It expanded its publications programs and produced a video on the Fund's form, functions, and policies; organized seminars at headquarters and abroad on macroeconomic policies and financial reforms for government officials and local academics; made public its surveys and scenarios on the world economy; strengthened and expanded its training programs at the IMF Institute; and in general began a program to reach out to and service the academic communities, government officials, and the general public.

In the 1990s, galvanized by the suddenness of the Mexican (q.v.) financial crisis and the lack of information and transparency that contributed to the crisis, the Fund went further to bring about as much transparency as possible in its own activities. It encouraged members of its staff missions abroad to consult with important segments of opinion makers, to appear on television and radio to explain the programs that were being implemented; published its staff economic reports on member countries; made public Executive Board (q.v.) comments from its Article IV consultations with members and the reviews of member-country programs (PINs) (q.v.); and made public on its web site (subject to the consent of the country authority involved) letters of intent from members undertaking Fund-supported adjustment programs. The bibliography includes a list of the Fund's publications.

Drawings. The term "drawing" is used synonymously with the term "purchase" (q.v.) in the Fund's lexicon. Technically, all operations with the Fund's General Department (q.v.) (i.e., its ordinary resources) are termed "purchases" and "repurchases" (q.v.). These terms reflect the fact that the Fund's resources (q.v.) consist of a pool of currencies (q.v.) (the Fund's holdings of gold [q.v.] are no longer used in any transaction) that has been subscribed by members. A member using the Fund's resources will purchase from the Fund a currency it needs by exchanging an equal amount of its own currency. When that member repays the Fund, it will repurchase its own currency by exchanging an equal amount of another member's currency, as designated by the Fund. "Purchases" and "repurchases" are not terms used in ordinary banking business and are often substituted by the more generally understood terms "drawings" and "repayments."

-E-

Economic Counselor. A position created on the staff of the Fund in May 1966, when Jacques J. Polak (q.v.), who was Director of the Research Department, was also appointed to the position of Economic Counselor. At that time, the Group of Ten (q.v.) and its Deputies began to meet regularly to discuss the problem of international liquidity (q.v.) and the need for a contingency mechanism for reserve creation. Jacques Polak was one of the two representatives of the Fund to attend the meetings of the Deputies and report back to the Executive Board (q.v.). After its creation, the position became permanent, and has been automatically conferred on the Director of the Research Department. Since Jacques Polak's retirement from the staff of the Fund, the Director of the Research Department has been recruited from outside the Fund and has generally been an esteemed member of the academic community.

Economic Development. Unlike the World Bank (q.v.), the Fund is not an organization whose primary or direct purpose is to promote economic development. The Fund is directly concerned with a member country's balance of payments (q.v.) position and the domestic monetary and fiscal policies that produce an imbalance in that position. But this concern has broader implications, because experience demonstrates that the domestic economic and financial policies of a country, its external economic position, and its rate of sustainable growth are all inextricably linked. Although not directly involved in economic development, the Fund's actions and policies have a crucial impact on economic development itself. The secondary, and indirect, purpose of the Fund's work, therefore, is to be supportive of the development efforts of its members and to help national governments raise the standard of living everywhere.

Fund policy is based on the belief that a stable economy, free from inflation and operating without artificial restrictions, affords the most promising grounds for sustainable economic development. It is a belief supported by many research and case studies conducted inside and outside the Fund. The key factors in a Fund-supported adjustment program (q.v.) also lead to the prerequisite conditions for growth and development. These include an appropriate balance between government revenue and expenditure, prudent monetary policies to avoid inflation, realistic exchange rates to promote a balance between a country's receipts from abroad and its external expenditures, the elimination of foreign exchange restrictions (q.v.) that hamper the growth of world trade, an open trading system to foster outward-orientated productive activities, and prudent policies on external borrowing. In addition, an extensive range of structural adjustments could include specific taxation policies, economic pricing of government services, free-market pricing wherever possible elsewhere in the economy, reduction of subsidies, privatization of loss-making state enterprises, and the development of institutions, such as securities exchanges, central banks, and investment banking, that would improve the economic management of the economy.

Moreover, a country adopting a stabilization program (q.v.) supported by the Fund sends a signal to the international financial community that it is putting its house in order and, therefore, is likely to attract finance, both official and private, for its economic development. Indeed, for many countries experiencing economic and financial difficulties, the Fund's seal of approval is critical in their efforts to attract external financing. During the 1980s, when international indebtedness was at its peak and many developing countries (q.v.) were having difficulty in debt servicing, the Fund was the only international organization in a position to initiate and coordinate efforts to round up external financing, including long-term finance, from other international organizations, national governments, and commercial banks in support of stabilization programs supported by Fund stand-by arrangements (q.v.).

Economies in Transition. With the end of central planning in many countries of Eastern Europe and the breakup of the Soviet Union in the early 1990s, the Fund entered into a close relationship with the economies in transition. Since 1990, the Fund has provided a vast amount of financial and technical assistance to these 27 countries, most of which have made good progress, with the resumption of economic growth, macroecomic stabilization, and the inception of structural reforms. Progress has been mixed, however, with some countries forging ahead of others, depending to a large extent on the nature of their initial problems and the steadfastness with which they pursued their goals.

Overall, between January 1, 1990, and December 31, 1997, the Fund committed a total of SDR 30.7 billion (about $40.3 billion) to the 27 economies in transition. These commitments were made through all the facilities of the Fund, such as under regular and extended stand-by arrangements (q.v.); the concessional window, enhanced structural adjustment facility (q.v.); the special temporary facility created for these economies, the systemic transformation facility (q.v.); and the compensatory and contingency financing facility (q.v.). At the end of January 1998, outstanding credit amounted to SDR 15.6 billion (about $20.3 billion). The largest commitment was to the Russian Federation (q.v.), amounting to SDR 14.1 billion (about $18.2 billion); followed by Poland (q.v.), SDR 2.7 billion (about $3.5 billion); Ukraine, SDR 2.5 billion (about $3.2 billion); Hungary, SDR 2.1 billion (about $2.7 billion); Romania, SDR 1.8 billion (about $2.3 billion); and Bulgaria, SDR 1.7 billion (about $2.2 billion).

Technical assistance provided by the Fund to the economies covered four broad categories: design and implementation of fiscal and monetary policies; institution building (such as improving tax collection and through the strengthening of tax administration); collection and refinement of statistical data; and reviewing legislation and providing assistance, when asked, in its drafting. Technical assistance also included training officials at the IMF Institute at headquarters and at the Joint Vienna Institute (q.v.). By the end of 1997, 8,300 participants from 33 countries had received training through courses and seminars at the Joint Vienna Institute.

Although the experience of the countries remains diverse, most of them have started on the growth process and have reduced inflation to moderate levels (e.g., Poland, the Baltic countries, Croatia, the Czech and Slovak Republics, Hungary, and Slovenia). In Russia, the long-awaited renewal of the growth in output began very modestly only in 1997, and it remains to be seen whether contagion from the Asian crisis (q.v.) will negate the progress that was beginning to be achieved at the end of 1997. Overall GDP in 1997 for all economies in transition grew by 1.7 percent, compared with negative results of 1.3 percent and 0.2 percent in 1995 and 1996, respectively. Overall inflation for the group fell from 119 percent in 1995, to 40 percent in 1996 and 31 percent in 1997.

Assessing the situation at the beginning of 1998, the Fund recognized that many challenges remained to be addressed to safeguard and further extend the progress that had been achieved. In many of the less advanced transition economies, there was a critical need to establish institutions essential to a market economy. Underdeveloped financial systems were plagued by nonperforming loans, the restructuring of former state-owned enterprises had not gone very far, and governments were often unable to honor obligations for lack of tax revenues. Fragile banking systems, in particular, posed a significant inflation threat, to the extent that governments may feel obliged to bail out insolvent financial institutions. To sustain and enhance countries' longer run growth performance and ensure that the benefits of initial reforms were more widely shared, the Fund called for the implementation of a second generation of reforms in all transition economies. These included the strengthening of bank regulation and supervision; further privatization and enterprise reform; the minimization of monopoly power; legal and institutional reforms to make it easier to exercise property rights and enforce contracts; improvements in tax systems and governance; health and education reforms; and pension reforms to lessen the fiscal pressures caused by an aging population. *See also* Transitional Economies.

Egypt. In the early 1990s, Egypt faced severe financial imbalance evidenced by high inflation, large external deficits, and accumulated external arrears. With support from the Fund by means of two successive financial arrangements, in 1991 and 1993, the country made important progress toward reducing these imbalances. Real GDP growth accelerated to over 4 percent in 1995-96, from virtual stagnation in 1991-92, while the rate of inflation declined to 7 percent, from over 21 percent. The overall balance of payments (q.v.) remained in surplus, leading to a substantial accumulation of international reserves (q.v.), equivalent to about 17 months of imports. With limited external borrowing and further debt relief from the Paris Club (q.v.), the ratio of external debt to GDP fell to 47 percent in mid-1996 from about 75 percent in 1991-92. Nevertheless, despite these promising development, economic performance remained below potential, particularly in regard to structural reforms.

Against this background, Egypt adopted an ambitious reform program, in support of which the Fund approved a two-year standby arrangement (q.v.) in October 1996. In light of Egypt's strong external reserve position (q.v.), the authorities viewed the arrangement as precautionary and had no intention to draw on it. The program focused on consolidating the gains on macroeconomic stabilization, while broadening and intensifying the structural reform agenda through privatization, deregulation, trade liberalization, and a revamping of the financial sector.

During the two-year period under the program, the aim was to achieve a further increase in real GDP to 6 percent and to maintain a viable external position, although the external current account position was expected to weaken slightly, reflecting the strong growth of imports driven by the recovery and higher investments. Structural reforms were aimed at expanding the private sector, in order to promote investment, growth, and employment. The central goal was to bring about a fundamental change in the ownership structure of the Egyptian economy, where public enterprises accounted for as much as one-third of Egypt's manufacturing sector, half of investment expenditure, and about 15 percent of total employment. To this end, the program was based on a continued divestiture of nonfinancial sector enterprises.

Other key structural reforms included further liberalization of Egypt's international trade system; fiscal reforms, including the transformation of the general sales tax into a value-added tax; the rationalization of the income tax to make it simpler, broader-based, and more transparent and equitable; a medium-term program for improving the civil service; and an acceleration of financial sector reform, including the privatization of banks and insurance companies, and a further strengthening of banking supervision. At the same time, the authorities are committed to improving the country's health and education systems, to a further strengthening of the social safety net, and to providing increased assistance to displaced workers through compensation pay, retraining, and redeployment.

Emergency Assistance. Although no formal facility has been established to provide emergency assistance, since 1962 the Fund has provided such assistance in the form of outright purchases (q.v.) in the first and second credit tranches (q.v.) to member countries facing payments problems arising from unforeseeable natural disasters. These purchases do not involve performance criteria or the phasing of disbursements; they must be repurchased in three-and-a-quarter to five years.

Emergency Financing Mechanism. After the 1944 Mexican crisis (q.v.), the Fund took a number of measures to strengthen its ability to respond promptly in support of its members. These included an agreement to formalize the procedures to be used in activating an emergency financing mechanism. The essence of the mechanism is that it would allow the Executive Board (q.v.) to give rapid approval for Fund financial support, while ensuring that appropriate conditionality (q.v.) would apply. In certain circumstances, it was also agreed that there might be a need for large and front-loaded access to Fund resources (q.v.). The procedures were used extensively in 1997 to provide emergency financing for the Fund-supported adjustment programs for Korea, Indonesia, and Thailand (qq.v.).

In agreeing on the elements for such a procedure, the Board expressed caution on how it should be activated; it was to be used only in circumstances representing or threatening to give rise to a crisis in a member's external accounts that required an immediate response from the Fund. One consideration, but not necessarily an exclusively determining factor, would be whether there would be a spillover or contagion effects. The Board considered that the procedures should be used only in rare cases. Conditions for its activation would include the readiness of the member to engage immediately in accelerated negotiations with the Fund, with the prospect

of an early agreement on and implementation of measures sufficiently strong to address the problem. A member's past cooperation with the Fund would be a factor in the speed at which the Fund could assess the situation and agree on necessary corrective measures; and until the emergency was resolved, there would be frequent assessments of the effectiveness of the member's policies. The Board also made it clear that there would be no automatic link between use of the emergency financing procedures and the General Arrangements to Borrow (q.v.) or other supplementary borrowing arrangements. Further, the availability of the mechanism would not represent a guarantee against sovereign default. It was to be understood that if the financial crisis was resolved quickly, the member would make early repayments of resources drawn under the emergency procedures.

On another aspect relating to use of the emergency procedures, the Board also agreed that the Fund should be ready to give technical and financial assistance to post-conflict countries. Such cases would include situations where the country's institutional and administrative capacity had been disrupted as a result of conflict. In these circumstances, a member might not be able to develop and implement a comprehensive economic program that could be supported by a Fund arrangement. Nevertheless, Fund support could be part of a concerted international effort to catalyze support from other official sources when there was an urgent balance of payments (q.v.) need to rebuild reserves (q.v.) and meet essential external commitments and the country had sufficient capacity and commitment to plan and implement policy. It was foreseen, however, that the Fund would most probably not be the lead institution in such an internationally coordinated effort.

Directors agreed that access to Fund resources (q.v.) in these cases should as a rule be limited to one credit tranche (q.v.) (25 percent of a member's quota [q.v.]) and that access policy under the existing emergency financing mechanism would provide sufficient flexibility to handle exceptional needs. The proposed financing would be available only if the member intended to move within a relatively short time to an upper credit tranche or enhanced structural adjustment facility (ESAF) arrangement. The financing would be supplemented by a comprehensive technical assistance (q.v.) program, including the building and rebuilding of institutions.

Enhanced Structural Adjustment Facility (ESAF). The ESAF was part of the Fund's efforts to help its low-income members to bring about reforms and structural adjustments to their economic and financial systems. The facility became operational in April 1988 and was extended and enlarged in December 1993. It followed the structural adjustment facility (SAF) (q.v.), which was established in March 1986 and had been virtually phased out by 1995. In September 1996, the Executive Board (q.v.) decided to make the ESAF a permanent rather than a temporary facility, as the centerpiece of the Fund's strategy to help low-income countries. Subsequently, the ESAF was supplemented by the initiative to assist the heavily indebted poor countries (HIPCs) (q.v.). In December 1996, the Board approved an extension of the commitment period to December 31, 2000, with a corresponding extension through December 2003 of the drawdown periods in the agreements with lenders.

In establishing the SAF in March 1986, it had been recognized that the resources available under the facility might be insufficient to support the strong and comprehensive adjustment programs (q.v.) that the poorest countries needed to undertake to restore and maintain balance of payments (q.v.) viability while achieving high and sustainable rates of economic growth. The ESAF was thus established to continue the work of the SAF, and the conditions on its use by members were basically similar to those pertaining to the SAF. The facility was financed mainly by loans and grants from member countries to the ESAF Trust and, following the facility's extension in 1986, by the participation of a broad cross section of the Fund's membership.

As had been the case with the SAF, the Trust conducted its operations through three separate accounts—a Loan Account, which received loans from contributors for on-lending to members under ESAF arrangements; a Subsidy Account, which received contributions, including grants from members and earnings from the ESAF Administered Accounts, to subsidize the rate of interest charged on borrowings from the Trust; and a Reserve Account, which was set up to provide added security to lenders' claims on the Trust Fund and was financed mainly by resources provided by repayments of SAF and ESAF loans.

Borrowings by members from the ESAF Trust covered a three-year period under three annual arrangements (as under the SAF). Disbursements take place semiannually, the first disbursement coinciding with the approval of the arrangement, followed by a second disbursement after completion of a midyear performance review. Interest on ESAF loans has been kept at half of one percent. Access under the ESAF arrangements depends on a member's balance of payments need, the strength of its adjustment efforts, the amount of the member's outstanding credit with the Fund, and the record of its past performance. Total access is subject to a maximum of 190 percent of quota (q.v.), with a provision that this limit may be exceeded in exceptional cases.

At the end of April 1998, 33 ESAF arrangements were in effect, and cumulative commitments under the ESAF and SAF arrangements had risen to SDR 10.3 billion, with over 60 developing countries (q.v.) benefiting from the Fund's concessional assistance.

The Fund's staff has conducted two internal reviews of the experience of countries under the ESAF and its precursor, the SAF. In regard to the first study, covering 19 countries and completed in March 1993, the Executive Board found that the experience under SAF/ESAF-supported programs had been generally favorable. The second study, completed in July 1997, covered 36 countries that had availed themselves of SAF and ESAF financing in support of 68 multiyear reform programs approved prior to December 31, 1994. This review was also positive, suggesting that countries undertaking reform and adjustment programs supported by the SAF/ESAF had brought their economies a long way from the doldrums of the early 1980s. By 1995, average real per capita output growth among ESAF users (excluding transitional economies [q.v.]) had caught up with that in other developing countries. The social indicators in most countries improved. Roughly three-quarters of ESAF-using countries moved closer to a viable external position. Budget deficits were trimmed and instances of very high inflation virtually eliminated.

The review made four recommendations for future programs:
(1) stronger fiscal adjustment based on durable budget econo-

mies, particularly from civil service reform and reduced support for public enterprises, while protecting growth-enhancing expenditures on health and education;

(2) more resolve in reducing inflation to single-digit levels by using monetary and exchange rate anchors, where appropriate;

(3) a more concerted effort to adopt "second generation" structural reforms, especially trade liberalization, public enterprise reform, bank restructuring, and strengthened property rights; and

(4) steps to reduce policy slippage and encourage more sustained policy implementation by more intensive program monitoring, greater use of contingency planning in program design, and more proactive technical assistance (q.v.) to build institutional capacity.

This internal review was complemented by an external evaluating panel, which presented its report for discussion by the Executive Board in March 1998. The panel, established in October 1996, comprised Dr. Kwesi Botchwey, Harvard Institute for International Development; Professor Paul Collier, Oxford University; Professor Jan Willem Gunning, Free University, Amsterdam; and Professor Koichi Hamada, Yale University. In accordance with its terms of reference, the panel concentrated on three specific areas: social policies and the composition of government spending, developments in countries' external position, and the determinants and influences of national ownership on ESAF-supported programs.

In its report the panel recommended the following:

(1) At a sufficiently high management level, the Fund should engage in intensive and informal policy dialogue with the country's political leadership to understand a country's political constraints and possibilities.

(2) The timing and duration of Fund staff missions should be arranged to allow adequate time for country preparation in advance of negotiation and consensus-building during the negotiation.

(3) Steps should be taken to relieve concerns about the Fund's perceived inflexibility in negotiations through the introduction of an element of choice in the negotiation of the design of programs.

(4) The Fund should develop a more systematic mechanism for providing ex-post support for country-initiated programs, enabling the Fund to play an important role in countries with balance of payments need but where agreement is impossible or delayed, although the areas of convergence between the Fund and government are substantial, or where a government feels unable to accede to formal agreement with the Fund for mainly political reasons.

(5) Ways should be found to both humanize and demystify the Fund's image, so as to assuage the political hazard that countries

perceive to be associated in dealing with the Fund.

(6) The Fund/World Bank (q.v.) relations should be better coordinated.

(7) Resident missions should be strengthened or established in all ESAF countries to reinforce strategies, foster country ownership, and assess the social impact of reform programs.

Enhanced Structural Adjustment Facility Subsidy Account. To enable enhanced structural adjustment financing to be provided at low concessional interest rates, subsidy contributions are received by the Trust Subsidy Account. Contributions to the Account take a variety of forms, including direct grants and deposits. At the end of the financial year on April 30, 1998, resources available in the Account totaled SDR 1.4 million; cumulative contributions by 22 countries amounted to SDR 1.6 million.

Enlarged Access Policy (EAP). Introduced as a temporary measure in 1981, the enlarged access policy was terminated in November 1992, when the increase in members' quotas (q.v.) under the ninth general review of quotas (q.v.) became effective. The policy had served its purpose by allowing members to use the Fund's financial resources (q.v.) over and above the normal limits established by the Fund in a period when many countries, particularly developing countries (q.v.), were suffering severe imbalance in their payments. The policy had been financed by Fund borrowing (q.v.), in lieu of an adequate increase in its ordinary resources through a quota increase. When the quota increases under the ninth general review of quotas became effective in November 1992 (and it took over five years from the start of the exercise to its completion), the Fund was able to meet members' needs for financing from its ordinary resources. Expressed in terms of the new quotas, the new access limits (q.v.) under stand-by (q.v.) and extended arrangements in support of members' economic programs were set at 68 percent of quota per annum and 300 percent of quota cumulatively, net of repayments falling due to the Fund during the period of the arrangement.

The EAP succeeded the supplementary financing facility (q.v.), which was introduced in 1979, and came into effect when all available resources in that facility had been committed. Access limits under the enlarged access policy were determined by guidelines adopted periodically by the Fund.

Environment and the Fund. Early in 1991, the Executive Board (q.v.) informally considered the extent to which the Fund should address environmental issues. It was agreed that the staff should recognize linkages among economic policies, economic development, and the environment. This would help the Fund to avoid policies that could have undesirable environmental consequences, while ensuring that the thrust of its actions promoted balance of payments (q.v.) viability and sustainable growth. The Fund consults with other organizations with expertise in environmental matters, including the World Bank (q.v.), the Organization for Economic Cooperation and Development (OECD), the United Nations Environmental Program (UNEP), and the United Nations Development Program (UNDP).

Equal Value Principle. The equal value principle is designed to ensure that a member country transferring SDRs (q.v.) in exchange for currency (q.v.) would receive equal value for the SDRs it was transferring, regardless of which currency was being provided in return for the SDRs received. Under the first amendment of the Articles (q.v.), this requirement was met by the stipulation that a member receiving SDRs in exchange for currency had to supply currency convertible in fact (q.v.). Under the second amendment to the Articles, this provision was changed, and a recipient of SDRs in exchange for currency had to supply "freely usable" currency (designated by the Fund as the deutsche mark, French franc, Japanese yen, pound sterling, and U.S. dollar).

Erb, Richard D. (1941-). Richard Erb (United States) was appointed Deputy Managing Director in 1984 and served for two five-year terms. Before his appointment as Deputy Managing Director, he had served the U.S. government in the Treasury Department. Upon the termination of his tenure in 1994, three Deputy Managing Directors were appointed, the first major change in the Fund management structure (q.v.) since the institution's founding.

Euro. The common currency established on January 1, 1999, by the European Monetary Union (q.v.). Eleven countries—Austria, Belgium, Finland, France, Germany, Ireland, Italy, Luxembourg, the Netherlands, Portugal, and Spain—participated in the launch of the new currency. Four countries did not join in the first wave—Denmark and the United Kingdom opted out, Sweden stood aside, and Greece did not qualify on macroeconomic grounds. *See also* European Monetary Union.

European Currency Units (ECUs). ECUs were issued by the European Monetary Cooperation Fund to the central banks of participating countries in exchange for contributions of 20 percent of their gold (q.v.) holdings and 20 percent of their gross dollar holdings. These contributions were made under revolving swaps, of three months' duration, and could be unwound at the initiative of the participant at short notice. Furthermore, each participating central bank could, under contract, invest and manage the assets it had contributed. The exact amount of ECU holdings depended on the price of gold, the exchange rate for the U.S. dollar, and the amount of each asset held by the participating central banks. ECUs were used for partial settlements between participants on a monthly basis. At the end of 1996, ECUs accounted for about 5.9 percent of identified reserve currency (q.v.) holdings by all countries.

European Economic and Monetary Union (EMU) and the Fund. January 1, 1999, marked the planned start of the European Economic and Monetary Union (EMU), when a new single currency (q.v.), the euro (q.v.), would be used by 11 members of the European Union for trade throughout the world. Unlike other monetary reforms, the euro will replace the national currencies of participating members, a number of whose currencies are already widely used for international transactions.

A single currency had been seen as a necessary element to complete the European Union's single market. The signing of the Single European Act in 1986 led to the adoption, in April 1989, of the Maastricht Treaty, which set the path by which the European Union would proceed to the EMU. The Treaty, which amended and supplemented the Treaty of Rome, proved to be highly controversial in a number of states and was signed by the heads of governments of the member states only after Denmark and the United Kingdom had negotiated their right to "opt out." The Treaty came into force on November 1, 1993, and imposed an obligation on the 13 states that had not negotiated to opt out to merge their currencies into a single currency if they met four macroeconomic criteria, relating to inflation, exchange rate stability, long-term interest rates, and government debt.

In May 1998, 11 member states were judged to have met the criteria, and a European Central Bank (ECB) was established. With the launch of the euro on January 1, 1999, the conversion rates of the national currencies for the euro were established and locked in; the euro became the currency of the participating states, and national currency units became denominations of the euro. The ECB took over control of monetary policy for the euro zone, and all new issues of government debt were to be issued in euro. In 2001, euro banknotes and coins would be introduced and all obligations denominated in national currency units would be redenominated in euro. On June 30, 2002, national banknotes and coins were to cease being legal tender.

The establishment of the EMU raised a number of issues for the Fund. These included how surveillance (q.v.) would be carried out, whether and how Fund resources (q.v.) should be made available to EMU members, how Fund quotas (q.v.) might be affected, whether the SDR (q.v.) would need to be redefined, and how the euro would be used in Fund operations. On September 30, 1998, the Fund announced that after the launch of the EMU on January 1, 1999, the euro would replace the currency amounts of the deutsche mark and the French franc in the SDR valuation basket.

It remained to be seen how these matters were worked out, but it seemed likely that EMU members would opt to remain individual members of the Fund, rather than choose to merge into a single Fund member with a single quota. The main reason for retaining individual membership seemed to be that the EMU implied only a limited transfer of decisionmaking at the supranational level. The transfer of competence would mainly concern the Union's monetary policy, which would be the exclusive responsibility of the ECB, and its exchange rate policy, which would be in the hands of the Council of Economic and Finance Ministers (ECOFIN) and the ECB. EMU member states would retain ultimate responsibility for other economic policies, and for this reason EMU members might wish to retain close individual relationships with the Fund.

Furthermore, a decision to merge EMU members into a single Fund membership with a single quota would imply a loss of national sovereignty, a step that many members would find hard to accept.

European Monetary System (EMS). The EMS began operating in March 1979 with the aim of establishing a zone of monetary stability among members of the European Community. Members of the Community electing to participate in the system were required to establish a central rate in terms of the European Currency Unit (ECU) (q.v.). The ECU consisted of a basket of currencies (q.v.) containing agreed to amounts of currency of each Community member. Adjustment in central rates (q.v.) were subject to agreement by other members and the European Commission. Participants had to observe limits of 2.25 percent above and below the cross rate arising from their central rates established in terms of the ECU. They were given the option of observing a 6 percent margin upon entering the system, but this wider margin was to be gradually reduced to 2.25 percent. The establishment of this regional monetary system was seen as a step toward full economic and political integration of the European Community. It has been superseded by the establishment of the common European Union currency, the euro (q.v.).

European Recovery Plan. On June 5, 1947, the U.S. Secretary of State, General George Marshall, in a commencement address at Harvard University, announced a far-reaching plan (known forever after as the Marshall Plan) to aid the recovery of a dollar-scarce Europe in the postwar period. The plan, formally called the European Recovery Program, in addition to providing substantial amounts of financing, called for a number of macroeconomic reforms in the recipient countries—reforms that would have otherwise fallen under the aegis of the Fund. Much discussion ensued in the Fund's Executive Board (q.v.) as to what should be the reaction of the Fund to the Marshall Plan. The U.S. view was that in making substantial amounts of dollars available under the aid program, it would not be necessary for the countries receiving Marshall Plan aid to use resources from the Fund. In the event, the Executive Directors accepted this view and reached a decision that it would be in the best interest of members if the Fund's dollar resources were not used prematurely. A later clarification indicated that even drawings of currencies (qq.v.) other than U.S. dollars by Marshall Plan recipients would be exceptional.

These decisions had important repercussions on the Fund's activities. Most of the previous drawings on the Fund had been by European members, and use of the Fund's resources (q.v.) by Western European members subsequently dropped precipitously. The decisions aroused widespread criticism of the U.S. authorities and the Fund, especially from the academic community, who felt that in shifting away from the Bretton Woods (q.v.) institutions, which they had helped to create, the Executive Board had moved the Fund to the sidelines for several years. Just when a new economic internationalism was about to be born, the Fund and Bank were shorn of much of their power and still awaited the dawn of the Bretton Woods age.

Exchange Controls. Exchange controls or exchange restrictions (q.v.), imposed or maintained by member countries on current transactions, require the prior approval of the Fund. This was a major authority given to the Fund under the Bretton Woods system (q.v.), and it has been perpetuated in subsequent amendments to the Articles (q.v.), even though the second amendment (1978) no longer required member countries to obtain the Fund's prior approval for exchange rate changes (q.v.). Restrictions on trade are closely linked to exchange restrictions, and although they are technically outside the Fund's jurisdiction, the Fund maintained a special and close relationship with the General Agreement on Tariffs and Trade (GATT) (q.v.) and this has continued with its successor organization, the World Trade Organization (WTO) (q.v.).

Exchange Cross Rates. Broken cross rates, that is to say, rates between two currencies (q.v.) in a third market that differ from the bilateral relationship of the two currencies derived from their par values or central rates (qq.v.), were a problem in the early years of the Bretton Woods system (q.v.). As the convertibility (q.v.) of currencies spread, restrictions were lifted, and exchange markets (q.v.) became more integrated, broken cross rates ceased to be a factor. Under the current Articles of Agreement (q.v.), broken cross rates, if they exist, would be of concern to the Fund if they contributed to disorderly exchange rates or were judged to be a factor in the manipulation of the international monetary system (q.v.).

Exchange Markets. Made up of monetary authorities (q.v.), commercial banks, brokers, and assorted finance houses, exchange markets exist in every country, although at different levels of sophistication, for the purpose of converting one currency (q.v.) into another. Only a few markets are broad enough to support reliable forward exchange market operations. Markets can be tightly controlled by monetary authorities or can operate freely. Dual exchange markets, auction markets, and other forms of regulated markets, once fairly widespread, are tending to be phased out in the developing world in favor of freely operating markets, enabling capital and financial flows to move around the world on a scale and at a speed never previously experienced. Under the Fund's Articles of Agreement (q.v.), all member countries are obliged to collaborate with the Fund and other members to assure orderly exchange rate arrangements (q.v.) and to promote a stable system of exchange rates.

Exchange Rate Arrangements. A term synonymous with exchange rate regime and exchange rate system. It refers to all the optional elements that can characterize a system: floating, crawling and sliding pegs (q.v.), flexible and fixed rates (qq.v.), including central rates and par values (qq.v.), as well as dual exchange markets, exchange auctions, and multiple exchange rates.

Exchange Rate Changes. Changes in exchange rates have not been subject to prior approval by the Fund, in practice since the collapse of the par value system (q.v.) in 1973, and legally since the second amendment (1978) of the Articles of Agreement (q.v.). Under the current system, members are required to notify the Fund promptly of any change in their exchange arrangements (q.v.), but this may be after the event. Under the Articles of Agreement, each member undertakes to collaborate with the Fund and other members to assure orderly exchange arrangements and to promote a stable system of exchange rates. In addition, members must avoid manipulating exchange rates or the international monetary system (q.v.) in order to prevent effective balance of payments (q.v.) adjustment or to gain an unfair competitive advantage over other members.

Exchange Rate Margins. Fixed or pegged exchange rates (qq.v.) imply that a margin exists beyond which a movement of the exchange rate will not be allowed. Under the par value system (q.v.), exchange rates had to be maintained within 1 percent either side of parity, allowing a maximum fluctuation between two currencies of 2 percent. Under the Smithsonian agreement (q.v.) (1971), which was followed by an implementing decision by the Executive Board (q.v.) of the Fund, the margins were widened to 2.25 percent either side of parity or central rates (q.v.), allowing a maximum fluctuation between two currencies (q.v.) of 4.5 percent. This was followed by the European narrow margins arrangement (known as the "snake") among a number of European countries whereby it was agreed that among their own currencies the maximum fluctuation should be reduced to 2.25 percent, and within this group of countries the Benelux countries (Belgium, Luxembourg, and the Netherlands) maintained an arrangement (called the "snake within a tunnel"), which terminated in 1976, that reduced the margins to 1.5 percent either side of parity.

The European Monetary System (q.v.) was established in 1979, under which members of the European Community agreed, in effect, to establish a regional par value system, based on the European Currency Unit (ECU) (q.v.). In spot exchange transactions between currencies, participants had to observe limits of 2.25 percent above and below the bilateral relationship derived from the central rates established for their currencies in terms of ECUs. In May 1998, 11 members of the European Union agreed to participate in the EMU (q.v.) and convert their national currencies into a single currency, the euro.

Exchange Restrictions. The Fund began operations in 1947 in a world that, apart from the U.S. dollar, was inundated with inconvertible currency (q.v.) and heavily enmeshed in trade and exchange trade controls, bilateral trade and payments arrangements, and restrictions on international trade of all kinds. The history of the first 25 years of the Fund's influence was the gradual disentanglement of its member countries from restrictions, first by the major trading countries and then later, more slowly and hesitantly, by developing countries (q.v.). Indeed, it was only in the late 1980s and early 1990s that many major developing countries, in Latin America and Asia, finally took steps to sweep away their restrictive exchange and trade practices.

The record of this progress to a freer world economy was neither steady nor without setbacks. The early attempt in 1947 to make the pound sterling convertible for current transactions failed and it was not until toward the end of the 1950s that the industrialized countries of Europe were able to eliminate restrictions and to establish external convertibility (q.v.) for their currencies. Full currency convertibility was not established with the Fund until 1961. The Fund's Articles of Agreement (q.v.) had envisaged a period of transitional arrangements (q.v.) and after five years had called for annual reports on restrictions. The first of these annual reports, the *Annual Report on Exchange Restrictions*, appeared in 1952, and such reports—renamed in the 1970s as the *Annual Report on Exchange Arrangements and Exchange Restrictions* (q.v.)—have been published each year since then.

Although progress toward a free trade and payments system had been slower than originally envisaged, in some respects the removal of some restrictions—those on capital movements (q.v.)—has gone beyond what was thought possible, or desirable, by the founders of the Fund. Indeed, the freedom with which capital, particularly short-term capital, was allowed to flow through the world's exchange markets (q.v.) was perceived to be one cause of instability in the international monetary system (q.v.) during the 1960s and led to renewed attempts by some countries (notably the United States and the United Kingdom) to restrain such flows. The growth of international capital flows, and the accompanying economic and financial crises of the 1990s, led the Fund to seek new and expanded authority over international capital movements.

The progress toward a free trade and payments system was accompanied by international reductions in tariffs under a series of negotiations held by the General Agreement on Tariffs and Trade (GATT) (q.v.), beginning with the initial round at Geneva (1947) and continuing in growing importance at Annecy (1949), Torquay (1950-51), Geneva (1956, 1960-61, 1964-67), Tokyo (1973-79), Geneva (1982), and finally the Uruguay Round (1986-93). The result was a sharp increase in international trade, open exchange markets (q.v.), the growth of multinational and transnational corporations, and the integration of the world's financial markets. Simultaneously, as the multinational transactions of private corporations, banks, and other interests have overrun national borders, national monetary authorities (q.v.) have attempted to close their ranks through summit, regional, and international meetings in an effort to harmonize policies, promote cooperation, and retain official influence over what has become an interdependent world.

Exchange Surcharges. The practice of adding a surcharge to the buying rate of an exchange rate was adopted by a number of countries in the late 1940s and early 1950s. Usually, it was introduced as a temporary expedient in order to stem imports and correct an imbalance in the country's external accounts. Such a surcharge could also be used to raise revenue, as an alternative to raising tariffs. Surcharges can be applied to different categories of exchange purchases, such as financial remittances or nonessential imports. They are considered multiple currency practices (q.v.) and require approval by the Fund.

Executive Board. Consisting of 24 Executive Directors (q.v.), the Board is responsible for conducting the day-to-day business of the Fund. It exercises for this purpose the powers assigned to it under the Articles of Agreement (q.v.) and those delegated to it by the Board of Governors (q.v.). The Board is chaired by the Managing Director (q.v.). Of the 24 Executive Directors making up the Board in August 1998, five were appointed by member countries with the largest quotas (the United States, Germany, Japan, the United Kingdom, and France); China, Russia (q.v.), and Saudi Arabia each had sufficiently large quotas and thus sufficient votes to elect their own Executive Directors; and 16 others were elected by groups of member countries forming constituencies.

The number of countries in a constituency varies, ranging up to 24. Each Executive Director appoints an Alternate Director (q.v.), who, in the absence of the Executive Director, is authorized to act on his behalf. An appointed Executive Director holds office until a successor is appointed. Elections for elected Executive Directors are held every two years—in practice, at the time of the Annual Meetings (q.v.) in even-numbered years—or when needed. In recent years, as the number of countries in the electoral constituencies has grown to accommodate the enlarged Fund, Executive

Directors have been authorized to appoint Advisors and Technical Assistants.

The Board functions in continuous session and is required to meet as often as the Fund business dictates. A quorum for the meeting exists when a majority of the Executive Directors having not less than one-half of the total voting power is present. Board meetings are held on a specific agenda, circulated in advance. Usually, the staff prepares the recommendations on which the policies and decisions taken by the Executive Board are based. Decisions on the more routine issues may be reached on a lapse-of-time basis, but the vast majority of decisions on matters of substance are reached by the Chairman ascertaining the "sense of the meeting."

Although Directors have the right to call for a formal vote, it has become a policy to try to avoid them, and formal votes are rare. If a vote is called for, an appointed Executive Director casts the number of eligible votes held by the member appointing him or her, and an elected Executive Director casts the total of eligible votes held by the members of his constituency. In the case of elected Executive Directors, they must cast their votes as one unit and cannot record individual country votes within their constituency. Most voting decisions of the Board are made by a majority of the votes cast. *See also* Voting Provisions in the Fund

Executive Board Committees. Executive Directors (q.v.) are aided by a number of Board Committees, such as the Committee on Administrative Procedures, and, when needed, by several ad hoc committees, such as on the terms of membership (q.v.) for applicant countries or on regulations for the conduct of the biennial election of Executive Directors. Although such committees are established with a smaller, specified membership than the full Executive Board, all Executive Directors are entitled to attend them and to speak to the business at hand. There is no voting in committee.

Executive Board Procedures. The responsibilities of the Executive Board (q.v.) are comprehensive in relation to the day-to-day business of the Fund, covering the formulation of new policies and the establishment of new facilities, the approval of stand-by arrangements (q.v.) and other financial operations, country consultations (q.v.), and staffing policies, as well as a range of housekeeping matters. Usually, the Managing Director (q.v.) and staff take the initiative in proposing the agenda and preparing the necessary papers for discussion and decision, but the influence of the Board and the need to obtain its final approval for any business of significance permeates all the work of the Fund. The management and staff may propose, but it is the Board that disposes.

Normally, the Board meets at fixed times in the mornings of Mondays, Wednesdays, and Fridays, allowing those Executive Directors (q.v.) who are also Executive Directors of the World Bank (q.v.) to meet with the Bank's Board on Tuesdays and Thursdays. The pressure of work on the Executive Board, though varying with the extent of international and country business, has tended to escalate over the years, as the Fund's membership (q.v.) grew and its operational work expanded sharply.

Routinely, the Executive Directors meet as a Board, and it is in that format that Directors must approve decisions. Occasionally, in discussing particularly sensitive subjects, the Board meets in executive session, when attendance is restricted to management, members of the Board, and, if deemed appropriate, selected staff members. Executive Directors may also meet as a Committee of the Whole on important issues on which discussion is likely to be prolonged, affecting a large number of members, and requiring frequent referrals by Executive Directors to their monetary authorities (q.v.). One such issue has traditionally been the general review of quotas (q.v.), which in the past has required many Board papers and meetings of the Committee of the Whole over a period of many months before a proposal could be agreed to by the Executive Board for submission to and approval by the Board of Governors (q.v.).

Also, Executive Directors may meet in informal session, sometimes when a major, sensitive topic or a new policy is to be discussed, when the management and staff, as well as Executive Directors, welcome the opportunity of sounding out views without taking firm positions. A similar format is used for discussion of the Fund's *World Economic Outlook* (q.v.), a twice-yearly review of the world economic situation and outlook prepared by the management and staff. Before the report is issued to the public, the staff takes into account factual comments made by Executive Directors, but the report remains a management and staff document.

The degrees of official status in these various formats of the Executive Directors' sessions are reflected in the character of the minutes of the meetings. Regular Board meetings are reported on in extensive (near verbatim) minutes and carefully checked by all those involved in the discussions. A summing up of the discussion prepared by the Managing Director is read to the meeting and later disseminated to the offices of Executive Directors and selected staff members. Since the beginning of 1998, the summings up by the Managing Director have been made available to the public in the form of Public Information Notices (PINs) (q.v.). Minutes of the other meetings are brief and deal only in outline with the substance of the discussion. Minutes become part of the official archives of the Fund and are tightly held, even among the staff.

Executive Directors. Executive Directors are officers of the Fund, appointed or elected by members and remunerated by the Fund. Unlike the Managing Director (q.v.) and staff, however, Executive Directors do not owe their duty entirely to the Fund in the discharge of their official functions. Because they are appointed or elected by member countries, they have to balance their duties to the Fund with the interests of the countries that they represent.

The role and status of Executive Directors was much discussed at the Bretton Woods Conference (q.v.), where it was the view of some that Executive Directors should be high officials of national governments, that they would attend Executive Board (q.v.) meetings, which would be called for only periodically, and that much of the day-to-day business of the Fund would be left in the hands of the management and staff. This was not how the Articles of Agreement (q.v.) finally emerged, however, and the requirement that the Board be in continuous session meant that Executive Directors would necessarily have to be full-time Fund officials, rather than practicing, hands-on members of their own governments. In fact, however, many Board members have been senior officials in their home governments, particularly in the earlier years of the Fund. With the revolution in the speed of communication since the 1960s, the tendency has been for governments to put forward less senior members of their administration, although a position on the Board is regarded as a prestigious experience. The closeness of the control exercised over Executive Directors by their home authorities differs for each incumbent, depending on personal factors and on national characteristics.

Expenditures of the Fund. *See* Income and Expenditures of the Fund.

Extended Fund Facility (EFF). Extended arrangements were introduced in 1974, on a recommendation of the Committee of Twenty (q.v.). They come into effect when the Fund supports medium-term programs that usually run for three years (or up to four years in exceptional circumstances) and are aimed at overcoming balance of payments (q.v.) difficulties arising from structural as well as macroeconomic problems. The program sets out the general objectives and policies for the three-year period and the policies and measures for the first year; policies for subsequent years are established in annual reviews. The Fund's continued support and financing over the period of the arrangement is dependent on the country achieving performance criteria established for the program. Repayments begin after four years and must be completed within 10 years after making the drawing (q.v.) from the Fund. After the quota (q.v.) increases under the ninth general review of quotas came into effect in November 1992, members' access limits (q.v.) to the extended facility was established at 100 percent of quota per annum, with a cumulative limit of 300 percent of quota.

External Audit Committee. The Articles of Agreement (q.v.) provide for the Fund's financial accounts to be audited annually and for the auditor's report to be published in the Fund's *Annual Report of the Executive Board* (q.v.). The audit is conducted by an External Audit Committee consisting of either three or five persons, each of whom is nominated by a different member of the Fund and confirmed by the Executive Board (q.v.). At least one person serving on each audit committee is nominated by one of the six members of the Fund having the largest quotas, and at least one person is nominated by a member that is a participant in the SDR Department (q.v.). The procedures for conducting the audit are outlined in the By-laws (q.v.).

External Debt. Indebtedness assumed crisis proportions for many developing countries (q.v.) in 1982. The disruptions caused by the sharp increases in oil prices in the 1970s, together with the easy availability of private financing and imprudent lending by some commercial banks as they recycled "oil dollars," led to the emergence of acute external debt-servicing problems in the 1980s, a problem that persisted in the 1990s.

The causes of the problems were varied and manifold: the inefficient use and control over borrowed funds by the recipient countries; inadequate investment returns to cover the cost of servicing the debt; the use of short-term debt for long-term projects; excessive debt levels in general; and adverse and unexpected international developments beyond the control of any individual country, such as rising interest rates, unfavorable terms of trade, restrictive and weak markets abroad, and a general decline in the growth of world trade and economic activity. The situation was compounded by a sharp reversal in the flow of external finance from the industrial countries to developing countries, principally caused by the commercial banks' need to cut back on new lending to the developing world in order to cope with their own portfolio and balance sheet problems.

Thus, some $130 billion of new private funds was lent to developing countries in 1981-82, whereas only $30 billion (most of which was part of a package connected with Fund adjustment programs [q.v.]) was made available in 1982-83. Thereafter, although existing debt was restructured, virtually no new money was made available through the second half of the 1980s. Subsequently, however, as confidence returned and international financial markets became more closely integrated, capital movements (q.v.) began to flow in increasing volume, a significant amount of which was of a short-term character. The 1994 Mexican crisis (q.v.) and the 1997 Asian crisis (q.v.) were compounded by large capital flows, in the form of both capital flight and the reversal of short-term capital movements.

The Fund played an active role in helping countries cope with the crisis, by assisting in their domestic debt management programs, by expanding the access of these countries to Fund financing under the enlarged access policy (q.v.), by taking the lead in coordinating the supply of external resources (from both official and private sources), and by helping countries to formulate and support adjustment programs that would bring effective domestic demand into balance with the available internal and external resources (q.v.).

During the 1980s, the Fund played an increasingly important role in facilitating discussions between its member countries and their creditors. It assisted countries in preparing statistical documentation, acted in many cases as "go-between" in bringing the debtor countries and private creditors together, and played a major role in supplying information and advice in the multilateral debt renegotiations held under the aegis of the Paris Club (q.v.), which is the main forum for dealing with debt owed to or guaranteed by governments and official agencies of the participating creditor countries.

In some instances, the Fund went further and played a more positive role in debt renegotiations. It helped to devise programs that, on the one hand, required discipline and domestic restraint to meet a specified financing "gap" and, on the other, required external creditors to assemble a financial package of official grants, concessional financing, trade credits, and commercial loans to cover the country's internal financing gap. While preserving the confidentiality of Fund-membership relations, creditors were kept informed about the country's policies and the progress of their implementation. The link between debt restructuring and Fund-supported adjustment programs was, on the one hand, on an arms-length basis and, on the other, based on trust.

-F-

Financial Packages. Financial packages consist of the Fund's financial resources (q.v.) and additional financing from international and national aid agencies, as well as the private sector of other Fund members. The assembly of financial packages became a regular practice in the late 1970s and 1980s and was aimed at assisting developing countries (q.v.) to cope with serious balance of payments (q.v.) problems through a coordinated approach of aggregating all available external resources in support of a country's adjustment program (q.v.) that tailored domestic absorption to available resources.

From its early days, a Fund stand-by arrangement (q.v.) with a member country has been accepted by the international financial community as a signal that the country was undertaking corrective programs to put its house in order. The adoption of a Fund-supported program has often been a catalyst to spur foreign aid and investment and, eventually, to enable the country to borrow in the world's financial markets. Thus, the relatively modest initial amount of financing received from the Fund often led to the inflow of funds several times the size of the Fund's commitment. The expectation that additional external financing would be forthcoming in connection with a successful Fund stand-by arrangement was one manifestation of growing international financial cooperation. Conversely, member countries came to understand that failure to reach agreement on a Fund-supported stand-by arrangement threatened isolation from regular sources of outside finance. The connection between a Fund-supported program and additional outside financing became stronger after the experiences of the 1970s, particularly as a result of the debt crises in 1982 and the 1990s.

Financial Programming. Financial programming is a set of coordinated policy measures—mainly in the monetary, fiscal, and balance of payments (q.v.) fields—intended to achieve certain economic targets in a relatively short period of time. In preparing such a program, the assumption is that a relatively stable relationship exists between financial variables (such as money and domestic credit) and nonfinancial variables (such as real national income and prices) and that in controlling the financial variables the monetary authorities (q.v.) can also control the real side of the economy.

In targeting a balance between real income and real absorption (consumption plus investment), a determination has to be made as to what changes are to take place in prices, international reserves (q.v.), and the exchange rate, and what, if any, will be the resources flowing in from abroad. Short-term financial programs usually concentrate on establishing reasonable price stability and a given target for reserves by restraining domestic demand and by eliminating the most evident impediments to production, without attempting to tackle the more deep-seated problems. Longer term programs also address the more fundamental problems, such as measures to stimulate investment, implement appropriate exchange rate and pricing policies, promote financial markets, and initiate tax reforms.

A number of techniques can be used to draw up a financial program, including the construction of an econometric model. Experience in developing countries (q.v.) suggests that linkages between the relevant variables are not always stable, that the data used is not wholly reliable, and that accurate specification of the model can be extremely difficult. In the last analysis, therefore, judgmental considerations often dominate final decisions on the shape of the program. *See also* Balance of Payments Adjustment; Stabilization Programs.

Fischer, Stanley (1943-). Stanley Fischer, a national of the United States, became First Deputy Managing Director (q.v.) of the Fund on September 1, 1994. He received his B.Sc. (Econ.) and M.Sc. (Econ.) from the London School of Economics and obtained his Ph.D. in economics at the Massachusetts Institute of Technology (MIT) in 1969. He was Assistant Professor of Economics at the University of Chicago until 1973, when he returned to MIT as Associate Professor in the Department of Economics. Stanley Fischer became Professor of Economics at MIT in 1977, and held visiting positions at the Hebrew University, Jerusalem, and the Hoover Institution at Stanford. From January 1988 to August 1990, he served as Vice President, Development Economics, and Chief Economist at the World Bank (q.v.). He has also held consulting appointments and has published extensively.

Fixed Exchange Rates. The Bretton Woods par value system (q.v.) was a fixed exchange rate (q.v.) system, based on gold (q.v.). Changes could be made in the value of a currency only with the concurrence of the Fund. Otherwise, exchange rate movements were to be confined to a margin of 1 percent either side of the declared parity.

The European Monetary System (q.v.), established in 1979, is an example of a regional par value or fixed-rate system, in which a participant fixes a central rate (q.v.) for its currency (q.v.) in terms of the European currency unit (ECU) (q.v.). Under this system, the value of a currency could be changed by the mutual consent of the other participants, but otherwise participants had to observe, in "spot" transactions, a margin of 2.25 percent above and below each bilateral relationship with any other currency in the system. The system used a "divergence indicator" to give a signal that the exchange rate of a currency was moving out of line with the average exchange rate of all other currencies. If a currency crossed its "threshold of divergence," there was an intimation that the participant would take action to correct the situation.

The second amendment to the Articles of Agreement (q.v.) provided for a return to a par value system, if a majority of 85 percent of the Board of Governors (q.v.) voted for such a system. The

Articles specifically preclude par values from being based on gold or a unit of currency. The evident intent of the drafters was that any new par value system operated by the Fund would be based on the SDR (q.v.). Under the system proposed in the Articles, the margin between pairs of currencies would be 4.5 percent, but the margin could be changed by an 85-percent-majority vote of the Board of Governors. Since the amendment to the Articles of the Fund there has never been a serious proposal to return to the par value system.

Floating Exchange Rates. The Bretton Woods system (q.v.) had ushered in a system of fixed but adjustable exchange rates, and one under which the countries themselves declared and notified the Fund of the par value of their currencies (qq.v.). The system did allow countries to float their currencies, but such practices were regarded as temporary expedients in order to arrive at a realistic par value, and floating was tolerated for only a few countries and in exceptional circumstances. Basically, the system was one of fixed exchange rates (q.v.), and the only major trading country that maintained a floating exchange rate (q.v.) for any length of time was Canada.

The breakdown of the Bretton Woods par value system (q.v.) in 1971 led to the generalized floating of currencies in 1973, signaling the abandonment, in the short term at least, of the fixed-rate system—both the par value system, which had prevailed up to 1971, and the central rate system (q.v.), which had been hastily put together at the end of that year. But the approach to floating was not a uniform one, and a fundamental disagreement rapidly emerged among the leading industrial nations as to whether currencies should be allowed to float freely in the exchange markets (q.v.) (the U.S. position) or whether movements in the exchange rate should be influenced by central bank intervention—mainly the European view. These two approaches came to be known as "clean" and "dirty" floating.

The new system, or "nonsystem" as some referred to it, evolved essentially into three currency blocs—the U.S. dollar, the Japanese yen, and the deutsche mark—each floating against the other. Within this floating system, the central bank of each country would, from time to time, try to influence the short-term movements of its currency in the market, and, more dramatically, sometimes the long-term movement of a particular currency (such as the

U.S. dollar) in concert with other central banks. (A notable example of such a planned move was by the Group of Seven in the Plaza Agreement [qq.v.], New York, in September 1985, when it was announced that the participating national monetary authorities (q.v.) would cooperate to bring about a reduction in the value of the U.S. dollar. At the subsequent Louvre [q.v.] Palace agreement, in Paris, in February 1987, the Group announced that existing exchange rates were broadly consistent with the economic fundamentals and that they would "cooperate closely to foster stability around current levels"). A number of countries pegged (q.v.) their currencies to the U.S. dollar, some to the pound sterling, and others to the French franc, which itself was linked to the deutsche mark through the European Monetary System (q.v.).

Fluctuating Exchange Rates. The system of flexible or floating exchange rates (q.v.) that came into effect in 1973 proved to be more than just flexible. Indeed, since the floating rate system came into effect, rates have fluctuated quite sharply, often overshooting and undershooting without any clear relationship to the underlying fundamentals. At the outset, national monetary authorities (q.v.) that had chafed under what they had come to regard as the excessive rigidity of the fixed-rate system (q.v.) were disappointed to discover that the degree of freedom in setting their own national interest rate and monetary policies under the new fluctuating rate system was also severely constrained. Indeed, the European countries began to integrate their exchange rate policies into the European Monetary System (q.v.) as a move toward a fully fledged economic and political community. As a result of the marked fluctuations experienced in exchange rates the main thrust of the Fund's surveillance (q.v.) role has been to place greater emphasis on the international coordination of monetary (q.v.) and exchange rate policies.

Foreign Exchange. Foreign exchange is the market in which national currencies (q.v.) are bought and sold by persons, corporations, or entities that wish to convert a sum of money in one currency to that of another currency. Such transactions may be derived from exports and imports, corporate and business operations. or private remittances by individuals across national borders. The actual conversion of currency is carried out by brokers, banks, and other dealers, who charge a small commission for the operation.

With the growth of rapid means of communication in recent years, the dismantling of exchange controls (q.v.), and the sharp expansion in international transactions, the exchange markets (q.v.) in individual countries have become almost instantaneously linked by an informal network of exchange dealers, where arbitrageurs buy and sell in the various markets to keep exchange rates, and their exchange cross rates (q.v.) with third currencies, in line throughout the world. Transactions in the exchange markets may be "spot," in which one currency is exchanged directly with another, or "forward," in which an exchange of currency is contracted for a future date. There are no official statistics on worldwide exchange transactions, but in 1998 it was estimated that the average daily turnover in the eight leading exchange markets amounted to over $1,600 billion, of which the London market accounted for about 40 percent, the U.S. market for about 20 percent, and the Japanese market for about 10 percent.

Fund Management Structure Change. On June 6, 1994, the Fund announced that it would increase the number of Deputy Managing Directors (q.v.) from one to three, and name Stanley Fischer (U.S.A.), Alassane D. Ouattara (Côte d'Ivoire), and Prabhakar R. Narvekar (q.v.) (India) to the positions. The three Deputies succeeded Richard Erb, who had been appointed in 1984 and had served two five-year terms in the position.

This was the first major change in the structure of the Fund's senior management since 1949, when the position of Deputy Managing Director was established. The enlarged management structure was in response to the increased burden of responsibilities for a greatly expanded membership (q.v.) since the Fund's establishment in 1946. Traditionally, the Deputy Managing Director's position had always been filled by a U.S. national and to preserve the status of the United States in the management team, Stanley Fischer was designated First Deputy Managing Director. In this capacity, he has broad responsibilities across the whole range of issues facing the institution, and exercises comprehensive oversight.

Working under the direction of the Managing Director (q.v.), each Deputy Managing Director has the authority to chair Executive Board (q.v.) meetings and to maintain contacts with officials of member governments, Executive Directors, and other institutions.

Fundamental Disequilibrium. The concept of a "fundamental disequilibrium" was essential to the working of the Bretton Woods system (q.v.). Under the original Articles (q.v.) of the Fund, a member was not allowed to propose a change in the par value (q.v.) of its currency (q.v.) except to correct a fundamental disequilibrium. The drafters of the Articles had, it was thought, deliberately left the term undefined in order not to tie the hands of the Fund in its future operations. The Fund, itself, never defined the term "fundamental disequilibrium," although numerous attempts were made, both inside and outside the Fund, to do so. In practice, the Fund assessed each proposed change in a member's par value on a case-by-case basis.

Fund-Bank Relations. Both the International Monetary Fund and the International Bank for Reconstruction and Development, the formal name of the World Bank (q.v.), were created at the Bretton Woods Conference (q.v.) of July 1944. Despite their common origin, however, they are separate, independent organizations, each with its own Articles of Agreement (q.v.), its own governing body and staff, and its own defined terms of reference. The Fund is responsible for an international code of conduct governing exchange rates and international payments among countries, and has available to it a pool of currencies (q.v.) that can be drawn upon, under suitable safeguards, by member governments that are in balance of payments (q.v.) difficulties. The World Bank, on the other hand, was conceived as an institution concerned with long-term economic development (q.v.) and has available to it resources from which it can make long-term loans to its member governments. After the reconstruction phase of the postwar world had been completed, when many warring nations, including Germany and Japan, had been helped in financing the rehabilitation of their war-torn economies, the World Bank concentrated entirely on the economic development of the Third World.

Both institutions were founded by farsighted but practical visionaries, who were dedicated to bringing about an essentially cooperative, open, free-market, postwar order. While the Fund was to oversee the international financial structure and the World Bank the world's economic development, a third institution, the International Trade Organization (ITO), was proposed to ensure fair and equitable arrangements for international trade. Aimed at the dismantling of tariffs, quotas (q.v.), and other barriers to free trade between nations, the International Trade Organization never came into existence, although its ideals lived on, in a somewhat diluted form, in the General Agreement on Tariffs and Trade (GATT) (q.v.). Nearly fifty years later, however, the ITO was resurrected when the new international organization, the World Trade Organization (WTO) (q.v.), replaced the GATT in 1995.

Facing each other across the street in Washington, D.C., cooperation between the World Bank and the Fund is close and practiced at all levels, both formally and informally. The World Bank's Articles of Agreement prescribe that a government must be a member of the Fund before it can become a member of the World Bank, and membership in the two institutions is virtually identical.

The Fund and the World Bank differ in their structure and size. The Fund has remained a single organization, with a relatively small staff, which had risen, after more than 40 years of operating, to only about 2,100. Most of its staff members work at its headquarters in Washington, D.C., although its has small offices in Geneva, Paris, Tokyo, and at the United Nations in New York, as well as a training institute in Singapore and another in Vienna (see Singapore Regional Training Institute; Vienna Institute), in which it participates jointly with other international organizations. The World Bank, on the other hand, has developed into the World Bank Group, comprising the World Bank, the International Development Association, the International Finance Corporation, the International Center for Settlement of Investment Disputes, and the Multilateral Investment Guarantee Agency. The World Bank Group has a staff of over 7,000 and maintains about 40 offices throughout the world, although the main work of the Group is carried on at its headquarters in Washington, D.C. Whereas the Fund employs mainly professional economists specializing in macroeconomics, fiscal, and financial matters, the World Bank employs a vast range of professionals, such as economists, engineers, agronomists, urban planners, educationists, and experts in health care, water supply, sewage, transportation, rural development, communications, and other disciplines required to bring about the conditions of a modern state.

A member's use of the Fund's resources is determined by its need in terms of its balance of payments need in relation to its quota (q.v.) in the organization (the larger its economy, the larger the quota), whereas the World Bank Group invests its resources in member countries with creditworthy governments for viable development projects and sectoral and structural development programs. Both the Fund and the World Bank have funds available to them subscribed by their members, but most of the World Bank's resources for its lending is raised from private market operations, whereas the Fund relies heavily on the resources subscribed by members and borrows only exceptionally, and then only from official sources. The International Development Association, which provides concessional loans to poorer members, derives its resources from donations by wealthier members. Whereas the World Bank Group lends only to developing countries, the resources of the Fund are available to all countries, rich and poor, and over the years nearly all Fund members have used its resources.

The Fund's financing is available to its members at rates slightly below the market rate and is generally repayable in three to five years, and never more than 10 years. The World Bank loans have a maturity of 12 to 15 years and bear rates of interest slightly above the rate at which the World Bank pays for the funds from the market. Loans from the International Development Association, however, are interest free and have a maturity of 35 to 40 years.

During the first two decades of their operations, the Fund and the World Bank fulfilled clearly defined roles and conducted very different kinds of operations; the World Bank financed mainly specific long-term projects, such as dams, power stations, and transportation, and the Fund concentrated on an international code of conduct and providing medium-term financing to its members in support of corrective balance of payments programs. In the 1970s, however, following the world oil price increases, the resulting structural imbalances in the economies of many developing countries (q.v.), and the subsequent debt crisis, both organizations were forced to broaden their respective roles. It became evident that the World Bank could no longer finance projects in isolation from general developments in the economy. Similarly, it became obvious that short-term balance of payments adjustment programs (q.v.) did not measure up to the severe structural problems persisting in many developing member countries.

The result was that the World Bank moved into structural and sector adjustment loans, while the Fund moved to longer term adjustment through extended arrangements, the structural adjustment facility, and the enlarged access policy (qq.v.). This broadening of the range of policies in both organizations brought them closer to each other operationally, with greater overlap and the necessity for even closer cooperation. Since the early 1980s, the two institutions have fielded a number of parallel and joint missions, cooperated in helping to prepare policy framework papers for the structural adjustment and enhanced structural adjustment facilities (q.v.), and have intensified their cooperation at all levels. At the same time, they have maintained their regard for each other as independent institutions and upheld the confidential relationship that each has with its members. In particular, the two organizations have been careful to avoid "cross conditionality," whereby the conditionality (q.v.) established by one organization for providing finance to a member is not a condition for receiving finance from the other. In the case of overdue obligations (q.v.) to either organization, the World Bank and the Fund cooperate closely with each other and the member, as well as with the regional development banks, such as the Inter-American Development Bank (IDB) and the Asian Development Bank (ADB), to bring about normalization of the relations with the member. More recently, the Fund and Bank have agreed on a common approach under the heavily indebted poor countries (HIPC) (q.v.) initiative.

-G-

General Account of the Fund. The General Account came into existence as a result of the first amendment to the Articles of Agreement (q.v.) in 1969, which created SDRs (q.v.). The first amendment to the Articles designated the General Account as the operating account for the type of operations conducted by the Fund under the original, largely unchanged Articles, and established the SDR Account to handle the allocation and transfers of SDRs. The second amendment to the Articles (1978) changed the name from General Account to General Department (q.v.).

General Agreement on Tariffs and Trade (GATT). The Fund had a special relationship with GATT, dating from 1950. In that year agreement was reached between the Fund and GATT under which the Fund would advise the Contracting Parties of the GATT as to whether a member's balance of payments (q.v.) position justified the imposition or maintenance of trade restrictions. In complying with this agreement, the Fund provided a report on the factual situation of the member in question and gave an evaluation of those facts in an advisory capacity. The Fund's office in Geneva maintained day-to-day contact with the GATT.

GATT was signed in October 1947 and came into existence after negotiations for the establishment of the International Trade Organization failed to reach fruition. The Contracting Parties to GATT, although not universal, accounted for the overwhelming value of world trade. GATT was a form of multilateral trade agreement, in accordance with which signatories agreed, based on the principles of "reciprocity and mutual advantage," to negotiate a substantial reduction in customs tariffs and other impediments to trade and to eliminate discriminatory practices in international trade.

In addition to monitoring and negotiating bilateral trade agreements and helping to settle disputes between trading partners, GATT negotiated a series of worldwide tariff reductions at meetings such as those held in Geneva (1947), Annecy (1949), Torquay (1950-51), Geneva (1956, 1960-61, and 1964-67), Tokyo (1973-79), and Geneva (1982). The latest of these, known as the Uruguay Round (q.v.), began in 1986, was expected to be completed in December 1990, but was delayed by protracted disagreements among the major trading countries on a number of sensitive issues, particularly agriculture. Finally completed at the end of 1993, the agreements not only brought about important tariff reductions, but also headed off a spate of protectionist measures awaiting in the wings, and reached agreement on the establishment, in the place of GATT, of a new international organization, the World Trade Organization (WTO) (q.v.), based on international law and with wider powers.

General Arrangements to Borrow (GAB). These arrangements came into existence in October 1962 when the Fund arranged to borrow, in certain circumstances, specified amounts of currencies (q.v.) from 11 industrial countries, consisting of 10 members of the Fund (Belgium, Canada, France, Germany, Italy, Japan, the Netherlands, Sweden, the United Kingdom, and the United States) and Switzerland, which was not a member at that time. The 10 member countries of the GAB originated the Group of Ten (q.v.), which became prominent in international monetary affairs in later years.

The GAB were the first borrowing (q.v.) arrangements entered into by the Fund. They provided for the Fund to borrow up to a total of $6.0 billion in lenders' currencies to help to finance purchases by GAB participants when such financing would forestall or cope with an impairment of the international monetary system (q.v.). The arrangements recognized that in the event of a financial crisis of any one of the participants, the Fund might not have sufficient resources (q.v.) of its own to cope with drawings (q.v.) of the magnitude required.

In 1982, faced with serious strains in the international financial system caused by the debt crisis, a thorough review of the arrangements was initiated, culminating in the completion of major reforms by the end of 1983. Under these new arrangements, the total of individual credit lines was increased to SDR 17 billion; the Swiss government became a participant in the arrangements, as distinct from an associate; provision was made for the Fund to enter, in association with the GAB, into borrowing arrangements with members that were not participants; and arrangements were agreed with Saudi Arabia to associate that country, on a bilateral basis, with the GAB. The revised arrangements also allowed the Fund, for the first time, to call on the participants to finance drawings by nonparticipants. Such drawings by nonparticipants are, however, subject to stricter conditionality (q.v.) than those made by participants. The GAB were renewed for a further period of five years from December 26, 1998, to December 25, 2003.

The credit amounts of the 11 participants in the GAB, totaling SDR 17 billion, and that for the associate participant, Saudi Arabia, are as follows (in millions of SDRs):

United States	4,250.0
Deutsche Bundesbank	2,380.0
Japan	2,125.0
United Kingdom	1,700.0
France	1,700.0
Saudi Arabia (associate)	1,500.0
Italy	1,105.0
Swiss National Bank	1,020.0
Canada	892.0
Netherlands	850.0
Sveriges Riksbank	382.5

Between 1964 and 1970 the GAB were activated six times to help the Fund finance four large drawings by the United Kingdom and two by France. In the 1970s, the arrangements were activated three times, to help finance drawings by the United Kingdom (1977), Italy (1977), and the United States (1978). In July 1998, in connection with increased financial assistance that was to be disbursed to Russia, and following the heavy commitments made to the Asian economies, the Fund announced that it would activate the GAB, the first time for 20 years. The New Arrangements to Borrow (q.v.) had not yet been ratified by all the participating parties.

General Counsel. This staff position was created in May 1966, when Sir Joseph Gold (q.v.), who was the Director of the Legal Department, was also appointed as the General Counsel. He participated in the discussions of the Deputies of the Group of Ten (q.v.) as a representative of the Managing Director (q.v.) and was one of the main drafters of the amendment to the Articles (q.v.) establishing the creation of the SDR (q.v.) facility. The title is honorific and was also given to François P. Gianviti, of France, who became Director of the Legal Department and General Counsel in 1985.

General Department. The General Department consists of the General Resources Account (q.v.), the Special Disbursement Account (q.v.), and the Investment Account, which by the end of 1998 had not been activated. The Borrowed Resources Suspense Account (q.v.) was established in May 1981 within the General Department.

General Reserve. The General Reserve is one of three precautionary balances maintained by the Fund to protect its assets from impairment and to demonstrate a sound financial management of the organization. The General Reserve is fed from the Fund's income (q.v.) after covering operational and administrative expenditures and any distributions to members that the Fund may decide upon. Apart from the first few years of its existence, the Fund has consistently had a surplus income over expenditure, yielding a net income that has been accrued in the General Reserve.

Periods of stringency have occurred, however, such as in 1970-71 and during the 1980s, when some members were unable to meet their repayments and other obligations to the Fund. To meet this situation, the Fund established two Special Contingency Accounts (q.v.), the first in 1987 and the second in 1990. The establishment of the first contingency account (SCA 1) was derived from the concept of burden sharing (q.v.), when it was decided that both creditor members of the Fund and those paying charges (q.v.) on the use of the Fund's resources (q.v.) should contribute to the cost of covering the overdue repayments (repurchases [q.v.]) and charges. The second contingency account (SCA 2), an extension of the burden-sharing principle, was established to safeguard purchases (drawings) (qq.v.) by a member that had been previously delinquent in its obligations to the Fund, but had accumulated sufficient "rights" (q.v.) to resume drawing on the Fund's resources.

General Resources Account (GRA). The General Resources Account is one of four accounts maintained in the General Department (q.v.); the other three are the Special Disbursement Account (SDA) (q.v.), the Investment Account (which has not yet been activated), and the Borrowed Resources Suspense Account (BRSA) (q.v.). The bulk of transactions between member countries and the Fund takes place through the General Resources Account, including the receipt of quota subscription, purchases and repurchases (qq.v.), receipt and refunding of charges (q.v.), payment of remuneration on members' loan claims and on creditor positions in the Fund, and repayment of principal to the Fund's lenders. The assets in the account are held in the form of currencies (q.v.) of member countries, and the Fund's own SDR and gold (qq.v.) holdings.

Ghana. When Ghana became independent in 1957 it enjoyed the highest per capita income in sub-Saharan Africa. It was the world's largest producer of cocoa, had a strong balance of payments position (q.v.), and held external reserves equivalent to three years of imports. Over the 25 years economic mismanagement led to an almost complete dissipation of these advantages. Government interventionist policies over all the critical areas of the economy, including foreign exchange (q.v.), prices, credit, and imports; the absence of any discipline over public sector finances, leading to surging inflation and a negative balance of payments; and, finally, a severe drought and falling cocoa prices in 1982-83, all brought the economy to the point of collapse.

Faced with a crisis situation, Ghana launched an ambitious economic recovery program, involving a progressive shift away from direct controls and government intervention toward greater reliance on market mechanisms. Over the next 15 years, with the support of several Fund-supported programs and its considerable financial backing, the government struggled to implement its program, but with only limited success. At the beginning of 1998, it was clear that the Ghanaian economy was still a work in progress. The market-oriented program had initially achieved some positive results: inflation had been reduced to 10 percent by the end of 1991, the distorted exchange rate and trade system had been liberalized, and real GDP growth was averaging about 5 percent a year, resulting in appreciable increases in real per capita income. Nevertheless, inflation remained high and variable; private sector saving and investment continued to be inadequate; and the implementation of critical structural reforms in the financial, parastatal, and agricultural sectors was progressing, but only slowly. Export growth was disappointing and the country continued to depend on external assistance.

In 1992, a fiscal imbalance reemerged, with the primary domestic deficit jumping from 1.9 percent of GDP in 1991 to 4.9 percent in 1992, accompanied by a rapid growth in the money supply and the reemergence of inflationary pressures. For the next four years the government's record of economic management was marked by recurrent lapses in financial discipline. In 1995, the Fund approved a series of loans for Ghana over the next three years under the enhanced structural adjustment facility (ESAF) (q.v.) totaling SDR 164.4 million (about $258 million) in support of the government's 1995-97 economic program. The implementation, however, of policies under the first year of the program was uneven, with the budgetary outturn falling well short of the target, resulting in the growth of arrears to private contractors and an annual rate of inflation of 71 percent. On the positive side, the privatization program remained on track, there was a bumper cocoa crop, an increase in foreign exchange reserves, and a GDP growth rate of 4.5 percent. In 1996, performance under the program was again mixed; most quantitative indicators and several structural benchmarks under the program were missed. Large fiscal slippages raised the budget deficit to 10.6 percent of GDP, 6 percent above the targeted amount. A bumper cocoa crop, however, helped to raise GDP growth to 5.2 percent, and inflation fell to 33 percent. The external deficit widened and gross international reserves (q.v.) declined. At the rate and pattern of economic growth that had been established over the previous years, it was estimated that it would take 30 years for the average poor in Ghana to cross the poverty line.

In 1997, the government launched a fiscal adjustment plan aimed at restoring budgetary discipline and thus generating the domestic primary surplus needed to reduce public borrowing and to lower inflation and interest rates. The plan succeeded in moderating the overall budget deficit, with a decline in tax receipts being more than offset by a decline in expenditures, brought about largely by a fall in capital outlays, where overruns had been concentrated in 1996. Owing mainly to a recovery in domestic foodstuff production and a slowdown in aggregate demand, inflation fell from 33 percent at the end of 1996 to 21 percent at the end of 1997. By the end of the year, a decade of reform had brought about some encouraging results, such as a drastic reduction in government regulations and interventionist policies; the enactment of significant legislation to provide the framework for private sector participation in the economy; and the divestitures of a total of 48 state-owned enterprises, from a predetermined list of 110 such enterprises.

In March 1998, in approving the second annual loan under the ESAF program, the Fund announced that the loan had been augmented by SDR 27 million (about $37 million) at the authorities' request, by rephasing the remaining amount available under the three-year program. The commitment period of the three-year ESAF arrangement had also been extended by one full year, to June 1999. In announcing its approval of the loan disbursement, the Fund said that the key macroeconomic targets of the 1998 program were (1) to achieve an annual rate of growth of real GDP of 5.6 percent; (2) to reduce annual inflation from 21 percent to 11 percent by the end of 1998, and to further halve it to 5.5 percent by the end of 1999; and (3) to contain the current account deficit at 7.3 percent of GDP, while maintaining gross official reserves at 2.7 months of imports. These objectives were to be achieved through an improvement in tax collection and the introduction of a value-added tax (VAT) in December 1998, an intensification of tax reform, and tighter control over the money supply. Under the program of structural reform, the government would further deregulate the petroleum and cocoa sectors, and aggressively pursue its divestiture program, liberalize the financial sector, and reform the civil service and autonomous government agencies. Under the government's social programs, priority would be given to education, health, and roads.

Ghana is implementing its policies under an ESAF economic and financial policy framework paper covering the years 1998-2000, prepared by the government in collaboration with the staffs of the Fund and the World Bank (qq.v.). The paper, which is available on the Fund's web site, sets out in detail the medium-term objectives, strategies, and policies up to the year 2000. It covers fiscal and monetary policies (q.v.), external sector policies, structural and sectoral policies, the rationalization of government operations,

improvements in agriculture and the environment, a strengthening of the infrastructure, the development of human resources, improvements in the quality and timeliness of reporting on core economic statistics, and details the support through technical assistance (q.v.) that Ghana will be receiving from the Fund, the World Bank, and several bilateral and multilateral agencies.

Gold, Sir Joseph (1912-). Sir Joseph Gold was a member of the Fund's Legal Department from October 1946 to July 1979. He was Director of the Legal Department from 1960 to 1979 and was also given the title of General Counsel (qq.v.) in 1966. Sir Joseph represented the Managing Director (q.v.) at the meetings of the Deputies of the Group of Ten (q.v.) and accompanied the Managing Director to the ministerial meetings of the Group. He was responsible for advising the Managing Director on a wide range of topics and for making many innovative proposals. He played a major role in drafting the first amendment to the Articles of Agreement (q.v.) and was the principal drafter of the second amendment.

Upon his retirement, Sir Joseph was appointed to the position of Senior Consultant in the Fund. He was knighted by the Queen of England in 1980. Sir Joseph has published numerous books and articles on the Fund and international monetary law and has contributed greatly to the development of international law in the fields of money and finance. Sir Joseph was a major influence in molding the shape and influence of the Fund over its first 50 years.

Gold. Referred to by central bankers and bullion brokers as "the metal," gold played a central role in the international monetary system established at Bretton Woods (qq.v.). It was the common denominator of the par value system (q.v.), and the value of each currency (q.v.) had to be expressed in terms of the fixed, official price of gold or in terms of the U.S. dollar, which had a fixed valuation in terms of gold of the weight and fineness in effect on July 1, 1944. The United States maintained the gold value of the U.S. dollar by undertaking to buy and sell gold freely for officially held U.S. dollars. The SDR (q.v.), which had been introduced into the international monetary system under the first amendment to the Articles (q.v.) in 1968, was also initially defined in terms of gold. Gold was thus the primary reserve asset (q.v.) of the international monetary system, as it had been in the nineteenth century.

Originally, members had to pay one-fourth of their subscriptions (q.v.) to the Fund in gold (or, as an authorized exception, in U.S. dollars). This led to the concepts of the gold tranche and credit tranches (qq.v.), which set a basic framework for the use of the Fund's resources (q.v.). The second amendment to the Articles of Agreement (1978) eliminated gold from the Fund's operations and transactions, provided for the sale of a portion of the Fund's gold holdings, and envisioned a gradual reduction in the role of gold in the international monetary system.

Gold and Foreign Exchange Reserves. *See* International Reserves.

Gold Auctions. The Fund held 45 gold (q.v.) auctions between 1976 and 1980, selling a total of 23.52 million ounces of gold at prices ranging from $108.76 an ounce in September 1976 to $718.01 an ounce in February 1980, for a total profit of $4.6 billion. The auctions were held in accordance with an agreement reached in the Interim Committee (q.v.) in August 1975, whereby it was agreed that one-sixth (25 million ounces) of the Fund's gold holdings should be sold for the benefit of the developing countries (q.v.) and another sixth should be "restituted" (distributed) to members.

Because under its Articles of Agreement (q.v.) then in effect, the Fund could sell its gold only to members with creditor positions in the Fund, only at the official price, and only to replenish its holdings of a member's currency (q.v.), it was necessary to adopt a circuitous, but legal, method of auctioning the gold. Thus, the gold was sold at the official price to creditor members, who then resold the gold, also at the official price, to the Trust Fund (q.v.). The Fund conducted the auctions on behalf of the Trust Fund, the proceeds of which were held by the Trust Fund and made available to a selected group of least developed countries under agreed upon adjustment programs (q.v.). *See also* Restitution.

Gold Markets. *See* Gold Pool.

Gold Pool. The gold pool was formed in 1961 by the central banks of Belgium, France, Germany, Italy, the Netherlands, Switzerland, the United Kingdom, and the United States to intervene in the London gold market to keep the price of gold (q.v.) at its official level. The London market was the leading gold bullion market, and by keeping the price of gold at its official price in the London market, the authorities were able to keep the price in other markets, in Europe and elsewhere, in line.

In 1967 and in 1968, following the devaluation (q.v.) of the pound sterling and a continuing deficit in the U.S. balance of payments (q.v.), a sharp loss of confidence in the U.S. dollar ensued and the demand for gold became so great that the market had to be closed. The gold pool arrangements were brought to an end in March 1968, when the eight central banks participating in the arrangements announced that they would continue official sales and purchases at the official rate, but that the price of gold in private transactions would henceforth be determined by supply and demand. The announcement ushered in a two-tier market for gold that lasted until the eight central banks that had formed the gold pool agreed that they would be free to sell gold from their official reserves in the private markets.

Gold Sales by the Fund. The Fund had substantial holdings of gold (q.v.), accounting for about 12 percent of world gold holdings at the end of April 1998. The Fund acquired most of its gold holdings as a result of its original Articles (q.v.) requiring members to pay 25 percent of their subscriptions (q.v.) to the Fund in gold. It was from this provision that the concept of the gold tranche (q.v.) originated. In addition to these gold payment subscriptions, the Fund also accumulated gold as a result of the provision requiring members to pay charges (q.v.) in gold.

Until the second amendment to the Articles of Agreement (q.v.) (1978) came into effect, the Fund regularly sold gold to replenish its holdings of currencies (q.v.) that were in demand and in short supply. Borrowings (q.v.) from participants in the General Arrangements to Borrow (q.v.) were also often accompanied by sales of gold to participants that were lending resources to the Fund, seemingly to compensate them for lending the Fund their currencies. In 1976-80, the Fund reduced its gold holdings by one-third (50 million ounces), half through a series of sales by gold auctions (q.v.) and half through restitution (q.v.) to members.

Since 1980, the Fund has not used gold in any of its operations, the SDR (q.v.) having replaced gold in the Fund's accounts and operations. At the end of the 1980s, the Executive Board (q.v.) agreed, in principle, that in the event of the rights accumulation (q.v.) procedure not succeeding in eliminating arrears (q.v.) to the Fund it would sell three million ounces of gold to cover such overdue obligations. The provision was a precautionary measure to give assurance to the Fund's creditors, and no decision has been made as to how such sales would be conducted, or at what price.

Gold Tranche. This term originated under the Bretton Woods system (q.v.) and was replaced after the second amendment to the Articles of Agreement (q.v.) by the reserve tranche (q.v.). Under the original Articles, a member normally paid one-fourth of its subscription (q.v.) in gold (q.v.) and three-fourths in its own currency (q.v.). In accordance with the Articles, the Executive Board (q.v.) took a number of decisions, dating from 1952, framing the tranche policies: (1) a member could purchase currencies that it desired (usually U.S. dollars) up to the point where the Fund's holdings (q.v.) of its currency reached 100 percent of its quota (q.v.), that is, a member could purchase the equivalent of its gold tranche, virtually without conditionality (q.v.); and (2) a member may normally have total purchases (q.v.) outstanding from the Fund up to the point where the Fund's holding of that member's currency did not exceed 200 percent of quota. A member's gold tranche was the difference between the Fund's holding of a member's currency and its quota. If a member's currency is purchased (drawn) by other members, that member's gold tranche (reserve tranche) increases correspondingly. After the first amendment to the Articles the gold tranche became a floating facility, and after the second amendment it was renamed the reserve tranche and could be drawn upon without challenge.

Good Governance. The declaration of *Partnership for Sustainable Global Growth* that was adopted by the Interim Committee (q.v.) at its meeting in Washington on September 29, 1996, identified "promoting good governance in all its aspects, including ensuring the rule of law, improving efficiency and accountability of the public sector, and tackling corruption" as an essential element of a framework within which economies can prosper. The Fund's Executive Board (q.v.) then met a number of times to develop guidance on the issue and adopted in July 1997 a Guidance Note. The guidelines seek to promote greater attention by the Fund to governance issues, in particular through:

(1) A more comprehensive treatment, in the context of both Article IV consultations and Fund-supported programs, of those governance issues within the mandate and expertise of the Fund;

(2) A more proactive approach in advocating policies and the development of institutions and administrative systems that eliminate the opportunity for bribery, corruption, and fraudulent activity in the management of public resources;

(3) An evenhanded treatment of governance issues in all member countries; and

(4) Enhanced collaboration with other multilateral institutions, in particular the World Bank, to make better use of complementary areas of expertise.

The guidelines seek to set boundaries for the Fund's involvement and specify that since the Fund is primarily concerned with macroeconomic stability, external viability, and orderly economic growth in member countries, the Fund's contribution to good governance arises principally in two spheres:

(1) improving the management of public resources through reforms covering public sector institutions (e.g., the treasury, central bank, public enterprises, civil service, and offices of official statistics), including administrative procedures (e.g., expenditure control, budget management, and revenue collection); and

(2) supporting the development and maintenance of a transparent and stable economic and regulatory environment conducive to efficient private sector activities (e.g., price systems, exchange and trade regimes, and banking systems and their related regulations).

The guidelines stress that the Fund does not have a mandate to adopt an investigative role in member countries, but that the staff should address governance issues, including instances of corruption, on the basis of economic considerations within its mandate. This would involve an assessment of whether poor governance would have an impact on macroeconomic performance and the government's ability to pursue appropriate and agreed-upon economic policies, taking into account the need to safeguard the use of the Fund's resources (q.v.). It is recognized, however, that there are practical limitations to the ability of the staff to identify deficiencies in governance, and it is proposed that the staff should urge governments to adopt greater transparency in their operations, so as help build private sector confidence in government policies. In this regard, the Fund's technical assistance (q.v.) should contribute to improving transparency and the economic aspects of good governance.

Finally, the staff is asked to keep abreast of activities in partner organizations and specific efforts in member countries to address governance issues. It should strengthen its collaboration on these issues with other multilateral institutions, in particular with the World Bank (q.v.).

Governors, Board of. *See* Board of Governors.

Group of Five. This group consisted of France, Germany, Japan, the United Kingdom, and the United States, but subsequently evolved into the Group of Seven (q.v.) with the addition of Canada and Italy.

Group of Eight. The Russian Federation (q.v.) was invited to join the annual summit meetings of the Group of Seven (q.v.) in 1998 and fully participated in the meetings for the first time in May of that year, when the group met in Birmingham, England

Group of Nine. During the 1960s, especially in connection with the establishment of the SDR (q.v.) facility, the nine Executive Directors (q.v.) elected by the developing countries (q.v.) in the Fund used to meet informally to discuss their common problems and objectives. Subsequently, additional Executive Directors were appointed or elected to an enlarged Board—Saudi Arabia in the 1970s, China in the 1980s, and Russia and Switzerland in the 1990s.

Group of Seven. Consists of seven industrial countries—Canada,

France, Germany, Italy, Japan, the United Kingdom, the United States—and was an expansion of the Group of Five (q.v.), with the addition of Canada and Italy. The leaders of these countries have had annual economic summit meetings since 1974. Their discussions and decisions are important for continued cooperation among the major industrial nations (q.v.) of the world, and often set the agenda for the Group of Ten (q.v.) meetings, the meetings of the Interim Committee (q.v.), and the Fund itself. Beginning in 1998, the Russia Federation was invited to attend the annual summit meetings of the group, making it a Group of Eight (q.v.).

Meeting in Bonn on February 20, 1999, the group endorsed a proposal to establish a "financial stability forum." The forum would meet regularly and establish more formal coordination among finance ministers, central bankers, and other financial regulators to more effectively promote international financial stability, improve the functioning of markets, and reduce systemic risk. The forum will initially include only the Group of Seven countries, but over time it is envisaged additional national authorities would be included in the process.

Group of Seventy-Seven. This group of countries emerged from the United Nations Conference on Trade and Development (UNCTAD) held in 1964, when the developing countries (q.v.) joined together to defend and promote their common interests. Subsequently, the number of developing countries in the group increased to over 100.

Group of Ten. The group consists of the 10 member countries that agreed to participate in the General Arrangements to Borrow (q.v.) established in 1962. These countries are: Belgium, Canada, France, Germany, Italy, Japan, the Netherlands, Sweden, the United Kingdom, and the United States. The group played a prominent role in shaping the SDR (q.v.) facility established by the first amendment to the Fund's Articles of Agreement (q.v.) and in the provisions of the second amendment, establishing the post-Bretton Woods international monetary system (q.v.). The group, made up of the principal industrial countries, is a dominating influence in international monetary negotiations and has tended to spawn counter groups from developing countries (q.v.). *See also* Group of Seventy-Seven; Group of Thirty-One; Group of Twenty-Four.

Group of Thirty-One. In 1966, developing countries (q.v.) briefly got together to put forward their views as to how the international monetary system (q.v.) should evolve, particularly in connection with the problem of the adequacy of international liquidity (q.v.). The activity of the group was provoked by discussions in the Group of Ten (q.v.) proposing that a scheme to create international reserves (q.v.) should be confined to the leading industrial

Group of Twenty-Four. An intergovernmental Group of Twenty-Four on International Monetary Affairs was set up in 1971, in part to have a counterbody to the Group of Ten (q.v.). The group consists of 24 Finance Ministers or senior monetary or financial authorities, eight appointed by the African, eight by the Asian, and eight by the Latin American members of the Group of Seventy-Seven (q.v.). Although the group is formally limited to 24 members, in practice any member of the group of Seventy-Seven can attend its meetings. The group played an active role in discussions of a reformed international monetary system (q.v.), and in the final phase of those negotiations it held two joint, informal sessions with the Executive Board (q.v.) of the Fund. In addition to helping to shape the reformed system, the group is credited with having been responsible for promoting several innovations within the Fund and elsewhere. It remains an active body, and meets regularly, usually twice a year at the time that the Group of Ten meets.

Group of Twenty-Two. This group consists of finance ministers and central bank governors of the Group of Seven (q.v.) plus those of 15 emerging developing countries (q.v.)—Argentina (q.v.), Australia, Brazil, Canada, China, France, Germany, Hong Kong SAR (q.v.), India, Indonesia (q.v.), Italy, Japan, Korea (q.v.), Malaysia (q.v.), Mexico (q.v.), Poland, Russia, Singapore, South Africa, Thailand (q.v.), the United Kingdom, and the United States. The group met in April 1998 to examine issues related to strengthening the international financial architecture. The initiative was intended to complement ongoing efforts in the Fund, the World Bank (q.v.), and other international institutions and fora and to help develop a broad international consensus on these important issues. At this meeting, three working groups were established, on enhancing transparency and accountability, on strengthening financial systems, and on international financial crises. Each working group comprised representatives from finance ministries and central banks of countries in the Group of Seven, as well as those from developed and emerging market economies; international organizations were also invited to participate in the discussions; and contributions and views were sought from other international groups, countries not represented in the working groups, and the private sector.

Meeting for a second time, in October 1998, the group received the reports prepared by the working groups on the outcome of their discussions. The report of the working group on enhancing transparency and accountability attached particular importance to enhancing the relevance, reliability, comparability, and understandability of information disclosed by the private sector and recommended that priority be given to compliance with and enforcement of high-quality accounting standards. It agreed on the need to improve coverage, frequency, and timeliness with which data on foreign exchange (q.v.) reserves, external debt, and financial sector soundness were published. Furthermore, it recommended that consideration be given to compiling and publishing data on the international exposures of investment banks, hedge funds, and other institutional investors. Stressing the importance of transparency, the report recommended that international financial institutions adopt a presumption in favor of the release of information, except where release might compromise a well-defined need for confidentiality. It also emphasized the importance of being transparent about transparency and recommended that the Fund prepare a Transparency Report summarizing the extent to which an economy meets internationally recognized disclosure standards.

The report of the working group on strengthening financial systems identified several areas—corporate governance, risk management (including liquidity management), and safety net arrangements—where standards for sound practices needed to be enhanced and developed. It recognized that cooperation and coordination among national supervisors and regulators and international groups and organizations were crucial to the strengthening of domestic financial systems and set out several options for enhancing international cooperation, such as the establishment of a Financial Sector Policy Forum that would meet periodically to discuss financial sector issues.

The report of the working group on international financial

crises stressed the need to encourage better management risk by the public and private sectors, and it recommended that governments limit the scope and clarify the design of guarantees that they offer. Effective insolvency and debtor-creditor regimes were identified as important means of limiting financial crises and facilitating rapid and orderly workouts from excessive indebtedness. The report urged countries to make the strongest possible efforts to meet the terms and conditions of all debt contracts in full and on time. Unilateral suspensions of debt payments were inherently disruptive and the report proposed a framework to promote the collective interest of debtors and creditors in cooperative and orderly debt workouts, with principles that could guide the resolution of future international financial crises. The working group added that its report should not be considered an agenda for addressing problems that were currently being experienced in many emerging markets.

The reports were forwarded to the Fund and other international financial organizations for further consideration and were published on the Fund's web site.

Gutt, Camille (1884-1971). Camille Gutt, of Belgium, was the Fund's first Managing Director (q.v.), from 1946 to 1951. Before taking up his appointment with the Fund, he served in the Belgium government as Minister of State and Finance Minister.

-H-

Heavily Indebted Poor Countries (HIPCs). In September 1996, the Managing Director (q.v.) of the Fund and the President of the World Bank (q.v.) submitted to meetings of the Interim Committee and the Development Committee (qq.v.) a joint report on a Program of Action to Resolve the Debt Problems of the HIPCs. The program was designed to address the problems of he HIPCs that follow sound policies, but for which traditional debt relief mechanisms would be inadequate to secure a sustainable external debt (q.v.) position over the medium term. The Committees endorsed the report and requested the implementation of the program.

The key features of the program are as follows: The initiative would be open to all members that are eligible to use the enhanced structural adjustment facility (ESAF) (q.v.) and the resources of the International Development Association (IDA), that is, only the poorer countries eligible to receive concessionary loans from IDA.

Eligibility: The Boards of the Fund and the World Bank would decide on a country's eligibility typically after three years of strong performance under adjustment and reform programs supported by the World Bank and the Fund (the first stage). To qualify for exceptional assistance under the program, countries would have to face an unsustainable debt situation at the completion point after the full application of traditional debt-relief mechanisms and would reform. This completion point would be reached after a successful second three-year period of adjustment and reform (the second stage). This six-year performance period would be implemented on a case-by-case basis, with countries receiving credit for programs that were already under way.

Debt Sustainability: The objective would be to bring a country's debt burden to sustainable levels, subject to satisfactory policy performance. This is defined as when the ratio of the net present value of a country's debt to exports is below the range of 200 to 250 percent and its debt service is below 20 to 25 percent of the value of its exports.

The First Stage: The program builds on the existing mechanisms for providing debt relief, including those of the Paris Club (q.v.), which in December 1994, at a meeting in Naples, had raised its rescheduling target to afford a 67 percent reduction in the net present value of eligible debt. During this first three-year period countries would need to establish a track record of good performance.

Possible Country Situation: At the end of the first stage, the Fund and the World Bank would prepare an analysis of the country's situation to determine whether all the efforts being made by the country itself, the Paris Club, other supporting institutions, and its creditors were sufficient to put the country into a sustainable debt position in the following three years. In the event that they find that the current efforts are sufficient (i.e., that the debt situation would be sustainable without further relief), the country would not be eligible for the program.

The Second Stage: For countries deemed eligible for support under the program, all creditors will commit at the decision point to provide the relief necessary to attain the targeted debt ratios in support of the country's continued reform efforts.

Action at the Completion Point: The Paris Club will provide a reduction in debt stock of up to 80 percent in present value terms on eligible debt, and comparable reductions will be sought from other bilateral official and commercial debtors, with the multilateral institutions also participating, but, at the same time, preserving their preferred creditor status.

Action by All Creditors: All creditors are expected to participate in providing the exceptional assistance needed by the country to reach debt sustainability.

The Fund's Participation: The participation of the Fund in the program would be through special ESAF operations and would take the form of a reduction in the present value of the Fund's claims on a country.

Use of Fund Reserves: It was agreed that if the need should arise, the Fund would have to be prepared to use its reserves (q.v.) to secure full financing under the program, and consideration would be given to the sale of up to five million ounces of the Fund's gold (q.v.) for this purpose. Not all Board members were in favor of such use of the Fund's gold reserves and it was further understood that only the proceeds from investments of the profits from such sales would be used to contribute to the financing of the debt reduction.

First Country Case: In April 1997, the Fund's Board approved Uganda's (q.v.) eligibility for assistance under the HIPC initiative, with an envisaged completion point one year later. The shortening of the second stage to one year was recognized as being exceptional, reflecting Uganda's success in implementing policies under previous Fund programs. Subsequently, five other countries—Bolivia, Burkina Faso (q.v.), Guyana, Côte d'Ivoire, and Mozambique—were judged to be eligible under the program, and discussions were being held on Guinea-Bissau and Mali.

Hedge Funds. Hedge funds are collective investment vehicles, often organized as private partnerships and resident offshore for tax and regulatory purposes. Their legal status places few restrictions on their portfolios and transactions and allows their managers freedom to use short sales, derivative securities, and leverage to raise returns and cushion risk. The Asian financial crisis (q.v.) led to the collapse of one of the largest, most leveraged, and, up to then, one of the most successful of hedge funds. Its collapse, and the need for a bail-out, was thought to have exacerbated the international financial crisis and led authorities, bankers, and other lenders to consider whether such funds should be subject to greater surveillance.

Holdings by the Fund. The Fund's holdings consist of currencies, gold, and since 1972, SDRs (qq.v.). These holdings are derived from subscription (q.v.) payments by members, either reflecting their quotas (q.v.) when they joined the Fund or subsequent increases in those quotas. In addition, the Fund's holdings are increased by charges (q.v.) and service fees on the use of its resources (q.v.), less the cost of remunerating members holding creditor positions in the Fund and interest payments on SDRs. *See also* Resources of the Fund.

Hong Kong SAR. The return of Hong Kong to the People's Republic of China took place on July 1, 1997. The terms of the transfer, which are embodied in the Basic Law, included the establishment of the Hong Kong Special Administrative Region (SAR). The Basic Law also provides for Hong Kong to have a considerable degree of autonomy over economic and other policies and includes a commitment to continue the existing free-market system for 50 years.

The Basic Law's requirements in the area of fiscal policy include the avoidance of fiscal deficits and the principle of keeping the budget commensurate with the growth rate of GDP. The Basic Law also requires Hong Kong's currency (q.v.) to be fully backed by foreign reserves (q.v.), and the exchange rate linked to the U.S. dollar under a currency board-type arrangement. At the end of December 1997, foreign currency assets totaled $92.8 billion.

The Asian crisis (q.v.) contributed to substantial volatility in the Hong Kong markets during 1997. Stock and property prices rose strongly during the first half of the year—by the middle of the year property prices were a third higher than their trough in the second quarter of 1994, and the Hang Seng price index had reached a historic peak in early August, having risen by around 50 percent during the previous 12 months. Spillovers from the regional turmoil, however, caused the Hong Kong dollar to come under speculative attack in the latter half of 1997.

These pressures were successfully resisted by means of intervention in the foreign exchange (q.v.) market and a corresponding tightening of domestic liquidity. Nonetheless, higher interest rates, which resulted from spillovers from the financial turmoil in the region and the resultant pressures on the exchange rate, contributed to a substantial correction in stock and property markets. By the end of January 1998, the Hang Seng index was roughly 45 percent below its 1997 peak, and property prices appeared to have fallen by 15 to 20 percent on average since mid-1997. Pressure on the financial markets continued throughout the first nine months of 1998 and the markets continued to react with volatility, but the downward slide slowed markedly. Pressure on the currency remained strong, but a devaluation was resisted, with foreign exchange reserves strengthening somewhat over the year.

Reviewing Hong Kong SAR's situation in February 1998, the Fund's Executive Directors (q.v.) observed that, notwithstanding the recent turmoil in the region, developments during the previous year had been satisfactory in many respects. The handover had been achieved smoothly, and confidence in a continuation of the existing economic and legal framework had been maintained under the "one country, two systems" framework. In addition, the economy had continued to recover during 1997 from the slowdown of 1994-95, consumer inflation had been contained, the fiscal position strengthened markedly, and foreign exchange reserves increased significantly. More recently, Hong Kong SAR's solid fundamentals and

decisive policy actions had helped it withstand the regional financial crisis and the bouts of speculative attacks. In particular, the Directors welcomed the stance taken by the government in allowing a prompt tightening of domestic monetary conditions under the linked exchange rate system to counter the pressures in the foreign exchange market.

The Directors agreed that the linked exchange rate system had provided an important anchor for economic stability since 1983 and that it currently played a vital role in demonstrating the commitment to an independent monetary and exchange rate policy in Hong Kong SAR and in maintaining confidence in its status as an international financial center. They emphasized the importance of the exchange rate link of maintaining substantial foreign exchange reserves, a fiscal surplus, and flexible factor markets. In this connection, they welcomed the Chinese authorities' commitment not to devalue the renminbi, which should further enhance confidence in the maintenance of Hong Kong SAR's linked exchange rate system.

The Directors commended the authorities for the firm, prudential regulatory oversight of the financial sector and for the recent improvement in disclosure requirements. They welcomed the willingness of the authorities to allow weaker financial institutions to fail, in line with its overall noninterventionist approach to policies. They noted the efforts to improve the timeliness and accuracy of economic data, but called for further early progress, particularly with regard to the data on foreign reserves and the availability of data on capital account of the balance of payments, including short-term liabilities, as well as data on the banking and corporate sectors.

Given the openness of the Honk Kong economy, it was inevitable that economic activity would be strongly affected by the falling demand in regional countries. Although the economy showed remarkable flexibility, the cost of adjustment was substantial, both in terms of a recession and rising unemployment. The outlook for 1999 remained subject to great uncertainty, depending to a large extent on the course of regional markets and the world economy. Nevertheless, after falling sharply in 1998, GDP was expected to recover in the second half of 1999.

-I-

IMF Institute. *See* Organization of the Fund; Technical Assistance and Training.

Income and Expenditure of the Fund. The Fund aims to be financially self-sufficient, covering its expenditure from income, and providing for a prudent financial reserve.

Income is derived from and determined by its financial operations with members, including the extent of the use of the Fund's resources (q.v.), the rate of interest on SDRs (q.v.), the rate of remuneration (q.v.) paid by the Fund to members, and the rate of charge (q.v.) on the use of the Fund's general resources (q.v.). About 90 percent of the Fund's income is derived from charges on the use of the Fund's resources, and the remainder is derived from interest on the Fund's holdings of SDRs and service charges on purchases of currency (qq.v.) from the Fund.

The Fund's current expenditures are made up of two categories, operational expenditures and administrative expenditures. Operational expenditures include mainly remuneration on creditor positions in the Fund and interest payments on the Fund's borrowings (q.v.). Administrative expenses are all those expenditures covered in the Fund's administrative budget (q.v.), which includes personnel expenditures and travel expenses.

The Fund's net income, which is defined as operational income minus operational and administrative expenditures, is either distributed to members or placed in reserve. In the financial year ended April 30, 1998, the Fund increased its total reserves by SDR 164 million, to SDR 2.1 billion. As part of the effort to strengthen its financial position in the face of a substantial volume of overdue obligations (q.v.), the Fund established Special Contingency Accounts (q.v.) in 1987 and 1990. Total precautionary balances (reserves, plus the two Special Contingency Accounts—SCA-1 and SCA-2) amounted on April 30, 1998, to SDR 4.0 billion, equivalent to 8 percent of credit outstanding to member countries in the General Resources Account (q.v.) at that date. Financing of SCA-2, planned to amount to SDR 1 billion and to cover the risks associated with the rights accumulation (q.v.) programs, was completed in 1996-7. In April 1998, the Board considered the level of the Fund's precautionary balances against the background of heavy use of its resources and decided to accelerate the rate of accumulation of the precautionary balances by adding during the following 12 months the equivalent of 5 percent to general reserves (q.v.) and an equal amount to SCA-1. *See also* Administrative and Capital Budgets of the Fund.

Indonesia. Indonesia had used various Fund facilities in the 1960s and early 1970s, but it had not requested a stand-by arrangement (q.v.) since the mid-1970s. The economic and financial crisis that swept through the region during 1997 thus caught Indonesia by surprise. Even though the country introduced measures to combat the situation during the middle of 1997 and called in the Fund while its exchange reserves (q.v.) were strong, the measures taken at that early stage were insufficient to restore confidence.

On November 5, 1997, the Fund approved a stand-by credit for Indonesia, authorizing drawings (q.v.) up to SDR 7.3 billion (about $10.1 billion) over a three-year period in support of the country's macroeconomic stabilization and structural reform program. Of the total, SDR 2.2 billion (about $3 billion) was available immediately, and a further SDR 2.2 billion was to be made available in March 1998, provided that performance targets had been met and the first review of the program had been completed. Subsequent disbursements, on a quarterly basis, were to be made available subject to the attainment of performance targets. The stand-by credit was made available under the Fund's emergency financing mechanism (q.v.).

In addition to the Fund financing, the reform program was supported by financing from the World Bank (q.v.) and the Asian Development Bank, which, together with Indonesia's substantial reserves, provided a first line defense of $23 billion.

After signing the agreement, substantial resistance surfaced in Indonesia to a number of aspects of the program. The poorer sections of the population revolted against the prospect of higher prices on a number of consumer staples, as well as gasoline, because of a reduction or elimination of subsidies, while some members and friends of the President's family resisted the proposed closing of nonviable banks and the dismantling of several government monopolies, with which they were closely identified. The delay in the program's implementation, and the likelihood that the second installment of Fund financing would not be approved, resulted in a further decline in confidence. This, in turn, led to heightened activity on the part of the Fund's Managing Director, Michel Camdessus (qq.v.), and the First Deputy Managing Director, Stanley Fischer (qq.v.), who, together with a staff mission, visited Jakarta to discuss with President Suharto and his officials a strengthening of the program in the face of a deteriorating situation. This unusual participation of the Fund's management in direct negotiations with the Indonesian authorities demonstrated the concern with which the Fund viewed the situation.

On January 15, 1998, however, the Fund's Managing Director was able to announce in Jakarta that agreement had been reached on the financial and structural reform program. He said that President Suharto had indicated that he would take personal responsibility for the program and would, himself, sign the Letter of Intent. Further, in order to ensure that the program would be fully implemented and its objectives realized, President Suharto would appoint a high council of ministers that would report directly to him to oversee the implementation of the program.

Indonesia's economic performance over the previous years had ranked among the best in the developing world, with real GDP growth averaging about 7 percent annually since 1970. This success had been based on a consistent adherence to prudent macroeconomic policies, high investment and savings rates, and market-oriented trade and exchange regimes. Broad-based labor-intensive growth, together with sustained improvement in basic education and health services, had dramatically reduced the incidence of poverty—from over 60 percent in the late 1960s to 11 percent by the mid-1990s.

The strong overall performance, however, masked the emergence of a number of underlying structural weaknesses that made Indonesia vulnerable to adverse external developments. Rigidities in the form of domestic trade regulations and some import monopolies impeded economic efficiency and competitiveness. At the same time, lack of transparency in business decisions adversely affected the business environment, while deficiencies in data weakened investor confidence. In addition, large capital flows intermediated through a weak banking system exposed Indonesia to a shift in financial market sentiment. Thus, Indonesia's banking system was not prepared to withstand the financial turmoil that swept Southeast Asia starting in July 1997. Similarly, the corporate sector was vulnerable to adverse external developments. Prompted by large interest rate differentials between domestic and foreign interest rates, private companies borrowed abroad to finance domestic operations, which in the context of a relatively stable exchange rate were largely unhedged. With the abrupt change in market sentiment, Indonesia was faced with a major crisis of confidence; the depreciation of its currency, the rupiah, and the fall in equity prices were among the largest in the area.

In announcing the renegotiated agreement in January, the Fund's Managing Director summarized the program as follows:

(1) The program was designed to avoid a decline in output, while containing inflation to 20 percent in 1998, with the aim of bringing it back to single digits the following year.

(2) The 1998-99 budget would be revised, to accord with the newly agreed macroeconomic framework, while still adhering to Indonesia's long-standing balanced-budget principle. This would imply a small deficit of about one percent of GDP.

(3) To promote further transparency, the accounts of the Resto-

ration and Investment Funds would be brought into the budget.

(4) Under current conditions, public spending would be limited only to those items of vital importance to the country. Twelve infrastructure projects would be canceled and a number of other government commitments would be discontinued.

(5) The Bank of Indonesia would be given full autonomy to conduct monetary policy and begin immediately unilaterally to decide interest rates.

(6) It was vitally important for the bank and corporate sectors to be restructured and specific plans formulated.

(7) On structural reforms, virtually all of the restrictions that were currently in place would be swept away, including the monopoly on the import and distribution of sugar, as well as the monopoly over the distribution of wheat flour. Domestic trade in all agricultural products would be fully deregulated; the Clove Marketing Board would be eliminated; all restrictive marketing arrangements would be abolished and the cement, paper, and plywood cartels would be dissolved; all formal and informal barriers to investment in palm oil plantation would be removed, while all restrictions on investment in wholesale and retail trades would be lifted.

(8) Measures would be taken to alleviate the suffering caused by the drought.

Subsequently, the Fund's Director of the Fund's Asia and Pacific Department, Hubert Neiss, announced on April 8, 1998, that Indonesia and the Fund team had concluded discussions on the first review of the stand-by arrangement approved by the Fund on November 5, 1997. He said that the economic program agreed upon with the government had adapted macroeconomic policies to the deteriorated economic situation and had expanded the structural and banking reforms agreed to on January 15, 1998. He went on to say that the credibility of the program depended on its full implementation, which would be assured through daily monitoring by the Executive Committee of the Resilience Council, in close cooperation with the Fund, the World Bank, and the Asian Development Bank. Substantive actions would be required prior to approval of the program by the Fund's Executive Board (q.v.), and there would be frequent program reviews by the Board. The Board would review the program, so as to make a determination on the next disbursement to Indonesia, after the agreed to prior actions had been implemented. Several of these measures had already been put in place, while others were expected to be implemented shortly.

Finally, the Fund announced the appointment of Prabhakar Narvekar (q.v.), a former Deputy Managing Director of the Fund, as resident special advisor to the President of Indonesia.

Despite the attempts to soften the impact of the austerity program on the more vulnerable sections of the population, implementation of the program was followed by widespread riots and political turmoil. In the face of growing civil unrest and demands for his resignation, President Suharto announced on May 20, 1998, his resignation from the presidency, and his Vice President, B. R. Habibie, was sworn in as president.

A Fund team visited Jakarta to renegotiate a new adjusted program in a situation where economic and financial conditions had deteriorated sharply. On June 24, 1998, the Fund and the Indonesian authorities announced agreement on a new program and financial package. As a result of the social and political upheavals in May, the economic situation and outlook had worsened considerably, and the economy was facing a very serious crisis. The distribution network had been badly damaged, economic activity, including exports, had been generally disrupted, and business confidence had been severely shaken. As a result, the exchange rate had weakened substantially, rather than appreciated, as had been envisaged in the April program, and inflation was running at higher levels than had been projected.

Because of shortfalls in budgetary resources, expenditures had had to be compressed to unsustainable levels, thereby weakening the social services and economic activity. In additional, large-scale liquidity support had had to be provided to meet a run on a major private bank, which was then placed under the control of the bank restructuring agency.

Under the revised macroeconomic scenario, in 1998 GDP was expected to decline by 10 percent, the exchange rate to stabilize at around 10,000 rupiahs to the dollar, and inflation to be about 80 percent, but an improvement in the situation was seen for 1999. A central feature of the program continued to be limiting the budget deficit to a level that could be offset by additional foreign financing. The pressure on the budget, however, had intensified in the deepening crisis, and, in view of its particular impact on the poor, there was an urgent need to strengthen the safety net to cushion the impact of higher unemployment and the greater incidence of poverty (q.v.). Although some savings were envisaged in greater efficiency in the management of state-run operations, most of the savings were to come from cuts in infrastructure projects, amounting to about 2.5 percent of GDP. It remained the objective to phase out subsidies on staple foods and fuels, but these measures would have to await the recovery of household income. Taken together, the budgetary actions were aimed at reducing the budget deficit to 8.5 percent of GDP in 1998-99—a level that would be unsustainable over the long run and would require further measures to raise revenues and cut subsidies in the following years.

Fiscal policy was to be supported by a tight monetary policy and a switch from setting interest rates administratively on central bank paper to a system of auctions. The further weakening that had occurred in the banking system meant that the implementation of comprehensive reforms were to be given the highest priority. The revised strategy involved measures to strengthen relatively sound banks partly through infusion of new capital and to recapitalize weak banks or close them. Decisions regarding individual banks would be based on uniform and transparent criteria, drawing on the results of portfolio reviews by international accounting firms. In the area of financial restructuring of the corporate sector, it was envisaged that domestic as well as foreign creditors would participate in debt workouts for individual companies, with all creditors sharing in the burden of providing the necessary relief. In support of the negotiation of such restructuring, the government had issued a regulation, in lieu of legislation, that had modernized the bankruptcy system. A critical aspect of the program would be the government's efforts to improve food security by placing considerable emphasis on ensuring that there were adequate supplies of essential commodities, especially rice, and that these would be available through the distribution system at affordable prices.

Finally, the government remained committed to implementing all of the structural reforms agreed to earlier, in collaboration with the World Bank. The privatization program was proceeding on schedule and the projected receipts from privatization, at $1.5 billion, would be achieved. The Monetary Monitoring Committee, comprising representatives of Indonesia, the Fund, the U.S. Treasury, and the Bundesbank, that had been meeting since April 1998, would continue to meet regularly. Regarding external financing needs, despite the considerable support that was being provided by bilateral and multilateral sources, additional balance of payments (q.v.) support amounting to about $4-6 billion, would be required in 1998-99 to close the financing gap. At this critical juncture, the government would be seeking further support from the international community to bring about success in the program.

The Fund completed its first review of the program in July 1998 and announced an increase of about $1.3 billion in the financing available to Indonesia, bringing the total financing available under the three-year arrangement to about $11.3 billion. Following completion of the review, about $1 billion was made available immediately, bringing total disbursement under the arrangement to $4.9 billion. The Fund also announced that additional financing was to be made available from Australia, China, the Asian Development Bank, and the World Bank amounting to nearly $5 billion, all to be made available before the end of March 1999.

The Executive Directors commended the authorities for their good policy implementation in very difficult circumstances. They welcomed the economic priorities set by the government to prevent further economic decline, reduce inflation, and to substantially intensify its efforts to protect the poor from the worst effects of the crisis. By the end of 1998, there were signs that the worst may be over. Interest rates were declining, the currency was appreciating, and usable external reserves had risen sharply. A modest recovery was expected to begin during 1999, with a marked fall in the rate of inflation by the end of the year. *See also* Asian Financial Crisis.

Ineligibility to Use Fund Resources. If a member fails to fulfill any of its obligations under the Articles of Agreement (q.v.), the Fund has the right to declare that member ineligible to use the Fund's general resources (q.v.). Nonpayment of charges (q.v.) or failure to fulfill repayment (repurchase [q.v.]) obligations would, in the absence of an explanation satisfactory to the Fund, be reason to declare a member ineligible. The Fund has used this right sparingly and as a last resort. Typically, when a member has shown good faith, the Fund has made an effort to reschedule repayments or enter into new programs that would restore the member's position of "good standing."

A declaration of ineligibility by the Fund carries harsh repercussions for the member concerned, as it signals to the international financial community that the member in question is not honoring its commitments, and it generally leads to cutting off funds from private and other official sources.

An early test of the Fund's authority occurred in connection with the decision to demonstrate its authority in the sphere of exchange rates, and particularly in its authority to approve a multiple exchange rate system established by a member. The test of this nascent policy came early in January 1948 over the Fund's objections that a French proposal for a free market for some transactions would destroy the country's whole system of fixed and stable par values (q.v.). The French went ahead, anyway, and devalued the franc and, at the same time, established a free exchange market alongside the official rate. In response, the Fund declared France to be ineligible to use the Fund resources—a disbarment that lasted for six years.

In the 1980s, with the outbreak of an acute debt crisis among many developing countries, the amount of overdue obligations (q.v.) reached substantial proportions, rising from about $1.2 billion in 1987 to $3.5 billion in 1992. The number of members with overdue obligations to the Fund reached a peak in 1993 at 12, and the number of countries that had been declared ineligible to use the Fund's resources rose to 10 in 1990. In that year, the Fund adopted a strengthened cooperative approach designed to prevent cases of overdue obligations arising in the first place, tightening the deterrent measures against delinquent members and organizing a collaborative approach on the part of members of the international financial community—designated as the "rights" (q.v.) approach—aimed at helping delinquent members to restore their good standing. Thereafter, with the implementation of these strategies, by April 30, 1998, the number of members with overdue obligations had fallen to seven and the number of ineligible members to four. *See also* Overdue Obligations.

Information and Publications. *See* Documents and Information.

Interim Committee. The Interim Committee of the Board of Governors on the International Monetary System (qq.v.) is one of two committees (the Development Committee [q.v.] is the other) that succeeded the Committee of Twenty (q.v.) in 1974. The terms of reference of the Committee are to advise and report to the Board of

Governors on (1) supervising the management and adaptation of the international monetary system, including the operation of the adjustment (q.v.) process; (2) considering proposals by the Executive Board (q.v.) to amend the Articles of Agreement (q.v.); and (3) dealing with sudden disturbances that pose a threat to the international monetary system. In carrying out these functions, the Committee reviews developments in global liquidity (q.v.) and, in this connection, the transfer of real resources to developing countries. The Committee also reports to the Board of Governors on any matter on which the Board seeks advice.

The aim in establishing the Committee was to bring into existence a group of officials who held high office in their own countries and who, meeting from time to time, would bring informed authority into the affairs of the Fund. Accordingly, the committee is composed of Governors of the Fund, ministers, or persons of comparable rank. Each Fund member that appoints an Executive Director (q.v.), and each group of Fund members that elects an Executive Director, is entitled to appoint one member and up to seven associates to the Committee. In addition, the Managing Director (q.v.), or his representative, is entitled to participate in the meetings and Executive Directors, or in their absence their Alternates (q.v.), are entitled to attend the meetings of the Committee. Meetings of the Committee are generally held twice a year and are usually attended by more than 200 officials, as were the meetings of the earlier Committee of Twenty.

The Committee is named as an interim body because it was the intention of the drafters of the second amendment to the Articles of Agreement that the Committee would eventually be replaced by a Council. The Council, which requires an 85 percent majority vote of the Board of Governors to come into effect, would have terms of reference, composition, and functions comparable to the Interim Committee. The principal difference is that the Committee is not an organ of the Fund and cannot exercise the powers of the Fund, such as taking decisions that bind members or the Fund. It can only make recommendations, and although these recommendations may carry great weight, the Board of Governors and the Executive Directors have the legal right to disregard them. The high majority of votes required under the Articles of Agreement to bring the Council into existence makes it unlikely that it will be established in the near future.

International Bank for Reconstruction and Development (IBRD). *See* World Bank.

International Capital Movements. *See* Capital Movements.

International Liquidity. The adequacy of international liquidity was of central concern under the Bretton Woods fixed exchange rate (qq.v.) system. The relatively fixed supply of gold (q.v.), together with an obvious limit to the role that could be played by the U.S. dollar as a reserve currency (q.v.) when those dollars could be converted, on demand, into gold at a fixed rate, raised questions of how an expansion of the world economy could be sustained on a relatively fixed reserve base. The issues, discussed with growing intensity both inside and outside the Fund in the 1960s, posed a number of questions: whether there was a need for more effective adjustment programs (q.v.) on the part of countries in balance of payments (q.v.) disequilibria or an increase in global reserves (q.v.); whether the undersupply or oversupply of reserves would be deflationary or inflationary; and whether any increase in international liquidity should be in the form of conditional liquidity, through an increase of members' quotas (q.v.) in the Fund, or in the form of unconditional liquidity (i.e., owned reserves in the form of gold, the creation of SDRs (q.v.) as an unconditional form of international liquidity, in accordance with the first amendment to the Fund's Articles of Agreement (q.v.) in 1969. The amendment called upon members and the Fund to make "the special drawing right the principal reserve asset in the international monetary system."

Two years after creating the SDR facility, the convertibility (q.v.) of the U.S. dollar into gold was suspended, and 18 months later the adjustable peg (q.v.) system established at the Bretton Woods Conference (q.v.) had completely collapsed. Although discussions on the adequacy of international liquidity and a possible mechanism for controlling its growth were part of the negotiations on reform of the international monetary system (q.v.), the legalization of the freely floating exchange rate (q.v.) system authorized by the second amendment (1978) effectively brought the debate to a close. Since the beginning of the 1980s, the issue of international liquidity has not been of concern, in part because the need for international liquidity had been substantially reduced in a freely floating exchange rate system, and in part because of the abundant supply of international credit that became available in the 1970s as a result of the recycling of "petrodollars" and subsequently through the integration of capital markets.

SDRs have continued to play a very minor role in the international monetary system and have not become the principal reserve asset (q.v.) envisaged under the 1978 amendment. Instead, there has been an explosion in foreign exchange holdings, which now are by far the largest component of international reserves (q.v.). With the integration of the world's financial markets, liquidity for creditworthy governments has not been a critical problem. For many developing countries (q.v.), a shortage of reserves has been chronic, but the attention of the international community has been focused more on their need for adequate development finance (q.v.) and for the maintenance of stable domestic economic conditions, rather than their liquidity needs.

International Monetary System. There are many definitions of the international monetary system, but basically the system is concerned with a member's economic and financial policies as they affect other members. It is concerned with the process of how a member influences its balance of payments (q.v.) positions, since one member's surplus is the obverse of a deficit or deficits elsewhere in the system, and vice versa. A country's balance of payments position is influenced, in some degree, by almost anything that happens in or to the economy, especially in an interdependent world economy, such as has developed over the past 20 years. Nevertheless, the main factors that impact on the international monetary system are (1) a country's exchange rate, (2) the openness and nondiscriminatory character of the payments system, (3) the free and prudential movements of capital across borders, (4) the form in which international reserves (q.v.) are held.

In the area of exchange rates, the world has moved from the fixed and unalterable exchange rates under the gold (q.v.) standard at the beginning of the century, through the floating era and "beggar-thy-neighbor" policies of the 1930s, to the Bretton Woods fixed (q.v.) but adjustable system of the postwar world, and finally to the freely floating (q.v.) system of exchange rates functioning under Fund surveillance (q.v.).

The mechanism for settling accounts between countries has also gone through parallel developments. Dating from the nineteenth century, the pound sterling was the principal transactions currency (q.v.), and operation of the gold standard hinged on London as the world's financial center. The interwar years saw the breakdown of the gold standard (or, more accurately, the gold exchange standard) and the emergence of a chaotic system, in which the pound sterling and the U.S. dollar were the principal transaction currencies, but where bilateral trade and payments agreements and discriminatory arrangements proliferated.

This interwar period was followed by the postwar Bretton Woods system (q.v.), which recognized that setting exchange rates was a matter of international concern and that the international behavior of nations should be governed by a code of conduct and monitored by a central international institution, the International Monetary Fund. The Bretton Woods system saw the gradual elimination of bilateral and discriminatory arrangements; the emergence of the U.S. dollar, based on gold, as the main vehicle and reserve currency; an attempt to introduce special drawing rights (SDRs) (q.v.) into the international monetary system to supplement international reserves; a gradual lowering of the barriers to trade; a reduction in government interventionist policies and greater reliance on free markets; the spread of convertibility (q.v.) among currencies; a transformation in global communications brought about by the computer and sophisticated international telecommunications systems; and a growing integration of the world's financial markets.

With the collapse of the Bretton Woods system in the early 1970s, the U.S. dollar still remained the dominant reserve currency (q.v.) and currency of payment, but other currencies, such as the deutsche mark and the Japanese yen, grew in importance. The link with gold was severed, and although the Fund and central banks continued to hold substantial quantities of gold in reserve (although some central banks decided to reduce their gold holdings in the 1990s), official convertibility of currencies into gold had been eliminated. International reserves increased sharply over the past 25 years, mainly in the form of U.S. dollars, but with a significant shift away from the dollar to other currencies. SDRs remained a neglected component of the international monetary system. *See also* Par Value System; Reform of the International Monetary System.

International Reserves. Reserves perform the same function for national economies as shock absorbers do for a car. They protect an economy from having to make sharp, and perhaps disruptive policy adjustments to cope with adverse domestic or external developments affecting its balance of payments (q.v.) position. The aim of allowing countries sufficient time to make orderly adjustment (q.v.) was one reason for establishing the Fund with a pool of currencies (q.v.). The Fund is a large supplier of conditional liquidity (q.v.) (i.e., the use of the Fund's resources [q.v.] on condition that a country will adopt an appropriate adjustment program [q.v.]), but for unconditional liquidity, a country has to look mainly to the reserve assets (q.v.) that it owns and can use without challenge.

Reserve assets consist of gold, foreign exchange reserves, reserve positions in the Fund, and SDRs (qq.v.). The role of gold in international reserves (q.v.) is ambiguous. It is the traditional reserve asset of last resort, and still esteemed by central bankers, although there has been an incipient movement by some central banks to sell small amounts of gold on the markets, and there has been a slight decline in total gold reserves. However, there is no official price for gold, and any substantial sales of gold on the free market by a national monetary authority (q.v.) runs the risk of endangering its market price.

Gold is held mainly by industrial countries, with the United States holding about 30 percent of the world total. For official valuation purposes, in both its own accounts and those relating to its members, the Fund continues to value gold at SDR 35 per fine troy ounce, about one-seventh of its market price in 1998. In April 1998, with gold valued at its market price, the value of reserves held by all countries amounted to over SDR 1,420, of which gold accounted for about 15 percent of the total. By this measurement, total reserves have increased by about 65 percent since April 1992.

At the end of April 1998, foreign exchange holdings accounted for about 81 percent of total reserves (with gold valued at market prices), of which U.S. dollar holdings accounted for about 57 percent, the deutsche mark 13 percent, the Japanese yen 5 percent, and the pound sterling 3 percent. Foreign exchange is the fastest growing component of international reserves, growing fivefold in the decade of the 1970s, doubling in the 1980s, and increasing by nearly 70 percent in the first seven year of the 1990s.

The two remaining components of international reserves, reserve positions in the Fund and SDRs, accounted for 5 percent of total reserves.

Reserves are computed on a gross, not net, basis, mainly because there is no international agreement as to what would constitute a liability on reserve holdings.

Investment by the Fund. From the period 1956 to 1972 the Fund invested a small amount of its resources (q.v.) to supplement its operational income (q.v.). The second amendment to the Articles of Agreement (q.v.) authorized the establishment of an Investment Account, which specifically would allow the Fund to invest its holdings of gold and currencies (qq.v.) in interest-bearing assets of member countries. No decision has been taken by the Fund to set up such an account, and the account is not yet operative.

-J-

Jacobsson, Per (1894-1963). Per Jacobsson, a Swedish national, was the third Managing Director (q.v.) of the Fund, serving in that position from 1956 until he died in office in 1963. He had joined the Bank for International Settlements (q.v.) in 1931 as economic advisor and became General Manager of the Bank in 1946.

Jamaica Agreement. The meeting of the Interim Committee (q.v.) in Jamaica in January 1976 put into place the last pieces of the second amendment to the Articles of Agreement (q.v.). At this meeting new provisions for the Articles of Agreement were concluded on exchange arrangements, the role of gold (q.v.) in the international monetary system (q.v.) and in the Fund, and a number of other technical problems that the Executive Board (q.v.) of the Fund had been unable to resolve. The Committee requested the Fund's Executive Directors (q.v.) to complete the work of amending the Articles and submit the amendments, along with a report, to the Board of Governors (q.v.) in a matter of weeks. The Jamaica meeting virtually brought to an end the negotiations on a reformed international monetary system. The initial proposals for a new system had been put forward by the Fund's staff in 1971, taken up by the Committee of Twenty (q.v.) in 1972, formulated in broad principles by an *Outline of Reform* in June 1974, discussed and completely changed by the Interim Committee and the Executive Board over the next two years, and finally came into effect in 1978. *See also* Reform of the International Monetary System.

Joint Fund-Bank Library. An early example of cooperation between the Fund and the World Bank (q.v.) was to establish the Joint Fund-Bank Library, to serve the staff of each institution. The library is administered by the Fund, under the aegis of a joint Fund-Bank Staff Advisory Committee, and its cost is shared by both institutions. The library's collection concentrates on contemporary works, rather than on historical, rare treatises and manuscripts. It has over 200,000 volumes, subscribes to over 4,000 separate journals, receives newspapers from nearly every member country, and has files of the major newspapers dating back to 1946. The library has an on-line cataloging system, subscribes to a nationwide commercial data base, and is a member of a national network of library catalogs. It is not open to the general public.

-K-

Keynes, Lord (1883-1946). John Maynard Keynes, the British economist, journalist, and financier, was the most outstanding economist of the twentieth century, best known for his *General Theory of Employment, Interest, and Money*, published in the mid-1930s, which changed the focus of economic theory and public policy throughout the noncommunist world. Working for the British Treasury during World War II, Keynes was one of the chief architects of the International Monetary Fund and played a dominant role in negotiating the drafts of the agreements establishing the Fund and the World Bank (q.v.) at the Bretton Woods Conference (q.v.) of July 1944.

Keynes Plan. First published in 1942, the Keynes plan was titled *Proposals for an International Currency (or Clearing) Union* and was conceived as an international central bank for national central banks. The unit of account was to be Bancor (q.v.), the value of which was to be fixed in terms of gold (q.v.), but not unalterably so. Debit balances, when they arose, were to take the form of overdrafts and not of specific loans. Reflecting Keynes' view that adjustment of balance of payments (qq.v.) disequilibria should be shared by countries in deficit and surplus, the Union was to charge a rate of interest on credit as well as debit balances. Exchange rates were to be fixed in terms of Bancor and were not to be altered without permission of the Governing Board, except when the member had a debit balance with the Union of more than one-fourth of its quota (q.v.), when it would be entitled to reduce the value of its currency (q.v.) by 5 percent annually. Persistent and growing debtors to the Union were to take increasingly severe action to correct their external position. At the same time, creditor countries were to be subject to similar action in reverse. As put forward by Keynes, the plan dealt only with the Clearing Union, but it did envisage the establishment of a number of parallel organizations, including international bodies charged with postwar relief, rehabilitation, and reconstruction.

The Keynes Plan was being drafted at the same time as the White Plan (q.v.) was being put together in the United States. Subsequently, other plans were also issued, such as the French plan, the Canadian plan, and the U.S. Federal Reserve Board plan. Discussions on these plans intensified in 1943 and culminated in the Bretton Woods Conference (q.v.) of July 1944. All the plans went through mergings and major revisions, but it is generally agreed that the final Articles of Agreement (q.v.) owed more to the White Plan than to Keynes.

Korea. Over a period of 50 years Korea, like other Asian economies, has passed through periods of poverty, stagnation, and miracle growth. It had used the Fund's resources (q.v.) under a variety of stand-by arrangements (q.v.) for many years, but by the end of 1987, Korea had repaid all its outstanding credits and loans to the Fund and had begun to build up its reserve position (q.v.). For several decades per capita GDP growth had risen by 7 percent annually, and by the end of the 1980s a once poor agrarian economy had been transformed into an advanced industrial economy. It was thus a great shock, both to those at home and abroad, when the deep economic and financial crisis broke in 1997.

During 1996 warning signs of financial stress began to emerge, but they were largely ignored by the authorities. Reflecting a weaker external demand, a collapse in computer chip prices, and loss of competitiveness as result of the depreciation of the Japanese yen, export growth slowed markedly. Productive capacity became increasingly underutilized, raising costs when sales were already weakening. Corporate profits deteriorated, leading to losses and debt servicing problems, and to an unusually high number of bankruptcies, including the large conglomerates (chaebols).

These ailing enterprises increased the pressures on the banking sector, which in turn adversely affected overseas creditors' confidence. By mid-November, confidence had fallen so low that foreign creditors began declining requests to roll over maturing debts. At the same time, a number of merchant banks faced serious liquidity problems and were virtually insolvent. Finally, the political uncertainty brought on by the presidential elections in December 1997 triggered a financial crisis, intensifying the pressures that the market had already been facing following the decline in the Hong Kong (q.v.) stock market prices late in October. The exchange rate for the won declined precipitously in a chaotic market, as did stock market prices. The country was perilously close to bankruptcy.

On November 7, 1997, the Korean authorities asked the Fund for support in implementing an economic stabilization (q.v.) and reform program. The Fund's Executive Board (q.v.) approved the request for a three-year stand-by credit for $21 billion on December 4, 1997, in support of the government's program, under its emergency financing mechanism (q.v.). The Board subsequently reviewed the situation three times—on December 18 and 30, 1997, and January 8, 1998, and disbursed substantial installments of the credit after each meeting.

In addition to the Fund's financing, the World Bank stood ready to provide up to $10 billion in support of specific structural reforms, and the Asian Development Bank indicated a willingness to provide a further $4 billion in support of policy and institutional reforms. At the same time, no less than a dozen industrial countries announced that they would be willing, in the event of unanticipated adverse circumstances, to provide a second line of defense, expected to be in excess of $20 billion, in support of the program.

The first objective of the program was to restore overseas and domestic confidence in order to stabilize the money, foreign exchange (q.v.), and stock markets and reverse the capital flows. The macroeconomic framework was designed to continue an orderly reduction in the external current account deficit, which had almost tripled from 1995 to nearly $24 billion in 1996, but had begun to fall in 1997; to rebuild international reserves (q.v.); and to contain inflationary pressures through a tighter monetary stance and temporary fiscal adjustments.

The centerpiece of the government's program, however, was a comprehensive restructuring and strengthening of the financial system to make it sound, transparent (i.e., open), and more efficient. This involved an exit strategy that would ensure the rapid resolution of troubled financial institutions in a manner to minimize systemic stress and avoid moral hazard (q.v.). Nine insolvent merchant banks were suspended and other merchant banks that were not able to submit appropriate restructuring plans were warned that they would have their licenses revoked. All banks were to meet the Basle Committee's (q.v.) capitalization standards. The deposit guarantee system that was currently in place would be eliminated by the year 2000 and would be replaced by a deposit insurance system, financed solely by contributions from the financial sector.

To improve transparency in the financial sector and upgrade accounting and disclosure practices to international standards, large financial institutions would be required to have their financial statements audited by internationally recognized firms. Disclosure standards would require the publication of key data by financial institutions twice a year, including nonperforming loans, capital structure, ownership, and affiliations.

Supervision of the financial sector would be strengthened by setting up a central agency that would consolidate all the supervisory functions that were currently distributed among a number of agencies. Early legislation would be sought to make the Bank of Korea independent, with price stability as its overriding mandate. To promote competition and efficiency, the authorities would allow foreigners to establish bank subsidiaries and brokerage houses by mid-1988.

To further the substantial trade liberalization that had taken place since the early 1980s, the program called for a timetable to be set up in line with the World Trade Organization (WTO) (q.v.) commitment to eliminate trade-related subsidies, restrictive import licensing, and the import diversification program. The government also undertook to accelerate its ongoing capital account liberalization program, raising the ceiling on aggregate foreign ownership of listed shares to 55 percent by the end of 1998 and the ceiling on foreign ownership from 7 percent to 50 percent by the end of 1997. Finally, labor market flexibility was to be enhanced by easing the restrictions on dismissals under mergers and acquisitions and corporate restructuring, so as to reduce the time-consuming court rulings. To ease the burden of layoffs and to expedite reemployment, the employment insurance system would be strengthened and private job placement agencies and temporary employment agencies would be allowed to operate.

The impact of the crisis on the real economy was severe and after growth of 5.5 percent in 1997, the real GDP contracted by 3.8 percent in the first quarter of 1998 and was not expected to recover until later in the year. The slowdown in recovery was hampered by the continued recession in the Japanese economy, for although exports to Europe and the United States expanded, this positive development was negated by a fall in exports to Japan. In its consultations with Korea at the end of May 1998, Executive Directors commended the authorities for their steadfast implementation of their wide-ranging stabilization and reform program. In the third quarter, the won stabilized at around 35 to 40 percent below its pre-crisis level and short-term interest rates were around 8 to 9 percent.

There was promise of resumed growth in 1999, when the GDP was expected to grow 2-3 percent. By the end of 1998, Korea's external reserves had grown to $47 billion, against $4 billion a year earlier, and it was able to repay the Fund $2.8 billion of drawings made under the SRF. Interest rates continued to moderate and the stock market turned bullish. Unemployment, however, remained high, at 9 percent, compared with a pre-crisis level of 3 percent. *See also* Asian Financial Crisis.

-L-

Language of the Fund. The working language of the Fund is English, and all its transactions, papers, Board discussions, policy decisions and documentation are conducted or prepared in English. Several key publications are, however, translated and issued in French and Spanish, and other selected documents (q.v.) and publications of special interest to selected non-English-speaking countries are translated from the English into Arabic, Chinese, French, German, Portuguese, Russian, and Spanish.

Libraries. The Fund maintains separate fiscal and legal libraries, and, in conjunction with the World Bank (q.v.), the main library, the Joint Fund-Bank Library (q.v.), which serves both organizations.

Liquidity, International. *See* International Liquidity; International Reserves.

Liquidity of the Fund. The liquidity of the Fund determines its lending capacity, that is, the maximum amount of financing that the Fund can make available to its members. The liquid resources (q.v.) of the Fund consist of usable currencies and SDRs (qq.v.) held in the General Resources Account (q.v.), supplemented as necessary by borrowed resources. Usable currencies, the largest component of liquid resources, are the currencies of members whose balance of payments (q.v.) and gross reserve positions are considered sufficiently strong to warrant inclusion of their currencies in the operational budget (q.v.) for use in financing Fund operations and transactions (q.v.). On April 30, 1998, the Fund's uncommitted resources had fallen to a level of about $30 billion, compared with $59 billion a year earlier. After the end of the financial year, the Fund's resources fell further, with the liquidity ratio reaching a record low of 36 percent, compared with a ratio of 121 percent at the end of April 1997. This drawdown of the Fund's resources reflected the heavy calls made on the Fund as a result of the Asian crisis (q.v.). The Fund repaid all its outstanding debt to lenders in March 1996, and on April 30, 1998, had no outstanding borrowings (q.v.). A further strengthening of the Fund's resources was due to become effective when the 45 percent increase in quotas (q.v.) under the eleventh general review of quotas (q.v.), approved by the Board of Governors (q.v.) in January 1997, became effective. In the absence of further exceptional demands on the Fund's financial resources, it was expected that the Fund's operations would continue to be based on its subscribed resources, but in August 1998, as a result of the pressure on the Fund's resources caused by the world crisis and with the Fund's liquidity at historically low levels, the General Arrangements to Borrow (GAB) was activated for the first time in 20 years.

Louvre Accord. The Louvre Accord of February 1987 among the Group of Seven (q.v.) industrial countries meeting in the Louvre, Paris, was meant to stem an excessive depreciation of the U.S. dollar and to stabilize currencies (q.v.) around the then current levels, which were considered to be "broadly consistent with underlying economic fundamentals." These objectives were to be supported by central bank intervention and agreed macroeconomic policies. Since 1988, the Group of Seven has held discussions covering a broad range of macroeconomic policy issues. The group has made specific efforts, including coordinated intervention, to resist exchange rate movements regarded as unwarranted by economic fundamentals or contrary to policy objectives, but it has made no commitment to a more formal arrangement. *See also* Plaza Agreement.

-M-

Madrid Declaration. Meeting in Madrid in 1994, the Interim Committee (q.v.) issued a *Declaration on Cooperation to Strengthen Global Expansion.* Two years later, meeting in Washington, D.C., the Committee noted that the strategy set out in the *Declaration,* which emphasized sound domestic policies, international cooperation, and global integration, remained valid. It reiterated the objective of promoting full participation of all economies, including the low-income countries, in the global economy. Favorable developments in, and prospects for, many industrial, developing, and transitional economies (q.v.) owed much to the implementation of sound policies consistent with the common medium-term strategy.

The Committee saw a need to update and broaden the *Declaration* in light of the new challenges of a changing global environment, and to strengthen its implementation, in a renewed spirit of partnership. In the new *Declaration on Partnership for Sustainable Global Growth,* known informally as the 11 commandments, the Committee attached particular importance to the following:

(1) It stressed that sound monetary, fiscal, and structural policies were complementary and mutually reinforcing: steady application of consistent policies over the medium term was required to establish the conditions for sustained noninflationary growth and job creation, which were essential for social cohesion.

(2) The implementation of sound macroeconomic policies and the avoidance of large imbalances were essential to promote financial and exchange rate stability and to avoid significant misalignments among currencies.

(3) Creation of a favorable environment for private savings.

(4) Consolidation of the success in bringing inflation down and building on the hard-won credibility of monetary policy.

(5) Maintenance of the movement toward trade liberalization, resistance against protectionist measures, and the upholding of the multilateral trading system.

(6) Encouragement of current account convertibility (q.v.) and careful progress toward increased freedom of capital movements (q.v.) through efforts to promote stability and financial soundness.

(7) Achievement of budget balance and strengthened fiscal discipline in a multiyear framework. Continued fiscal imbalances and excessive public indebtedness, and the upward pressures they put on global real interest rates, were threats to financial stability and durable growth. It was essential to enhance the transparency of fiscal policy by persevering with efforts to reduce off-budget transactions and quasi-fiscal deficits.

(8) Improvement of the quality and composition of fiscal adjustment by reducing unproductive spending while ensuring adequate basic investment in infrastructure. Because the sustainability of economic growth depended on the development of human resources, it was essential to improve education and training; reform public pension and health systems to ensure their long-term viability and enable them to provide effective health care; and alleviate poverty and provide well-targeted and affordable social safety nets.

(9) Bold structural reform, including labor and product market reforms, with a view to increasing employment and reducing other distortions that impeded the efficient allocation of resources, so as to make members' economies more dynamic and resilient to adverse developments.

(10) The promotion of good governance (q.v.) in all its aspects, including adherence to the rule of law, improvements in the efficiency and accountability of the public sector, and tackling corruption, as essential elements of a framework within which economies could prosper.

(11) Strong prudential regulation and supervision of the banking system to ensure its soundness, improved coordination, better assessment of credit risk, stringent capital requirements, timely disclosure of banks' financial conditions, action to prevent money laundering, and improved management of banks.

Malaysia. Since the late 1980s, Malaysia's economy, sustained by high levels of investment (over 40 percent of GDP in recent years) and savings (well over 30 percent of GDP)—a federal government surplus and a favorable balance of trade—and generally strong macroeconomic fundamentals, had achieved considerable success, reflected in high growth and a very substantial reduction in poverty. In 1997, however, Malaysia was seriously affected by regional developments, although it avoided the most serious market pressures and economic difficulties experienced by some other countries. Nevertheless, from the second half of 1997, economic activity slowed and there was a large outflow of short-term capital; from the end of 1996 through April 1998, gross international reserves (q.v.) fell by $7 billion, to $20 billion. The ringgit depreciated by 44 percent, and the stock market fell by almost 50 percent between mid-1997 and January 1998. In the next three months, however, the ringgit strengthened by 20 percent and the stock market recovered by 9 percent.

In March 1998, the government announced a new package of measures, which built on earlier initiatives and was designed to broaden the overall policy response within the changed macroeconomic framework. The measures included action to strengthen the financial sector and address emerging problems in financial institutions. Fiscal policy was aimed at ensuring a small surplus, despite an increase in spending to strengthen the social safety net. There was to be a significant reduction in credit and monetary growth, and a more active use of interest rates to stabilize the foreign exchange (q.v.) market and restrain inflation. The government also renewed its commitment to improve transparency and steadily to implement structural measures aimed at improving corporate governance and competition.

Upon the conclusion of the Executive Board's consultations (qq.v.) with Malaysia in April 1998, the Directors welcomed the package of measures announced by the Malaysian authorities in March, noting that it constituted a more comprehensive approach to restructuring the Malaysian economy. Directors placed strong emphasis on the tightening of monetary policy, on improvements in corporate governance and fiscal transparency, and on the early implementation of commitments to deepen structural reform.

As contagion spread, however, the Malaysian economy was subjected to continuing pressure, and in August 1998, following a course set by Prime Minister Mahathir, the authorities imposed currency controls on capital movements, imposed a temporary moratorium on short-term debt, and introduced measures to reflate the economy. At the end of 1998, prospects for a medium-term recovery were uncertain. Although economic and monetary policy had become more expansionary, their effects were being jeopardized by the damage to investors' confidence caused by the imposition of capital controls. *See also* Asian Financial Crisis.

Managing Director. The Managing Director of the Fund is selected by the Executive Board (q.v.) for an initial term of five years. He is Chairman of the Executive Board and participates in meetings of the Board of Governors, the Interim Committee, and the Development Committee (qq.v.). The Managing Director is also chief of the Fund's staff (q.v.) and, under the direction of the Executive Board, conducts the ordinary business of the Fund. Subject to the general overview of the Executive Board, he is also responsible for the organization, appointment, and dismissal of staff. The position has traditionally been filled by a national of one of the Fund's European members. The Deputy Managing Director (q.v.) has traditionally been from the United States.

Membership of the Fund. Membership in the Fund is open to every country that controls its foreign relations and is able and prepared to fulfill the obligations of membership contained in the Fund's Articles of Agreement (q.v.). At the end of April 1997, membership was virtually universal, amounting to 182 members, compared with only 30 original members in 1946. The collapse of communism and the breakup of the U.S.S.R. (q.v.) was followed by the memberships of the three Baltic states, the other 12 newly independent countries that formerly made up the Soviet Union, the rest of the former communist countries in Eastern Europe that had not already joined the Fund, and Switzerland.

The Board of Governors (q.v.) is the only authority in the Fund to approve applications for membership, and it does so by a simple majority vote. In matters of procedure, a committee of five or six Executive Directors (q.v.) is formed which, along with the staff (q.v.) of the Fund, helps the applicant gather the necessary economic data and agrees with the applicant on the terms of membership. The most critical aspects of the Membership Resolution (q.v.) are the size of the new member's quota (q.v.) and the form in which the subscription (q.v.) is to be paid.

In determining whether an applicant is a country, and thus

eligible to become a member, the Fund makes its own finding, although it will take into account the recognition given to it by other members and by the United Nations (q.v.). Membership of the UN, however, is not a sufficient condition for membership in the Fund. The sole determinants for membership are that the applicant is a country able to control its foreign relations and fulfill the obligations of its membership. Membership does not depend on the geographic or economic size of the country, or whether it has its own currency or central bank, or whether it is a centrally planned economy. The Fund has accepted into membership many small states (q.v.), several countries not possessing their own currencies or central banks, and countries in various parts of the world having centrally planned economies.

Membership Resolution. A country is admitted to membership in the Fund after the Board of Governors (q.v.) has voted on a Membership Resolution and the terms of the Resolution have been complied with by the member. The Resolution specifies the size of the member's quota (q.v.), the method of paying the subscription (q.v.), notification by the member of its exchange arrangements, the terms on which it can engage in transactions (q.v.) with the Fund, confirmation that it has taken all legal steps necessary under its own constitutional arrangements to become a member, and the period of time for accepting membership.

Mexican Crisis. Mexico has a long history of financial relations with the Fund and from the early years made frequent use of the Fund's resources (q.v.) in moderate amounts. It was not until the late 1970s that Mexico's drawings (q.v.) on the Fund became substantial in a period when international payments were badly out of balance because of escalating oil prices. Mexico's difficulties partly resulted from inconsistent policies that encouraged domestic consumption spending, and from the practice that sprang up among the international banks of making unwise loans to developing countries (q.v.) through syndicated lending in their efforts to recycle the petrodollars deposited with them by the oil-producing countries

It was Mexico's 1982 debt crisis that led the Fund into new fields of international finance. As the weight of international debt grew dramatically, mounting concern about Mexico's financial viability spread through the international financial community. The international banks suddenly stopped lending to Mexico and, in order to avoid declaring a default on its loans, the country turned to the Fund for support. Up to this point, the Fund had always followed a passive role in cofinancing: it had established the amount of financing that it could itself provide under its institutional rules and then it ascertained what other creditors would be willing to contribute, framing the adjustment program (q.v.) to the total external resources available. In the situation that Mexico and many other developing countries found themselves in the early 1980s, the international banks were unwilling to make any further new loans or to roll over existing loans.

This led to what became known as concerted lending. The Managing Director (q.v.) of the Fund went before a meeting of creditor banks in New York and informed them that the Fund would lend Mexico $3.8 billion over three years under an extended Fund facility (q.v.) only if he received a written assurance from the banks that, as a group, they would increase their own lending to Mexico by $5.8 billion. His perception was that the banks' long-term common interest in saving Mexico from default was greater than the dubious short-term advantage that they would achieve if, as individual institutions, they attempted to reduce their exposures unilaterally. Concerted lending became the wave of the future for the next three or four years, until debt-reduction strategies were put in place.

A remarkable economic transformation had been achieved by Mexico through prudent macroeconomic programs and structural reforms since the 1982 crisis. These programs emphasized three aspects:

(1) Fiscal and budgetary reforms that brought about a broader tax base, an increase in revenues, lower tax rates, and the elimination of loopholes, which, combined with cuts in government expenditures, converted a deficit amounting to 7 percent of GDP in 1982 to a surplus of 8 percent of GDP in 1990.

(2) Privatization, which first focused on making the private sector self-sufficient and weaning it away from subsidized inputs and interest rates, and then converted state-owned enterprises into private hands so that by 1991 the government owned only 257 firms, compared with 1,155 at the end of 1982.

(3) Trade liberalization, which included unilateral initiatives, as well as reciprocal trade liberalization under the General Agreement

on Tariffs and Trade (GATT) (q.v.), which Mexico joined in 1985, in time to participate in the Uruguay Round.

Despite the progress made since 1982, concerns about the sustainability of the current account deficit began to rise sharply in 1994. Dramatic political unrest, intense foreign competition for savings in other emerging markets, and generally higher interest rates abroad led to a sharp decline in capital inflows and even to significant outflows. To stem capital outflows, the Mexican authorities raised interest rates, allowed the currency (q.v.) to depreciate, and substituted short-term indebtedness denominated in foreign currency for local currency-denominated debt. The level of reserves (q.v.) was stabilized for about six months during 1994, but in October of that year a resurgence of investors' fears put further pressure on the foreign exchange (q.v.) and financial markets, forced the government to float the peso, and precipitated another crisis.

Mexico again turned to the Fund. At first the Fund intended to lend Mexico $7.8 billion under a stand-by arrangement (q.v.), but when the U.S. Congress refused the U.S. Administration's request for $40 billion in loan guarantees late in the evening of January 30, the Fund promptly raised its loan amount by $10 billion, to $17.8 billion, said at that time to be the largest amount ever lent to anyone (although not all the credit was subsequently drawn on). In making such a huge loan available to Mexico, the Fund's rationale was not only to restore confidence in Mexico, but also to head off the contagion *(Tequila)* effect that the loss of confidence was having on other countries in the region and the broader threat to the international monetary system (q.v.). In addition to Fund resources, the U.S. Administration, despite the opposition by the U.S. Congress, agreed to provide $20 billion in credit from the Exchange Stabilization Fund, and the Bank for International Settlements (q.v.) raised its loan offer from $5 billion to $10 billion, thereby restoring the original amount of financing.

Tighter fiscal and monetary policy, along with greater privatization and other structural reforms, led to sharp economic and financial improvements. Interests rates, although remaining high, began to fall and the trade surplus increased dramatically. Overall, however, economic growth was slow to recover, although the country's external position improved markedly, with a strengthening of its international reserves (q.v.) and some recovery in its foreign exchange and financial markets. As a consequence, Mexico was able to resume borrowing from private markets abroad and to begin repaying its creditors ahead of schedule.

The 1994 Mexican crisis, as in the crisis 12 years earlier, was followed by a number of improvements in the international financial mechanism. Although there had been some earlier indications that the underlying economic conditions were not entirely satisfactory, the force and severity of the crisis when it did come took the international community by surprise and provoked a sharp overreaction by the international financial markets not justified by the economic fundamentals. In the succeeding years steps were taken to significantly strengthen the Fund's financial resources by establishing the New Arrangements to Borrow (NAB), the renewal of the General Arrangements to Borrow (GAB) (q.v.), and a general 45 percent increase in quotas under the eleventh general review of quotas (qq.v.). Its mechanism for coping with unexpected demands for resources was expedited by the emergency financing mechanism and the supplementary reserve facility (qq.v.). Finally, the data and other information made public by the Fund were improved and expanded; the Fund's surveillance (q.v.) procedures over members' economies were intensified; the Executive Board's views on members' policies under Article IV consultations (q.v.) were made available to the public in the form of Public Information Notices (q.v.); Letters of Intent, spelling out the adjustment programs (q.v.) supported by the Fund, were made available on the Fund's web site, subject to the consent of the member involved; Special Dissemination Standards for statistical data were established for improving the quality and transparency of the data supplied by member countries; and, in general, the range of the Fund's publications (q.v.) was expanded sharply to include staff reports on countries, working papers, and other analytical and explanatory material.

Military Expenditures. The Fund estimated that military spending in the early 1990s amounted to about 5 percent of the world's GDP. In discussing military expenditure and the role of the Fund toward the end of 1992, the Directors indicated that such expenditure had an important bearing on a member's fiscal policy and external position. They recognized, however, that judgments about the appropriate level of military spending were the prerogative of national governments and were not part of the Fund's work. The Executive Board (q.v.) emphasized that aggregate data on all fiscal expenditures, including off-budget items, should continue to be reported to the Fund.

According to a Fund staff analysis of 132 countries, military expenditures declined to 2.3 percent of GDP in 1996 and 1997, from 3.5 percent in 1990—allowing some $357 billion of resources to be applied to more productive endeavors, assuming the maintenance of the 1990 level of expenditures throughout the period.

The sharp drop and eventual leveling off of military expenditures during the 1990s were most notable in stand-by and extended Fund arrangements (qq.v.). This was mainly due to the significant number of transitional economies (q.v.) seeking Fund assistance under these arrangements and their high levels of military expenditures before they entered into the arrangements. Low-income countries, which typically enter into adjustment programs or enhanced structural adjustment arrangements, also managed to reduce their military expenditures significantly.

Military expenditures as a share of GDP in countries receiving Fund-supported programs have remained below the worldwide average, particularly in those countries with programs extending for two years or more. Military expenditures in countries with programs under the structural adjustment facility (SAF) (q.v.) and the enhanced structural adjustment facility (ESAF) had fallen from 4.4 percent of GDP in 1990 to 2.8 percent in 1997, in countries with extended Fund facility programs from 4.8 percent to 1.7 percent, and in countries with stand-by arrangements from 3.8 percent to 1.9 percent.

Ministates. *See* Small States.

Monetary Approach to Balance of Payments. In the 1950s, the Fund developed what came to be known as the Polak model, reflecting the work of Jacques J. Polak (q.v.), Director of the Research Department from 1958 to 1979, a monetary model that was designed to allow the Fund to judge whether a country's policies would be sufficient to restore economic balance. The main feature of the model was its simplicity, confining inputs to the economic data (banking data and trade data) generally available in many member countries at that time, and the necessity to keep the model based on the key variable that governments could control (domestic credit creation). The model contained two behavioral equations—a demand-for-money function that was proportional to income and a correlated demand-for-import function. The set of four equations in the model constitutes the logical core of the Fund's programming exercise, known as "financial programming" (q.v.). Over the years, for practical purposes the model has remained simple, with a limited number of standard variables. It has, however, been subject to elaboration on an ad hoc basis.

Monetary Authority. Monetary authorities are the treasury, central bank, stabilization fund, or any similar fiscal agency of a member country. Normally, a monetary authority is responsible for applying the rules governing the relationship between the country and

the Fund insofar as the country's balance of payments (q.v.) and related matters are concerned.

Monetary Policy. Monetary policy is one of several short-term policy instruments used as part of a broader approach to structural and balance of payments adjustment (q.v.) that may include fiscal and exchange rate policies, as well as institutional and structural reforms. Regulation of the money supply is controlled through central banking instruments of policy—interest rates, special central bank deposits, open-market operations, and other techniques. Adjustment programs (q.v.) supported by the Fund usually include quarterly credit ceilings—on the public and private sectors, and on overall bank credit. Curtailment of the money supply reduces domestic absorption (consumption and investment), releases resources for export, cuts down on imports, and brings about an improvement in the balance of payments (q.v.). Other factors, financial and nonfinancial, may need attention, and the relationship between the money supply and the balance of payments requires assumptions about the demand for money, which may differ from country to country, and over time. Nevertheless, the monetary approach to the balance of payments is a proven, pragmatic, practical approach, based on readily available and up-to-date statistics that are easy to monitor. *See also* Financial Programming.

Monetary Reserves. Used in the original Articles of Agreement (q.v.), the term has been eliminated from the current Articles. The term was never defined, but refers to reserve assets (q.v.). *See*

International Reserves.

Moral Hazard. As the Fund moved into crisis management, first
with the Mexican crisis (q.v.) in 1982 and subsequently with the
critical crisis that arose again with Mexico in 1994 and the Asian
crisis (q.v.) three years later, it came under strong criticism from
many quarters for what were labeled its "bail-out" policies. It was
contended by these critics that the marketplace was the appropriate
place to bring about any needed adjustment, that the chips should
fall where they may, and that the intervention of an international
organization was not only unnecessary but damaging to the long-
run health of the free enterprise system. It was charged that the
Fund, by providing assistance to countries in crisis, encouraged
more reckless behavior on the part of borrowers and lenders in the
future. Further, it was contended that the very participation of the
Fund in a country's economy, no matter what long-term benefit
there would be, sent a strong signal that in the short term the country was in trouble, and thus caused an exacerbation of the situation.

Addressing this issue in a speech given in February 1998, the
Fund's Managing Director, Michel Camdessus (qq.v.), said that the
notion that the availability of Fund programs encouraged countries
to behave recklessly was not plausible; no country would deliberately court such a crisis, even if it thought international assistance
would be forthcoming. The economic, financial, social, and
political price paid was simply too great. "Nor do countries," he
added, "show any great desire to enter Fund programs unless they
absolutely have to."

Further, the Managing Director noted, despite the constant talk
of bailouts, most investors were taking heavy losses in the crisis.
With stock markets and exchange rates plunging, foreign equity investors had lost nearly three-quarters of the value of their holdings
in some Asian markets. Many firms and financial institutions in
these countries would go bankrupt, and their foreign and domestic
lenders would share in the losses. International banks were also
sharing in the cost of the crisis.

The Managing Director concluded his defense of the Fund by
saying that the bottom line was that there was a trade-off in how
the international community chose to handle the Asian crisis. It

could step back, allow the crisis to deepen, bring additional suffering to the people of the region, and, in the process, possibly teach a handful of international lenders a better lesson. Or it could step in and try to do what it could to mitigate the undesired side effects. "In my view," he said, "the global interest lies in containing and overcoming the crisis as quickly as possible. And working through the Fund offers the most expeditious and cost-effective way of doing this." The controversy parallels the arguments that sometimes reappear in some countries as to whether central banks or other government authorities should indulge in bailouts for domestic banks. In practice, however, no country, however sparse its regulations over the financial sector may be, can stand aside and watch its national banking system collapse. And so far, no country has done so. Similarly, the Fund and other international institutions would be failing in their responsibilities to allow a major international financial crisis to develop to a point where there is a danger of the international system suffering severe disruption or even collapsing, as happened in the 1930s, when the troubles of a relatively small Austrian bank were followed by a worldwide depression.

On the question of "bailing-in" the private sector, the Interim Committee and the Executive Board (qq.v.) have given much consideration as to how private creditors can be encouraged to stay with a country in crisis, without pulling out their funds in unison, and as to how this can be done on a voluntary basis, without the creditors withdrawing their funds from other markets. The November 1998 agreement on the economic and financial program with Brazil (q.v.) was an experimental attempt along these lines.

Multilateral Exchange Rate Model (MERM). The MERM was an early worldwide econometric model devised by the Fund's staff that, in analyzing a country's overall competitiveness in terms of changes in its exchange rate (q.v.), calculated effective exchange rates by taking into account the commodity (q.v.) composition of a country's trade, the relevant elasticities of supply and demand, and the relative importance of other countries as trading partners and as competitors in third markets. The MERM was phased out during the 1980s and has been replaced by a more generalized model.

Multilateral Surveillance. *See* Surveillance Over Exchange Rates.

Multiple Currency Practices. Members must obtain the approval of the Fund before engaging in multiple currency practices. Despite the fact that under the second amendment to the Articles (q.v.) members have freedom to choose their exchange arrangements, unitary rates of exchange continue to be the principle to be upheld under the Articles. Multiple currency practices are objected to because they can be restrictive, discriminatory among members, and unfairly competitive. Under the original Articles, multiple rates were legally identifiable if some exchange transactions took place within the legal margins and others outside that margin. Under the current system of exchange arrangements, there are no legal margins, which are set by the market. As a guideline, therefore, in defining a multiple currency practice, the Fund has adopted a decision reasoning that official action should not cause spreads between a buying and selling rate for a currency, or discrepancies between cross rates among currencies, that differ unreasonably from the rates that would emerge if they were affected only by normal commercial costs and risks of exchange transactions. For the purpose of applying this decision, the Fund has established a margin of 2 percent. If a spread exceeds 2 percent without official action, it will not be considered a multiple currency practice. But if this is caused by official action, such as, say, a tax on exchange transactions of more than 2 percent, then the Fund will judge that to be a multiple currency practice.

Multiple Reserve Currency Proposals. A number of plans were advanced late in the 1950s and in the 1960s, mainly by private economists, proposing a deliberate diversification of foreign currency (q.v.) holdings by central banks, in order to reduce reliance on the U.S. dollar. The proposals had many variations in their details, but they were never seriously considered by the monetary authorities (q.v.). Instead, the SDR facility was established in the Fund under the first amendment of the Articles (q.v.) (1969). *See also* Mutual Currency Account Plan.

Mutual Currency Account Plan. A scheme to increase international liquidity (q.v.) and reduce the role of gold (q.v.) in the international monetary system (q.v.) was first put forward, in 1962, by Robert V. Roosa, at that time Undersecretary for Monetary Affairs of the U.S. Treasury. He suggested that the industrial countries should be prepared to hold each other's currencies (q.v.) in their monetary reserves (q.v.): a country in surplus in its balance of payments (q.v.) would receive and hold the currency of an industrial country in balance of payments deficit, thereby avoiding its conversion into gold, U.S. dollars, or sterling. At that time, the U.S. dollar and sterling were the principal reserve currencies (q.v.) and the effect of the Roosa scheme would have been to increase the number of currencies held in reserves.

Later in the same year, Reginald Maudling, of the United Kingdom, built on the idea put forward by Roosa by suggesting that the Fund establish a mutual currency account into which the mutual holdings of currencies could be converted into a reserve asset (q.v.) defined in terms of gold. The plan was cast in terms of voluntary action, but its details were never fully formulated, since the United States, which was in balance of payments deficit, resisted the idea of establishing a two-tier dollar holding structure, one with a defined and guaranteed value in terms of gold established under the mutual currency account and the other consisting of U.S. dollars held by countries in their reserves outside the mutual currency plan.

Although these early schemes to counter the shortage of international liquidity and to reduce the role of the U.S. dollar as a reserve currency did not get far, they laid the groundwork for a number of other proposals. These included a mechanism to control international liquidity put forward by Professor Robert Triffin and others; a reserve asset scheme suggested by Edward M. Bernstein (q.v.), who had played a prominent role in the negotiation of the original Articles of Agreement (q.v.); and the establishment of the special drawing rights (SDR) (q.v.) facility in the Fund in 1969. Although the concept of a substitution account was seriously considered and even outlined in some detail by the Committee of Twenty (q.v.), the differing proposals could not be reconciled. Subsequently, in 1980, the Interim Committee (q.v.) agreed to abandon further study of the proposal.

-N-

Narvekar, Prabhakar R. (1932-). Prabhakar Narvekar, a national of India, was appointed one of three Deputy Managing Directors in June 1994. He had been Special Advisor to the Managing Director (q.v.) of the Fund since August 1991. He joined the staff (q.v.) of the Fund in 1953 as a Research Assistant, and he held various positions in the Asian and European Departments before being appointed Director of the Asian Department in 1986. He holds degrees in economics from Bombay University and Columbia University and also studied at Oxford University. Narvekar retired from the Fund's staff in 1997 but was appointed by the Managing Director as Special Advisor to the President of Indonesia (q.v.) in 1998, following that country's economic crisis and the inauguration of a Fund-supported adjustment program (q.v.).

Need for Financing. *See* Requirement of Need.

New Arrangements to Borrow (NAB).   Under the NAB, approved by the Fund's Executive Board (q.v.) on January 27, 1997, 25 participant countries and institutions stand ready to lend the Fund additional resources—up to SDR 34 billion (about $47 billion)—to supplement its regular quota (q.v.) resources when needed to forestall or cope with an impairment of the international monetary system (q.v.) or deal with an exceptional situation that threatens the stability of the system. The NAB do not replace the supplemental credit lines available to the Fund under the General Arrangements to Borrow (GAB) (q.v.), which remain in force. Under the GAB, the Group of Ten (q.v.) industrial countries and Switzerland stand ready to lend up to SDR 17 billion (about $24 billion); in an associated agreement, Saudi Arabia is prepared to make available SDR 1.5 billion (about $2.1 billion). The NAB, however, will be the facility of first recourse.

It entered into force on November 17, 1998—for five years and subject to renewal—when it was approved by participants with credit arrangements totaling SDR 28.9 billion (about $40 billion), including the five participants with the largest credit arrangements. NAB credit lines may be drawn on for the benefit of all NAB participant countries, or for nonparticipant countries under circumstances similar to those under the GAB. Activation procedures for nonparticipants under the NAB credit lines may be drawn on for the benefit of all NAB participant countries, or for nonparticipant countries under circumstances similar to those under the GAB. Activation procedures for nonparticipants are, however, somewhat more flexible. A country or institution not currently a participant may become one when the NAB is renewed, if the Fund and participants representing 80 percent of credit arrangements agree.

Participants in the NAB
(Millions of SDRs):

Australia	810	Austria	412
Belgium	967	Canada	1,396
Denmark	371	Deutsche Bundesbank	3,557
Finland	340	France	2,577
Hong Kong Monetary		Italy	1,772
Authority	340	Japan	3,557
Korea	340	Kuwait	345
Luxembourg	340	Malaysia	340
Netherlands	1,316	Norway	383
Saudi Arabia	1,780	Singapore	340
Spain	672	Sveriges Riksbank	859
Swiss National Bank	1,557	Thailand	340
United Kingdom	2,577	United States	6,712

The wider participation under the NAB reflects the changing character of the global economy and a broadened willingness to share responsibility for managing the international monetary system. The credit contributions (except for the Hong Kong Monetary Authority) are based initially on the strength and size of the economies of the participating members as reflected by their quotas in the Fund. In approving the new arrangements the Board reiterated that they were in no way a substitute for the strengthening of quotas—which is the capital basis of the Fund.

The first activation of the NAB came in December 1998, when 21 countries lent a total of about $12.5 billion to the Fund to help finance the arrangement approved for Brazil.

Nonmetropolitan Territories of Members. Dependencies or nonmetropolitan territories of members cannot be admitted to membership (q.v.) of the Fund, even though the dependency may have a separate currency (q.v.) and a separate balance of payments (q.v.), full internal autonomy, and, in terms of economic size, may be far larger than many existing members of the Fund (e.g., as was Hong Kong [q.v.]). Members accepting the obligations of the Articles of Agreement (q.v.) do so for all the territory under their authority and are solely responsible for carrying out those obligations, which cannot be shared with a dependency.

-O-

Obligations Under Article VIII. Members accepting the obligations of the Articles of Agreement (q.v.) undertake to refrain from imposing restrictions on the making of payments for current international transactions or engaging in discriminatory currency arrangements or multiple currency practices (q.v.) without Fund approval. Members that are not in a position to accept Article VIII can avail themselves of the transitional arrangements (q.v.) set out in Article XIV. On April 30, 1998, 142 members had accepted Article VIII.

Offices Outside the United States. The Fund maintains two small offices in Europe. An office in Paris, with a staff of about 12, serves mainly as a liaison office for the Fund with the European Union, the Organization for Economic Cooperation and Development, and the national monetary authorities (q.v.) in Europe. Another in Geneva, with a staff of about six, maintains close contact with the General Agreement on Tariffs and Trade (q.v.) and its successor, the World Trade Organization (q.v.), and agencies of the United Nations (q.v.) based in Geneva, such as the United Nations Conference on Trade and Development and the International Labour Office. In January 1998, the Fund opened a Regional Office for Asia and the Pacific in Tokyo.

Oil Facilities. In 1974 and again in 1975 the Fund established a temporary facility to help members meet the increased costs of imports of petroleum and petroleum products as a result of the sharp rise in oil prices occurring at the end of 1973. These large increases in oil prices had given rise to balance of payments (q.v.) difficulties of unprecedented magnitude for most oil-importing countries. Drawings (q.v.) by these members under the Fund's normal credit tranche (q.v.) policies would have been inadequate to meet the serious imbalances caused by the oil price escalation, and would have virtually rendered the Fund a bystander at a time when a serious payments crisis was threatening to overwhelm the world economy.

The establishment of the oil facilities of 1974 and 1975 was based on the view that neither the oil-exporting countries nor the oil-importing countries could quickly adjust to their new payments situations. The capacity of the major oil-exporting countries to increase imports was limited in the short run, while measures to rectify the balance of payments of the oil-importing countries could only aggravate the general imbalance in payments through widespread deflationary policies or trade restrictions. Financing rather than adjustment was the principal objective to be achieved by establishing the oil facilities. The facilities were funded by borrowing from those members that were in balance of payments surplus, mainly the major oil-exporting countries, thereby recycling the so-called petrodollars.

In accordance with this policy, conditionality (q.v.) on the use of the two oil facilities was minimal, although the terms of the 1975 facility were tightened somewhat. Repayments of drawings (q.v.) under the facilities were to begin in the fourth year after purchase and be completed within seven years. All told, 55 members drew SDR 6.9 billion under the facilities, which were funded by borrowings from 17 lenders.

Oil Facility Subsidy Account. In August 1975 the Fund established a subsidy account to assist its most seriously affected members to meet the cost of using resources made available under the oil facility (q.v.). Members eligible to receive assistance from the subsidy account were 18 Fund members on the list of countries prepared by the Secretary-General of the United Nations (q.v.) that had been most seriously affected by the increased price of petroleum and petroleum products. Contributions to the subsidy account were made by 24 members of the Fund and Switzerland, in the amount of SDR 160 million. The account enabled the effective cost of using the resources of the oil facility to be reduced by about 5 percent, to about 2.75 percent a year. The account was administered by the Fund as trustee, and in that guise the resources of the account were able to be directed to a specific list of 25 developing countries (q.v.) without violating the spirit of the Articles of Agreement (q.v.), which imply that all members be treated equally. The subsidy account was the forerunner of the Trust Fund (q.v.), which was established the following year.

Operational Budget. The Fund's financial resources (q.v.) consist essentially of a pool of gold, SDRs, and national currencies (qq.v.) subscribed by members. Not all the currencies held by the Fund are usable at all times. Only currencies of members in sufficiently strong balance of payments (q.v.) and reserve positions are sold by the Fund in its transactions (q.v.) and operations. A considerable portion of its currency holdings is not, therefore, available for use.

Currencies to be used in drawings (purchases), repayments (repurchases) (qq.v.), and other Fund operations are selected by the Executive Board (q.v.) for successive quarterly periods by drawing up an operational budget. This budget specifies the amount of SDRs and currencies that the Fund is expected to use in the three-month period. In preparing the budget, the selection of currency is determined by the strength of the balance of payments and gross reserves of members and by developments in exchange markets (q.v.). In addition, the Fund tries to promote, over time, balanced positions in the Fund, so that the amount of individual currencies transferred through the budget are consistent with the member's gross holding of gold and foreign exchange (q.v.) reserves and with the need for the Fund to maintain minimum working balances in all currencies.

The operational budget is a practical example of members co-operating within the institution. Members that are in strong balance of payments and reserve positions make resources available to members experiencing balance of payments difficulties. In preparing the budget, the Fund makes a projection of the overall use of its resources that will be required in the following quarter and assesses which currencies will be available to use in drawings by other members. The purpose of the exercise is to ensure that only the stronger currencies are used, temporarily, to help the weaker currencies.

Organization of the Fund. The organizational structure of the Fund is set out in its Articles of Agreement (q.v.). They provide for a Board of Governors, an Executive Board, a Managing Director, and a staff (qq.v.) of international civil servants. The highest authority in the Fund is the Board of Governors, which consists of one Governor and one Alternate Governor appointed by each of the Fund's members. The Governors are usually ministers of finance or heads of central banks. The second amendment to the Articles provided for the Board of Governors to establish a Council as a permanent body at the ministerial level to supervise the management and functioning of the international monetary system (q.v.) and to consider any proposals to amend the Articles of Agreement, but the

Board has not done so. Instead, the Interim Committee (q.v.), which was to have been a temporary committee to precede the establishment of the Council, has remained in existence. In 1974, the Board of Governors also established the Development Committee (q.v.) to advise and report to the Fund and Bank Boards of Governors on developing issues.

The Board of Governors has delegated many of its powers to the Executive Board, which is the day-to-day decisionmaking authority. The Executive Board selects the Managing Director (q.v.) of the Fund, who serves as its Chairman and the head of the Fund's staff. The Deputy Managing Directors (q.v.) are selected by the Managing Director, subject to the approval of the Executive Board.

Beneath the Office of the Managing Director, and reporting directly to it, are 16 Departments, two Bureaus, two offices and a Secretariat at headquarters, and four offices outside Fund headquarters.

The Departments consist of six area departments, African, Asia and Pacific, European I, European II, Middle Eastern, and Western Hemisphere; eight functional and special services departments, Fiscal Affairs, IMF Institute, Legal, Monetary and Exchange Affairs, Policy Development and Review, Research, Statistics, and Treasurer's, and an information and liaison department, External Relations; and two support services department, Administration and Secretary's.

The area departments advise management and the Board on the economies and economic policies of the countries in their areas, assist in the formulation of Fund policies toward these countries, and carry out these policies. Area departments also negotiate arrangements for the use of Fund financial resources (q.v.) and review performance under Fund-supported arrangements. Together with other departments, the area departments provide member countries with policy advice and technical assistance and maintain contact with regional organizations and multilateral institutions in their area. Much of the Fund's bilateral surveillance (q.v.) work is carried out by the area departments through their direct contacts with member countries, supplemented by staff in functional departments. More than 70 staff members are assigned to countries as resident representatives.

Functional and special services departments are individually responsible for a wide range of activities. The Fiscal Affairs Department is responsible for all activities involving the public finance of member countries. It participates in area department missions on fiscal matters, reviews the fiscal content of Fund policy advice and of Fund-supported adjustment programs (q.v.), and provides technical assistance in public finance. It also conducts research and policy studies on fiscal issues, as well as on income distribution and poverty, social safety nets, public expenditure policy issues, and the environment.

The IMF Institute provides technical assistance through training officials of member countries, particularly developing countries (q.v.), in such topics as financial programming (q.v.) and policy, external sector polities, balance of payments (q.v.) and government statistics, and public finance.

The Legal Department advises management, the Board, and the staff on the applicable rules of law. It prepares most of the decisions and other legal instruments necessary for Fund activities. It serves as counsel to the Fund in litigation and arbitration cases, provides technical assistance on legislative reform in member countries, and responds to inquiries from national authorities and international organizations on the law of the Fund.

The Monetary and Exchange Affairs Department provides technical assistance to central banks in such areas as monetary (q.v.) and exchange rate policies, banking supervision, and prudential regulation, and on issues related to payments systems. Experts are assigned to central banks requesting assistance. The department works with area departments by reviewing topics in the area of its expertise in the context of surveillance and requests for the use of Fund resources, and contributes to the exercise of Fund jurisdiction on exchange practices and restrictions.

The Policy Development and Review Department plays a central role in the design and implementation of Fund financial facilities and operations, in surveillance policies, and in other areas. Together with the Research Department, it takes a lead in the areas of multilateral surveillance, policy coordination, and associated review and support activities. With area departments, it helps to mobilize other financial resources for members using Fund assistance, including work on debt and program financing (through the Paris Club [q.v.] and international banks).

The Research Department carries out policy analysis and research in areas relating to the Fund's work. The department also plays a prominent role in the development of Fund policy concerning the international monetary system (q.v.) and surveillance. It cooperates with other departments in formulating the Fund's policy advice to member countries. It also coordinates the semiannual World Economic Outlook (q.v.) exercise and the *International Capital Markets Report*, as well as analysis for the Group of Seven (q.v.) policy coordination exercise and for the Board's seminars on World Economic and Market Developments. The department also develops the Fund's contacts with the academic community and with other research organizations.

The Statistics Department maintains a data base of country, regional, and global economic and financial statistics and reviews country data in support of the Fund's surveillance role. It is also responsible for developing statistical concepts in balance of payments, government finance, and money and financial statistics, and for producing methodological manuals. The department provides technical assistance and training to help members to develop statistical systems and produces the Fund's statistical publications. In addition, it is responsible for the development and maintenance of standards for the dissemination of data by member countries.

The main functions of the Treasurer's Department are formulating the Fund's financial policies and practices; conducting financial operations and transactions in the General Department, the SDR Department (q.v.), and the Administered Accounts (including the enhanced structural adjustment facility [ESAF] (q.v.) Trust and related accounts); controlling expenditures under the administrative and capital budgets (q.v.); and maintaining the Fund's accounts and financial records. The department's responsibilities include work on quotas, borrowing, the Fund's liquidity (qq.v.), the Fund's policies on the SDR (q.v.), its policies on its currency and gold (qq.v.) holdings, and its policies on accounting and on financing its capital projects and expenditures.

The External Relations Department is responsible for the editing, production, and distribution of the Fund's nonstatistical publications; providing information services to the press and the general public; and maintaining contacts with nongovernmental organizations and parliamentary bodies.

The Fund's offices in Geneva, Paris, Tokyo, and the special representative in New York at the United Nations maintain close contacts with other international and regional institutions in the areas of their responsibilities.

The Fund's support services are provided by the Administration Department and the Secretary's Department. The Administration Department manages recruitment, training, and career planning programs; supervises the operations of the headquarters building and leased space; provides administrative services to the Fund; and administers the Joint Fund-Bank Library (q.v.). The Secretary's Department assists in preparing and coordinating the work program of the Board and other official bodies, including scheduling and assisting in the conduct of Board meetings. The department also manages the Annual Meetings (q.v.), in cooperation with the World Bank (q.v.), and is responsible for the Fund's archives (q.v.), communications, and security program.

The Fund's bureaus and offices (at headquarters) are responsible for such aspects as computer services, language services, auditing, budget matters, technical assistance, work practices, and investment under the staff retirement plan. *See also* Staff of the Fund.

Ossola Group. The Ossola Group was established by the Deputies of the Group of Ten (q.v.) in June 1964 to study the various proposals for the creation of reserve assets (q.v.), headed by Rinaldo Ossola, of the Bank of Italy. The Group's report, submitted in May 1965, was an important step in the subsequent formulation of the Special Drawing Rights (q.v.) facility.

Ouattara, Alassane D. (1942-). Alassane Ouattara was appointed a Deputy Managing Director of the Fund in 1994. He studied at the Drexel Institute of Technology and the University of Pennsylvania, where he received his Ph.D. in economics. He joined the staff (q.v.) of the Fund in 1968 as an economist in the African Department, leaving in 1973 to join the Central Bank for West African States (BCEAO), where he became Vice Governor in 1983. He rejoined the Fund's staff in November 1984 as Director of the African Department and was appointed Counselor in May 1987. Ouattara returned to the BCEAO as Governor in November 1988, was appointed Chairman of the Economic Committee of the Government of Côte d'Ivoire in April 1990, and between November 1990 and December 1993, served as Prime Minister of Côte d'Ivoire.

Overby, Andrew (1909-1984). Andrew Overby, who had been

appointed to the Executive Board (q.v.) by the United States in July 1947, was appointed as Deputy Managing Director (q.v.) from February 1949 to January 1952. He was formerly Assistant Vice President of the Federal Reserve Bank of New York, and immediately before becoming Deputy Managing Director was Special Assistant to the Secretary of the Treasury in charge of international and monetary affairs.

Overdue Obligations to the Fund. Members' overdue obligations to the Fund began to be a serious problem in the second half of the 1980s. In the financial year ending April 30, 1986, 11 members had obligations overdue by six months or more, amounting to a total of SDR 489 million. The amount overdue rose dramatically in the following years, reaching a peak of SDR 3.5 billion at the end of the 1991-92 financial year, accounted for by 10 members. By April 30, 1998, total arrears (q.v.) had fallen to SDR 2.3 billion, and the number of delinquent members had fallen to seven, after rising to a peak of 12 five years earlier. On April 30, 1998, seven members—Liberia, Sierra Leone, Somalia, Sudan, Vietnam, Zaire, and Zambia—had been declared ineligible to use the Fund's resources (q.v.) and three of them, Liberia, Sudan, and Zaire, had been declared to be not cooperating with the Fund.

In 1990, the Fund introduced a strengthened cooperative strategy on overdue obligations, consisting of three key elements—prevention, deterrence, and intensified collaboration. Preventive measures seek to make certain that adjustment (q.v.) programs are drawn up so that members will be able to meet their obligations to the Fund when they fall due. Potential risks and dangers are highlighted, and every effort is made to address these risks in the design, implementation, and financing of the program. Deterrent and remedial measures include a tightening of the timetable for dealing with members with overdue obligations by shortening the period between the emergence of arrears and the declaration of ineligibility (q.v.) and by setting a specific date for a declaration of noncooperation and the initiation of the procedures for compulsory withdrawal.

The collaborative approach requires the "ineligible" member to embark on and adhere to an adjustment program that is monitored by the Fund. Although the member would not be eligible to receive Fund financing, successful completion of the program, together with clearance of its arrears to the Fund, would place it in a position to acquire "rights" (q.v.) to use the Fund's financing under a successor program. The member would be expected to obtain the financing and other assistance needed for a Fund-monitored program from a support group, whose assembly would be encouraged by the Fund. At a minimum, the financing generated for such a program would include funds to settle financial obligations falling due to the Fund and the World Bank (q.v.) during the program period. The rights approach allows a member following a comprehensive economic program to restore its good standing in the Fund and accumulate rights toward future drawings. Encashment of accumulated rights would take place only after clearance of arrears to the Fund and would be associated with a successor financial arrangement. The new program would involve some Fund financing beyond that provided for the encashment of rights.

-P-

Par Value System. The par value system established at the Bretton Woods Conference (q.v.) was a major departure from the experience in the period between World War I and World War II, when countries held the view, and acted accordingly, that the setting of an exchange rate was a sovereign decision and beyond the purview of other countries. In addition to bringing exchange rates under international supervision, a second objective of the Bretton Woods system (q.v.) was to avoid the rigidity of the gold (q.v.) standard and establish a stable system of exchange rates, but at the same time allow them to be adjusted, with the approval of the Fund, if a country was faced with a fundamental disequilibrium (q.v.) in its balance of payments (q.v.).

The rules for operating the par value system were both broad and specific. Competitive exchange (q.v.) alterations were forbidden. The value of each member's currency (q.v.) was fixed in terms of gold (q.v.) or in terms of the U.S. dollar of the weight and fineness in effect on July 1, 1944. The fixed rate (q.v.) of exchange of one currency against another was determined by the ratio between the two currencies based on their par values (q.v.), and transactions had to be kept within a specified margin of 1 percent either side of parity. Floating exchange rates (q.v.) were not allowed, although temporary floating in order to reach a viable par value for a currency was tolerated in a few cases by the Fund. Exchange systems were to be unitary; multiple currency practices (q.v.), discriminatory exchange rates, and exchange restrictions (q.v.) were to be outlawed.

The Bretton Woods par value system was fatally disrupted on August 15, 1971, when the United States suspended the conversion of official dollar balances into gold, and it finally expired in March 1973 when all the major trading countries had resorted to letting their currencies float on the world's exchange markets (q.v.). The second amendment to the Articles of Agreement (q.v.) legalized the freely floating exchange rate system (q.v.) that had emerged, but included provisions for a return to a par value system (one that would not be based on gold) if 85 percent of the total voting power of the Board of Governors (q.v.) voted in favor of its restoration. *See also* International Monetary System; Reform of the International Monetary System.

Par Values. Par values were the central feature of the Bretton Woods system (q.v.). The Articles of Agreement (q.v.) gave the Fund authority to bring exchange rates under international supervision. Exchange rates were to be unitary, fair, and no longer regarded as the sole preserve of national authorities. Under the Bretton Woods system, a member had to notify the Fund of the initial par value of its currency (q.v.) expressed in terms of gold (q.v.) as a common denominator or in terms of the U.S. dollar of the weight and fineness in effect on July 1, 1944. Agreement of the Fund was necessary when an initial par value was communicated to the Fund, and the concurrence of the Fund was required when a change in par value was proposed going beyond a cumulative 10 percent from the initial par value. A member was entitled to change the par value of its currency after consulting with and obtaining the concurrence of the Fund, but only to correct a fundamental disequilibrium (q.v.) in its balance of payments (q.v.). Temporary balance of payments disequilibria were not grounds for a change in a par value. The member was expected to finance short-term disequilibria, with the assistance of the Fund's financial resources (q.v.), if necessary. Exchange transactions taking place in the territory of a member were not permitted to differ from parity by more than 1 percent for spot transactions.

Paris Club. The Paris Club is an informal group of creditor governments mainly from industrial countries that has met regularly in Paris since 1956, with the French Treasury providing the Secretariat. The Club assumed importance after many developing countries (q.v.) in the 1970s incurred a sharp increase in external debt (q.v.) that led to debt-servicing difficulties and to payment arrears (q.v.). Meetings of the Club are usually called on the initiative of the debtor country in order to bring all its creditors together at one meeting to discuss possibilities of a multilateral debt relief, instead of bilateral negotiations with each creditor. In addition to the debtor and creditor countries, meetings are attended by the Fund, the World Bank (q.v.), the Organization for Economic Cooperation and Development, and the United Nations Conference on Trade and Development. The international organizations do not attend in official capacities, but provide technical assistance (q.v.) and information. The Fund's role is primarily to act as a "go-between," to help the debtor country prepare its submission to the meeting and, if requested, to make presentations analyzing the impact that various levels of debt restructuring would have on the debtor's financial programming (q.v.) and its balance of payments (q.v.) situation over the medium term. Over the years, the meetings of the Paris Club became more formal, and debt relief became linked to an understanding that a debtor country would enter into a stand-by arrangement (q.v.) with the Fund to implement a stabilization program (q.v.).

In the 1980s, the Paris Club became extremely active, and the Fund also took the initiative in embarking on a more innovative and broader role in multilateral debt negotiations. At first, in its early attempts to provide relief in the new indebted situation, the Club creditors provided reschedulings for low-income countries on nonconcessional standard terms, with relatively short grace (five years) and maturity periods (10 years), and on market-related interest rates. Many countries, however, continued to have difficulties in adhering to their new payments schedules and it became obvious that such repeated reschedulings over a prolonged period would not solve their debt problems. In the late 1980s, therefore, the Paris Club creditors, meeting in Toronto, agreed to provide concessional rescheduling on what became to be known as the Toronto menu (q.v.)—a menu of options for debt and debt-service reduction to reduce the net present value of rescheduled amounts by up to one-third. These new terms provide substantial relief, but within a few years it again became obvious that more far-reaching measures would be required. Thus, meeting in London in December 1991, creditors introduced what came to be known as the London terms, which increased the level of debt relief up to 50 percent. Subsequently, meeting in Naples at the end of 1994, the level of concessionality was increased to 67 percent—the Naples terms.

Under the Naples terms eligibility is determined on a case-by-case basis, based primarily on a country's income level. Most countries receive a reduction in eligible nonofficial development assistance debt of 67 percent of net present value terms, with somewhat less easier terms for countries with a per capita income of $500 or more and a ratio of debt to exports in present value terms of less than 350 percent. The coverage of the debt to be included in the rescheduling is also decided on a case-by-case basis, but previously rescheduled debts are not excluded from the Naples terms. Creditors have a choice of two concessional options: a debt reduction option, with repayment over 23 years with a six-year grace period, or, a debt-service reduction option, under which the net present value reduction is achieved by concessional interest rates, with repayments over 33 years. There is a third option that allows creditors to enter into a commercial or long-term maturities option, providing for no net present value reduction, with repayment of 40 years with 20 years' grace. Finally, a stock-of-debt operation is available under which the entire stock of eligible debt is rescheduled concessionally. This option is reserved for countries with a satisfactory track record for a minimum of three years with respect to both payments under rescheduling agreements and performance under Fund arrangements. Creditors must be confident that the country will be able to respect the debt agreement as an exit rescheduling (with no further rescheduling required), and there must be a consensus among creditors to choose concessional options.

To ensure concerted support by the international community, Paris Club rescheduling agreements include a comparability clause under which the rescheduling country commits itself to seek at least comparable debt relief from commercial and non-Paris Club bilateral creditors.

On September 30, 1997, 31 countries had graduated from reschedulings, made up of eight low-income countries, 11 lower-middle-income countries, and 12 other middle-income countries. At that time, another 22 countries had rescheduling agreements in effect, of which 17 were low income, three were lower-middle-income, and two were other. A further 14 countries, mostly low-income, had had previous rescheduling agreements, but had not graduated from reschedulings and were without current agreements. All told, a total of 67 countries were or had been participating in the Paris Club debt-relief operation.

Payments Arrears. *See* Arrears in Payments.

Pegging of Exchange Rates. After the collapse of the fixed exchange rate system (q.v.) in 1973, each country was faced with the choice of letting its currency float freely in the exchange market (q.v.) (and thus have its value determined by supply and demand) or of pegging to another currency or composite unit. While the national monetary authorities (q.v.) of the major currencies (q.v.), such as the U.S. dollar, the Japanese yen, and the deutsche mark, chose to allow their currencies to float (the deutsche mark in the context of the European Monetary System [q.v.]), many smaller economies chose to peg their currencies to one of the major currencies, to a composite unit made up of a basket of currencies of their main trading partners, or to the SDR (q.v.). On April 30, 1997, 21 currencies were pegged to the U.S. dollar, 15 to the French franc, and nine currencies to other single currencies; 22 currencies were pegged to a composite currency, (including two to the SDR); 16 had a flexible arrangement (12 linked under a cooperative agreement and four to a single currency); 47 currencies were operating under a managed float; and nine currencies were floating independently. *See also* Crawling Pegs; Floating Exchange Rates.

Per Jacobsson Foundation. Established in 1964, the Per Jacobsson Foundation was founded as a permanent memorial to Per Jacobsson (q.v.), the third Managing Director (q.v.) of the Fund, who died in office in May 1963. The Foundation was sponsored by the Fund, the Bank for International Settlements (q.v.), and a group of 45 former finance ministers, heads of central banks, and other friends of Per Jacobsson.

The Foundation sponsors a lecture series, to be given by an authority in the field of international economics and finance. The lectures are usually held annually at the same time and place as the Fund-World Bank Annual Meetings (q.v.) and are thus convened for two consecutive years in Washington, D.C., followed by a meeting every third year outside the United States.

Peru. The government that took office in 1990 immediately began to address the crisis facing the Peruvian economy by carrying out a program of macroeconomic adjustment and structural reform aimed at sharply reducing inflation, and creating the conditions for sustained economic growth and a progressive return to external viability. At that time, Peru had heavy external indebtedness and had overdue obligations (q.v.) to the Fund. The program was initially supported by a Fund-monitored rights accumulation program (RAP) (q.v.) through the end of 1992. Following through on the improvement of economic performance under that program, the government developed a three-year program that was supported by an extended Fund arrangement (EFF) in an amount equivalent to SDR 1,018 million (about $1,467 million), which expired in March 1996. After an initial disbursement of SDR 642.7 million (about $926 million), Peru opted not to make any further drawings (q.v.) under the arrangement. All quantitative performance criteria through December 1995 were met with margins to spare, reflecting an impressive real performance; during 1993-95, output grew at an average of 8.5 percent a year, inflation was reduced to 10 percent during 1995, and the net international reserve (q.v.) position of the Central Reserve Bank improved significantly. These results were the fruits of prudent fiscal and monetary polices (q.v.), a comprehensive program of structural reform, and continued support from the international financial community, including Paris Club (q.v.) rescheduling of debt.

In July 1996, the Fund approved a second three-year extended arrangement in the amount equivalent to SDR 248.3 million (about $358 million) in support of the government's medium-term economic and reform program during the period 1996-98. Building on the progress that had been made under the previous program, performance under the new program was again strong. In 1997, output grew by 7.4 percent, inflation dropped to 6.5 percent, from 11.8 percent in 1996, and the external current account narrowed somewhat. About two-thirds of the external current account was covered by long-term capital flows, and the net international reserves of the Central Reserve Bank rose by $1.6 billion in 1997, with gross reserves reaching the equivalent of nearly 12 months of goods and services by the end of the year. This performance took place in the context of a flexible exchange rate regime, with open trade and capital account. As in the previous years, all performance criteria under the program were observed.

During 1997, the Fund supported a disbursement of SDR 160.5 million (about $223 million) to support Peru's debt and debt-service reduction operation with its external commercial creditors. After the completion of this operation, the ratio of Peru's debt-service obligations to commercial banks was reduced to 3.1 percent of exports of goods and nonfactor services in 1997, from 7.4 percent in 1995. A debt rescheduling, granted in July 1996 by the Paris Club creditors, provided additional debt relief over the medium term, substantially improving the prospects of Peru's external viability by the end of 1998.

In a May 1998 Letter of Intent to the Fund from the Minister of Economy and the President of the Central Reserve Bank, it was noted that, as in previous years, all performance criteria had been observed in 1997; real GDP rose by 7.4 percent, the external current account deficit narrowed to 5.2 percent, and net international reserves rose by $1.6 billion. In 1998, as a result of the adverse affects on the economy by El Niño, real GDP was expected to grow 4-5 percent, with inflation in the range of 7 to 9 percent. The efforts to reduce tax evasion would be intensified, government expenditure kept under strict control, and the flexible exchange rate policy maintained. The government would continue to implement its policy on privatization, reform the pension system, continue in its efforts to improve education and health, and maintain open trade, capital, and exchange regimes. Finally, it would be the main priority of the government's program to reduce poverty (q.v.), it being noted that the share of the population living in extreme poverty had been reduced from 24 percent in 1991 to 18 percent in 1996 and that access to basic services, such as drinking water and electricity, had increased significantly over the past five years.

Philippines. At the time that the economic and financial crisis spread through Southeast Asia, the Philippines was in the third year of a Fund-assisted program under its extended Fund facility (EFF) (q.v.) that was due to expire on July 23, 1997. While the macroeconomic program remained broadly on track in the first quarter of 1997, the economy began to face a number of stresses in the second quarter, including increasing turbulence in the foreign ex-change (q.v.) market, slippages in fiscal performance, and delay in the passage of proposed tax reforms. Following the float of the Thai baht on July 2, 1997, the foreign exchange market in the Philippines came under increased pressure, causing a significant depletion in the Philippines' international reserves (q.v.).

The authorities responded decisively to the pressures on the peso by floating the currency on July 11 and supporting this action by strong fiscal and monetary policies (q.v.). They requested an extension and augmentation of the EFF program until the end of 1997 to allow passage of tax reforms and completion of the final review of the EFF credit, and also to support their action to float the peso to discourage speculative capital flows. The amount under the EFF credit, originally set at $650 million, was augmented by an additional $435 million, bringing the total immediately available to the Philippines to about $700 million.

Under the extended program, the government sought passage of a comprehensive tax reform package, to strengthen the financial sector by the adoption of measures to tighten the limits of exposure of banks to the real estate market, to discourage the growth of foreign currency liabilities through new liquidity requirements, and by removing tax disincentives to peso deposits.

At the end of March 1998, the Fund approved financial assistance amounting to $1.4 billion under a two-year stand-by arrangement (q.v.). The arrangement was regarded as a precautionary measure and the authorities had expressed their intention to draw on it only if necessary. The program under the stand-by addressed the dual goals of managing the current crisis while creating the conditions for sustained growth over the medium term, providing for an orderly adjustment to lower capital inflows in the wake of the crisis. The main macroeconomic objectives for 1998 and 1999 were to contain the slowdown of real GDP growth to 3 percent in 1998 and to 5 percent in 1999; limit inflation to 8 percent in 1998 and to 6 percent in 1999; and reduce the current account deficit to 3.1 percent of GNP in 1998 and 2.7 percent in 1999, compared with a 5.7 percent deficit in 1997. The program also included banking sector reforms, such as increasing capital requirements, tightening regulatory oversight, and dealing with problem banks.

The program also addressed the need to reduce poverty (q.v.), on which progress had lagged behind other countries in the region. This involved a strengthening of agriculture and improvements in education and health services, with a focus on primary education and the rural areas.

On October 30, 1998, the Fund's Deputy Managing Director, Shigemitsu Sugisaki (qq.v.), announced that the Executive Board (q.v.) had completed first and second reviews under the stand-by credit and had approved the release of the first credit tranche (q.v.), amounting to $280 million, for the Philippines. The Philippine authorities had decided to draw on the credit, which up to that point they had treated as precautionary. The statement also said that the program had been modified to take into account the continued difficult economic environment and to incorporate the policy agenda of the new government, which had taken office in July 1998. The revised program for 1998-99 aimed at deepening the stabilization gained, cushioning the impact of the financial crisis on vulnerable sections of the population, and setting the stage for an early, strong, and sustainable recovery. Sugisaki emphasized the need for the government to proceed quickly and forcefully with the structural reform agenda, with emphasis on banking, tax, and public reform issues. *See also* Asian Financial Crisis.

Plaza Agreement. Meeting at the Plaza Hotel, New York, in September 1985, the Group of Five (q.v.) reached an understanding on a specific coordinated action to intervene in the exchange markets (q.v.) to reduce the value of the U.S. dollar. In the succeeding months, the monetary authorities (q.v.) of the five countries sold U.S. dollars in their markets and brought about a substantial reduction in the value of the dollar. Meeting at the Louvre Palace, Paris, in February 1987, the Group of Seven (q.v.) announced that existing exchange rates were broadly consistent with the economic fundamentals and they would "cooperate closely to foster stability around current levels." The lessons of that episode were variously interpreted: some commentators saw it as an example of what coordinated policy action could achieve; others felt that the value of the dollar was due to decline in any event, and that central bank intervention had only assisted in the movement of the market. *See also* Louvre Accord.

Polak, Jacques J. (1914-). Jacques J. Polak, of the Netherlands, joined the staff of the Fund in 1947, became Director of the Research Department in June 1958, and later, while he continued to hold that position, was appointed Economic Counselor (q.v.). After his retirement from the staff of the Fund in 1979, Polak served briefly as advisor to the Managing Director (q.v.) and then, in January 1981, he was elected as Executive Director (q.v.) for the constituency of Cyprus, Israel, the Netherlands, Romania, and Yugoslavia. Polak contributed greatly to the work of the Fund by furthering its research work (he was a leading exponent of the monetary approach to the balance of payments [q.v.]) and by the development of the Fund's operational policies. He also made a particular contribution in the 1960s with his analytical work on international liquidity (q.v.) and was a leading authority and proponent on the establishment of Special Drawing Rights (SDRs) (q.v.), the world's first international reserve asset (q.v.) to be created by international treaty. *See also* Monetary Approach to Balance of Payments.

Poland. Poland was an original member of the Fund, but withdrew voluntarily from membership in 1950 on the grounds that the Fund was no more than a mouthpiece for the U.S. government. It rejoined the Fund in 1986 and since then has been one of the most successful economies of the East European countries. Poland adopted an ambitious economic program supported by a stand-by arrangement (q.v.) in 1990 with the aim of reducing hyperinflation and shifting the economy to market mechanisms, involving measures to liberalize prices and the foreign exchange (q.v.) and trade systems, as well as introducing a wide range of market economy institutions. Poland continued its program of converting to a free-market economy with the support of a series of arrangements with the Fund through 1996, making only partial drawings (q.v.) on the finances available to it, and for the most part reducing its debtor position in the Fund.

In concluding the Executive Board's (q.v.) Article IV consultations (q.v.) with Poland in March 1998, it was noted that Poland had been able to combine strong economic growth—the fastest in Eastern and Central Europe over the previous four years—with substantial declines in inflation. Close to two-thirds of all jobs in the economy were in the private sector, illustrating that the country's transition was firmly on track. Strong investment-spending and the fastest real retail sales since the transition began resulted in a real GDP growth of 6.9 percent during 1997 (compared with increases of 6.1 percent in 1996 and 7.0 percent in 1995) with a marked decline in unemployment. The strong domestic demand, however, had led to a deterioration in the current account of the balance of payments (q.v.), from a surplus of more than 3 percent of GDP in 1995 to a 3.2 percent deficit in 1997.

The monetary authorities (q.v.) tightened policy several times in 1997, both by raising reserve requirements and raising interest rates. In the foreign exchange market, the zloty, which was being managed via a currency (q.v.) basket arrangement with a plus or minus 7 percent band and a crawling (q.v.) central rate that was allowed to depreciate by one percent each month, weakened in the second half of 1997 under the impact of the Asian currency gyrations, but strengthened markedly in the first three months of 1998.

The Fund's Executive Directors (q.v.) praised the Polish authorities for the progress that had been made in advancing structural reforms and saw Poland as a leader among the transitional economies (q.v.). Nevertheless, they expressed concern that the current account position had deteriorated sharply over the past two years, mainly because they considered real domestic demand had been increasing at an unsustainable rate. The main challenges for economic policy in 1998 were to stabilize the current account and maintain the momentum of disinflation, which in the previous four years had fallen dramatically from 37.6 percent in 1993 to about 13 percent in 1997.

Policies on the Use of Fund Resources. *See* Use of Fund Resources.

Poverty and Fund-Supported Adjustment Programs. As governments of developing countries (q.v.) increasingly took steps in the 1970s and early 1980s to respond to adverse shocks and to correct for earlier excess borrowing and spending, the burden of these adjustments often fell on the most vulnerable groups in society. Social disturbances occurred in several countries, resulting from the severe strains caused by adjustment programs (q.v.). The Fund came under increasing criticism from nongovernmental organizations (NGOs), academics, and other organizations for paying insufficient attention to the social consequences of its adjustment programs. In March 1989, in a letter published in major newspapers, the Fund's Managing Director, Michel Camdessus (qq.v.), responded to this criticism by pointing out that it was the prerogative of member states to decide for themselves what measures were required for recovery, however unpleasant those measures might be.

The Fund's staff (q.v.), however, carried out much research on the effect of adjustment programs and on how their adverse effects could be mitigated. In a number of cases it could demonstrate to the relevant government authorities what effects a program would have on income distribution, and provide them with alternative scenarios. Nevertheless, the staff has not been able to come up with a watertight theory defining the relationship of income distribution to economic growth and, thus, is unable to recommend to governments the "right" type of income distribution that should result from structural adjustments. As a result of this work, however, the Fund is able to focus on programs that benefit the poor, to help in setting up social safety nets for the disadvantaged, to target subsidy programs to those who really need them, and, in general, to streamline and make more efficient, at less cost, existing social programs. Many countries implementing Fund-supported adjustment programs, particularly those of the former Soviet Union (FSU) and Africa, have benefited from the Fund's advice and technical assistance (q.v.) in improving their social policies (q.v.), including the establishment and reform of safety nets.

Press Information Notices. *See* Public Information Notices.

Price Controls. The Fund is a strong advocate of eliminating price controls, which hide underlying inflationary pressures, distort demand and production, and bring about bureaucratic rigidities in the economy. The freeing of prices, or setting them at realistic levels, is often a central feature of Fund-supported adjustment programs (q.v.), whether it be for agriculture, consumer goods, public services, interest rates, or foreign exchange (q.v.) rates.

Public Information Notices (PINs). On April 25, 1997, the Executive Board (q.v.) agreed to the issuance of Press Information Notices (PINs), subsequently called Public Information Notices, following the conclusion of Article IV consultation (q.v.)

discussions, for those members seeking to make known to the public the Fund's views about their economies.

The action, taken after the experience of growing, and sometimes volatile, capital flows was intended to strengthen the Fund's surveillance (q.v.) over the economic policies of member countries by increasing the transparency of the Fund's assessment of these policies, while preserving the integrity and confidentiality of the Article IV consultation process.

PINs are issued at the request of the member country shortly after the Executive Board discussion. They consist of a background section with factual information on the member country's economy and the Fund's assessment of the member country's economic policies and prospects, as reflected in the Executive Board's discussion of the Article IV review of the member country.

The first PIN was issued on May 27, 1997, and by the end of May 1998 74 PINs had been issued. The full texts of PINs are available on the Fund's web site (http//www.imf.org), and beginning in 1998 PINs were also reproduced in a Fund publication entitled, *IMF Economic Reviews*, which appears three times a year containing all the PINs that have been issued in the preceding four-month period. The publication carries the summary material on Article VI consultations previously included in the *Annual Report of the Executive Board* (q.v.).

Publications of the Fund. *See* Documents and Information; bibliography.

Purchases of Currency from the Fund. When a member uses the Fund's resources (q.v.), it purchases needed usable currencies (q.v.) by exchanging its own currency. Thus, for example, a member's initial position in the Fund may be a subscription (q.v.) held by the Fund consisting of 25 percent in SDRs (q.v.) and 75 percent in the member's domestic currency. When the country makes a drawing (q.v.) on the Fund, it purchases usable currency with its own currency. As a result, the Fund's holdings of the currency of the member making the drawing will rise and its holdings of usable currencies (such as U.S. dollars, deutsche mark, yen, and others) will fall. Similarly, repayments to the Fund will be effected by a reverse procedure, with the member repurchasing its own currency by providing a designated usable currency to the Fund.

The cycle of purchase and repurchase operations, effected over the short- to medium-term, illustrates the cooperative concept on which the Fund was founded. A member, by purchasing usable currency with its own currency, and then subsequently repurchasing its own currency with a usable currency designated by the Fund, returns to its initial accounting position, of being neither a debtor nor a creditor to the Fund. In this manner also, the Fund maintains its resources in the form of a revolving pool of currencies that can be drawn upon by members, always on the understanding that repurchases (q.v.) will be executed over the medium term. Technically speaking, therefore, Fund operations consist of purchases and repurchases, and are not loans and repayments.

In practice, only relatively few currencies held by the Fund are usable in international payments. The Fund draws up quarterly operational budgets (q.v.) based on estimates of the likely use of the Fund's resources and establishes the amounts for those currencies whose countries' economic positions and international reserves (q.v.) are sufficiently strong to be used in Fund operations and international payments.

-Q-

Quota Reviews. The Fund is required by its Articles of Agreement (q.v.) to conduct, at intervals of not more than five years, a general review of quotas and propose any adjustments that it deems appropriate. It may also, if it thinks fit, consider at any other time the adjustment of any particular quota (q.v.) at the request of the member concerned.

The Fund has completed eleven general reviews of quotas since it was founded, although in September 1998 the eleventh had yet to be fully subscribed and come into effect. The first general increase in quotas took place in 1959, when membership (q.v.) in the Fund had risen to 69, an increase of 40 members since 1945. A general increase of 50 percent in quotas, as well as special increases for four countries, raised total quotas to SDR 14.6 billion. No increase in quotas was proposed in the third quinquennial review, but the fourth general review (1965) and the fifth general review (1970) each approved general increases of 25 percent, raising total quotas to SDR 28.8 billion, with a membership of 116 countries. The sixth general review (1976) resulted in a substantial increase in total quotas, with increases distributed among members in a way that would provide more balance among the different groups of countries. The seventh general review (1978) raised total quotas by 50 percent; the eighth (1983) by 19 percent, along with substantial increases for individual countries; and the ninth (1990) by 50 percent, bringing total quotas to about SDR 145 billion.

By the end of the fiscal year, April 30, 1995, payments of quota increases under the ninth general review had been completed by all members that had consented to their increases. Including the quotas of new members, this brought the total amount of Fund quotas to SDR 145 billion. At the end of April 1995, six members had overdue obligations to the Fund's General Resources Account (qq.v.) and, as provided for in the Board of Governors (q.v.) Resolution on the ninth general review of quotas, they could not consent to their quota increase until their arrears (q.v.) were cleared.

The ninth general review of quotas was completed seven years after the previous review, and this delay in its completion meant that the tenth general review, which was to have been completed by March 31, 1993, in accordance with the five-yearly timetable specified in the Articles of Agreement, had to be extended. In December 1994, the Executive Board (q.v.) concluded that the ninth general review, which was then still being implemented, would provide the Fund with substantial additional usable resources and that the tenth general review should be concluded without an increase in quota.

The eleventh general review of quotas was completed early in January 1997, when the Board of Governors adopted a Resolution proposing an increase of 45 percent in the total Fund quotas, to approximately SDR 212 billion (about $288 billion) from SDR 146 billion. With the resurgence of a U.S. Congress dominated by the Republican Party after the 1996 congressional elections, resistance to U.S. participation in the quota increase stiffened, reflecting a variety of reasons ranging from a general distrust of international organizations, to a belief that adjustments to national economies were best left to free-market forces and that the policies and structure of the Fund, in any case, required radical reform.

Quotas. A member's quota in the Fund establishes its fundamental relationship with the organization. It determines how much the member will subscribe to the Fund, its maximum access (q.v.) to financing, its voting strength, and its share in Special Drawing Right (SDR) (q.v.) allocations.

The amount of a member's quota is expressed in terms of SDRs and is equal to the subscription (q.v.) the member must pay, in full, to the Fund. Up to 25 percent of the subscription is paid in reserve assets (q.v.) specified by the Fund (SDRs or usable currencies) and the remainder in the member's own currency. The maximum access of a member to Fund resources (q.v.), no matter to what facilities or under what policies, is determined in proportion to its quota. Similarly, allocations (q.v.) of SDRs are made to all participants as a percentage of quotas. Each member has 250 basic votes plus an additional vote for each SDR 100,000 of quota.

The size of members' quotas in the Fund is determined mainly by economic factors, but a judgmental approach is used to make the final determination. The original quotas in the Fund were determined in large part by the so-called Bretton Woods formula, which took into account such basic economic variables as the values of annual average import and export flows, gold (q.v.) holdings and U.S. dollar balances, and national income. In the 1960s, this formula was revised and has since undergone various permutations, changing the components of the formula and the weights attached to them, and using as many as 10 formulas in a single quota review (q.v.) for comparative purposes. The central purpose is to measure, in as comprehensive a way as possible, members' relative economic positions in the world economy.

-R-

Reconstitution of Special Drawing Rights (SDRs). Compulsory reconstitution of SDRs (q.v.) was a feature of the SDR facility from its inception in 1969 to April 1981, when the requirement was abrogated. At the time of the facility's inception, participants were obligated to maintain over a five-year period average holdings of SDRs at 30 percent of their net cumulative allocations (q.v.). In the ensuing years, however, as changes were made to widen the uses of SDRs and to increase the interest rate on holdings of SDRs to near market levels, the compulsory holding requirement was no longer considered necessary. Participants, however, are still expected to maintain over time a balanced relationship between their holdings of SDRs and their other reserves (q.v.).

Reconstitution was one of several difficult and divisive issues that preceded the establishment of the SDR facility. Many countries had basic doubts as to whether it was wise to put the power to create international liquidity (q.v.), that is, create an international reserve asset (q.v.), into the hands of officials of an international organization that was, in the last analysis, controlled by national political influences. During the course of the negotiations, the concept of a reserve unit, to be distributed to an exclusive group of countries, was changed to a universal drawing rights scheme designed only to supplement international reserves (q.v.). The decision, moreover, to allocate SDRs—normally over a basic period of five years—was hedged around with a complicated procedure and required approval of 85 percent of the participants' total voting power. As part of this cautious approach, the reconstitution provisions were made compulsory, partly to obligate national monetary authorities (q.v.) to accept and hold this new and unfamiliar supplement to reserves (dubbed in the press "funny money"), and partly because of the strongly held view by some members that reserves should not be a mechanism to effect the permanent transfer of real resources from industrial countries to developing countries (q.v.) in order to finance economic development.

Reform of the Fund. Reform of the Fund refers to the first amendment to the Articles of Agreement (q.v.), which became effective in 1969, as distinct from reform of the international monetary system (q.v.), brought about by the second amendment to the Articles of Agreement, which became effective in 1978. The principal object of the first amendment was to establish a facility in the Fund based on Special Drawing Rights (SDRs) (q.v.). The establishment of the SDR facility necessitated the addition of 12 new Articles and a number of related changes in the rest of the text. At the same time, however, the opportunity was taken to make minor amendments to a number of other Articles affecting the technical operations of the Fund. The most important of these was the amendment to clarify that a member's gold tranche (q.v.) (now the reserve tranche [q.v.]) could be drawn upon without challenge from the Fund, and thus could be counted as part of a member's unconditional liquidity. Among other changes were a simplification of the complicated and technical provisions governing repurchase (q.v.) requirements, a provision to allow members to use their gold tranche to meet capital transfers, and a clarification in the definition of a member's monetary reserves (q.v.).

Reform of the International Monetary System. Reform of the international monetary system (q.v.) did not start out as an attempt to replace the Bretton Woods par value system (qq.v.) in its entirety. After the par value system broke down, the immediate reaction of the Group of Ten (q.v.) was to try to patch up the system, pending agreement on a more thoroughgoing reform. Meeting at the Smithsonian Institution (q.v.) in Washington, D.C., in December 1971, the Group of Ten countries (plus Switzerland) introduced the option of central rates (q.v.)—fixed but alterable—with wider margins. This interim system lasted for about 15 months, during which time all the major countries, one by one, gradually abandoned the fixed exchange rate (q.v.) for their currency. By March 1973, all the major countries had abandoned their par values (q.v.) or central rates and had let their currencies (q.v.) float against each other.

Within the Fund, staff (q.v.) studies on a reformed system had begun almost immediately after the U.S. action of August 1971, and when the Board of Governors (q.v.) approved a Resolution just six weeks later at the 1971 Annual Meeting requesting Executive Directors (q.v.) to prepare a report on the reformed system, the staff was able to produce a sketch of a new system early in 1972 for consideration by the Executive Board (q.v.). The drafting of the report by the Executive Board revealed deep differences of viewpoints among member countries. Although there was a general desire to return to a par value system, with modifications to the Bretton Woods system, there was no agreement on other proposed improvements, such as asset convertibility and the role of the U.S. dollar. When the report was published in August 1972 under the title of *Report on Reform of the International Monetary System*, it contained a number of new ideas and proposals but its tone was tentative, suggesting that a great deal more work was required on a number of fundamental issues.

Meanwhile, as a result of initiatives taken within the Fund, a committee of governors, known as the Committee of Twenty (q.v.), or more formally the Committee of the Board of Governors on Reform of the International Monetary System and Related

Issues, was established in July 1972. The committee replicated the structure of the Executive Board at the ministerial or central bank governor level, but included seven associate members and observers—about 200 officials in all. At its first meeting, the Committee established a Committee of Deputies, which, in turn, established seven technical groups. The Committee met six times over a period of two years, the Deputies met 12 times, and the technical groups held innumerable formal and informal sessions. The Committee's progress was slow and uncertain, and when the Organization of Oil Exporting Countries (OPEC) quadrupled international oil prices in December 1973, placing unprecedented strain on the world payments system, the Committee concluded that a fully reformed system was out of reach.

The Committee's report was published in June 1974, together with an incomplete *Outline of Reform*. Part I of the *Outline* indicated the general direction in which the Committee believed that the system could evolve. However, recognizing that a new system could not come into being for some time, the Committee recommended in Part II of the *Outline* that a number of immediate steps be taken in the interim to begin an evolutionary process of reform. Among the recommendations included in Part II was a proposal to establish an Interim Committee of the Board of Governors on the International Monetary System that would examine draft amendments to the Articles of Agreement (q.v.) "for possible recommendation at an appropriate time for the Board of Governors." The Committee of Twenty was dissolved and the Interim Committee (q.v.) came into existence.

The Interim Committee is structured on the same lines as was the Committee of Twenty, replicating the representation on the Fund's Executive Board and, like the Committee of Twenty, providing for each committee member to appoint seven associates to attend meetings, along with the Managing Director, his Deputy, Executive Directors (qq.v.), and a limited number of observers. In its new metamorphosis, however, there are no Committee of Deputies or outside working groups; these roles are performed by the Executive Board and the Fund's staff.

The staff provided the Executive Board with drafts, redrafts, and explanatory memoranda for nearly two years. The Executive Directors, on their part, debated and negotiated the amendments for 280 hours over 146 sessions, and were in constant communication with their national authorities, reporting on each stage of the discussions and receiving directions from them. Sensitive and divisive issues were referred to the Interim Committee, but the Committee itself had difficulty in reaching a decision on a number of key issues, and did so on several occasions only after government-to-government agreements had been negotiated. In April 1976, the prolonged negotiations were ended and the proposed second amendment was submitted to members for acceptance.

The key areas of disagreement related to the exchange rate system, the growth of international liquidity (q.v.), and the role of gold (q.v.) in the system. In the end, the idea of returning to a par value system was abandoned, at least for the foreseeable future, but the new system did not go much further than legitimizing existing practices. It allows members to choose their own exchange rate arrangements (q.v.), including floating (q.v.). It upheld the authority of the Fund by requiring members to collaborate with the Fund in an endeavor to promote stability and order through economic and financial policies, and to avoid manipulating exchange rates to gain an unfair advantage over other members. The Fund, on its part, is required to oversee the compliance of each member with its obligations and exercise firm surveillance (q.v.) over the exchange rate policies of its members. The official price of gold was abolished and the role of gold in the system was to be gradually reduced; the denomination of any exchange rate arrangement in terms of gold was prohibited and the obligation of the Fund and members to receive gold under the Articles was eliminated. At the same time, the Fund was required to dispose of a portion of its gold holdings. In place of gold, the amendment sets out a clear objective of making the Special Drawing Right (SDR) the principal reserve asset (q.v.) of the international monetary system.

More than two decades after the reform of the 1970s, the onset of a worldwide economic and financial crisis (*see* Asian Crisis) generated another wave of concern and proposals for reforming the international monetary system. The central problem was seen to be the volatility of free capital flows, particularly short-term capital movements (q.v.). Several initiatives were floated, including greater international control over the liberalization of capital markets, the setting up of some kind of insurance institution to cover the risks associated with capital movements, a new facility within the Fund to protect countries in a sound position from being overthrown by unjustified adverse capital movements, as well as a variety of measures to make the existing facilities and instruments more effective. Clearly, the more adventurous of these proposals raise critical practical problems and the history of international monetary negotiations, now involving over 180 countries, indicates that the more far-reaching proposals will not be easily or swiftly agreed upon.

Remuneration of Members. The Fund remunerates (pays interest) on that portion of a member's currency (q.v.) holdings that the Fund uses to meet the outstanding drawings (q.v.) of other members, referred to as the remunerated reserve tranche (q.v.) position. A remunerated reserve tranche position exists whenever the Fund's holdings of a member's currency falls below the norm. A member's norm is the total of 75 percent of its quota (q.v.) prior to the second amendment of the Articles of Agreement on April 1, 1978, plus the amounts of any subsequent increases. For countries that become members of the Fund after April 1, 1978, the norm is the weighted average of the norms applicable to all other members on the date the member joined the Fund plus any increase in its quota after that date. As quotas are increased, the norm will gradually rise over time.

Repurchases. The Fund's resources (q.v.) consist of a pool of currencies (q.v.) subscribed by members, and whenever a member draws from that pool by exchanging its own currency for that of another member's currency in the pool (i.e., by making a purchase [q.v.]), it is under an obligation to reverse that process as and when its balance of payments and international reserves (qq.v.) allow it to do so (i.e., it must repurchase [q.v.] its own currency by using SDRs [q.v.] or a currency selected by the Fund). The Articles of Agreement (q.v.) prescribe that normally repurchases should be made over a term of three to five years from the date of purchase. The objective is to maintain the revolving character of the Fund's financial resources.

The Fund's repurchase policies, however, are flexible, and longer terms may be allowed in exceptional cases of hardship. In addition, the Executive Board (q.v.) can vote to establish policies under individual facilities that reflect the changing needs and circumstances of members. The extended Fund facility (EFF) (q.v.), which addresses structural adjustment, has repurchase schedules up to 10 years, and facilities financed by borrowed funds have repurchase terms of up to seven years.

The overriding principle is that a member is obligated to make repurchases when its balance of payments and international reserves (q.v.) strengthen, even if such repurchases would be in advance of its repurchase schedule. Such early repurchases can, if desired by the member, be effected by the Fund selling its currency to another member in a purchase operation when that member is making a drawing (q.v.) on the Fund. A member that wishes to effect repurchases by having the Fund's holdings of its currency reduced in this manner must notify the Fund in advance, so that the transaction can be accommodated in the operational budget (q.v.).

Requirement of Need. Any use of the Fund's resources (q.v.) is subject to the representation of a balance of payments (q.v.) need by the member. All such representations are subject to challenge by the Fund, except for reserve tranche (q.v.) purchases. The balance of payments need of a member is assessed both as to the magnitude of the financing required and the adjustment program (q.v.) to be followed by the member to correct the underlying balance of payments disequilibrium. The Fund's assessment is determined by three elements—a member's balance of payments position, its international reserve (q.v.) position, and developments in its reserve position. The assessment may be made on the basis of any single one of these elements, or by a combination of all three. In addition, some individual facilities may stipulate a requirement of need of a particular character, such as the compensatory and contingency financing facility (CCFF) (q.v.), which is aimed at addressing temporary balance of payments deficits caused by export shortfalls, increased costs of cereal imports, or other factors that are largely beyond the control of the member.

A similar requirement of need also pertains to transactions in SDRs (q.v.) under the Fund's designation procedure. Under this procedure, the Fund may designate a participant to provide currencies (q.v.) in exchange for Special Drawing Rights (SDRs) on the basis of the strength of its balance of payments. A participant's obligation to provide currency, however, does not extend beyond the point at which its SDR holdings amount to three times its cumulative SDR allocations (q.v.). Participants can also exchange SDRs against currency by agreement. These transactions can be effected without balance of payments need, and in recent years all transactions of SDRs for currency have taken place by agreement between members, without the Fund's designation.

Reserve Assets. The attributes of a reserve asset are that it must maintain its value over time, be known and widely accepted internationally, and be in adequate but not excessive supply. Currently, reserve assets are reserve currencies, SDRs, gold, reserve positions in the Fund, and European Currency Units (ECUs) (qq.v.). During the 1950s and 1960s, the U.S. dollar was the principal currency held in countries' reserves and accounted for the major part of total reserves. Since the mid-1970s, the growth of reserve currency holdings has continued, but the earlier movement away from the U.S. dollar has not continued in the 1990s. At the end of 1996, total currency reserves of all countries amounted to SDR 1,030 billion, of which about 59 percent was accounted for by the U.S. dollar, 14 percent by the deutsche mark, 6 percent by the Japanese yen, 3 percent by the pound sterling, and 2 percent by the French franc. Holdings of gold (valued at market prices) were SDR 224 billion and of SDRs and reserve positions in the Fund, SDR 18 billion and SDR 36 billion, respectively. Holdings of ECUs accounted for 6 percent of total identified official holdings of foreign exchange (q.v.) at the end of 1996.

Reserve Creation Plans. The problem of an expanding world economy and a relatively fixed level of international reserves (q.v.) attracted the intense attention of international economists in the 1950s and 1960s. In addition, there was a somewhat visionary view, held by a number of economists, that the world ought to have a central institution—and the International Monetary Fund was the only existing organization that could possibly fulfill the role—that would, eventually, be able to regulate the supply of international reserves in accordance with need. The establishment of a mechanism that would allow a deliberate incremental increase or decrease in world reserves would be a first step toward creating an international central bank.

Proposals for deliberately creating international reserves began to come forward in the latter part of the 1950s and continued through the 1960s. Early suggestions centered around so-called multiple-currency (q.v.) accounts, by which means central banks would hold controlled amounts of each other's currency and have reciprocal claims on such an account. A proposal of this kind was studied at some length in the Fund in 1963-64, calling for the establishment of members' special accounts in the Fund. These special accounts would enlarge members' potential drawing rights, but in such a way that members with a zero net position in the Fund would be able to draw on the account without conditionality (q.v.), while drawings (q.v.) of members with a net debtor position would be subject to conditionality.

A second set of schemes revolved around the creation of collective or composite reserve units (CRUs). All these composite unit schemes differed in detail, but basically they envisioned the creation of a reserve unit that would be transferable among central bank or national monetary authorities (q.v.) and not for trading in private markets. The units would be established, in a trustee organization, in exchange for liabilities from each participating country, in the form of either claims on gold (q.v.) or promissory notes. CRU schemes were usually conceived as being confined to a select group of countries, such as the industrial countries.

The end result of the many ideas propagated was the establishment of the Special Drawing Right (SDR) (q.v.) facility in the Fund, created by the first amendment to the Articles of Agreement (q.v.) in 1969. The new asset was a breakthrough in international money; neither a monetary unit nor credit, and dubbed by the press "funny money," the new mechanism did have several unique characteristics. First, the facility was a universal one, although participation in it was voluntary. Second, the SDR itself was an unconditional drawing right backed by an international agreement (the Fund's Articles of Agreement) and not a unit backed by financial claims or liabilities. Third, SDRs were to be allocated to members in proportion to their quotas (q.v.) in the Fund. And fourth, the allocations (q.v.) of SDRs were to be made as a result of deliberate decisions, based on an informed assessment of need, concurred in by participants, and approved by 85 percent of the Fund's total voting power. With the growing integration of international financial markets in the 1980s and 1990s, fears of a scarcity of international liquidity faded. Indeed, the survival of the SDR and the SDR system is becoming questionable, as more and more academics and officials see the SDR as an anachronism of the past.

International liquidity (q.v.) had been an underlying concern of the founders of the Bretton Woods system (q.v.) and a growing concern for a quarter of a century throughout the postwar era. The establishment of the SDR facility was welcomed as a significant follow-through in an ongoing attempt to instill stability and order into the international monetary system (q.v.).

Reserve Currency. During the nineteenth century and in the early part of the twentieth century, the United Kingdom was the leading industrial and trading country, and the pound sterling, its value based on gold (q.v.), was the primary reserve currency. During the interwar years, the United Kingdom's trading position weakened, the gold exchange standard was abandoned, and the pound sterling lost its preeminent position as a reserve currency to the U.S. dollar. Under the Bretton Woods system (q.v.) established after World War II, the United States became the principal industrial and trading country, and the U.S. dollar, which was the only currency convertible into gold, became the principal reserve currency. After the U.S. authorities abrogated the gold convertibility (q.v.) obligation for the dollar in 1971, the dollar remained the preeminent reserve currency, but other currencies, notably the deutsche mark and the Japanese yen, began to be widely held by national monetary authorities (q.v.) as reserve currencies. *See also* International Reserves.

Reserve Position in the Fund. A member's reserve position in the Fund comprises the reserve tranche (q.v.) position and its creditor position under various borrowing arrangements. A member's reserve position is equivalent to a reserve asset (q.v.) owned by a member and can be drawn upon without challenge.

Reserve Tranche. A member's reserve tranche (before the second amendment to the Articles [q.v.] it was known as the "gold tranche" [q.v.]) is equal to the amount by which a member's quota (q.v.) exceeds the Fund's holdings (q.v.) of its currency (q.v.) after excluding those holdings that reflect the member's use of Fund credit. Excluding holdings that reflect the use of a member's Fund credit means that the member can preserve its reserve tranche, even though it makes a drawing (q.v.) in the credit tranches (q.v.). Reserve tranche positions are liquid claims of members on the

Fund arising from that part of quota subscriptions (q.v.) that are paid in reserve assets (q.v.), plus any outstanding sales by the Fund of the member's currency to other members that are drawing on the Fund.

Reserves. *See* International Reserves.

Resources of the Fund. The resources of the Fund consist of ordinary resources and borrowed resources. Ordinary resources arise from members' subscriptions (q.v.) to the Fund in accordance with their quotas (q.v.) and from undistributed net income derived from the use of those resources. The value of these resources is established and maintained in terms of Special Drawing Rights (SDRs) (q.v.), the Fund's unit of account. An amount not exceeding 25 percent of a member's quota is paid in reserve assets (q.v.) specified by the Fund (SDRs or usable currency) and the remainder in the form of promissory notes in the member's own currency.

Although quota subscriptions are the basic source of Fund financing, the Fund is authorized to borrow from its members and does so if it believes that a particular size, duration, or distribution of payments imbalances warrants a large temporary expansion of Fund credit. In this way, borrowing (q.v.) can provide a prompt and temporary supplement to usable quota resources and thus avoid the delay of a Fund-wide quota increase. There is nothing in the Fund's Articles of Agreement (q.v.) to preclude it from borrowing in private markets, but so far the Fund has borrowed only from official sources, such as from member governments, central banks, and the Bank for International Settlements (q.v.).

The liquid resources of the Fund consist of usable currencies (q.v.) and SDRs held in the General Resources Account (q.v.), supplemented as necessary by borrowed resources. In the fiscal year ended April 30, 1998, the Fund's usable resources declined to SDR 47.3 billion, compared with SDR 62.7 billion a year earlier, reflecting a historically high level of outstanding drawings (q.v.) at the end of the year. The stock of uncommitted usable resources, that is, usable resources less the amount of resources committed under current arrangements and considered likely to be drawn, also declined sharply during the period, to SDR 32 billion at the end of April 1998, from SDR 55.7 billion a year earlier. The Fund's liquidity ratio had thus declined precipitously to 44.5 percent, compared with a ratio of 120.5 percent a year earlier. The pressure on the Fund's resources continued throughout the rest of 1998, and in July the General Arrangements to Borrow (GAB) had to be activated for the first time in 20 years. These developments lent great urgency to the need for the eleventh quota increase, which would raise total quotas by 45 percent to SDR 212 billion, to be fully subscribed and become effective as soon as possible.

Resident Representatives. These posts, typically filled by a single staff member, are intended to enhance the provisions of the Fund's policies and Fund-supported arrangements in the country concerned. At the end of the financial year ended on April 30, 1998, the Fund had 70 resident representatives in 64 countries.

Restitution. The term *restitution* relates to the distribution of the Fund's gold (q.v.) in four annual installments beginning in January 1977. The decision, reached by the Interim Committee (q.v.) in August 1975, was to sell one-third of the Fund's gold holdings, or 50 million ounces. One-half of this amount, 25 million ounces, would be sold at gold auctions (q.v.), and the remaining 25 million would be distributed, or "restituted" to members at the official price for gold (SDR 35 per fine ounce). This was the first and only occasion on which the Fund had made an across-the-board distribution of gold to its members, although it had on many occasions previously sold gold to individual members in connection with specific operations of the Fund, mostly to replenish its depleted holdings of members' currencies (q.v.). The term *restitution* was, itself, an attempt to mask a difference of view on the ownership of the gold. Gold subscribed by members belongs solely to the Fund, but some members felt that in the case of a general disposition of gold held by the Fund, the gold ought to be returned to those members that had subscribed it.

The agreement reached in the Interim Committee to dispose of a portion of the Fund's gold was an attempt to remove gold from the central position in which it had been placed under the Bretton Woods par value system (qq.v.) and reflected the treatment given to gold in the 1978 amendments to the Articles of Agreement (q.v.). One-sixth (25 million ounces) of the Fund's gold was to be sold at auction in order to maximize the sale proceeds so as to yield a surplus or profit over the official price that would be available to the Fund to lend to low-income countries. The Trust Fund (q.v.) was established to receive these surplus proceeds and to lend them to 55 low-income countries.

Rights Accumulation. Aimed at resolving a member's overdue obligations (q.v.) to the Fund, the rights accumulation program allows a member to earn "rights" toward future financing through the implementation of a comprehensive economic program that the Fund would monitor but not assist in financing. Upon successful completion of such a program, and once the payments arrears (q.v.) to the Fund and the World Bank (q.v.) had been cleared, the member would be eligible to use the Fund's resources under a Fund-supported successor program. The Board extended the deadline for entry into the rights program until May 1999, but also decided that the future of the scheme would be considered at that time. Of the 11 countries eligible to take advantage of the rights program, five had cleared their arrears without recourse to the rights approach, three other members had adopted the rights accumulation program and had successfully cleared their arrears with the Fund, and three others have continued to have overdue obligations.

Rooth, Ivar (1888-1972). Ivar Rooth, of Sweden, was the Fund's second Managing Director (q.v.), serving from 1951 until 1956. He had been Governor of the Riksbank from 1929 to 1948, and for three years preceding his Fund appointment had been chairman of the Economic Research Institute of Sweden.

Rules and Regulations of the Fund. The Rules and Regulations supplement the Articles of Agreement and the By-Laws (qq.v.) and are subordinate to both. The Rules and Regulations deal with the day-to-day business of the Fund and are periodically reviewed, amended, and published.

Russian Federation. The systemic transformation facility (STF) (q.v.), established in April 1993, was designed to help the Fund assist countries of the former Soviet Union (FSU) to transform themselves from command economies to market economies. In accordance with this objective, the Fund mounted a vast assistance program for the 15 former countries of the Soviet Union, among which the Russian Federation was the largest former member and absorbed the greatest amount of the Fund's resources, both in terms of manpower and finances.

Russia signed its first program with the Fund in June 1993, and received disbursements of $1.5 billion that year and a further $1.5 billion in 1994. The programs were aimed at eventually sweeping away the framework of the preceding communist command economy and substituting freely working private markets. Because, perhaps, of the very size of Russia, combined with the established decentralization of controls operated by autonomous institutions under the former communist regime, the progress in transforming Russia to a free enterprise system was slower than in many other FSU countries.

In the two years under the 1993 STF program, an important start had been made on the transformation of the economy, but the extent of the progress had been disappointing. In 1995, the Fund approved a request by the Russian Federation for a 12-month stand-by arrangement (q.v.), authorizing drawings (q.v.) up to $6.8 billion, an amount at that time exceeded only by the Mexican (q.v.) arrangement signed three months earlier. The stand-by credit was aimed at bringing about decisive progress in stabilization and structural reform in 1995 and set the stage for a sustained recovery in output and living standards. The key objectives were to bring inflation down to an average of one percent a month in the second half of the year and to accelerate the move to a market economy through wide-ranging structural reforms. In 1993, real GDP fell by 12 percent, in 1994, by 15 percent, and in 1995, by 4 percent. Inflation remained high, although falling from an annual rate of nearly 900 percent in 1993, to 300 percent in 1994, and to 190 percent in 1995. At the end of 1995, the monthly increase had fallen to a single digit—an improvement, however, that was not maintained in the following year.

In 1996, the Fund approved an extended Fund facility (EFF) (q.v.) for the Russian Federation authorizing drawings amounting to about $10.1 billion over a period of three years. Progress under this program finally became markedly more positive, and in 1997, for the first time since 1992, the economy grew, albeit barely. At the end of 1997, the situation seemed to be positive. The current account of the balance of payments (q.v.) was in surplus; the Central Bank of Russia had proved its professionalism by overseeing a further decline in inflation, successfully fighting off contagion from the Asian financial crisis, and maintaining the currency band, which had been established in 1995. In 1998, however, the internal political situation weakened considerably, legislative progress on fiscal and structural reforms slowed sharply, and contagion from the Asian crisis all combined to halt the reform effort and throw the economy into a deep crisis.

Going into the third year of the EFF, a major problem still to be overcome was a deficit in the Federal budget, amounting to about 7.5 percent of GDP, reflecting a complex and inadequate tax system that, together with a weak tax collection system, discouraged domestic and foreign investment, encouraged tax evasion, and fostered the expansion of underground activities. On the expenditure side, needed improvements were: the strengthening of management and control over expenditures; reform of the civil service and the shedding of redundant workers; downsizing of the workforce in public health and education; improved targeting of social benefits and strengthening of the social safety net; and reform of public pension schemes.

Urgent structural reforms included faster, more transparent privatization and improved management of state-owned enterprises; the restructuring and pricing of natural monopolies (gas, electric power, district heating, and railways); urban land and real estate reform; further development of the capital market; development of a sound and efficient banking system; setting up a legal and institutional framework to make it easier to exercise and transfer property rights and to enforce contracts; liberalization of the housing market; the promotion of agricultural efficiency and productivity; a continued open economy to foreign trade and investment; elimination of arbitrary and corrupt practices by public officials.

The situation deteriorated progressively, however, as 1998 wore on. The Russian economy was impacted by the Asian crisis, the recession in Japan, unfavorable developments in Russia's external markets, notably oil, and the failure on the part of the Russian parliament, the Duma, to pass critical reform legislation. On February 19, 1998, the Fund's Managing Director, Michel Camdessus (qq.v.), and the Prime Minister of Russia, Victor Chernomyrdin, announced that, following a review of the medium-term strategy supported by the EFF, they had reached agreement on an extension of one year to the three-year agreement signed in April 1996 and on an augmentation of the financial support for the program. In a communiqué issued after the meeting, they said that they "shared a common assessment of the situation, of the strategy, and of the policies needed to bring the program to full success."

The communiqué went on to say that, notwithstanding substantial achievements in the areas of macroeconomic stabilization and the establishment of market mechanisms and institutions, a number of remaining challenges required decisive action without delay. These included, as noted in the communiqué, structural reform to promote the principles of good corporate governance and reduction in the fiscal imbalance. The draft 1998 budget as amended by the government, the communiqué said, was fully consistent with the EFF program, which also envisaged a strengthening of structural reforms in areas such as private sector development, fiscal institutions, banking, and natural monopolies.

The pronouncement of these measures, however, did nothing to halt the deteriorating situation, and in mid-1998 the Russian economy was in the midst of serious economic, financial, and political crisis, facing the specter of having to devalue the ruble and/or default on its external debts (q.v.). In July 1998, bearing in mind the risks associated with a collapse of the Russian economy, the Fund again reached agreement with the authorities on a new financing plan, along with an undertaking by the government that it would, either by legislative action or under presidential authority, implement the reforms that had been previously agreed to, particularly in regard to the budget for 1999 and voluntary debt restructuring scheme. Under the terms of this latest agreement, the budget for 1999 was expected to produce a deficit of 2.8 percent of GDP, which would be about one-half of the deficit of 5.6 percent expected in 1998. In addition, authorities had agreed to convert, on a voluntary basis, GKOs, or treasury bills, maturing through June 1999, into longer term dollar denominated liabilities of seven and 20 years maturity. This scheme was expected to help in avoiding the problem of rolling over GKOs and save substantial amount in interest payments.

The financial package (q.v.) negotiated with the Russian authorities included an additional $11.2 billion from the Fund for

1998. In addition, there would be two tranches, each of $670 million under the previous arrangement, that would be disbursed when conditions were met on schedule in 1998. Thus, in 1998, if the economy stayed on track, Russia would be eligible for another $12.5 billion in financing from the Fund. In addition, the Russian Federation requested that the EFF arrangement be replaced by a new EFF, starting at the beginning of 1999, that would last for three years. Under that arrangement, the Fund's Managing Director said that he would recommend to the Executive Board (q.v.) disbursements on roughly the same scale as the current EFF, that is to say, $2.6 billion a year. By the end of 1999, therefore, if the Russians carried out the program, the Fund would have disbursed about $15.1 billion.

Under separate arrangements, the World Bank (q.v.) would be disbursing $1.25 billion in the second half of 1998 and a further $3 billion in 1999. With further money in the pipeline, it was expected that during the second half of 1998 through the end of 1999 total assistance from the World Bank would be $6 billion. Further, the Japanese government had agreed to provide $1.5 billion in balance of payments support in cofinancing with the World Bank. All told, the total financing available to Russia would thus amount to $22.6 billion—a figure that had been announced in the Russian press and slightly in excess of the amount that the Russian government was reported to have been requesting. In order to secure the financing, the Fund announced that it would be activating the General Arrangements to Borrow (GAB) (q.v.).

On July 20, 1998, the Executive Board announced that the package represented a strong and appropriate response to overcome Russia's current difficulties. It noted, however, that parliamentary backing had not been forthcoming for needed action relating to personal income tax, nor had there been permanent measures to strengthen the pension fund. The Board welcomed the government's intention to seek parliamentary approval of measures in these areas in a special parliamentary session scheduled for August.

Subsequently, the Duma rejected the tax measures, the voluntary debt restructuring scheme became a nonstarter, and the government was unable to deliver on its policy commitments. Faced with the choice of devaluation (q.v.), debt restructuring, and default, the government chose all three. The ruble was let float, theoretically in a band from six to nine to the U.S. dollar, but promptly fell to 16; the restructuring was imposed unilaterally; and a temporary moratorium was imposed on private debts payments.

The new government, which contained for the first time since the overthrow of communism, several members in important positions who were known to be lukewarm or even opposed to the market orientation policy, announced that it was proceeding to put together an economic plan, but at the same time indicated that it would be resorting to controls and money printing. In October 1998, the international community awaited Russia's return to stability and the reform movement, to determine whether it might be able to financially reengage with Russia.

Talks between the Russian authorities and the Fund staff (q.v.) continued through the second half of September and at the time of the Fund-Bank Annual Meetings (q.v.) in October. The negotiations resumed in Moscow during the last 10 days of October, but a low-key statement issued by the Fund's staff in Moscow after the meeting indicated that no agreement had yet been reached on a full program. In the Fund's view. A critical priority was the elaboration of a realistic budget for 1999 as part of a policy program that could be supported by the international community. *See also* U.S.S.R. and the Fund.

-S-

Scarce Currency Clause. Article VII, Section 2, of the Articles of Agreement (q.v.) states that "if the Fund finds a general scarcity of a particular currency [q.v.] is developing, the Fund may so inform members and may issue a report setting forth the causes of the scarcity and containing recommendations designed to bring it to an end." Section 3 goes further and authorizes the Fund to declare a currency scarce if demand for it seriously threatens the Fund's ability to supply that currency and it allows members to impose restrictions on operations in that currency. The provisions survived the first, second, and third amendments to the Articles, but neither Section 2 nor Section 3 has ever been invoked.

Article VII was a compromise, one of many, reached by the drafters of the original Articles. Lord Keynes (q.v.) and others felt that the responsibility for adjusting balance of payments (q.v.) imbalances should not necessarily fall only on countries in deficit and that countries in surplus had a responsibility to pursue policies that were compatible with their surplus positions. The United States negotiators, however, understanding that there would be a global dollar shortage after World War II and that application of the scarce currency clause would negate any progress that could be made toward a free and open trading and financial system, held out for only the milder sanction—of a report by the Fund—as provided for in Section 2. Acceptance by the United States of Section 3, which would have authorized other members to use a potentially powerful weapon of discrimination (q.v.) against the United States, was regarded as a generous and good-faith concession on the part of that country, demonstrating the spirit of cooperation that was to prevail in the postwar world.

Schweitzer, Pierre-Paul (1912–1994). A French national, Pierre-Paul Schweitzer became the fourth Managing Director (q.v.) of the Fund in September 1963. He had been Deputy Governor of the Bank of France since 1960 and before that Director of the French Treasury. In 1947-48, he had been Alternate Executive Director (q.v.) of the Fund for France. Schweitzer completed two terms as Managing Director, serving until August 1973. During the crisis of 1971, he had appeared on television seemingly endorsing a proposal to devalue the U.S. dollar in terms of gold (q.v.). The U.S. authorities were shocked, even outraged, and a third term for him as Managing Director was thereby placed out of reach.

SDR. The special drawing right was the first international reserve asset (q.v.) to be created by international law, coming into existence under the authority of the first amendment to the Articles of Agreement (q.v.) in 1969. SDRs are purely book entries maintained by the Fund, and they do not have any traditional reserve backing, such as gold or reserve currencies (qq.v.), or any other tangible property. They were created as a supplement to existing reserves (q.v.) and are neither reserve units nor credits, but combine features of both. They are for use among nations participating in the SDR facility—for settling accounts between national monetary authorities (q.v.), but not for conducting private transactions or buying and selling in private markets, including foreign exchange (q.v.) markets. The actual coming into existence of SDRs occurred in 1970-72, the first so-called basic period, when a total of SDR 9.3 billion was allocated. A second allocation (q.v.) of SDRs was made in the third basic period, 1978-81, for a total of SDR 12.1 billion, bringing total allocations to SDR 21.4 billion.

The acceptability of the SDR in settlements, the use to which they can be put, and the value to be placed on them are mandated and circumscribed by international law, namely that of the Articles of Agreement. The unit value of the SDR was originally defined in the first amendment to the Articles as being 0.888671 gram of fine gold, equivalent to SDR 35 per one ounce of gold, but from 1974 until 1980, after the Bretton Woods system (q.v.) had collapsed, it was valued daily in terms of an SDR basket (q.v.) of 16 currencies, each currency in the basket carrying a weight determined by its share of world exports and services over a five-year period, with a special weight for the U.S. dollar. Subsequently, the valuation process was simplified to a weighted average of five major currencies (q.v.) (U.S. dollar, deutsche mark, Japanese yen, pound sterling, and French franc). On December 31, 1998, the conversion rate for the U.S. dollar was SDR 1 = $1.4083. The Fund publishes daily the exchange rates (q.v.) for nearly 50 currencies in terms of the SDR.

The amount of SDRs allocated to each participant is based on the size of its quota (q.v.) immediately preceding the allocation. Participants may exchange SDRs for usable currencies from other participants, either by agreement between the participants or by designation. Transfers by agreement with participants are now the predominant method for using SDRs. Under this procedure, there is no requirement of need (q.v.) and the Fund acts only as an intermediary in bringing the parties together. Transactions by agreement can be used for a wide range of purposes—to obtain usable currency, in currency swap arrangements (q.v.), in forward operations, to make loans, to settle financial obligations, as security for financial obligations, and for donations. In the first few years of the life of the SDR facility, however, most transfers were conducted under the designation procedure, whereby the Fund can designate a participant to receive SDRs if its gross reserves and balance of payments (q.v.) position is considered sufficiently strong. A designated participant is obliged to provide usable currency in exchange for SDRs only up to three times its net allocations (i.e., allocations, minus cancellations). The designations procedure can be used only to meet a balance of payments need.

After the second amendment to the Articles came into effect, several measures were taken to enhance the attractiveness of SDRs. The requirement that participants must hold, over a five-year period, an average of 30 percent of their net allocations (called the reconstitution [q.v.] provisions) was abrogated. The rate of interest on holdings of SDRs was raised to market levels and is calculated weekly, using the weighted average of interest rates of short-term instruments in the money markets of the five countries whose currencies comprise the SDR valuation basket.

Although SDRs are allocated only to participants, the Fund is authorized to prescribe other official institutions as holders of SDRs. By the end of 1998, 15 such institutions had been prescribed by the Fund, including three central banks, three intergovernmental agencies, and nine development banks. These designated entities can acquire and use SDRs in transactions by agreement and in operations with participants and other holders under the terms and conditions prescribed by the Fund for participants.

Cumulative allocations of SDRs amount to less than 2 percent of the world's total nongold reserves, an amount too small to make it the principal reserve asset (q.v.) of the international monetary system (q.v.), the goal stipulated in the current Articles of Agreement. Nevertheless, the SDR is used as a unit of account in a number of international and regional organizations, as well as a limited number of private arrangements. SDRs can be held and traded only by official entities, and thus they have only a limited role as a medium of exchange. In 1980 and 1981, bonds and other financial instruments denominated in SDRs were placed in the private capital markets, but the demand for the private SDR has faded.

Since the allocation of SDRs in 1979-81, no further SDRs have been allocated because 85 percent of the Fund's voting (q.v.) membership could not agree on whether there was a need for a further allocation. Several major countries believed that there was no need for an allocation, since the world's liquidity (q.v.) needs had been taken care of by the global movement of funds through private international capital markets and that, therefore, the SDR was something of an anachronism in the modern world.

On the other hand, a broad array of members, including many developing countries (q.v.), felt strongly that there was a need for an allocation of SDRs, partly in terms of a distribution of real resources, partly in terms of equity, and partly to keep the SDR in play as an international reserve (q.v.) asset. They pointed out that

39 of the current members of the Fund had never received SDRs and that another 37 members had participated in some, but not all, allocations.

Within the Executive Board (q.v.), there had been broad agreement that the Fund should make a special "equity" allocation of SDRs to correct for the fact that many members had either never received SDRs or had not participated in all the allocations made. The Interim Committee (q.v.), at its meeting in September 1996, endorsed an Executive Board proposal for a special one-time allocation—through an amendment to the Articles of Agreement—that would raise each member's ratio of cumulative allocations to quota (q.v.) to a common benchmark level. This would have enabled all members of the Fund to participate in the SDR system on an equitable basis. The Committee, at the time, emphasized that this would not affect in any way the Fund's existing power to allocate SDRs on the basis of a finding of a long-term, global need to supplement reserves as and when that need arose.

At its April 1997 meeting, the Interim Committee welcomed the progress in the Board toward a proposed amendment of the Articles of Agreement that would provide for a special one-time allocation of SDRs and requested it to continue its work. Later, at the 1997 Annual Meetings in Hong Kong SAR (qq.v.), the Board of Governors adopted a Resolution approving the special one-time allocation, amounting to SDR 21.4 billion, that would equalize all the ratio of SDRs to quotas for all members at 29.3 percent, allow the 38 members that have never received an allocation to participate in the SDR system, and double the total amount of SDRs in existence. The proposed amendment will become affective when approved by three-fifths of the membership with 85 percent of the total voting (q.v.) power.

SDR Department. An accounting entity rather than an organizational unit of the Fund's staff (q.v.), this department records and administers transactions and operations in SDRs (q.v.). SDRs do not constitute claims by holders against the Fund to provide currency (q.v.), except in connection with termination of participation or liquidation. Participation in the SDR Department is voluntary, but currently all Fund members are participants.

SDR Transfers. Total transfers of SDRs during the financial year ended April 30, 1998, amounted to SDR 20.3 billion, compared with SDR 19.8 billion in 1996-97, and annual average of SDR 18.7 billion over the past nine years. Transfers among participants and prescribed holders in 1997-98 amounted to SDR 9.8 billion, compared with SDR 8.4 billion in the previous year, and an annual average of SDR 5.8 billion over the past nine years. Since September 1987 there have been no transactions with designation because potential exchanges of SDRs for currency (q.v.) have been accommodated through voluntary transactions.

SDR Valuation Basket. The current SDR valuation basket comprises the currencies (q.v.) of the five member countries in the Fund with the largest export of goods and services in terms of value during the period 1990-94. The percentage weights of the five currencies making up the basket, as of January 1, 1996, are as follows: the U.S. dollar, 39 percent; the deutsche mark, 21 percent; the Japanese yen, 18 percent; the French franc, 11 percent; and the pound sterling, 11 percent. On December 22, 1998, the Fund announced that effective January 1, 1999, the deutsche mark and the French franc would be replaced by equivalent amounts of euros. This currency basket will be in effect until January 1, 2001.

The financial instruments included in the current SDR interest rate basket are the market yield for three-month U.S. Treasury bills; the three-month interbank deposit rate in Germany; the rate on three-month certificates of deposit in Japan; the rate for three-month treasury bills in France; and the market yield for three-month U.K. treasury bills. The weekly (Monday through Sunday) yield on the Special Drawing Right (SDR) (q.v.) is computed as the sum, rounded to the nearest two decimal places, of the products of the respective interest rates, the currency amounts, and the exchange rates in effect on the preceding Friday.

Singapore Regional Training Institute. The Fund and the government of Singapore inaugurated the Singapore Training Institute on May 4, 1998. The establishment of the Institute will allow the Fund to expand its training in Asia. It planned to offer 12 training courses for officials in the Asian-Pacific region during the next twelve months. The Fund jointly participates with other international organizations in a training institute in Vienna. *See* Vienna Institute.

Small States. Geographic size, population, the existence of a national currency (q.v.), possession of its own central bank, or the strength of its economy have no bearing on whether a country is eligible to become a member of the Fund. There are only three criteria: the applicant must be a country, it must be in formal control of its external relations, and it must be able and willing to perform the obligations of membership (q.v.) contained in the Articles of Agreement (q.v.).

The Fund's weighted voting provisions (q.v.) for its members have avoided most of the problems that membership of small states has posed in other international organizations. In 1998, for instance, after the 45 percent increase in quotas (q.v.) under the eleventh general review of quotas became effective, the United States was the largest member of the Fund with a voting power with 17.521 percent of total votes, whereas the Republic of Palau, the smallest member, will have a tiny voting power of 0.003 percent of the total power. The weighted voting system has facilitated the policy of not denying membership to small countries and of judging all applications on the criterion of whether the applicant has the ability to perform the obligations of membership, as set out in the Articles of Agreement. Denial of membership in the Fund would automatically deny the applicant membership in the World Bank (q.v.), and thus cut off development finance (q.v.) to the country in question.

The sharp increase in membership of small states has, however, created a number of problems for the Fund. The sheer increase in the number of members has sharply expanded the constituencies of some Executive Directors (q.v.) and complicated their responsibilities in representing a diversity of interests. It has added to the workload and size of the staff (q.v.), with more overseas missions, greater demands for technical assistance (q.v.), and the need for policy prescriptions on problems that can be almost as intractable as in more sophisticated economies. Decisionmaking in the Fund has also become more difficult, especially at the level of the Board of Governors (q.v.), when majorities are specified in terms of a proportion of the number of Governors and total votes.

Smithsonian Agreement. The Finance Ministers and central bank governors of the Group of Ten (q.v.) (Belgium, Canada, France, Germany, Italy, Japan, the Netherlands, Sweden, the United Kingdom, and the United States), Switzerland, and the Managing Director (q.v.) of the Fund met in Washington, D.C., in the Old Red Castle of the Smithsonian Institution on December 17 and 18, 1971, to negotiate a new pattern of exchange rate (q.v.) relationships among currencies (q.v.). The United States agreed to devalue the dollar by 7.89 percent against gold (q.v.), France and the United Kingdom were to maintain the par values (q.v.) for their currencies, and the Canadian dollar was to continue to float (q.v.). The other six countries agreed to establish central rates (q.v.), involving revaluations against the dollar of 16.88 percent for the yen, 13.58 percent for the deutsche mark, 11.57 percent each for the Belgian franc and the Netherlands guilder, 7.48 percent for the Italian lira, and 7.49 percent for the Swedish krona.

It was the first time that the major trading countries had sat around a table and reached agreement on a new pattern of exchange rates for their currencies. It was hailed as a milestone in international monetary cooperation, and seen by many as a reconstitution of the fixed rate system (q.v.). The new exchange rates were not to last, however, and 14 months later they had been overwhelmed by underlying economic developments and by speculative attacks in the exchange markets (q.v.). By March 1973 the mixed par value and central rate system had been overthrown and all the major currencies were floating against each other.

Social Policies and Fund Programs. The Fund's mandate is to promote international monetary cooperation, balanced growth of international trade, and a stable system of exchange rates, and it is the belief in the Fund that fulfilling this mandate is its primary contribution to sustainable economic and human development. In general terms, social development requires a strategy of high-quality economic growth, macroeconomic stability to generate low inflation, and promotion of the agriculture sector, where many of the poor work.

During the 1950s and 1960s, when the Fund provided financial assistance mainly to industrial countries, its policy advice concentrated primarily on macroeconomic policies. With the shift to lending to developing countries (q.v.) since the 1970s and economies in transition (q.v.) since the late 1980s, much greater attention has been given to structural reform, and the interrelationship between macroeconomic policies and social issues. Experience has shown the need to protect vulnerable groups during the adjustment period by constructing well-targeted social safety nets and by safeguarding their access to basic public services, such as primary health and education. Such measures make structural reforms (which tend to bring benefits in the longer term) more acceptable to the vulnerable and to be politically sustainable.

The major components of social safety sets (SSNs) are typically as follows: (1) targeted commodity (q.v.) subsidies and cash compensation schemes aimed at protecting the consumption of basic food items by the poor in the face of rising prices, while reducing budgetary expenditure; (2) adaptation of permanent social security arrangements, such as pension and disability insurances, and child allowances, which can be improved and bolstered through restructuring, targeting, and improved incentives; and, (3) the enhancement of unemployment benefits, severance pay, and public works schemes to cope with a temporary increase in unemployment brought about by structural reforms.

The aim of targeting is to reduce fiscal costs by limiting social benefits to those most in need. Where sophisticated means testing is not possible, resort to category targeting can be a useful substitute, whereby the benefits are limited to children or pensioners, or to households in certain regions. Commodity subsidies can be limited to goods consumed disproportionately by the poor or by limiting the quantity that each household can consume, for example, via coupons. The construction of incentives to encourage beneficiaries to move out of social safety nets is a question of tailoring social programs to the tax structure. Social safety nets must be crafted taking into account the specific circumstances of each country, including its administrative capacity, the strength of its informal and formal social support systems, and the characteristics of the poor.

Examples of the advice and technical assistance (q.v.) provided by the Fund in recent years cover a wide range of countries and a variety of social measures. Thus, in Italy, where the expenditure on public health care services was similar to other Organization for Economic Cooperation and Development (OECD) countries, but the quality of the care was seen to be declining as costs rose, the Fund counseled in its Article IV consultations (q.v.) with Italy in 1992 that health care spending should avoid untargeted across-the-board cuts and should aim for long-lasting savings. It recommended a strategy of increasing local responsibility for expenditure decisions, reinforcing the managerial authority and financial account-ability of local health administrators, and giving patients a greater degree of choice.

In Jordan, a generalized system of food subsidies was replaced in 1990 by subsidies targeted through a coupon scheme. The scheme allowed coupon recipients to purchase fixed quantities of subsidized sugar, rice, and powdered milk equal to quantities con-sumed, on average, by the poorest 10 percent of the population. As a result, the budgetary costs of the subsidy declined from 3.4 per-cent of GDP in 1990 to 1 percent of GDP in 1994, while the real consumption of the poor was shielded. In another variation of a subsidy scheme, general subsidies in the Kyrgyz Republic were re-placed by a cash compensation scheme to pensioners and families with three or more children, together with the introduction of means testing.

In Ghana (q.v.), where a comprehensive program of economic and structural reform was being supported by the Fund, the impact of a reduction of more than 32,000 positions in the civil service was cushioned by a comprehensive severance scheme that paid a lump sum to departing workers based on length of service and provided employment counseling and retraining, credit facilities, and food-for-work programs for those unable to find alternative employment.

In Sri Lanka, which in 1989-94 implemented successive pro-grams supported by the Fund and the World Bank (q.v.), the main programs designed to alleviate poverty (q.v.)—the JanaSaviya, the Midday Meal, and the Food Stamp Program—were all poorly tar-geted and cost some 3 percent of GDP. After reform, when the benefits were confined to those in need, the cost declined substan-tially without a reduction in the benefits available to the vulnerable.

In Uganda (q.v.), after almost a decade of war and civil strife, the infrastructure was devastated, agricultural lands widely aban-doned, public services paralyzed, and its population largely impov-erished. Real GDP fell by 8 percent between 1983 and 1986, exter-nal financing declined, and inflation rates were at extreme levels. A series of Fund-supported adjustment programs (q.v.), starting in 1987, restored economic stability, reduced inflation to single-digit levels in 1993, and revived economic growth, which averaged 5 percent a year in the period 1987-94. More than 40,000 ghost workers were eliminated from public payrolls, and the public sector was reorganized. The reorganization, combined with a system of mainly donor-financed severance payments, allowed the retrenchment of 66,000 temporary public employees and 14,000 civil servants. Moreover, more than 23,000 soldiers were reintegrated into civilian life through the provision of a support package that included a six-month subsistence allowance, the distribution of construction materials and agricultural inputs, as well as labor-intensive public works, and training programs. The peace dividend, in combination with the efficiency gains from the public sector reorganization, set free resources to effectively double the share of health expenditure and increase the share of education in government expenditures.

In Peru (q.v.), as part of its efforts to stabilize and liberalize the economy in 1990, the authorities entered into a series of programs supported by the Fund and the World Bank (q.v.). The programs were successful in reducing annual inflation to 16 percent by the end of 1994, from an annual average of 3,800 percent during 1988-90, and raised economic growth in 1994 to 11 percent. Hyperinflation had led to the virtual collapse of revenues, with the consequence that real wages of civil servants and critical government services had declined dramatically. As a result of fiscal reforms, current revenues rose from 7 percent of GDP in 1989 to 12 percent in 1994, allowing a gradual recovery in social and other expenditures. In 1991, the government stepped up its efforts to combat poverty (q.v.) by establishing a social investment fund to improve the access of the poor to social services and, in 1994, launched a basic social program to coordinate efforts in five priority areas—education, health services, nutrition, justice, and the creation of jobs. Through privatization of public enterprises, better targeting of social programs, enhanced budgetary expenditures, and improved management, the effectiveness of social spending was substantially improved.

Southard, Frank A., Jr. (1907-1989). A U.S. national, Frank Southard was the third Deputy Managing Director (q.v.) of the Fund, serving from October 1962 to March 1974. Before becoming Deputy Managing Director, he had been the Executive Director (q.v.) appointed by the United States since February 1949. Prior to that appointment, He had held senior posts in the U.S. Treasury and the Federal Reserve Board. Earlier he had taught economics at the University of California and at Cornell University, where he became Chairman of the Department of Economics in 1946. Frank Southard spent 25 years with the Fund in its most formative years and, more than any other individual, was a major influence on its evolution and development.

Special Contingency Accounts (SCAs). In view of protracted overdue obligations (q.v.) to the Fund on the part of members, beginning in 1987, the Fund decided to establish Special Contingency Accounts, in addition to the precautionary balance that it maintained in its general reserve (q.v.). At the end of April 1998, these balances amounted to SDR 1.9 billion, held in two different accounts, designated as SCA-1 and SCA-2. SCA-1 was established in 1987 with an initial balance of SDR 26.5 million and has been fed by amounts derived from higher charges (q.v.) and lower rates of remuneration (q.v.) under a burden-sharing (q.v.) mechanism.

A second contingency account, SCA-2, was established in 1990 to raise SDR 1 billion over a five-year period from a further increase in the rate of charge and a further adjustment in the rate of remuneration. The SCA-2 reached its target of one billion U.S. dollars in 1996 and further accumulation in the account has been terminated. The amounts in reserve are to safeguard drawings (q.v.) made on the Fund after a rights accumulation (q.v.) program has been successfully completed by members with protracted arrears (q.v.) to the Fund at the end of 1989, and they will also be used to finance such drawings.

When overdue obligations have been cleared, balances held in SCA-1 will be returned to those members that paid additional charges or received reduced remuneration. Similarly, balances held in SCA-2 will be refunded to contributors when the credits have been repaid, or earlier at the discretion of the Fund. At the end of the 1997-98 financial year, the general reserves, together with the precautionary balances, amounted to SDR 4.0 billion, equivalent to 8.1 percent of total outstanding General Resources Account (GRA) (q.v.) credit as of April 30, 1998.

Special Data Dissemination Standard (SDDS). The SDDS was established in April 1996 to encourage the timely publication of economic data used by market participants in evaluating a country's policies and prospects. It was one of a number of improvements to the international monetary system (q.v.) introduced by the Fund following the 1994 Mexican crisis (q.v.). Participation in the SDDS is voluntary and is aimed at members that have, or seek to have, access to international capital markets. Countries that subscribe to the SDDS undertake to make the necessary changes to statistical practices to meet the requirements of the SDDS during a transition period (set to end December 31, 1998), and to follow good practices with respect to the four areas covered by the standard: coverage, periodicity, and timeliness of data; access by the public; integrity; and quality. As of October 1998, 45 countries and territorial entities had subscribed to the SDDS.

In September 1996, the Fund opened to public access, through the Internet, an electronic bulletin board, the Dissemination Standards Bulletin Board (DSBB). This board posts information on the data dissemination practices of subscribers as well as steps they have taken to move toward full observance of the standard. It also provides up-to-date information on future release dates of data, identifies contacts in the subscribing country, and gives information on how to obtain the data. The Internet address of the DSBB is http://dsbb.imf.org. The bulletin board may also be accessed through the Fund's public Internet site (http://www.imf.org).

In April 1997 electronic links (hyperlinks) were established that allow users to move directly from the DSBB to subscribers' Internet data sites to access the latest economic and financial data. By October 1998, links were in place for 17 countries.

In March 1997, the Executive Board (q.v.) agreed to establish a General Data Dissemination System (GDDS). Unlike the SDDS, which is aimed at member countries with or seeking access to capital markets, the GDDS is focused on the improvement of data quality and systems for the production and dissemination of statistics for all Fund members. The GDDS framework consists of setting standards of "good practices" for data production, for the development of country statistical systems, and for data users in helping them to assess the practices of participating countries.

Special Disbursement Account (SDA). The Special Disbursement Account, activated in 1981, received transfers from the Trust Fund (q.v.) derived from repayments of loans and interest payments to the Trust, which in 1992 was in the process of being wound up.

Amounts received by the Special Disbursement Account were transferred to the supplementary financing facility subsidy account (q.v.), which was established for the purpose of reducing the cost to eligible members that used the Fund's resources (q.v.) under the supplementary financing facility (SFF) (q.v.). In 1985, the Fund determined that the resources in the Subsidy Account (q.v.) were sufficient to meet its estimated needs, and transfers to that account from the Special Disbursement Account were terminated. Thereafter, amounts received from the Trust Fund were held in the Special Disbursement Account pending their use in loan arrangements under the structural adjustment facility (SAF) and the enhanced structural adjustment facility (ESAF) (qq.v.). At the end of the 1997-98 financial year, the balance held in the Special Disbursement Account was SDR 0.9 billion.

Special Drawing Right. *See* SDR.

Special Facilities. The Fund's special facilities consist of the compensatory and contingency financing facility (CCFF) (q.v.) and the buffer stock financing facility (BSFF) (q.v.).

Stabilization Programs. The terms *stabilization program* and *adjustment program* (q.v.) are used synonymously, but a stabilization program has the connotation of policy measures aimed at correcting a financial imbalance, and is usually short-term, whereas an adjustment program may address structural maladjustments, as well as financial instability, and be for the longer term. A stabilization program is basically directed at restoring equilibrium to the economy in the near term through demand management policies, such as fiscal, monetary, and exchange rate policies.

Most of the early Fund-supported programs were of this character. In the mid-1970s, however, when many of the newly independent developing countries (q.v.) were experiencing the effects of unfavorable trends in their primary export markets, increased oil import prices, overambitious domestic development plans, and inflation, more fundamental and more enduring structural problems emerged. Demand management policies were by themselves no longer sufficient and needed to be underpinned by a broader economic strategy involving the mobilization of the country's resources, the integration of the various sectors of the economy, the removal of bottlenecks, the modernization of the taxation and banking systems, and policies to increase domestic savings and expand food production. These reforms could not be completed in the traditional 12 months of a stabilization program, and required implementation over the course of several years.

Stabilization measures are basic to all adjustment programs, for without financial stability, economic development and a viable balance of payments (q.v.) position cannot be sustained. In the postwar era, many earlier Fund stabilization programs included measures of structural adjustment that were introduced under 12-month stand-by arrangements (q.v.) and were only fully implemented after the duration of the arrangement.

All Fund programs are based on the understanding that deficits that are neither temporary nor self-reversing cannot be financed indefinitely and must be corrected through internal policy adjustments. Commitment on the part of a government to an appropriate Fund-supported adjustment program can bring in financing from other public, as well as private, sources, and thus provide breathing space for corrective policies to be implemented with less disruption than would otherwise be possible. *See also* Financial Programming.

Staff of the Fund. Unlike the United Nations, the Fund is not subject to nationality quotas in recruiting its staff. The Articles of Agreement (q.v.) specify that the staff owes its duty entirely to the Fund and to no other authority. In recruiting staff, the Managing Director (q.v.) is charged, subject to the paramount importance of securing the highest standards of efficiency and of technical competence, to pay due regard to the importance of recruiting personnel on as wide a geographical basis as possible. The Fund's professional staff is predominantly composed of economists, mostly with advanced qualifications and/or specialized knowledge in national accounts and macroeconomics.

The regular budgeted staff of the Fund at all levels has grown from 1,444 on April 30, 1980, to 2,181 on April 30, 1997, of which 46 percent were women and 54 percent men. Of this total, 693 were support staff (593 women and 100 men); 1,179 were professional staff (390 women and 789 men), of which 770 were economists (150 women and 620 men) and 409 other career streams

(240 women and 169 men); and 309 were managerial staff (31 women and 278 men).

Distribution of professional staff by nationality and region was as follows: Africa, 5.2 percent; Asia, 15.0 percent, of which Japan 1.6 percent; Europe, 33.2 percent, of which France was 4.5 percent, Germany was 3.8 percent, Italy was 2.8 percent, the United Kingdom was 7.0 percent, and other Europe was 15.1 percent; Middle East, 6.1 percent; Western Hemisphere, 40.5 percent, of which Canada was 3.5 percent, the United States was 25.5 percent, and other Western Hemisphere was 11.5 percent.

On April 30, 1997, the Fund's regular staff numbered 2,181. In addition to its regular staff, the Fund had 480 authorized positions for outside experts and consultants. *See also* Organization of the Fund.

Stand-by Arrangements. A stand-by arrangement is a decision of the Fund by which a member is assured that, in accordance with the terms of the decision, the member will be able to purchase the currency (q.v.) of other members from the Fund during a specified period and up to a specified amount. Analogous to a confirmed line of credit, the stand-by arrangement was a novel instrument of international law and finance devised in the early years of the Fund. Since the first arrangement, with Belgium in 1952, the stand-by arrangement—either of 12-month or extended duration—has become the main instrument for making the resources (q.v.) of the Fund available to members.

By the end of the financial year on April 30, 1998, 1,174 arrangements had been approved by the Fund, in the total amount of over SDR 316 billion. Of the total arrangements, 792 were stand-by arrangements accounting for SDR 156 billion, 46 were under the extended Fund facility (EFF) (q.v.) accounting for SDR 132 billion, 35 under the structural adjustment facility (SAF) (q.v.) accounting for SDR 5.4 billion, and 39 under the enhanced structural adjustment facility (ESAF) (q.v.) accounting for SDR 27 billion. The largest amount of funds committed in any one year was in the financial year ending April 30, 1998, when SDR 32.1 billion was committed.

The first stand-by arrangement, with Belgium in 1952, was for a duration of 6 months, but shortly thereafter the standard period for a stand-by arrangement became 12 months until 1974, when the

EFF was established, providing for three-year programs.

As noted above, a stand-by arrangement provides an assurance to a member that a specified amount of financing will be made available to that member over the life of the arrangement, but this assurance is dependent on the member observing the terms and conditions set out in the arrangement. Normally, the stand-by document will include economic performance criteria, such as budgetary and credit ceilings, exchange rate (q.v.) policies, interest rate policies, avoidance of restrictions on current payments and transfers, limits on indebtedness, and minimum levels of net foreign exchange (q.v.) reserves. In addition, the arrangement may provide for periodic reviews of the progress being made under the program and set out a schedule for the disbursement of finance at quarterly or half-yearly intervals. In the case of extended arrangements, members are expected to present a program outlining their objectives and policies for the whole period of the arrangement, as well as a detailed statement of policies and measures that will be followed during each 12-month period. Under these arrangements, the program will establish the macroeconomic criteria, as well as the structural maladjustments that are to be reformed.

Structural Adjustment Facility (SAF). This facility, established in 1986, enables the Fund to provide financial resources on highly concessional terms to support medium-term macroeconomic and adjustment programs (q.v.) in low-income countries facing protracted balance of payments (q.v.) problems. The programs are explicitly directed toward the elimination of structural imbalances and rigidities in the economies of the poorer countries, for which the facility has been specifically established. Under its terms, the member develops and updates, with the assistance of the staffs (q.v.) of the Fund and the World Bank (q.v.), the framework of a medium-term policy for a three-year period. Within this framework, detailed yearly policy programs are formulated and supported by financing from the Fund in the form of annual loan disbursements. The programs include quarterly benchmarks to assess performance. The overall access limit (q.v.) for the SAF was set in November 1992 at 50 percent of quota (q.v.) over a three-year period, with annual limits in the first, second, and third years of the program of 15 percent, 20 percent, and 15 percent, respectively. The rate of interest on SAF loans was set at 0.5 percent a year, and repayments were to be made in five-and-a-half to 10 years. The SAF was gradually phased out after an Executive Board (q.v.) decision was made in 1993 to extend and enlarge its successor, the enhanced structural adjustment facility (ESAF) (q.v.).

Subscriptions to the Fund. A member's subscription is equal to its quota (q.v.) and must be paid in full before membership (q.v.) becomes effective. An amount not exceeding 25 percent of quota has to be paid in reserve assets (q.v.) specified by the Fund (currently in SDRs or usable currencies, but formerly in gold [qq.v.] until the second amendment to the Articles in 1978) and the balance in the member's own currency. Normally, that part of the quota subscription paid in the member's own currency is provided in the form of promissory notes.

Subsidy Accounts. *See* Enhanced Structural Adjustment Facility Subsidy Account; Oil Facility Subsidy Account; Supplementary Financing Facility Subsidy Account.

Suez Crisis. The Suez crisis provided the opportunity for the Fund to become a major player on the international financial scene at a time of crisis after a period in which it had been sidelined in Europe by the introduction of the Marshall Plan and had played only a marginal role elsewhere. Egypt (q.v.) nationalized the Suez Canal in July 1956 and three months later Egypt was attacked by France, Israel, and the United Kingdom. The Suez Canal remained closed for many months and all four combatants approached the Fund for financial assistance. The first to do so was Egypt, which, making its first use of the Fund's resources (q.v.) since joining the Fund as a founding member (q.v.), drew $15 million in its gold tranche (q.v.) and subsequently a further drawing of $15 million in its first credit tranche (q.v.). Second was France, which obtained in September 1956 a one-year stand-by arrangement (q.v.) for its gold and first credit tranches, amounting to $262.5 million. In December the British government also drew out its gold and first credit tranches, amounting to $561.5 million, and entered into a one-year stand-by arrangement for $738.5 million. Finally, early in 1957, Israel drew out its gold and credit tranches, amounting to $3.8 million.

Thus, 1956-57 was a turning point for the Fund. The volume

of drawings (q.v.) made on the Fund during the year, amounting to nearly $1.7 billion, was larger than the total resources (q.v.) made available by the Fund in the preceding nine years. In addition, new stand-by arrangements, amounting to $1.2 billion, were approved during the year, completely dwarfing the volume of stand-by arrangements that the Fund had previously approved. Of the total drawings, nearly $1 billion (or 59 percent) had been drawn by the four principals in the Suez affair.

Sugisaki, Shigemitsu (1941-). Shigemitsu Sugisaki, a national of Japan, was appointed Deputy Managing Director (q.v.) for a five-year term, beginning February 3, 1997. Before his appointment as Deputy Managing Director, he had served as Special Advisor to the Managing Director (q.v.) since August 1994. A graduate of the University of Tokyo and Columbia University, Sugisaki joined Japan's Ministry of Finance in 1964 as a member of the Minister's Secretariat. He held various positions in the International Finance Bureau and the Tax Bureau, and was appointed Personal Assistant to the President, Asian Development Bank. After rejoining the Ministry of Finance in 1979, he held a number of positions, including that of Deputy Director General of the International Finance Bureau in 1991-92 and Commissioner of the Tokyo Regional Taxation Bureau in 1992-93. From mid-1993 until his appointment to the Fund, he held the position of Secretary-General of Executive Bureau, the Securities and Exchange Surveillance Commission. *See also* Fund Management Structure Change.

Super Gold Tranche. The super gold tranche, now an outdated term, referred to the amount that the Fund's holdings (q.v.) of a member's currency (q.v.) fell below 75 percent of its quota (q.v.) (assuming that the member had paid 25 percent in gold [q.v.]) because of net outstanding use of its currency by other members. Gold (q.v.) was eliminated from the Fund's operations by the second amendment to the Articles (q.v.) in 1978, and the terms *gold tranche* (q.v.) and *super gold tranche* no longer apply. Although the term *gold tranche* has been replaced by *reserve tranche* (q.v.), the use of the prefix *super* has been dropped.

Supplementary Financing Facility (SFF). Widening payments imbalances throughout the 1970s resulted in the need for financing balance of payments needs (q.v.) that were large in relation to members' quotas (q.v.) and, building on the experiences of the borrowing (q.v.) arrangements for the 1974 and 1975 oil facilities (q.v.), the Fund entered into borrowing agreements with 13 members and the Swiss National Bank to borrow the equivalent of SDR 7.8 billion as supplementary financing to meet the rising demand for Fund resources (q.v.) that could not be met from ordinary resources. Available resources in the facility were fully committed by March 1981 and repurchases (q.v.), which had a maximum repayment term of seven years, were completed by 1991. Use of the facility was subject to the standard requirement of balance of payments need and also to three other criteria: (1) that the period required for satisfactory adjustment of the balance of payments must normally be longer than one year; (2) that the financing required by the member must exceed the amount available in the credit tranches (q.v.) or under the extended Fund facility (EFF) (q.v.); and (3) that access must be in conjunction with an upper credit tranche stand-by arrangement (q.v.) or an extended arrangement with the Fund, and that purchases (q.v.) under the facility would be subject to the same conditionality (q.v.) as purchases under those arrangements.

Financing from the supplementary facility was mixed with financing from the ordinary resources of the Fund in varying proportions, depending on the type of arrangement that the facility supplemented and on the extent of the financing required. The Fund borrowed resources for the supplementary facility at market-determined interest rates, and its charges (q.v.) to members on outstanding balances under the facility were correspondingly higher than those on ordinary resources.

Supplementary Financing Facility Subsidy Account. The supplementary financing facility subsidy account, which was administered by the Fund and separated from all other accounts, was established in 1980 to assist low-income developing countries (q.v.) to meet the cost of using resources made available through the Fund's supplementary financing facility (SFF) (q.v.) and under the policy on exceptional use. Resources of the account were derived from contributions (SDR 57.4 million) and loans (SDR 4.6 million) from members and interest income earned on investments (q.v.) (SDR 61.4 million). The account also benefited by transfers of amounts received in interest and loan repayments from the Trust Fund through the Special Disbursement Account (qq.v.).

Subsidy payments to eligible members were made on a two-tier basis. Members with per capita incomes in 1979 equal to or below the per capita level used to determine eligibility for assistance from the International Development Association (the concessional lending facility of the World Bank [q.v.] Group) received the full rate of subsidy, with a maximum limit of 3 percent a year. Those with per capita income in 1979 above that level, but not more than that of the member with the highest per capita among the countries that were eligible to receive assistance from the Trust Fund, received subsidies at half the full rate (i.e., at 1.5 percent). The subsidy payment was calculated on the average daily balances of the Fund's holdings (q.v.) of a member's currency (q.v.) that resulted from purchases (q.v.) under the supplementary financing facility, but it was stipulated that the subsidy could not reduce the cost of using the facility below that of using the ordinary (unborrowed) resources of the Fund. After 1988, the rate of subsidy declined from the maximum of 3 percent and 1.5 percent, owing to the reduction in the charge (q.v.) on purchases under the supplementary financing facility in relation to the cost of the Fund's ordinary resources.

Supplemental Reserve Facility (SRF). Following the experience of the Mexican crisis (q.v.) of 1996 and the more recent Asian crisis (q.v.), which were marked by sharply adverse capital flows, the Fund introduced a new facility in December 1997 to provide financial assistance to a member experiencing exceptional balance of payments difficulties caused by a large short-term financing need resulting from a sudden and disruptive loss of market confidence, as reflected by movements in the member's capital account and reserves. Assistance under the facility will be available when there is a reasonable expectation that the implementation of strong adjustment policies and adequate financing will result, within a short period, in an early correction of the balance of payments difficulties.

Although resources of the Fund are available to all members, in setting up the SRF the Fund had in mind its use by members when the magnitude of an outflow created a risk of contagion that could potentially threaten the stability of the international monetary system (q.v.). In approving a request by a member to use the SRF resources, the Fund takes into account the financing provided by other creditors. To minimize moral hazard, a member using the SRF resources is encouraged to maintain the participation of creditors—both official and private—until the pressure on the balance of payments ceases. The facility is part of the Fund's efforts to strengthen its surveillance (q.v.) procedures and encourage members to implement appropriate policies in order to prevent crises from occurring.

Financing under the new facility will be available in the form of additional resources (q.v.) under a stand-by or extended arrangement (qq.v.) and be committed for up to one year, generally available in two or more tranches. The amount of financing available to a member under the facility will be determined by taking into account the financing needs of the member, its capacity to repay, the strength of its economic program, its outstanding use of Fund credit, and its record of cooperating with the Fund in the past. Countries will be expected to repay within one to one-and-a-half years after each tranche is drawn, although the Fund may extend this repayment period for up to a year. During the first year borrowers pay a surcharge of 300 basis points above the rate of charge on Fund drawings. This rate increases by 50 basis points at the end of the first year and every six months thereafter until the surcharge reaches 500 basis points. *See also* Brazil; Asian Crisis.

Surveillance Over Exchange Rates. The Fund is charged under its Articles of Agreement (q.v.) "to exercise firm surveillance over the exchange rate policies of its members" to help assure orderly exchange arrangements and promote a stable exchange rate system. The Fund has approved three principles to guide members in their conduct of exchange rates. The first of these reaffirms the obligation of members to refrain from manipulating exchange rates or the international monetary system (q.v.) in order to prevent balance of payments adjustment (q.v.) or to gain an unfair competitive advantage over other members. The second directs members to intervene in the exchange markets (q.v.) if necessary to counter disorderly conditions that may be characterized by, among other things, disruptive short-term movements in the exchange value of its currency (q.v.). The third requires members to take into account in their intervention policies the interest of other members, including those of the countries in whose currencies (q.v.) they intervene.

In applying these principles, developments that might prompt the Fund to have discussions with a member are: (1) a protracted large-scale intervention in one direction in the exchange market; (2) an unsustainable level of official or quasi-official borrowing, or excessive and prolonged short-term official or quasi-official lending, for balance of payments (q.v.) purposes; (3) the introduction, substantial intensification, or prolonged maintenance, for balance of payments purposes, of restrictions on, or incentives for, current transactions or payments, or the introduction or substantial modification for balance of payments purposes of restrictions on, or incentives for, the inflow or outflow of capital; (4) the pursuit, for balance of payments purposes, of monetary and other domestic financial policies that provide abnormal encouragement or discouragement to capital flows; and (5) behavior of the exchange rate that appears to be unrelated to underlying economic and financial conditions, including factors affecting competitiveness and long-term capital movements (q.v.).

The appraisal of a member's exchange rate policies is conducted within the framework of a comprehensive analysis of the general economic situation and the policy strategy of the members. First, the Executive Board (q.v.) regularly reviews each member's economic policies and performance and their interaction with economic developments in other countries. These reviews are based on staff reports prepared on the basis of regular Article IV consultation (q.v.) discussions with authorities of member countries, normally conducted on an annual basis. Second, broad developments in exchange rates are reviewed periodically by the Executive Board within the context of discussions on the world economic outlook, allowing members' policies to be reviewed and analyzed from a multilateral perspective. In this connection, the *World Economic Outlook* (q.v.) is prepared and published twice a year.

In addition, the Board holds, somewhat more frequently, discussions on exchange market developments in the major industrial countries. The Managing Director (q.v.) also participates in the meetings of finance ministers and central bank governors of the major industrial countries (the Group of Seven, increased to eight in 1998), to which he is able to provide a global view and analysis of national policies in terms of their international interactions.

Underlying the Fund's examination of members' exchange rate policies are the comprehensive data that the Fund routinely demands and receives on members' economic conditions, the close contact that the staff maintains with the officials in member countries responsible for formulating and implementing policy, and the comparative analysis that a multinational staff, in close contact with all member countries, can bring to the task of multilateral surveillance (q.v.). Among the numerous indicators that are monitored and analyzed are economic growth rates, inflation, unemployment rates, fiscal and monetary trends, external debt developments, structural indicators, trade and current account balances, capital flows, investment, savings, exchange rates, and reserves (q.v.). The staff prepares medium-term projections for these indicators as a means of monitoring and reviewing the policies and performances of the large industrial countries, and it draws up medium-term scenarios that illustrate the effects of alternative policies and identify potential conflicts. An important objective of the exercise is to examine the outlook for various categories of its members, such as advanced economies, developing countries (q.v.), debtor countries, heavily indebted countries, and oil-exporting countries.

As a complement to other approaches, the Fund also uses macroeconomic models to identify possible exchange rate misalignments. These involve (1) a trade equation model to calculate the underlying current account position that would emerge at prevailing market exchange rates if all countries were producing at their potential output levels; (2) a separate model to estimate normal or equilibrium level of the saving-investment balance consistent with medium-run fundamentals, including the assumption that countries were operating at their potential levels; (3) a calculation of the amount by which the exchange rate would have to change, other things being equal, to equilibrate the underlying current account position with the medium-term saving-investment norm; and (4) an assessment whether the estimates of exchange rates consistent with the medium-term fundamentals suggest that any currencies are badly misaligned, taking into account the prevailing cyclical conditions and the degree to which macroeconomic policies are appropriate.

Swaps. *See* Currency Swap Arrangement.

Systemic Transformation Facility (STF). This new temporary facility, established in April 1993, was designed to help member countries facing balance of payments (q.v.) difficulties arising from a disruption of their traditional trade and payments arrangements caused by a shift from reliance on trading at nonmarket prices to multilateral, market-based trade. The countries that were expected to benefit from the facility were those that belonged to the former Council for Mutual Economic Assistance, the republics of the former Soviet Union (FSU), and other countries experiencing similar transformation. Access to the facility was limited to no more than 50 percent of quota (q.v.), with financing being provided in two equal disbursements. Members using the facility were required to commit themselves to an interim program that could be succeeded by a full-fledged adjustment program (q.v.) with the Fund. Disbursements under the facility were made from the Fund's general resources (q.v.), the rate of charge (q.v.) was the same as for other use of those resources (q.v.), and the repayment period was set at from four-and-a-half to 10 years. *See also* Economies in Transition; Transitional Economies.

-T-

Technical Assistance and Training. The provision of technical assistance and training has been an important part of the Fund's activities almost since its inception, but during the 1990s, particularly in the aftermath of the demise of the communist regimes, requests for technical assistance escalated sharply. In the year ended April 30, 1998, technical assistance accounted for an estimated 16.5 percent of the Fund's total expenditures. The assistance provided by the Fund covers a wide range of fields, including fiscal, monetary and balance of payments (q.v.) policies, debt management, banking, exchange and trade systems, government finance, and statistics. Recipients are member countries, dependent territories of member countries, countries about to join the Fund, and some multinational institutions. Assistance is provided mainly through staff (q.v.) missions, field assignments by staff members or outside experts, and studies and recommendations prepared at headquarters. The technical assistance program is operated through the IMF Institute (q.v.), the Monetary and Exchange Affairs Department, the Fiscal Affairs Department, and the Statistics Department, with other departments, such as the Legal, Secretary's, and area departments, participating when their particular fields of competence are involved. *See* Organization of the Fund.

The IMF Institute trains officials from member and prospective member countries through courses at Fund headquarters, at the IMF-Singapore Regional Training Institute, the Joint Vienna Institute (q.v.), and in regional national centers. Courses in Washington, D.C., are offered in Arabic, English, French, and Spanish; courses in Vienna are offered in English, with Russian interpretation, and in French; and courses in other overseas locations are offered in Arabic, French, or Spanish, with interpretation into the local language, as needed. During 1996-97, the Institute in Washington, D.C., held 15 courses and three seminars, attended by 757 participants. In addition to the courses held at headquarters, the Institute conducts a large number of overseas training programs, participates in a Japan-IMF Scholarship program for Asia, financed by the Japanese authorities, and cooperates with the Research Department in conducting an in-house training program for Fund economists.

The Fiscal Affairs Department provides technical assistance in fiscal matters, catering to as many as 100 countries in any one year. Countries of the African continent, together with the Baltic countries, Russia, and other countries of the former Soviet Union were recipients of about half the assistance provided by the Department. Assistance to help country authorities with the building of tax administration and public expenditure management institutions absorbs about 80 percent of the Department's total technical assistance resources.

The Legal Department provides technical assistance in the areas of central banking, commercial banking, foreign exchange, fiscal, collateral, and bank insolvency laws. The assistance includes drafting legislation, commenting on draft legislation prepared by the authorities of member countries, drafting implementing regulations, and providing other legal advice. The assistance is directed to a broad range of countries, but in the 1990s the larger share was to members with economies in transition (q.v.).

The Monetary and Exchange Affairs Department in 1996-97

supervised the work of about 80 long-term experts in more than 50 countries. Assistance was provided to all regions of the Fund's membership (q.v.), but a comprehensive effort was being maintained in the 1990s in central and eastern Europe, the Baltic countries, Russia, and other countries of the former Soviet Union (FSU). In addition to finding, selecting, guiding, and supervising these experts, the Department provides a wide range of other technical assistance programs, which includes missions, seminars and workshops, and coordinates technical assistance with other organizations. Major areas for these activities are banking regulation, supervision, and restructuring foreign exchange (q.v.) operations and reserve (q.v.) management; central bank accounting, clearing, and settlement systems for payments; monetary operations and money market development; monetary analysis and research; and the development of government security markets. The Department has paid particular attention to China, which has absorbed as much as one-third of all workshops during any one year.

The Statistics Department, as other departments of the Fund, directs much of its technical assistance to countries in transition, centered on balance of payments, government finance, money and banking, national accounts, and price and international trade statistics. The Department has been active establishing the Special Data Dissemination Standard (SDDS) (q.v.) and guiding member countries that are seeking to participate in subscribing to the SDDS.

Other assistance provided by the Fund covers, from time to time, technical aspects of membership and operations, as well as help in the modernization of member countries' computer systems in central banks, ministries of finance, and statistical offices.

Thailand. Thailand had made extensive use of the Fund's resources (q.v.) in the period from 1976 to 1989, when it cleared its outstanding use of Fund credit and loans and had begun to build up its reserve (q.v.) position in the Fund. On August 20, 1997, in the face of an economic and financial crisis that quickly spread to other countries in the region, the Fund approved a stand-by arrangement (q.v.) for Thailand, authorizing drawings (q.v.) of up to $3.9 billion over the following 34 months to support the government's economic program. An additional total of over $12 billion was pledged by the World Bank (q.v.), the Asian Development Bank, and bilateral lenders in the region.

Thailand's economic crisis, like others in the region, came after a decade of robust and strong growth, aided by successful macroeconomic policies. Its current account deficit had been widening for several preceding years and reached a peak of 8 percent of GDP in 1996. An associated external debt burden rose to 50 percent of GDP, of which some 40 percent was short-term. As was the case in other countries in the region, Thailand became increasingly vulnerable, with a serious weakness in the financial sector, which was exacerbated by a sharp slowdown in exports and GDP growth, growing difficulties in the property market, and a sharp fall in stock market prices. The introduction of a managed float (q.v.) of the baht in July 1997 was followed by a 20 percent depreciation in its value.

Although the Thai authorities took some early measures to address the growing difficulties, their actions were inadequate to correct a deepening crisis. In the face of continuing widespread loss of confidence, the Thai authorities, with the support of the Fund, moved quickly to put together a comprehensive economic package designed to restore confidence and economic stability at an early stage and lay the foundation for sound growth over the medium term.

The principal objective of the program in the short run was to bring about an orderly adjustment to the domestic economy in the face of a sharp, forced reduction in the current account deficit. The main thrust of this short-term program was through fiscal policy, which aimed at restoring an overall surplus in the public sector by 1998 through an increase in the value-added tax, stronger monitoring of the expenditures of the state enterprises, and a greater emphasis on privatization. This involved significant increases in the prices of some utilities and petroleum products, although subsidies for bus and rail fares were left in place for social reasons.

In the monetary field, strict control over the monetary aggregates included ending the practice of providing open-ended, unconditional financial support to insolvent institutions; the development of additional monetary policy (q.v.) instruments; and improved public disclosure of key economic information. The rate of inflation was to be brought down from over 9 percent in 1997 to 5 percent in 1998.

The heart of the strategy, however, was the up-front, suspension, and restructuring of nonviable institutions, immediate steps to instill confidence in the rest of the financial system, strict conditionality (q.v.) on the use of the resources of the financial institutions' Development Fund (the lax use of which had intensified the earlier loss of confidence), and a phased implementation of broader structural reforms to restore a healthy financial sector. These reforms included a strengthening of the capital base of the financial institutions, as well as encouraging mergers of weaker institutions, and foreign capital injections.

On March 4, 1998, after reviewing the progress made under the economic program, the Fund made a further disbursement under the stand-by credit and strongly commended the Thai authorities for resolutely implementing the program in very difficult circumstances, noting the shift in the external current account from a deficit to a surplus. At the same time, a number of key changes were introduced into the program, including more flexible use of interest rate policy, a slight relaxation in the fiscal program, and intensified efforts to recapitalize the banking system.

Despite bouts of international nervousness caused by the burgeoning crises in Russia and Latin America, progress continued in Thailand throughout 1998. Inflation stayed lower than expected, money market rates fell below their pre-crisis level, and the baht appreciated. A large swing in the external current account led to a substantial build-up in external reserves. At the beginning of 1999, prospects were for a modest one percent growth in GDP for the year. *See also* Asian Financial Crisis.

Toronto Menu. In June 1988, the leaders of the Group of Seven (q.v.) major industrial countries, participating in the fourteenth economic conference in Toronto, endorsed a debt-relief plan for the official bilateral debts of low-income countries undertaking macroeconomic and structural adjustment (q.v.) programs. The relief measures consisted of a reduction in debt service, a rescheduling at concessional interest rates, or a rescheduling at longer maturities. Subsequently, the menu was enlarged at the Group of Seven meeting in Trinidad in September 1990 to encompass debt reduction and was adopted by the Paris Club (q.v.) in December 1991.

Training. *See* Technical Assistance and Training.

Transactions of the Fund. In the years since 1946 all industrial countries have purchased currencies (q.v.) from the Fund (although several, including the United States, have drawn only on their reserve tranche [q.v.]). Drawings (q.v.) on the Fund by industrial countries, however, dropped sharply in the 1970s, and no major industrial country has used the Fund's financial resources (q.v.) since 1976, when a total of SDR 2.6 billion was drawn by eight industrial countries. In 1976-84, several of the smaller industrial countries made limited use of the Fund's resources, but since 1984 no industrial country has found it necessary to approach the Fund for financing.

Developing countries (q.v.), on the other hand, have continued to make extensive use of the Fund's resources, with drawings reaching record levels through the 1980s and 1990s. The oil shocks of the 1970s, the debt crisis of the 1980s, and the economic and financial crises of the 1990s all posed serious problems for many developing countries, requiring a growing volume of resources from the Fund. In 1984, the Fund committed over SDR 28 billion under Fund-supported programs, and although the level declined thereafter in the 1980s, it began to rise again sharply in the 1990s, reaching a peak in 1997-98, when total Fund credit outstanding rose to a record SDR 56 billion, an increase of SDR 16 billion during the year. By April 1998, the Fund had committed a total of over SDR 310 billion under about 1,170 Fund-supported programs. In financing these programs, the Fund has drawn on its ordinary resources as well as loans made to it for the oil facilities, the enlarged access policies, the supplementary financing, and the Trust Fund (qq.v.), amounting to over SDR 30 billion, not taking into account the activations of the General Arrangements to Borrow (GAB) (q.v.) over the years of its establishment. *See also* Borrowing by the Fund.

Transitional Arrangements. Article XIV, Section 2, of the Articles of Agreement (q.v.) allows a member to avail itself of transitional arrangements under which it may maintain and adapt to changing circumstances the restrictions on payments and transfers for current international transactions that were in effect on the date on which it became a member. Members are under an obligation to withdraw such restrictions as soon as conditions permit. Originally, members were given a transitional period targeted at five years, but the provision was replaced by more general language in the second amendment to the Articles. Under its Articles the Fund must report annually on restrictions in force in countries that are availing themselves of the transitional arrangements, and the Fund does so by publishing the *Annual Report on Exchange Arrangements and Exchange Restrictions* (q.v.). By April 30, 1998, 144 members, including all the main trading countries, had accepted the obligations of Article VIII, under which they had undertaken to refrain from imposing restrictions on the making of payments and transfers for current international transactions or engaging in discriminatory currency arrangements or multiple currency practices (q.v.). At that time, about 40 members, all developing countries (q.v.), transitional economies (q.v.), or new members, were availing themselves of the transitional arrangements.

Transitional Economies. A group of countries, mainly from the former Soviet Union (FSU), that had unusual problems in changing from a command economy to one based on free markets. A temporary facility, the systemic transformation facility (STF) (q.v.), was established to help these countries take the initial steps in their transformation. *See also* Economies in Transition.

Trust Fund. The Trust Fund was established in 1976 as an intermediate agency to receive funds from the profits of sales of the Fund's gold (q.v.) holdings, transfers from some of the beneficiaries of direct distributions of gold sales (q.v.) profits, and income from investment (q.v.) of assets. These proceeds were then channeled to eligible developing countries (q.v.) in the form of concessionary loans, repayable in installments over a period beginning five-and-a-half years and ending 10 years after disbursement of the loan and bearing a rate of interest of 0.5 percent a year. During the 1976-81 period the Fund provided SDR 2.9 billion from the Trust Fund, in two successive periods of two years, to 61 eligible developing member countries, defined as those having a per capita income of SDR 300 or less in 1973 and SDR 520 or less in 1975. The Trust Fund made its final disbursements in March 1981. Thereafter, interest on and repayments of Trust

Fund loans were transferred to the Fund's Special Disbursement Account (q.v.).

-U-

Uganda and HIPC. Uganda was the first country to be declared eligible for assistance under the Heavily Indebted Poor Countries (HIPC) (q.v.) initiative in April 1997. On April 8, 1998, following the declaration of the country's eligibility, the Fund and the World Bank (q.v.) agreed that Uganda had met the requirements for receiving nearly $650 million in debt relief from its external creditors under the HIPC initiative—it was the first country to receive debt relief under the program.

Under the agreement, relief from all of Uganda's creditors would be worth $350 million (in terms of net present value), to which the World Bank would contribute about $160 million and the Fund $69 million. This total represented about 20 percent of Uganda's external debt (q.v.). The Fund's portion of the debt relief was to be made available in the form of a grant to pay part of the debt falling due to it. To relieve the country's debt to the International Development Association (IDA), the World Bank's contribution was to be made in three ways—partly in the form of a grant, partly as the payment or cancellation of debt, and partly by payment of Uganda's debt service by means of a grant from the HIPC Trust Fund.

In making the joint announcement, the Fund and World Bank press release noted that Uganda was one of the strongest performing economies in Africa, with an average annual economic growth over the past 10 years of 6 percent. Inflation had been contained and the economy was becoming increasingly diversified. The country had regained its position as Africa's premier coffee producer; the tea industry was being revitalized; a small horticulture industry was emerging; and maize exports were expanding. In addition, the country's transportation system was being rehabilitated, a national grid system to connect all parts of the country was being worked on, and the government had begun a program to bring about universal primary education.

In November 1997, the Fund approved a three-year arrangement under the enhanced structural adjustment facility (ESAF) (q.v.), in a total amount equivalent to about $138 million, to be drawn semiannually over the three years. In November 1998, the Fund approved the second annual loan for Uganda under the ESAF arrangement, equivalent to about $46 million, in support of the government's economic program for 1998-99. The loan is available in two annual installments, the first of which, equivalent to $23 million, would be disbursed on November 25, 1998.

The Fund noted that macroeconomic performance in 1997-98 was generally in line with the program. Real GDP, which was adversely affected by El Nino weather conditions in the first half of the year, recovered in the second half, rising by 5.5 percent for the year. Inflation had been low and international reserves (q.v.) had been rebuilt to a relatively comfortable level. Notable progress had been made in 1997-98 in a number of structural areas, particularly trade liberalization, civil service reform, tax administration, and financial sector reform, although privatization targets had not been fully achieved.

United Nations, Relations with. The Fund is a specialized agency within the United Nations family of agencies and, as noted in the 1947 agreement between the Fund and the United Nations, is an independent international organization. The responsibility for maintaining day-to-day contact with the United Nations rests with the Fund's Special Representative to the United Nations, who maintains an office in the headquarters of the United Nations and devotes his activities solely to sustaining the Fund's close relations with the United Nations.

The Managing Director (q.v.) of the Fund also participates in a number of functions of the United Nations and its specialized agencies. He attends the meetings of the Administrative Coordinating Committee of the United Nations, speaks at sessions of the Economic and Social Council, the Economic Commission for Latin America and the Caribbean, the United Nations Conference on Trade and Development, and, when invited, also addresses other meetings and conferences of the United Nations and its specialized agencies on matters of relevance to the Fund.

Uruguay Round. The Uruguay Round of Multilateral Trade Negotiations—the eighth in the series conducted under the General Agreement on Tariffs and Trade (GATT) (q.v.) since 1947—began in Punta del Este, Uruguay, in January 1986. Originally scheduled to be completed by 1990, the tortuous negotiations, frequently on the brink of a complete breakdown, dragged on for eight years. Completed at the end of 1993, it marked the biggest reform of international trade since 1948. In the end, the agreement succeeded in bridging great differences of opinion between Europe and the United States, as well as those among a number of other countries, especially on the question of agricultural subsidies. The issues included: (1) a significant reduction in trade barriers; (2) restoring to GATT the responsibility for monitoring trade in certain items that had moved outside multilateral trade negotiations, such as textiles and clothing; (3) bringing discipline to the trade-related aspects of intellectual property; (4) improving the rules and dispute settlement system; and (5) providing a framework for trade in services. Other matters under discussion include trade-related investment measures and the relations of GATT with the Fund and the World Bank (q.v.). In addition, and of most importance, the Uruguay Round approved a proposal to establish a new international trade organization, the World Trade Organization (WTO) (q.v.), based on international law and having wider responsibilities than GATT, which it replaced, effective January 1, 1995.

Use of Fund Resources. Use of the Fund's resources is defined by its Articles of Agreement (q.v.), which state in Article I(iv) that the Fund is to make the "general resources of the Fund temporarily available to them [members] under adequate safeguards, thus providing them with an opportunity to correct maladjustments in their balance of payments (q.v.) without resorting to measures destructive of national or international prosperity." The essential provisions are: first, a member may draw on the Fund only to meet a balance of payments need (q.v.); and second, use of the Fund's resources must be temporary (i.e., drawings [q.v.] must be repaid within a reasonable time). It follows, then, that in making finance available, the Fund must be assured that the member will adopt adjustment (q.v.) policies to correct the imbalance in its payments and be able to repay the Fund over the medium term. Influenced by the discussions held at the Bretton Woods Conference (q.v.), the Fund decided that repayments (repurchases [q.v.]) should be over three to five years, or earlier if warranted by an improvement in the country's balance of payments position.

Early in the 1950s, the Fund clarified the terms on which a

member could use its resources by establishing the so-called tranche policies. These consist of a reserve tranche and four credit tranches (qq.v.), normally each tranche amounting to 25 percent of a member's quota (q.v.). The reserve tranche is a floating tranche and can be used without challenge. Drawings in the credit tranches require safeguards in terms of policy adjustments; moderate safeguards for drawings in the first credit tranche, but more substantial ones for drawings in the upper credit tranches.

In 1952, the Fund devised the stand-by arrangement (q.v.), an original instrument under which members make almost all their drawings from the Fund. Since its inception, the Fund has approved over 800 stand-by and extended arrangements for its members. Nearly all stand-by arrangements in the upper credit tranches contain criteria linking performance under adjustment programs to phased disbursements under stand-by arrangements.

The simple schema for use of the Fund's resources soon became more complicated, however, as elements in the balance of payments were picked out for special treatment and as a deepening and structural imbalance in world payments required longer term adjustment programs, increased temporary resources through Fund borrowings (q.v.), and enlarged access limits (q.v.). The process began in 1963 with the establishment of the compensatory financing facility to provide financing to members, with little or no conditionality (q.v.) and in amounts over and above those available under credit tranche policies, to offset shortfalls in export earnings.

This was followed by a buffer stock financing facility (q.v.) in 1969; the oil facilities (q.v.), financed by Fund borrowings, in 1974 and 1975; the supplementary financing facility (q.v.), again financed by borrowings, in 1979; the enlarged access policy (q.v.), financed by a mix of ordinary and borrowed funds, in 1981; the structural adjustment facility (q.v.), providing loans on concessional terms and financed from reflows from the Trust Fund (q.v.), in 1986; the enhanced structural adjustment facility (q.v.), also providing loans on concessional terms and funded in part from resources derived from the structural adjustment facility and partly from donations and loans, in 1987; the compensatory and contingency financing facility (q.v.), combining the various elements of compensatory financing with contingency financing, in 1989; the systemic transformation facility (q.v.), for use by countries in transition to a market-based economy, in 1993; and, finally, the emergency financing mechanism (q.v.) in 1995.

The conditionality (q.v.) attached to use of the Fund's financial resources has been subjected to much public discussion and many periodic reviews within the Fund. In 1979 the Executive Board (q.v.) established a set of guidelines to clarify the standards for the drawing up of stand-by and extended arrangements. Although the guidelines largely codified existing practices, they gave developing countries (q.v.) an opportunity to define and express some of their concerns about Fund conditionality. One guideline, regarded as being of great importance by developing countries, is that in devising adjustment programs, the Fund will pay due regard to the domestic social and political objectives, the economic priorities, and the circumstances of members. Another is that performance criteria will normally be confined to macroeconomic variables. The guidelines have been reviewed by the Board several times since 1979, but have not undergone substantive change.

In general, these guidelines are intended to prevent Fund-supported adjustment programs from interfering with national policy objectives, such as consumer subsidies or military expenditures, adopted for social or national security purposes. Nevertheless, the preparation of a realistic adjustment program often poses difficult and unwanted choices for national policymakers, particularly if they approach the Fund as a last resort, when their economic and financial affairs are in an extreme state of disorder. When requested, the Fund's staff (q.v.) can help by providing optional scenarios showing the various means to attain the targeted macroeconomic variables. In the last analysis, however, member countries are responsible for accepting and implementing the details of their adjustment programs.

During the 1990s, the largest commitments of the Fund's resources—each over SDR 10 billion—were for Russia, Mexico, Korea, Indonesia, Argentina (qq.v.), and India, although not all the commitments were, in fact, disbursed.

U.S.S.R. and the Fund. The U.S.S.R. participated in the Bretton Woods Conference (q.v.) in July 1944 and was given a quota (q.v.) in the Fund, but ultimately decided against joining it. Thereafter, occasional and informal contacts between the Fund and the

U.S.S.R. took place until July 1990, when the Fund was asked to convene a joint study on the Soviet economy for the Group of Seven (q.v.), to be carried out in conjunction with the World Bank (q.v.), the Organization for Economic Cooperation and Development, and the European Bank for Reconstruction and Development. The joint study's recommendations were made public in December 1990, and in the following October the Fund and the U.S.S.R. entered into a Special Association. This enabled the Fund to develop closer links with the U.S.S.R., provide technical assistance (q.v.), and prepare and publish economic studies of all 15 states of the former Soviet Union (FSU) in mid-1992. The Fund's Executive Board (q.v.) completed pre-membership economic reviews of the 15 states, announced the quota calculations, and submitted membership resolutions (q.v.) to the Board of Governors (q.v.), which in May 1992 agreed to admit to membership (q.v.) all the countries of the FSU.

The quota for Russia was determined at SDR 2.9 billion, but was increased to SDR 5.9 billion under the eleventh general review of quotas (q.v.), which was expected to become effective in 1999. Russia has the ninth largest quota in the Fund, after Canada.

-V-

Vienna Institute. The Joint Vienna Institute opened in Vienna in October 1992 to train officials from former centrally planned economies in various aspects of public administration and economic management. The Institute is sponsored by the Fund, the Bank for International Settlements (q.v.), the Commission of the European Communities, the European Bank for Reconstruction and Development, the World Bank (q.v.), and the Organization for Economic Cooperation and Development. The Institute offered 50 courses in its first year, for approximately 1,600 participants. *See also* IMF Institute.

Voting Provisions in the Fund. The voting structure in the Fund is distinguished by the fact that, in contrast to the situation in the United Nations, voting power is not based on "one member, one vote" but is weighted according to a member's financial contri-bution (its quota [q.v.]) to the organization. Each member receives a basic allotment of 250 votes, and also receives one additional vote for each part of its quota equivalent to SDR 100,000. The basic allotment of 250 votes for each member was intended to ensure that all members, no matter how small, would have some weight in influencing the operations of the organization. Over the years, however, the basic allotment of votes per member has not changed, although general quota increases have raised total quotas more than fourfold. In 1958, for example, when the Fund had 69 members with total quotas of $9.2 billion, the basic votes of all members amounted to nearly 16 percent of total votes. In 1999, when the Fund had 182 members and total quotas under the eleventh general review of quotas (q.v.) had risen to SDR 212 billion, the basic votes of all members had fallen to just over 2 percent of total votes.

The Board of Governors (q.v.) is the senior organ of the Fund, and the Governor of each member is entitled to cast the votes of the member appointing him. He cannot cast fewer votes than he is entitled to, and must either cast all his votes or abstain. The Board of Governors has delegated most of its powers to the Executive Board (q.v.), but a number of powers that have a special institutional importance are confined to the Board of Governors. Basically, the Board of Governors takes decisions by a simple majority of the votes cast, but there are many decisions that require special majorities of 70 percent or 85 percent. Allocation (q.v.) and cancellation of Special Drawing Rights (SDRs) (q.v.), valuation of special drawing rights, rates of charge and remuneration (qq.v.), sale of gold holdings (qq.v.), increases or decreases in the number of Executive Directors, and compulsory withdrawal of members are just a few of the decisions that require special majorities.

Executive Directors cast the votes of the members that appointed or elected them. They cannot split their votes, however, and must either abstain from voting or cast all the votes of their constituency as a whole for or against a decision. In practice, the Executive Board rarely votes and reaches a decision by a "sense of the meeting." On particularly controversial issues, Executive Directors may meet in informal sessions, in seminar form, or in groups with the Managing Director (q.v.) as a precursor to reaching a consensus at a formal Board meeting. A well-informed Executive Director presenting a solid and persuasive case can have an influence far beyond his formal voting power, and it has become a tradition in the Executive Board to seek to accommodate the interests of as many Directors as possible in the final decision. In practice, however, decisions tend to reflect the position articulated by the Managing Director after he has taken note of the various statements made by each speaker and the voting strengths that they command.

The Interim Committee (q.v.) is an advisory body and its recommendations reflect a consensus view. The Articles of Agreement (q.v.) provide for the Committee to be succeeded by a Council (if voted into existence by an 85 percent majority of the Board of Governors), having the same structure and representation as the Committee, but with decisionmaking powers. Members of the Council would be able to split their votes, casting separately the number of votes allotted to each member in their constituencies.

-W-

White, Harry Dexter (1892-1948). Harry Dexter White and John Maynard Keynes (q.v.) were the men primarily concerned in founding the Fund. White joined the staff of the U.S. Treasury in 1934, becoming an Assistant Director in the Division of Research and Statistics in 1936, Director of the Division of Monetary Research in 1938, Assistant to the Secretary in 1941, and Assistant Secretary in 1945. He resigned that position the following year to take up the post of U.S. Executive Director of the Fund. Accused of being a communist, and even a spy (charges that were never proved), he resigned from the Fund in 1947 and died the following year.

White Plan. Harry Dexter White (q.v.) began working on a plan for a comprehensive international agreement in the monetary field as early as 1941 and produced a first completed version in March 1942 entitled *Preliminary Draft Proposal for a United Nations Stabilization Fund and Bank for Reconstruction and Development of the United Nations and Associated Nations.* Unlike the Keynes Plan (q.v.), White's Stabilization Fund required contributions from members and provided for members to be able to purchase currencies (q.v.) of other members. Foreseeing the disruption caused by the war, the plan called for the Stabilization Fund to accept blocked balances in return for usable currencies, to be repaid over time in units, called Unitas. Members were to eliminate within a year all restrictions and controls over foreign exchange (q.v.) transactions and to alter their exchange rate only to correct a fundamental disequilibrium (q.v.) in their balance of payments, and then only with the consent of the Stabilization Fund. These and other features were merged with Keynes' plan for a Clearing Union, as well as with other plans put forward later by other authorities. These plans were discussed for nearly two years and were finally negotiated as the Articles of Agreement (q.v.) of the International Monetary Fund at the International Monetary and Financial Conference of the United and Associated Nations at Bretton Woods (q.v.), New Hampshire, in July 1944.

Witteveen, H. Johannes (1921-). Johannes Witteveen, of the Netherlands, was the Fund's fifth Managing Director (q.v.) from September 1973 to June 1978. From 1948 to 1963, he had been Professor of Economics at the Rotterdam School of Economics; from 1963 to 1965, Minister of Finance; and from 1967 to 1971, he had been both Deputy Prime Minister and Finance Minister.

World Bank. The World Bank, officially known as the International Bank for Reconstruction and Development, came into existence at the same time as the International Monetary Fund at the United Nations International Monetary Conference held at Bretton Woods (q.v.), New Hampshire, in 1944. The Bank's primary responsibility is the financing of economic development. Its first loans were to finance the postwar reconstruction of Europe and other areas ravaged by the war. Since those days, the Bank has concentrated its efforts on assisting developing countries (q.v.), by financing the development of infrastructure (dams, bridges, roads, airports, hydroelectric supplies, education, sewage, water supply, telecommunications, population, and health care) and by promoting agriculture, urban development, and other sectors critical for economic development.

The World Bank comprises two major organizations: the International Bank for Reconstruction and Development and the International Development Association (IDA). Associated with the World Bank, but legally separate from it, are the International Finance Corporation (IFC), the International Center for Settlement of Investment Disputes (ICSID), and the Multilateral Investment Guarantee Agency (MIGA). Together, these five organizations are referred to as the World Bank Group.

The World Bank obtains most of the funds it lends to finance development by borrowing in world markets through the issuance of bonds (guaranteed by member governments) to individuals and private institutions. It lends to creditworthy governments of developing countries at an interest rate that is slightly above the market rate at which the Bank itself can borrow; its loans must generally be repaid in 12 to 15 years.

The International Development Association, on the other hand, obtains its funds largely by grants and donations from member governments. It lends only to governments of very poor developing countries, and its loans are interest free and have a maturity of 35 or 40 years.

The International Finance Corporation mobilizes funds for private enterprises in developing countries, providing both loan and equity capital in partnership with commercial banks and private corporations.

The International Center for Settlement of Investment Disputes, as its name suggests, brings together parties that are in conflict in an attempt to settle investment disputes between them.

The Multilateral Investment Guarantee Agency, the newest member of the World Bank Group, offers insurance coverage against certain risks connected with foreign investment in developing countries. *See also* Fund-Bank Relations.

World Economic Outlook (WEO). The Fund's World Economic Outlook exercise originated with an informal discussion by the Executive Board (q.v.) in 1969. It sprang to prominence in 1973, when the first oil price shock impacted the international payments system, creating imbalances between oil-exporting and oil-importing countries on a scale that had never been seen before. Within a few years it became a regular agenda item for both the Executive Board and the Interim Committee (q.v.), and much of its development was driven by the policy concerns of those governing bodies.

By the late 1970s, the WEO had become a major semiannual forecasting project, supplemented by analyses of trends and policy issues, evolving to include medium-term projections or "scenarios." By the mid-1980s, the role of the scenarios grew to the point where the primary focus of the WEO was no longer short-term scenarios where cyclical fluctuations dominated, but rather the policy requirements for sustainable, noninflationary growth and for consistency between countries. The economic analysis underpinning the scenarios also evolved during the 1980s, from one based primarily on Keynsian models of aggregate demand to one that emphasized neoclassical macroeconomics and incorporated a systematic role for structural policies.

The staff's (q.v.) ability to prepare scenarios representing viable policy options hinged on the development of increasingly sophisticated econometric models. That process also began in the 1960s, with the specification of the Multilateral Exchange Rate Model (MERM) (q.v.). Both MERM and the later World Trade Model, however, were static representations with only limited applicability to policy analysis. The breakthrough came in 1986 with the emergence of MINIMOD, a scaled-down version of a dynamic multicountry model developed elsewhere. Not only was the Fund version smaller and more manageable, it also incorporated endogenous, forward-looking, model-consistent expectations. The credibility gained from that exercise paved the way for the development of MULTIMOD, the staff's first full-scale dynamic model. MULTIMOD, and a separate system of developing-country models, enabled the staff to develop more detailed scenarios within the short lead times required for the WEO. After its discussion by the Executive Board, the *World Economic Outlook* is published twice a year, together with the staff's related analytical papers.

World Trade Organization (WTO). The WTO came into existence on January 1, 1995, and took over, amended, and expanded the responsibilities of the General Agreement on Tariffs and Trade (GATT) (q.v.), which were incorporated into the new WTO agreement. Whereas GATT dealt only with trade in goods, the WTO agreement covers services and intellectual property as well. In October 1997 the WTO had 132 members and 34 observer countries. The latter, which had all applied to join the WTO, included China (although not Hong Kong SAR [q.v.], which was a founding member), the Russian Federation (q.v.), and a large number of countries that were members of the former Soviet Union (FSU).

The Fund, which had a special relationship with GATT, signed a Cooperation Agreement with the WTO on December 9, 1996. The agreement seeks to formalize and build on the close, collaborative relationship that had evolved between the Fund and the contracting parties to GATT. It provides for the Fund to have observer status in the main bodies and committees of the WTO and for the two organizations to exchange an extensive range of their documents.

Statistical Appendix

Table 1. Selected Financial Indicators during the Financial Year Ended April 30
(Millions of SDRs)

	1994	1995	1996	1997	1998
Disbursements					
Total	5,903	11,178	12,303	5,644	19,924
Purchases by facility (GRA)[1]					
Total	5,241	10,592	10,826	4,939	18,981
Stand-bys[2]	1,052	7,587	9,127	1,836	16,127
EFF	746	1,595	1,554	2,820	2,824
CCFF	718	287	9	282	—
STF	2,725	1,123	136	—	—
SAF/ESAF loans	662	587	1,477	705	973
SDA resources	68	19	185	—	—
ESAF Trust resources	594	568	1,292	705	973
Repurchases and Repayments					
Repurchases	4,343	3,984	6,698	6,668	3,789
SAF/ESAF & Trust					
Fund repayments	166	247	402	528	596
Outstanding IMF Credit					
Total	29,889	36,837	42,040	40,488	56,026
Of which:					
GRA	25,533	32,140	36,268	34,539	49,701
SDA	1,835	1,651	1,545	1,220	922
Administered accounts					
Trust Fund	105	102	95	90	90
ESAF Trust[3]	2,416	2,944	4,132	4,639	5,314
Change in outstanding credit (%)					
	5	23	14	- 4	- 438
Number of indebted countries					
	93	99	97	95	94

1. Excludes reserve tranche purchases.
2. Includes first credit tranche drawings.
3. Includes Saudi Fund for Development associated loans.

Source: *Annual Report of the Executive Board, 1998.*

Table 2. Members' Quotas and Voting Power Under Eleventh Review of Quotas, January 1999

Member	Quota *Million SDRs*	Votes *Percent*
Afghanistan, Islamic State of	161.9	0.076
Albania	48.7	0.023
Algeria	914.4	0.431
Angola	286.3	0.135
Antigua and Barbuda	13.5	0.006
Argentina	2,117.1	0.998
Armenia	92.0	0.043
Australia	3,236.4	1.526
Austria	1,872.3	0.883
Azerbaijan	160.9	0.076
Bahamas, The	130.3	0.061
Bahrain	135.0	0.064
Bangladesh	533.3	0.252
Barbados	67.5	0.032
Belarus	386.4	0.182
Belgium	4,605.2	2.172
Belize	18.8	0.009
Benin	61.9	0.029
Bhutan	6.3	0.003
Bolivia	171.5	0.081
Bosnia and Herzegovina	169.1	0.080
Botswana	63.0	0.030
Brazil	3,036.1	1.432
Brunei Darussalam	215.2	0.101
Bulgaria	640.2	0.302
Burkina Faso	60.2	0.028
Burundi	77.0	0.036
Cambodia	87.5	0.041
Cameroon	185.7	0.088
Canada	6,639.2	3.004

Table 2. Members' Quotas and Voting Power *(continued)*

Member	Quota *Million SDRs*	Votes *Percent*
Cape Verde	9.6	0.005
Central African Republic	55.7	0.026
Chad	56.0	0.026
Chile	856.1	0.404
China	4,687.2	2.211
Colombia	774.0	0.365
Comoros	8.9	0.004
Congo, Dem. Rep. of	533.0	0.251
Congo, Republic of	84.6	0.040
Costa Rica	164.1	0.077
Côte d'Ivoire	325.2	0.153
Croatia	365.1	0.172
Cyprus	139.6	0.066
Czech Republic	819.3	0.386
Denmark	1,642.8	0.775
Djibouti	15.9	0.007
Dominica	8.2	0.004
Dominican Republic	218.9	0.103
Ecuador	302.3	0.143
Egypt	943.7	0.445
El Salvador	171.3	0.081
Equatorial Guinea	32.6	0.015
Eritrea	15.9	0.007
Estonia	65.2	0.031
Ethiopia	133.7	0.063
Fiji	70.3	0.033
Finland	1,263.8	0.596
France	10,738.5	5.065
Gabon	154.3	0.073
Gambia, The	31.1	0.015

Table 2. Members' Quotas and Voting Power *(continued)*

Member	Quota *Million SDRs*	Votes *Percent*
Georgia	150.3	0.071
Germany	13,008.2	6.135
Ghana	369.0	0.174
Greece	823.0	0.388
Grenada	11.7	0.006
Guatemala	210.2	0.099
Guinea	107.1	0.051
Guinea-Bissau	14.2	0.007
Guyana	90.9	0.043
Haiti	81.9	0.039
Honduras	129.5	0.061
Hungary	1,038.4	0.490
Iceland	117.6	0.055
India	4,158.2	1.961
Indonesia	2,079.3	0.981
Iran, Islamic Republic of	1,497.2	0.706
Iraq	1,188.4	0.560
Ireland	838.4	0.395
Israel	928.2	0.438
Italy	7,055.5	3.328
Jamaica	273.5	0.129
Japan	13,312.8	6.279
Jordan	170.5	0.088
Kazakhstan	365.7	0.172
Kenya	271.4	0.128
Kiribati	5.6	0.003
Korea	1,633.6	0.770
Kuwait	1,381.1	0.651
Kyrgyz Republic	88.8	0.042
Lao People's Democratic Republic	52.9	0.025

Table 2. Members' Quotas and Voting Power *(continued)*

Member	Quota *Million SDRs*	Votes *Percent*
Latvia	126.8	0.060
Lebanon	203.0	0.096
Lesotho	34.9	0.016
Liberia	129.2	0.061
Libya	1,123.7	0.530
Lithuania	144.2	0.068
Luxembourg	279.1	0.132
Macedonia, FYR	68.9	0.032
Madagascar	122.2	0.058
Malawi	69.4	0.033
Malaysia	1,486.6	0.701
Maldives	8.2	0.004
Mali	93.3	
Malta	102.0	0.048
Marshall Islands	3.5	0.002
Mauritania	64.4	0.030
Mauritius	101.6	0.048
Mexico	2,585.8	1.220
Micronesia, Federal States of	5.1	0.002
Moldova	123.2	0.058
Mongolia	51.1	0.024
Morocco	588.2	0.277
Mozambique	113.6	0.054
Myanmar	258.4	0.122
Namibia	136.5	0.064
Nepal	71.3	0.034
Netherlands, The	5,162.4	2.435
New Zealand	894.6	0.422
Nicaragua	130.0	0.061
Niger	65.8	0.031

Table 2. Members' Quotas and Voting Power *(continued)*

Member	Quota *Million SDRs*	Votes *Percent*
Nigeria	1,753.2	0.827
Norway	1,671.7	0.788
Oman	194.0	0.091
Pakistan	1,033.7	0.488
Palau, Republic of	3.1	0.003
Panama	206.6	0.097
Papua New Guniea	131.6	0.062
Paraguay	99.9	0.047
Peru	638.4	0.301
Philippines	879.9	0.415
Poland	1,369.0	0.592
Portugal	867.4	0.409
Qatar	263.8	0.124
Romania	1,030.2	0.486
Russia	5,945.4	2.804
Rwanda	80.1	0.038
Samoa	11.6	0.005
San Marino	17.0	0.008
São Tomé and Principe	7.4	0.003
Saudi Arabia	6,985.5	3.295
Senegal	161.8	0.076
Seychelles	8.8	0.004
Sierra Leone	103.7	0.049
Singapore	862.5	0.407
Slovak Republic	357.5	0.169
Slovenia	231.7	0.109
Solomon Islands	10.4	0.005
Somalia	81.7	0.039
South Africa	1,868.5	0.881
Spain	3,048.9	1.438

Table 2. Members' Quotas and Voting Power *(continued)*

Member	Quota *Million SDRs*	Votes *Percent*
Sri Lanka	413.4	0.195
St. Kitts and Nevis	8.9	0.004
St. Lucia	15.3	0.007
St. Vincent and the Grenadines	8.3	0.004
Sudan	315.1	0.149
Suriname	92.1	0.043
Swaziland	50.7	0.024
Sweden	2,395.5	1.130
Switzerland	3,458.5	1.631
Syrian Arab Republic	293.6	0.138
Tajikistan	87.0	0.041
Tanzania	198.9	0.094
Thailand	1,081.9	0.510
Togo	73.4	0.035
Tonga	6.9	0.003
Trinidad and Tobago	335.6	0.158
Tunisia	286.5	0.135
Turkey	964.0	0.455
Turkmenistan	75.2	0.035
Uganda	180.5	0.085
Ukraine	1,372.0	0.647
United Arab Emirates	611.7	0.288
United Kingdom	10,738.5	5.065
United States	37,193.3	17.521
Uruguay	306.5	0.145
Uzbekistan	275.6	0.130
Vanuatu	17.0	0.008
Venezuela	2,659.1	1.254
Vietnam	329.1	0.155
Yemen, Republic of	243.5	0.115

Table 2. Members' Quotas and Voting Power *(concluded)*

Member	Quota *Million SDRs*	Votes *Percent*
Yugoslavia, Fed. Rep of	467.7	0.221
Zambia	489.1	0.231
Zimbabwe	353.4	0.167
Total	212,029.0	100.00

Note: No increase in quotas can take effect before the date on which the Fund determines that members having not less than 85 percent of the total quotas on December 23, 1997, have consented to the increase in their quotas. A member's quota cannot be increased until it has consented to the increase and paid the subscription.

Source: *Annual Report of the Executive Board*

Table 3. Stand-by and Other Arrangements Approved in the Financial Years Ended April 30, 1953-1998

	Number of Arrangements					SDRs
	Stand-bys	EFF	SAF	ESAF	Total	*Millions*
1953-57	20				20	1,368
1958-62	65				65	4,558
1963-67	108				108	7,016
1968-72	110				110	6,090
1973-77	73	5			78	8,931
1978	19	3			18	5,877
1979	15	5			20	2,643
1980	22	7			29	3,803
1981	22	15			37	10,795
1982	23	12			35	16,206
1983	30	9			39	25,035
1984	30	5			35	18,569
1985	27	3			30	11,675
1986	24	2			26	4,907
1987	23	1	10		34	5,391
1988	18	2	25		45	4,540
1989	14	2	23	7	46	6,608

Table 3. Stand-by and Other Arrangements *(concluded)*

	Stand-bys	EFF	SAF	ESAF	Total	SDRs *Millions*
1990	19	4	17	11	51	13,911
1991	14	5	12	14	45	14,652
1992	22	7	8	16	53	19,203
1993	15	6	4	20	45	15,279
1994	16	6	3	22	47	8,428
1995	19	9	1	27	56	23,385
1996	21	7	1	28	57	27,918
1997	14	11		35	60	17,996
1998	14	13		33	60	45,069
Total	**765**	**57**	**38**	**65**	**925**	**329,853**

Source: *Annual Report of the Executive Board.*

Table 4. Arrangements Under the Enhanced Structural Adjustment Facility in Effect during the Financial Year Ended April 30, 1998

(Amounts in Millions of SDRs)

Member	Arrangemment Dates Effective date	Expiration date	Amounts Approved Through 4/30/98	Undrawn Balances As of 4/30/98
Armenia	2/14/96	2/13/99	101	34
Azerbaijan	2/20/96	2/19/99	94	38
Benin	8/28/96	12/19/99	27	18
Bolivia	12/19/94	8/27/99	101	—
Burkina Faso	6/14/96	9/9/98	40	20
Cambodia	5/6/94	6/13/99	126	—
Cameroon	8/20/97	8/19/00	162	108
Chad	9/1/95	8/31/98	50	17
Congo, Rep. of	6/28/96	6/27/99	69	56
Côte d'Ivoire	3/11/94	6/13/97	333	—
Cote d''Ivoire	3/17/98	3/16/01	286	202
Ethiopia	10/11/96	10/10/99	88	74
Georgia	2/28/96	2/27/99	167	56

Table 4. Enhanced Structural Adjustment Facility *(concluded)*

| Member | Arrangement Dates | | Amounts Approved | Undrawn Balances |
	Effective date	Expiration date	Through 4/30/98	As of 4/30/98
Georgia	2/28/96	2/27/99	167	56
Ghana	6/30/95	6/29/99	164	69
Guinea	1/13/97	1/12/00	71	35
Guinea-Bissau	1/18/95	7/24/98	10	—
Guyana	1/13/97	4/17/98	54	—
Haiti	10/18/96	10/17/99	91	76
Honduras	7/24/92	11/26/99	47	—
Kenya	4/26/96	4/25/99	150	125
Kyrgz Republic	7/20/94	3/31/98	88	—
Lao PDR	6/4/93	5/7/97	35	—
Macedonia	4/11/97	4/10/00	55	36
Madagascar	11/27/96	11/26/99	81	15
Malawi	10/18/95	10/17/98	46	15
Mali	4/10/96	3/17/01	62	21
Mauritania	1/25/95	6/11/99	43	—
Mongolia	7/30/97	10/19/00	33	28
Mozambique	6/21/96	1/12/98	76	25
Nicaragua	6/24/94	6/23/97	120	—
Nicaragua	3/18/98	3/17/01	101	84
Niger	6/12/96	6/11/99	58	19
Pakistan	10/20/97	10/19/00	682	455
Senegal	8/29/94	1/12/98	131	—
Senegal	4/20/98	4/19/01	107	89
Sierra Leone	3/28/94	5/4/98	102	5
Tanzania	11/8/06	11/7/99	162	74
Togo	9/16/94	6/29/98	65	11
Uganda	9/6/94	11/17/97	12	—
Uganda	11/10/97	11/9/00	100	60
Vietnam	11/11/94	11/10/97	362	—

Table 4. Enhanced Structural Adjustment Facility *(concluded)*

Member	Arrangement Dates		Amounts Approved Through 4/30/98	Undrawn Balances As of 4/30/98
	Effective date	Expiration date		
Yeman	10/29/97	10/28/00	265	221
Zambia	12/6/95	12/5/98	702	40
Total			**4,048**	**2,165**

Source: *Annual Report of the Executive Board, 1998.*

Table 5. Extended Arrangements in Effect in the Financial Year Ended April 30, 1998
(Amounts Expressed in Million SDRs)

Member	Effective Date	Expiration Date	Undrawn Balance
Algeria	5/22/95	5/21/98	84
Argentina[1]	2/4/98	2/3/01	2,080
Azerbaijan	12/20/96	12/19/99	26
Croatia	3/12/97	3/11/00	324
Gabon	11/8/95	11/7/98	50
Jordan[2]	2/9/96	2/8/99	47
Kazakhstan[1]	7/17/96	7/16/99	309
Lithuania	10/24/94	19/23/97	—
Moldova	5/20/96	5/19/99	98
Pakistan	10/20/97	10/19/00	398
Panama	12/10/97	12/9/00	110
Peru[3]	7/1/96	3/31/99	140
Philippines[4]	6/24/94	3/31/98	—
Russia	3/26/96	3/25/99	3,065
Yemen	10/29/97	10/28/00	97
Total			**6,828**

1 The authorities indicated their intention not to draw under the arrangement.

2. Original amount of SDR 201 million increased by SDR 37 million.

3. Original amount of SDR 248 million increased by SDR 52 million for debt and debt service reduction.

4. Extendedfrom June 23, 1997, December 31, 1997, and January 31, 1998. Increased by SDR 317 million.

Source: *Annual Report of the Executive Board, 1998.*

Bibliography

Contents

Publications Issued by the Fund

General Bibliography

The following bibliography lists selective publications on the history and evolution of the International Monetary Fund. The Fund itself periodically published, from 1951 through 1985, comprehensive bibliographies in various issues of its quarterly economic journal, *Staff Papers*. Many of these bibliographies were compiled by Anne C. M. Salda, who on her retirement from the Joint Fund-Bank Library compiled an extensive and annotated bibliography, *International Monetary Fund*, which references publications on the Fund since its inception (*see* under General Bibliography).

The first section of this bibliography lists publications issued by the Fund. The second section concentrates on citing substantive material published outside the Fund dealing with its work and related matters. No attempt has been made to cover the many serious and interesting articles that have appeared in newspapers and news magazines.

The Fund's public web site was opened in September 1996 at the address http://www.imf.org. From the the home-page menu, hyperlinks lead to various submenus, including a catalogue of publications. A number of publications are also available in full text on the web site.

The Fund issues annually a catalog of available publications.

Publications Issued by the Fund

Reports and Documents

Agreement Between the United Nations and the International Monetary Fund, 1956.

Annual Report of the Executive Board, 1946 to date. Published also in French, German, and Spanish.

Annual Report on Exchange Arrangements and Exchange Restrictions, 1979 to date.

Annual Report on Exchange Restrictions, 1950 to 1978.

Articles of Agreement of the International Monetary Fund, Original Articles in 1946; as modified by the first amendment to the Articles, 1968; as modified by the second amendment to the Articles, 1978; and as modified by the third amendment to the Articles, 1992. Also in Arabic, French, Russian, and Spanish.

By-Laws, Rules and Regulations, issued periodically since 1947.

Establishment of a Facility Based on Special Drawing Rights in the International Monetary Fund and Modifications in the Rules and Practices of the Fund: A Report by the Executive Directors to the Board of Governors Proposing Amendment of the Articles of Agreement, 1968.

International Monetary Reform: Documents of the Committee of Twenty, 1974.

Proposed Third Amendment of the Articles of Agreement: A Report to the Board of Governors of the International Monetary Fund Containing the Managing Director's Proposal on the Allocation of Special Drawing Rights for the First Basic Period, 1969. Also in French and Spanish.

Schedule of Par Values, irregular, 1946 to 1971.

Selected Decisions of the International Monetary Fund and Selected Documents, irregular, 1st issue 1962, 23rd issue, 1998.

Summary Proceedings of the . . . Annual Meetings of the Board of Governors, 1946 to date.

Books

Adjustment and Financing in the Developing World: The Role of the International Monetary Fund, papers presented at a seminar sponsored by the IMF and the Overseas Development Institute, London, England, edited by Tony Killick, 1982.

Adjustment, Conditionality, and International Financing, papers presented at a seminar in Viña del Mar, Chile, sponsored by the Central Bank of Chile, the Frederico Santa Maria University, and the IMF, edited by Joaquín Muns, 1983.

Adjustment Policies and Development Strategies in the Arab World, papers presented at a seminar in Abu Dhabi, United Arab Emirates, at a seminar sponsored by the Arab Monetary Fund and the IMF, edited by Said El-Naggar, 1987.

Africa and the International Monetary Fund, papers presented at a symposium sponsored by the Association of African Central Banks and the IMF, edited by G. K. Helleiner, 1987.

Analytical Issues in Debt, by Jacob A. Frenkel, Michael P. Dooley, and Peter Wickham, 1989.

Approaches to Exchange Rate Policy, papers presented at a seminar on exchange rate policy in developing and transitional economies held by the IMF Institute, edited by Richard Barth and Chorng-Huey Wong, 1994.

Balance of Payments Adjustment, 1945 to 1986: The IMF Experience, by Margaret Garritsen de Vries, 1987.

Balance of Payments Compilation Guide, a companion document to the fifth edition of the *Balance of Payments Manual,* 1995.

Balance of Payments Manual, the fifth edition of this manual, revised and updated, 1993.

Balance of Payments Textbook, a companion document to the *Balance of Payments Manual,* 1996.

Bank Soundness and Macroeconomic Policy, by Carl-Johan Lindgren, Gillian Garcia, and Matthew I. Saal, 1996.

Banking Crises: Cases and Issues, edited by V. Sundarajan and Thomas J. T. Baliño, 1991.

Beyond Adjustment: The Asian Experience, edited by Paul Streeten, 1988.

Building Sound Finance in Emerging Market Economies, edited by Gerard Caprio, David Folkerts-Landau, and Timothy D. Lane, 1994.

Central and Eastern Europe: Roads to Growth, papers presented at a seminar moderated by George Winckler, organized by the IMF and the Austrian National Bank, 1992.

Central Banking Technical Assistance to Countries in Transition, proceedings of a joint meeting of central banking technical assistance held in St. Petersburg, Russia, in 1994, edited by J. B. Zulu, Ian S. McCarthy, Susan Almuiña, and Gabriel Sensenbrenner, 1994.

Central Bank Reform in Transition Economies, contains the background papers prepared for the second coordinating meeting of 23 participating central banks of the Baltic States and the Commonwealth of Independent States, edited by V. Sundarajan, Arne B. Petersen, and Gabriel Sensenbrenner, 1997.

Choosing an Exchange Rate Regime: The Challenge for Smaller Industrial Countries, edited by Victor Argy and Paul de Grauwe, 1990.

Coordinated Portfolio Investment Survey Guide, a guide for balance of payments compilers in conducting an internationally coordinated survey of security holdings conducted under the auspices of the IMF, 1996.

Coordinating Public Debt and Monetary Management: Institutional and Operational Arrangements, edited by V. Sundarajan, Peter Dattels, and Hans Blommestein, 1997.

Coordinating Stabilization and Structural Reform, papers presented in an IMF Institute seminar covering four case studies—China, Poland, Argentina, and The Gambia, edited by Richard C. Barth, Alan R. Roe, and Chorng-Huey Wong, 1994.

Current Legal Issues Affecting Central Banks, Vols. I, II, III, and IV, papers presented at four biennial seminars sponsored by the IMF for central banks, edited by Robert C. Effros, 1992, 1994, 1995, and 1997.

Deepening Structural Reform in Africa: Lessons from East Asia, the proceedings of a seminar involving policymakers and senior government officials from Africa and East Asia and senior staff of international organizations, edited by Laura Wallace, 1997.

Debt Stocks, Debt Flows and the Balance of Payments, prepared jointly by the BIS, IMF, OECD, and World Bank, 1994.

Economic Adjustment: Policies and Problems, the proceedings of a seminar held in Wellington, New Zealand, concentrating on economic adjustment problems in the South Pacific, edited by Sir Frank Holmes, 1987.

Economic Policy Coordination, the proceedings of a seminar held in Hamburg, Germany, moderated by Wilfred Guth, 1988.

Emerging Financial Centers: Legal and Institutional Framework, edited by Robert C. Effros, 1982.

Economic Adjustment: Policies and Problems, papers presented at a seminar sponsored by the IMF in Wellington, New Zealand, edited by Sir Frank Holmes,1987.

Economic Policy Coordination, papers presented at a seminar sponsored by the IMF in Hamburg, Germany, 1988.

Effective Government Accounting, by A. Premchand, 1995.

EMU and the International Monetary System, the proceedings of a seminar held in Washington, sponsored by the IMF and the Fondation Camille Gutt, 1997.

Evolving Role of Central Banks, papers presented at a seminar sponsored by the IMF at the Fund's headquarters, edited by Patrick Downes and Reza Vaez-Zadeh, 1991.

External Debt: Definition, Statistical Coverage and Methodology, a comparative description of statistics collected by the BIS, IMF, OECD, and the World Bank, 1998.

External Debt Management, papers presented at a seminar sponsored by the IMF, Washington, D.C., edited by Hassanali Mehran,1985.

External Debt, Savings, and Growth in Latin America, papers presented at a seminar sponsored by the Instituto Torcuato di Tella and the IMF in Don Torcuato, Argentina, edited by Ana María Martirena-Mantel, 1987.

Fifty Years After Bretton Woods: The Future of the IMF and the World Bank, the proceedings of a conference held in Madrid, Spain, sponsored by the IMF and the World Bank to commemorate the fiftieth anniversary of the two institutions, edited by James M. Boughton and K. Sarwar Lateef, 1994.

Financial Policies and Capital Markets in Arab Countries, the proceedings of a seminar held in Abu Dhabi, edited by Said El-Naggar, 1994.

Financial Programming and Policy: The Case of Hungary, edited by Karen A. Swiderski, 1992.

Fiscal Federalism in Theory and Practice, a series of papers on a number of countries examining the relationships among central, state, and local governments in respect to their spending and revenue-raising responsibilities, edited by Teresa Ter-Minassian, 1997.

Fiscal Policies in Economies in Transition, edited by Vito Tanzi, 1992.

Fiscal Policy, Economic Adjustment, and Financial Markets, papers presented at a seminar sponsored by the Centre for Financial and

Monetary Economics, Università Luigi Bocconi, in Milan, Italy, and the IMF, edited by Mario Monti, 1989.

Fiscal Policy in Open Developing Economies, papers presented at the 44th Congress of the International Institute of Public Finance, edited by Vito Tanzi, 1990.

Fiscal Policy, Stabilization, and Growth in Developing Countries, edited by Mario I. Blejer and Ke-young Chu, 1992.

Foreign and Inter-Trade Policies of Arab Countries, papers presented at a seminar sponsored by the IMF in Abu Dhabi, United Arab Emirates, edited by Said El-Naggar, 1992.

Framework for Monetary Stability: Policy Issues and Country Experience, edited by Tomás J. T. Baliño and Carlo Cottarelli, 1994.

The Functioning of the International Monetary System, Vols. I and II, a series of 30 analytical papers on the system as it functioned in 1987-91, edited by Jacob A. Frenkel and Morris Goldstein, 1996.

The Future of the SDR in Light of Changes in the International Monetary System, the proceedings of a seminar held at the IMF, edited by Michael Mussa, James Boughton, and Peter Isard, 1996.

Government Financial Management: Issues and Country Studies, edited by A. Premchand, 1990.

Growth-Oriented Adjustment Programs, papers presented at a symposium sponsored by the IMF and the World Bank in Washington, D.C., edited by Vittorio Corbo, Morris Goldstein, and Mohsin Khan, 1987.

How to Measure the Fiscal Deficit: Analytical and Methodological Issues, edited by Mario I. Blejer and Adrienne Cheasty, 1992.

IMF Glossary, English-French-Arabic, by the IMF Bureau of Language Services, 1996.

IMF Glossary, English-French-Spanish, by the IMF Bureau of Language Services, 1997.

IMF Glossary, English-French-Russian by the IMF Bureau of Language Services, 1998.

The IMF's Statistical Systems in Context of Revision of the United Nations' "A System of National Accounts," edited by Vicente Galbis, 1991.

Improving Tax Administration in Developing Countries, edited by Richard M. Bird and Milka Casanegra de Jantscher, 1992.

Inflation and Growth in China, the proceedings of a conference, edited by Manuel Guitián and Robert Mundell, 1996.

Interest Rate Liberalization and Money Market Development, a series of papers presented at a seminar held in Beijing, China, sponsored by the IMF and the People's Bank of China, edited by Hassanali Mehran, Bernard Laurens, and Marc Quintyn, 1995.

International Financial Policy: Essays in Honor of Jacques J. Polak, papers presented at a conference sponsored by the Netherlands Bank and the IMF in Washington, D.C., edited by Jacob A. Frenkel and Morris Goldstein, 1991.

International Monetary Cooperation Since Bretton Woods, a comprehensive history written by Harold James and published jointly by the IMF and Oxford University Press, 1996.

The International Monetary Fund, 1945-1965: Twenty Years of International Monetary Cooperation. Vol. I, *Chronicle,* by J. Keith Horsefield; Vol. II, *Analysis,* by Margaret G. de Vries and J. Keith Horsefield with the collaboration of Joseph Gold, Mary H. Gumbart, Gertrude Lovasy, and Emil G. Spitzer; and Vol. III, *Documents,* edited by J. Keith Horsefield, 1969.

The International Monetary Fund, 1966-1971: The System Under Stress. Vol. I, *Narrative,* by Margaret Garritsen de Vries; Vol II, *Documents,* edited by Margaret Garritsen de Vries, 1976.

The International Monetary Fund, 1972-1978: Cooperation on Trial. Vols. I and II, *Narrative and Analysis,* by Margaret Garritsen de Vries; and Vol. III, *Documents,* edited by Margaret Garritsen de Vries, 1985.

International Reserves: Needs and Availability, papers presented by a number of scholars and Fund staff members at a seminar convened at the Fund's headquarters, 1970.

Legal and Institutional Aspects of the International Monetary System: Selected Essays, Vols. I and II, by Joseph Gold, 1984.

Legal Effects of Fluctuating Exchange Rates, by Joseph Gold, 1990.

Macroeconomic Accounting and Analysis in Transition Economies, by Abdessatar Ouanes and Subhash Thakur, 1997.

Macroeconomic Adjustment: Policy Instruments and Issues, edited by Jeffrey M. Davis, 1992.

Macroeconomic Issues Facing ASEAN Countries, papers prepared for the ASEAN conference held in Jakarta, edited by John Hicklin, David Robinson, and Anoop Singh, 1997.

Macroeconomic Models for Adjustment in Developing Countries, edited by Mohsin S. Khan, Peter J. Montiel, and Nadeem U. Haque, 1991.

Macroeconomic Policies in an Interdependent World, edited by Ralph Bryant, David Currie, Jacob A. Frenkel, Paul Masson, and Richard Portes, 1989.

Macroeconomics and the Environment, the proceedings of a seminar held at the IMF at which experts from academic and research institutions, nongovernmental organizations, and staff from the IMF and World Bank shared their views on macroeconomic policies and the environment, edited by Ved P. Gandhi, 1996.

Manual on Government Finance Statistics, 1986.

The Monetary Approach to the Balance of Payments, edited by Rudolf R. Rhomberg, 1977.

Optimum Currency Areas: New Analytical and Policy Developments, a revisit to Robert Mundell's pioneering theory of optimum currency areas, with an update by Robert Mundell himself, edited by Mario I. Blejer, Jacob A. Frankel, Leonard Leiderman, and Assaf Razin, 1997.

The Payment System: Design, Management and Supervision, 12 papers by central bank experts from around the world, edited by Bruce J. Summers, 1994.

Payment System, Monetary Policy, and the Role of the Central Bank, by Otomunde E. G. Johnson, Richard K. Abrams, Jean-Marc Destresse, Tony Lybek, Nicholas Roberts, and Mark Swinburne, 1997.

Policies for African Development: From the 1980s to the 1990s, a collection of papers presented at a seminar in Gaborone, Botswana, edited by I. G. Patel, 1992.

Policies for Growth: The Latin American Experience, papers presented at a seminar in Rio de Janeiro, Brazil, moderated by André Lara Resende, 1995.

Privatization and Structural Adjustment in the Arab Countries, papers presented at a seminar sponsored by the IMF in Washington, D.C., edited by Said El-Naggar, 1989.

Public Expenditure Handbook: A Guide to Public Policy Issues in Developing Countries, edited by Ke-young Chu and Richard Hemming, 1991.

Public Expenditure Management, by A. Premchand, 1993.

Reforming China's Public Finances, the proceedings of a conference held in Shanghai, China, with supplemental papers, edited by Ehtisham Ahmad, Gao Qiang, and Vito Tanzi, 1995.

Report on the Measurement of International Capital Flows and Background Papers, 1992.

Report on the World Current Account Discrepancy, by the IMF and other international organizations, 1987.

The Social Effects of Economic Adjustment on Arab Countries, papers presented in a seminar sponsored by the Arab Fund for Economic and Social Development, the Arab Monetary Fund, the IMF, and the World Bank, edited by Taher H. Kanaan, 1997.

Strategies for Structural Adjustment: The Experience of Southeast Asia, papers presented at a seminar sponsored by the IMF in Kuala Lumpur, Malaysia, moderated by Ungku A. Aziz, 1990.

Structural Adjustment and Macroeconomic Policy Issues, papers presented at a conference in Lahore, Pakistan, moderated by V. A. Jafarey, 1992.

Supply-Side Tax Policy: Its Relevance to Developing Countries, by Ved P. Gandhi, Liam P. Ebrill, George A. Mackenzie, Luis Mañas-Anton, Jitendra R. Modi, Somchai Richupan, Fernando Sanchez-Ugarte, and Parthasarathi Shome, 1987.

System of National Accounts, prepared by the Joint Commission of the European Communities, IMF, OECD, UN, and World Bank, 1993.

Systemic Bank Restructuring and Macroeconomic Policy, sets out cross-country restructuring experiences, edited by William E. Alexander, Jeffrey M. Davis, Liam P. Ebrill, and Carl-Johan Lindgren, 1997.

Tax Law Design and Drafting, Vol. I and II, edited by Victor Thuronyi, 1996.

Tax Policy Handbook, edited by Parthasarathi Shome, 1995.

Trade Policy Issues, papers presented in a seminar sponsored by the IMF, edited by Chorng-Huey Wong, 1997.

Transition to Market Studies in Fiscal Reform, edited by Vito Tanzi, 1993.

The Uruguay Round and the Arab Countries, papers presented at a seminar sponsored by the IMF, the Arab Fund for Economic and Social Development, the Arab Monetary Fund, and the World Bank, edited by Said El-Naggar, 1996.

Value-Added Tax: International Practice and Problems, by Alan A. Tait, 1988.

Periodicals

Finance & Development, jointly published by the Fund and the World Bank up to June 1998, when the IMF became the sole publisher. The magazine contains articles in nontechnical language explaining the financial and development issues. Published quarterly, 1964 to date. In Arabic, Chinese, English, French, German, Portuguese, Spanish, and Russian *(free).*

IMF Economic Reviews, a triennial collection of PINs issued in the preceding trimester.

IMF Survey, maintains a running record of the Fund's policies, decisions, and activities, as well as country and world economic developments. Issued twice a month, 1972 to date. Also in French and Spanish.

Staff Papers, quarterly, 1950 to date.. The following are selected articles:

"Analysis of Proposals for Using Objective Indicators as a Guide to Exchange Rate Changes," by Trevor G. Underwood, Vol. 20 (Mar. 1973), pp. 100–117.

"The Appropriate Use of Monetary and Fiscal Policy for Internal and External Stability," by Robert A. Mundell, Vol. 9 (Mar. 1962), pp. 70–79.

"Are Exchange Rates Excessively Volatile? And What Does "Excessively Volatile" Mean, Anyway?" by Leonardo Bartolini and Gordon M. Bodnar, Vol. 43 (Mar. 1996), pp. 72-96.

"Balance of Payments Adjustment Among Developed Countries," by Anne Romanis Braun, Vol. 12 (Mar. 1965), pp. 17—34.

"Competitive Depreciation," by Walter Gardner and S. C. Tsiang, Vol. 2 (1951-52), pp. 399–406.

"Conditionality: Past, Present, Future," by Manuel Guitían, Vol. 42 (Dec. 1995), pp. 792–835.

"Consumption. Income, and International Capital Market Integration," by Tamim Bayoumi and Ronald MacDonald, Vol. 42 (Sept. 1995), pp. 552–76.

"Currency Unions, Economic Fluctuations, and Adjustment," by Tamim Bayoumi and Eswar Prasad, Vol. 44 (Mar. 1997), pp. 36-58.

"Corruption Around the World: Causes, Consequences, Scope, and Cures," by Vito Tanzi, Vol. 45 (Dec. 1998), pp. 559-4.

"The Determinants of Banking Crises in Developing Contraries," by Asli Demirgüç-Kunt and Enrica Detragiache, Vol. 45 (Mar. 1998), pp. 81–109.

"Devaluation Versus Import Restriction as an Instrument for Improving Foreign Trade Balance," by Sidney S. Alexander, Vol. 1 (1950–51), pp. 379–96.

"Developments in the International Payments System," by J. Marcus Fleming, Vol. 10 (Nov. 1963), pp. 461–84.

"Domestic Financial Policies Under Fixed and Floating Exchange Rates," by J. Marcus Fleming, Vol. 9 (Nov. 1962), pp. 369–80.

"Effectiveness of Exchange Rate Policy for Trade Account Adjustment," by Alfred Steinherr, Vol. 28 (Mar. 1981), pp. 199–224.

"Effects of a Devaluation on a Trade Balance," by Sydney S. Alexander, Vol. 2 (Apr. 1952), pp. 263–78.

"Effects of Various Types of Reserve Creation on Fund Liquidity," by J. Marcus Fleming, Vol. 12 (July 1965), pp. 163–88.

"The Exchange Rate Regime: An Analysis and a Possible Scheme," by Fred Hirsch, Vol. 19 (July 1972), pp. 259–85.

"Exchange Rates, Inflation, and Vicious Circles," by John F. O. Bilton, Vol. 27 (Dec. 1980), pp. 679–711.

"Fifty Years of Exchange Policy and Research at the International Monetary Fund," by Jacques V. Polak, Vol. 42 (Dec. 1995), pp. 734–61.

"Fiscal Policy and Long-Run Growth," by Vito Tanzi and Howell H. Zee, Vol. 44, (June 1997), pp. 179–209.

"Fixed and Flexible Exchange Rates: A Renewal of the Debate," by Jacques Artus and John H. Young, Vol. 26 (Dec. 1979), pp. 654–98.

"Fluctuating Exchange Rates in Countries with Relatively Stable Economies: Some European Experiences After World War I," by S. C. Tsiang, Vol. 7 (Oct. 1959), pp. 244–73.

"From Centrally-Planned to Market Economies: The Road from CPE to PCPE," by Guillermo A. Calvo and Jacob A. Frenkel, Vol. 38. (June 1991), pp. 268–99.

"The Fund and International Liquidity," by J. Marcus Fleming, Vol. 11 (July 1964), pp. 177–215.

"Fund Members' Adherence to the Par Value Regime: Empirical Evidence," by Margaret G. de Vries, Vol. 13 (1966), pp. 504–32.

"Government Spending, Taxes, and Economic Growth" by Paul Cashin, Vol. 42 (June 1995), pp. 237–69.

"The Historical Development of the Principle of Surveillance" by Harold James, Vol. 42 (Dec. 1995), pp. 762–91.

"Improving the Demand for Money Function in Moderate Inflation," by William H. White, Vol. 25 (Sept. 1978), pp. 564–607.

"Indexation of Wages and Salaries in Developed Economies," by Anne Romanis Braun, Vol. 23 (Mar. 1976), pp. 226–71.

"An Indicator of Effective Exchange Rates," by Fred Hirsch and Ilse Higgins, Vol. 17 (Nov. 1970), pp. 453–84.

"Indices of Effective Exchange Rates," by Rudolf R. Rhomberg, Vol. 23 (Mar. 1976), pp. 88–112.

"Interest Rate Differences, Forward Exchange Mechanism, Scope for Short-Term Capital Movements," by William H. White, Vol. 10 (Nov. 1963), pp. 485–503.

"International Monetary Fund: A Selected Bibliography," by Martin Loftus and Anne C. M. Salda, Vol. 1 (1951)–Vol. 25 (Dec. 1985), various issues.

"Liberalization and the Behavior of Output During Transition from Plan to Market," by Ernesto Hernández-Catá, Vol. 44 (Dec. 1997), pp. 405-29.

"The Macroeconomic Impact of Privatization," by G.A. Mackenzie, Vol. 45 (June 1998), pp. 363–400.

"The Management of International Liquidity," by Oscar L. Altman, Vol. 13 (July 1966), pp. 216–47.

"Monetary Analysis of Income Formation and Payments Problems," by Jacques J. Polak, Vol. 6 (Nov. 1957), pp. 1–50.

"The Monetary Approach to the Exchange Rate: Some Empirical Evidence," by John F. O. Bilson, Vol. 25 (Mar. 1978), pp. 48–75.

"A Multilateral Exchange Rate Model," by Jacques Artus and Rudolf R. Rhomberg, Vol. 20 (Nov. 1973), pp. 591–611.

"Official Intervention in the Forward Exchange Market: A Simplified Analysis," by J. Marcus Fleming and Robert A. Mundell, Vol. 11 (Mar. 1964), pp. 1–9.

"Openness, Human Development, and Fiscal Policies: Effects of Economic Growth and Speed of Adjustment" by Delano Villanueva, 41 (March 1994), pp. 1–29.

"The Peace Dividend: Military Spending Cuts and Economic Growth," by Malcolm Knight, Norman Loayza, and Delano Villanueva, Vol. 43 (Mar. 1996), pp. 1–37.

"The Present System of Reserve Creation in the Fund," by Hannan Ezekiel, Vol. 13 (Nov. 1966), pp. 398–420.

"The Productivity Bias in Purchasing Power Parity: An Econometric Investigation," by Lawrence H. Officer, Vol. 23 (Nov. 1976), pp. 545–75.

"Professor Triffin on International Liquidity and the Role of the Fund," by Oscar L. Altman, Vol. 8 (May 1961), pp. 151–92.

"The Purchasing-Power-Parity Theory of Exchange Rates: A Review Article," by Lawrence H. Officer, Vol. 23 (Mar. 1976), pp. 1–60.

"Restraining Yourself: The Implications of Fiscal Rules for Economic Stabilization," by Tamim Bayoumi and Barry Eichengreen, Vol. 42 (Mar. 1995), pp. 32–48.

"A Revised Version of the Multilateral Exchange Rate Model," by Jacques Artus and Anne Kenny McQuirk, Vol. 28 (June 1981), pp. 275–309.

"The Role of Incomes Policy in Industrial Countries Since World War II," by Anne Romanis Braun, Vol. 22 (Mar. 1975), pp. 1–6.

"The Role of the International Monetary Fund in Promoting Price Stability," by Walter Gardner, Vol. 7 (Apr. 1960), pp. 319–26.

"The SDR as a Basket of Currencies," by Jacques J. Polak, Vol. 26 (Dec. 1979), pp. 627–53.

"The SDR: Some Problems and Possibilities," by J. Marcus Fleming, Vol. 18 (Mar. 1971), pp. 25–47.

"SDRs and the Working of the Gold Exchange Standard," by Fred Hirsch, Vol. 18 (July 1971), pp. 221–53.

"Separate Exchange Markets for Current and Capital Transactions," by Anthony Lanyi, Vol. 22 (Nov. 1975), pp. 714–49.

"Some Economic Aspects of Multiple Exchange Rates," by Edward M. Bernstein, Vol. 1 (1950-51), pp. 224–37.

"Special Drawing Rights: Renaming the Infant Asset," by Joseph Gold, Vol. 23 (July 1976), pp. 295–311.

"Stabilization Programs in Developing Countries: A Formal Framework," by Mohsin S. Khan and Malcolm D. Knight, Vol. 28 (Mar. 1981), pp. 1–53.

"Strategic Factors in Balance of Payments Adjustment," by Edward M. Bernstein, Vol. 5 (Aug. 1956), pp. 205–49.

"A Survey of Literature on Controls Over International Capital Transactions," by Michael Dooley, Vol. 43 (Dec. 1996), pp. 639–87.

"The Vicious Circle Hypothesis," by John F. O. Bilson, Vol. 26 (Mar. 1979), pp. 1–37.

"Warning: Inflation May Be Harmful to Your Growth," by Atish Ghosh and Steven Philips, Vol. 45 (Dec. 1998), pp. 672–715.

"Why is China Growing So Fast?" by Zului F. Hu and Mohsin S. Khan, Vol. 44 (Mar. 1997), pp. 103–31.

Statistical Publications

(All four statistical publications are available on tape.)

Balance of Payments Statistics Yearbook, 1948 to date.

Direction of Trade Statistics, quarterly and yearbook issues, 1986 to date.

Government Finance Statistics Yearbook, 1977 to date.

International Financial Statistics, monthly and yearbook issues, 1948 to date.

World Economic and Financial Surveys

Developments in International Exchange and Payments Systems, by a staff team, 1991.

Developments in International Exchange and Trade Systems, by a staff team, 1989.

International Capital Markets: Developments and Prospects, annually, 1981 to date. Issues from 1981-85 were issued in the *Occasional Papers series.*

Issues and Developments in International Trade Policy, by a staff team headed by Margaret Kelly and Anne Kenny McQuirk, 1992.

Issues in International Exchange and Payments, by an IMF staff team, issued in 1989, 1992, and 1995.

Multilateral Official Debt Rescheduling: Recent Experience, by a staff team, 1987, 1988, and 1990.

Officially Supported Export Credits: Development and Prospects, by a staff team, 1986, 1988, 1989, 1990, and 1995.

Primary Commodity Markets, staff studies, annually from 1986 through 1990.

Private Market Financing for Developing Countries, staff study, 1991, 1992, 1993, and 1995.

Staff Studies for the World Economic Outlook. Supporting material for the analysis and scenarios depicted in *World Economic Outlook.*

World Economic Outlook: A Survey by the Staff of the IMF, from 1980 to date, biannually. Also in French, Spanish, and Arabic.

Occasional Papers (series)

International Capital Markets: Recent Developments and Short-Term Prospects, by a staff team headed by R. C. Williams, 1980. No. 1.

External Indebtedness of Developing Countries, by a staff team headed by Bahram Nowzad and Richard Williams, 1981. No. 3.

The Multilateral System of Payments: Keynes, Convertibility, and the International Monetary Fund's Articles of Agreement, by Joseph Gold, 1981. No. 6.

International Comparisons of Government Expenditure, by Alan A. Tait and Peter S. Heller, 1982. No. 10.

Effects of Slowdown in Industrial Countries on Growth in Non-Oil Developing Countries, by Morris Goldstein and Mohsin S. Khan, 1982. No. 12.

Currency Convertibility in the Economic Community of West African States, by John B. McLenaghan, Saleh M. Nsouli, and Klaus-Walter Riechel, 1982. No. 13.

Developments in International Trade Policy, by S. J. Anjaria, Z. Iqbal, N. Kirmani, and L. L. Perez, 1982. No. 16.

Aspects of the International Banking Safety Net, by G. G. Johnson, with Richard K. Abrams, 1983. No. 17.

Alternatives to the Central Bank in the Developing World, by Charles Collyns, 1983. No. 20.

Interest Rate Policies in Developing Countries, a study by the Research Department, 1983. No. 22.

Recent Multilateral Debt Restructuring with Official and Bank Creditors, by a staff team headed by E. Brau and R. C. Williams, with P. M. Keller and M. Nowak, 1983. No. 25.

The Fund, Commercial Banks, and Member Countries, by Paul Mentré, 1984. No. 26.

Exchange Rate Volatility and World Trade, a study by the Research Department, 1984. No. 28.

Issues in the Assessment of the Exchange Rates of Industrial Countries, a study by the Research Department, 1984. No. 29.

The Exchange Rate System—Lessons of the Past and Options for the Future, a study by the Research Department, 1984. No. 30.

Foreign Private Investment in Developing Countries, a study by the Research Department, 1985. No. 33.

Adjustment Programs in Africa: The Recent Experience, by Justin B. Zulu and Saleh M. Nsouli, 1985. No. 34.

The West African Monetary Union: An Analytical Review, by Rattan J. Bhatia, 1985. No. 35.

Formulation of Exchange Rate Policies in Adjustment Programs, by a staff team headed by G. G. Johnson, 1985. No. 36.

Export Credit Cover Policies and Payment Difficulties, by Eduard H. Brau and Champen Puckahtikom, 1985. No. 37.

A Case of Successful Adjustment: Korea's Experience During 1980–84, by Bijan B. Aghevli and Jorge Márquez-Ruarte, 1985. No. 39.

Recent Developments in External Debt Restructuring, by K. Burke Dillon, C. Maxwell Watson, G. Russell Kincaid, and Champen Puckahtikom, 1985. No. 40.

Fund-Supported Adjustment Programs and Economic Growth, by Mohsin S. Khan and Malcolm D. Knight, 1985. No. 41.

Global Effects of Fund-Supported Adjustment Programs, by Morris Goldstein, 1986. No. 42.

A Review of the Fiscal Impulse Measure, by Peter S. Heller, Richard D. Haas, and Ahsan H. Mansur, 1986. No. 44.

Switzerland's Role as an International Financial Center, by Benedicte Vibe Christensen, 1986. No. 45.

Fund-Supported Programs, Fiscal Policy, and Income Distribution, a study by the Fiscal Affairs Department, 1986. No. 46.

Strengthening the International Monetary System: Exchange Rates, Surveillance, and Objective Indicators, by Andrew Crockett and Morris Goldstein, 1987. No. 50.

The Role of the SDR in the International Monetary System, by the Research and Treasurer's Departments, 1987. No. 51.

Floating Exchange Rates in Developing Countries: Experience with Auction and Interbank Markets, by Peter J. Quirk, Benedicte Vibe Christensen, Kyung-Mo Huh, and Toshihiko Sasaki, 1987. No. 53.

Protection and Liberalization: A Review of Analytical Issues, by Max Corden, 1987. No. 54.

Theoretical Aspects of the Design of Fund-Supported Adjustment Programs, a study by the Research Department, 1987. No. 55.

Privatization and Public Enterprises, by Richard Hemming and Ali M. Mansoor, 1988. No. 56.

The Implications of Fund-Supported Adjustment Programs for Poverty: Experiences in Selected Countries, by Peter S. Heller, A. Lans Bovenberg, Thanos Catsambas, Ke-young Chu, and Parthasarathi Shome, 1988. No. 58.

Policies for Developing Forward Foreign Exchange Markets, by Peter J. Quirk, Graham Hacche, Viktor Schoofs, and Lothar Weniger, 1988. No. 60.

Policy Coordination in the European Monetary System, by Manuel Guitián, Maximo Russo, and Giuseppe Tullio, 1988. No. 61.

Common Agricultural Policy of the European Community: Principles and Consequences, by the European Department, 1988. No. 62.

Managing Financial Risks in Indebted Developing Countries, by Donald J. Mathieson, David Folkerts-Landau, Timothy Lane, and Iqbal Zaidi, 1989. No. 65.

The European Monetary System in the Context of the Integration of European Financial Markets, by David Folkerts-Landau and Donald Mathieson, 1989. No. 66.

The Role of National Saving in the World Economy: Recent Trends and Prospects, by Bijan B. Aghevli, James M. Boughton, Peter J. Montiel, Delano Villanueva, and Geoffrey Woglom, 1990. No. 67.

Debt Reduction and Economic Activity, by Michael P. Dooley, David Folkerts-Landau, Richard D. Haas, Steven A. Symansky, and Ralph W. Tryon, 1990. No. 68.

International Comparisons of Government Expenditure Revisited: The Developing Countries, by Peter S. Heller and Jack Drummond, 1990. No. 69.

The Conduct of Monetary Policy in the Major Industrial Countries: Instruments and Operating Procedures, by Dallas S. Batten, Michael P. Blackwell, In-Su Kim, Simon E. Nocera, and Yuzuru Ozeki, 1990. No. 70.

MULTIMOD Mark II: A Revised and Extended Model, by Paul Masson, Steven Symansky, and Guy Meredith, 1990. No. 71.

The Czech and Slovak Federal Republic: An Economy in Transition, by Jim Prust and an IMF staff team, 1990. No. 72.

German Unification: Economic Issues, by Leslie Lipschitz and Donogh McDonald, 1991. No. 75.

China: Economic Reform and Macroeconomic Management, by Mario Blejer, David Burton, Steven Dunaway, and Gyorgy Szapary, 1991. No. 76.

The Determinants and Systemic Consequences of International Capital Flows, by Morris Goldstein, Donald J. Mathieson, David Folkerts-Landau, Timothy Lane, J. Saul Lizondo, and Liliana Rojas-Suarez, 1991. No. 77.

Exchange Rate Policy in Developing Countries: Some Analytical Issues, by Bijan Aghevli, Mohsin Khan, and Peter J. Montiel, 1991. No. 78.

Domestic Public Debt of Externally Indebted Countries, by Pablo E. Guidotti and Manmohan S. Kumar, 1991. No. 80.

Currency Convertibility and the Transformation of Centrally Planned Economies, by Joshua E. Greene and Peter Isard, 1991. No. 81.

Characteristics of a Successful Exchange Rate System, by Jacob A. Frenkel, Morris Goldstein, and Paul R. Masson, 1991. No. 82.

Value-Added Tax: Administrative and Policy Issues, edited by Alan A. Tait, 1991. No. 88.

The Internationalization of Currencies: An Appraisal of the Japanese Yen, by George S. Tavlas and Yuzuru Ozeki, 1991. No. 90.

Economic Policies for a New South Africa, edited by Desmond Lachman and Kenneth Bercuson, 1991. No. 91.

Regional Trade Arrangements, by Augusto de la Torre and Margaret R. Kelly, 1991. No. 93.

Tax Harmonization in the European Community: Policy Issues and Analysis, by George Kopits, 1992. No. 94.

The Fiscal Dimensions of Adjustment in Low-Income Countries, by Karim Nashashibi, Sanjee Gupta, Claire Liuksila, Henri Lorie, and Walter Mahler, 1992. No. 95.

Policy Issues in the Evolving International Monetary System, by Morris Goldstein, Peter Isard, Paul R. Masson, and Mark P. Taylor, 1992. No. 96.

Rules and Discretion in International Economic Policy, by Manuel Guitián, 1992. No. 97.

Financial Sector Reforms and Exchange Arrangements in Eastern Europe, by Guillermo A. Calvo, Manmohan S. Kumar, Eduardo Borensztein, and Paul R. Masson, 1993. No. 102.

The Structure and Operation of the World Gold Market, by Gary O'Callaghan, 1993. No. 105.

Economic Adjustment in Low-Income Countries: Experience Under the Enhanced Structural Adjustment Facility, by Susan Schadler, Franek Rozwadowski, Siddarth Tiwari, and David O. Robinson, 1993. No. 106.

Recent Experiences with Surges in Capital Inflows, by Susan Schadler, Maria Carkovic, Adam Bennett, and Robert Kahn, 1993. No. 108.

Limiting Central Bank Credit to the Government: Theory and Practice, by Carlo Cottarelli, 1993. No. 110.

The Russian Federation in Transition: External Developments, by Benedicte Vibe Christensen, 1994. No. 111.

The Behavior of Non-Oil Commodity Prices, by Eduardo Borensztein, Mohsin Khan, Carneb M. Reinhart, and Peter Wickham, 1994. No. 112.

Exchange Rates and Economic Fundamentals: A Framework for Analysis, by Peter B. Clark, Leonardo Bartolini, Tamim Bayoumi, and Steven Symansky, 1994. No. 115.

Improving the International Monetary System: Constraints and Possibilities, by Michael Mussa, Morris Goldstein, Peter B. Clark, Donald J. Mathieson, and Tamim Bayoumi, 1994. No. 116.

Uganda: Adjustment with Growth, 1987-94, by Robert L. Sharer, Hema R. De Zoysa, and Calvin A. McDonald, 1995. No. 121.

Capital Flows in the APEC Region, by Mohsin S. Khan and Carmen M. Reinhart, eds., 1995. No. 122.

Saving Behavior and the Asset Price "Bubble" in Japan: Analytical Studies, by Ulrich Baumgartner and Guy Meredith, eds., 1995. No. 124.

The Adoption of Indirect Instruments of Monetary Policy, by a staff team headed by William E. Alexander, Tómas J. T. Baliño, and Charles Ecoch, 1995. No. 126.

Road Maps of the Transition: The Baltics, the Czech Republic, Hungary, and Russia, by Biswajit Banerjee, Vincent Koen, Thomas Krueger, Mark S. Lutz, Michael Marrese, and Tapio O. Saavalainen, 1995, No. 127.

IMF Conditionality: Experience Under Stand-by and Extended Arrangements, Part I: Key Issues and Findings, by Susan Schadler, Adam Bennett, Maria Carkovic, Louis Dicks-Mireaux, Mauro Mecagni, James H. J. Morsink, and Miguel A. Savastano, 1995. No. 128.

IMF Conditionality: Experience Under Stand-By and Extended Arrangements, Part II: Background Papers, by Susan Schadler, ed., Adam Bennett, Maria Carkovic, Louis Dicks-Mireaux, Mauro Mecagni, James H.J. Morsink, and Miguel A. Savastano, 1995. No. 129.

Capital Account Convertibility: Review of Experience and Implications for IMF Policies, by staff teams headed by Peter J. Quirk and Owen Evans, 1995. No. 131.

Financial Fragilities in Latin America: The 1980s and 1990s, by Liliana Rojas-Suárez and Steven R. Weisbrod, 1995. No. 132.

Policy Experiences and Issues in the Baltics, Russia, and Other Countries of the Former Soviet Union, by Daniel A. Citrin and Ashok K. Lahiri, eds., 1995. No. 133.

India: Economic Reform and Growth, by Ajai Chopra, Charles Collyns, Richard Hemming, Karen Parker, with Woosik Chu and Oliver Fratzscher, 1995. No. 134.

Aftermath of the CFA Franc Devaluation, by Jean A. P. Clément, with Johannes Mueller, Stéphane Cossé, and Jean Le Dem, 1996. No. 138.

Reinvigorating Growth in Developing Countries: Lessons from Adjustment Policies in Eight Economies, by David Goldsbrough, Sharmini Coorey, Louis Dicks-Mireaux, Balazs Horvath, Kalpana Kochhar, Mauro Mecagni, Erik Offerdal, and Jianping Zhou, 1996. No. 139.

Monetary and Exchange System Reforms in China: An Experiment in Gradualism, Hassanali Mehran, Marc Quintyn, Tom Nordman, Bernard Laurens, 1996. No. 141.

Adjustment for Growth: The African Experience, by Michael Hadjimichael, Michael Nowak, Robert Sharer, and Amor Tahari, 1996. No. 143.

Exchange Rate Movements and Their Impact on Trade and Investment in the APEC Region, by Takatoshi Ito, Peter Isard, Steven Symansky, and Tamim Bayoumi, 1996. No. 145.

Thailand: The Road to Sustained Growth, by Kalpana Kochhar, Louis Dicks-Mireaux, Balazs Horvath, Mauro Mecagni, Erik Offerdal, and Jiamping Zhou, 1996. No. 146.

The Composition of Fiscal Adjustment and Growth: Lessons from Fiscal Reforms in Eight Economies, by G. A. Mackenzie, David W. H. Orsmond, and Philip R. Gerson, 1997. No. 149.

Currency Board Arrangements: Issues and Experiences, by D. Mihalke, 1997. No. 151.

Hong Kong, China: Growth, Structural Change, and Economic Stability During the Transition, by John Dodsworth and Dubravko Mihaljek, 1997. No. 152.

Credibility Without Rules, by Carlo Cottarelli and C. Giannini, 1997. No. 154.

The ESAF at Ten Years: Economic Adjustment and Reform in Low-Income Countries, by the staff of the IMF, 1997. No. 156.

Central Bank Reforms in the Baltics, Russia, and the Other Countries of the Former Soviet Union, by a staff team headed by Malcom Knight, 1997. No. 157.

Transparency in Government Operations, by George Kopitz and Jon Craig, 1997. No. 158.

Fiscal Reforms in Low-Income Countries, by an IMF staff team headed by George Abed, 1998. No. 160.

Fiscal Policy Rules, by G. Kopits and S. Symansky, No. 162.

MULTIMOD Mark III: The Core Dynamic and Steady State Model, by David Laxton, Peter Isard, et al., 1998. No. 164.

Hedge Funds and Financial Market Dynamics, by B. Eichengreen and D. Mathieson, 1998. No 166.

Capital Account Liberalization: Theoretical and Practical Aspects, by a staff team led by Barry Eichengreen and Michael Mussa, with Giovanni Dell'Ariccia, Enrica Detragiache, Glan Maria Milesi-Ferretti, and Andrew Tweedie, No. 172.

Pamphlet Series

This series covers, in depth, various aspects of the Fund, its functions, policies, and legal concepts *(free).* The following is an incomplete listing.

1. *Introduction to the Fund,* by J. Keith Horsefield, 1964.
2. *The International Monetary Fund: Its Form and Function,* by J. Marcus Fleming, 1964.
3. *The International Monetary Fund and Private Business Transactions: Some Legal Effects of the Articles of Agreement,* by Joseph Gold, 1965.
4. *The International Monetary Fund and International Law: An Introduction,* by Joseph Gold, 1965.
6. *Maintenance of the Gold Value of the Fund's Assets,* by Joseph Gold, 1971.
7. *The Fund and Non-Member States; Some Legal Effects,* by Joseph Gold, 1971.
9. *Balance of Payments: Its Meaning and Uses,* by Poul Høst-Madsen, 1967.
10. *Balance of Payments Concepts and Definitions,* 1969.
12. *The Reform of the Fund,* by Joseph Gold, 1969.
13. *Special Drawing Rights: Character and Use,* by Joseph Gold, 1970.
14. *The Fund's Concepts of Convertibility,* by Joseph Gold, 1971.
16. *Some Reflections on the Nature of Special Drawing Rights,* by J. J. Polak, 1971.
18. *Valuation and Rate of Interest of the SDR,* by Jacques J. Polak, 1974.
19. *Floating Currencies, Gold, and SDRs: Some Recent Legal Developments,* by Joseph Gold, 1976.
20. *Voting Majorities in the Fund: Effects of the Second Amendment to the Articles,* by Joseph Gold, 1977.
21. *International Capital Movements Under the Law of the International Monetary Fund,* by Joseph Gold, 1977.
22. *Floating Currencies, SDRs, and Gold: Further Legal Developments,* by Joseph Gold, 1977.
23. *Use, Conversion, and Exchange of Currency Under the Second Amendment of the Fund's Articles,* by Joseph Gold, 1978.
25. *The Second Amendment of the Fund's Articles of Agreement,* by Joseph Gold, 1978.

26. *SDRs, Gold, and Currencies: Third Survey of New Legal Developments,* by Joseph Gold, 1979.
27. *Financial Assistance by the International Monetary Fund: Law and Practice,* by Joseph Gold, 1980.
28. *SDR,* by J. J. Polak, 1979.
31. *Conditionality,* by Joseph Gold, 1979.
32. *The Rule of Law in the International Monetary Fund,* by Joseph Gold, 1980.
33. *SDRs, Currencies, and Gold: Fourth Survey of New Legal Developments,* by Joseph Gold, 1980.
35. *The Legal Character of the Fund's Stand-By Arrangements and Why It Matters,* by Joseph Gold, 1980.
36. *SDRs, Currencies, and Gold: Fifth Survey of New Legal Developments,* by Joseph Gold, 1981.
37. *The International Monetary Fund: Its Evolution, Organization, and Activities,* by the staff, 1984.
38. *Fund Conditionality: Evolution of Principles and Practices,* by Manuel Guitián, 1981.
39. *Order in International Finance, the Promotion of IMF Stand-By Arrangements, and the Drafting of Private Loan Agreements,* by Joseph Gold, 1982.
40. *SDRs, Currencies, and Gold: Sixth Survey of New Legal Developments,* by Joseph Gold, 1983.
44. *SDRs, Currencies, and Gold: Seventh Survey of New Legal Developments,* by Joseph Gold, 1987.
45. *Financial Organization and Operations of the IMF,* by the Treasurer's Department, 1991.
46. *The Unique Nature of the Responsibilities of the International Monetary Fund,* by Manuel Guitián, 1992.
47. *Social Dimensions of the IMF's Policy Dialogue,* by the staff of the IMF, 1995.
48. *Unproductive Public Expenditures: A Pragmatic Approach to Policy Analysis,* by the Fiscal Affairs Department, 1995.
49. *Guidelines for Fiscal Adjustment,* by the Fiscal Affairs Department, 1995.
50. *The Role of the IMF: Financing and Its Interactions with Adjustment and Surveillance,* by Paul Masson and Michael Mussa, 1995.
51. *Debt Relief for Low-Income Countries: The HIPC Initiative,* by Anthony R. Boote and Kamau Thugge, 1997.
52. *The IMF and the Poor,* by the Fiscal Affairs Department, 1998.

Booklets

This new series, which was launched in 1996, is designed to make available to a readership of nonspecialists some of the economic research being carried out in the Fund. The papers are written in nontechnical language.

1. *Growth in East Asia: What We Can and What We Cannot Infer,* by Michael Sarel, 1996.
2. *Does the Exchange Rate Regime Matter for Inflation and Growth,* by Atish R. Ghosh, Ann-Marie Gulde, Jonathan D. Ostry, and Holger Wolf, 1996.
3. *Confronting Budget Deficits,* by Rozlyn Coleman, prepared from a working paper by Paul R. Masson and Michael Mussa, 1996.
4. *Fiscal Reforms That Work,* by C. John McDermott and Robert F. Wescott, 1996.
5. *Transformation to Open Market Operations: Developing Economies and Emerging Markets,* by Stephen H. Axilrod, 1996.
6. *Why Worry About Corruption?* by Paolo Mauro, 1997.
7. *Sterilizing Capital Flows,* by Jang-Yung Lee, 1997.
8. *Why Is China Growing So Fast?* by Zuliu Hu and Moshin S. Khan, 1997.
9. *Protecting Bank Deposits,* by Gillian G. Garcia, 1997.
10. *Deindustrialization—Its Causes and Implications,* by Robert Rowthorn and Ramana Ramaswamy, 1997.
11. *Does Globalization Lower Wages and Export Jobs?* by Matthew J. Slaughter and Phillip Swagel, 1997.
12. *Roads to Nowhere: How Corruption in Public Investment Hurts Growth,* by Vito Tanzi and Hamid Davoodi, 1998.
13. *Fixed or Flexible: Getting the Exchange Right in the 1990s,* by Francescp Caramazza and Jahangir Aziz, 1998.
14. *Lessons from Systemic Bank Reconstructing,* by Claudia Dziobek and Ceyla Pazarbasioglu, 1998.
15. *Inflation Targeting as a Framework for Monetary Policy,* by Guy Debelle, Paul Masson, Miguel Savastano, and Suni Sharma, 1998.

Papers on Policy Analysis and Assessment

Beginning in January 1999, this series was renamed Policy Discussion Papers (PDP). The series comprises staff studies in the area of policy design and research. They are aimed primarily at operational staff involved in mission work and economists elsewhere interested in policy issues. The following is a selective listing.

Japan's Corporate Groups and Imports, by Daniel A. Citrin, 1992, PPAA/92/2

The Operation of the Estonian Currency Board, by Adam G. G. Bennmett, 1992. PPAA/92/3

Real Exchange Rate Targeting in Developing Countries, by Peter J. Montiel and Jonathan D. Ostry, 1993. PPAA/93/2

Adjusting to Development: The IMF and the Poor, by James Boughton, 1993. PPAA/93/4

A Cautionary Note on the Use of Exchange Rate Indicators, by Peter Wickham, 1993. PPAA/93/5

The Strategy of Reform in the Previously Centrally Planned Economies of Eastern Europe: Lessons and Challenges, by Eduardo Borensztein, 1993, PPAA/93/6

The Capital Inflows Problem: Concepts and Issues, by Guillermo A. Calvo, Leonardo Leiderman, and Carmen Reinhart, 1993. PPAA/93/10

Options for Monetary and Exchange Arrangements in Transition Economies, by Delano Villanueva, 1993. PPAA/93/12

Aspects of the Design of Financial Programs with the Adoption of Indirect Monetary Controls, by Barry Johnston, 1993. PPAA/93/16

The Taxation of High Income Earners, by Parthasarathi Shome, 1993. PPAA/93/19

International Capital Transactions: Should They Be Restricted? by Norman S. Fieleke, 1993. PPAA/93/20

On the Political Sustainability of Economic Reform, by Carlos M. Asilis and Gian Maria Milesi-Ferretti, 1994. PPAA/94/3

The New Protectionism in Industrial Countries: Beyond the Uruguay Round, by Douglas A. Irwin, 1994. PPAA/94/5

Asset Prices, Monetary Policy, and the Business Cycle, by Garry J. Schinasi, 1994. PPAA/94/6

Emerging Equity Market: Growth, Benefits, and Policy Concerns, by Robert A. Feldman and Mammohan S. Kumar, 1994. PPAA/94/7

Establishing Monetary Control in Financial Systems With Insolvent Institutions, by Donald Mathieson and Richard D. Haas, 1994. PPAA/94/10

Use of Central Bank Credit Auctions in Economies in Transition, by Matthew I. Saal and Lorena M. Zamalloa, 1994. PPAA/94/11

Macroeconomic Management with Informal Financial Markets, by Pierre-Richard Agénor and Nadeem U. Haque, 1994. PPAA/94/12

Currency Arrangements in the Countries of the Former Ruble Area and Conditions for Sound Monetary Policy, by Thomas A. Wolf, 1994. PPAA/94/15

Currency Board: Issues and Experiences, by Adam G. G. Bennett, 1994. PPAA/94/18

Structural Policies in Developing Countries, by Eduardo Borensztein, 1994. PPAA/94/19

Russia and the IMF: The Political Economy of Macro-Stabilization, Ernesto Hernández-Catá, 1994. PPAA/94/20

The IMF and the Latin American Debt Crisis: Seven Common Criticisms, by James M. Boughton, 1994. PPAA/94/23

The Speed of Financial Sector Reform: Risks and Strategies, by R. Barry Johnston, 1994. PPAA/94/26

Social Safety Nets for Economic Transition: Options and Recent Experiences, by the Expenditure Policy Division Staff, 1995. PPAA/95/3

Non-G-10 Countries and the Basle Capital Rules: How Tough a Challenge Is It to Join the Basle Club? by Claudia Dziobek, Olivier Frécaut, and Maria Nieto, 1995. PPAA/95/5

Discretion with Rules? Lessons from the Currency Board Arrangement in Lithuania, by Wayne Camard, 1996. PPAA/96/1

Borrowing by Subnational Governments: Issues and Selected International Experiences, by Teresa Ter-Minassian, 1996. PPAA/96/4

Social Protection in Transition Countries: Emerging Issues, by Ke-young Chu and Sanjeev Gupta, 1996. PPAA/96/5

Fiscal Dimensions of EMU, by Paul R. Masdson, 1996. PPAA/96/7

The Definition of Reserve Money: Does It Matter for Financial Programs? by Kalpana Kochhar, 1996. PPAA/96/10

Conditionality as an Instrument of Borrower Credibility, by Pierre Dhonte, 1997. PPAA/97/2

The Macroeconomic Impact of Privatization, by G. A. Mackenzie, 1997. PPAA/97/9

Making a Currency Board Operation, by Charles Enoch and Anne-Marie Gulde, 1997. PPAA/97/10

Bank Soundness and Currency Board Arrangements Issues and Experience, by Veerathai Santiprabhob, 1997. PPAA/97/11

Transparency in Central Bank Operations in the Foreign Exchange Markets, by Charles Enoch, 1998. PPAA/98/2

The Payment System and Monetary Policy, by Omotunde E. G. Jouhnson, 1998. PPAA/98/4

Sequencing Capital Account Liberalization and Financial Sector Reform, by R. Barry Hohnston, 1998. PPAA/98/8

Systemic Banking Distress: The Need for aan Enhanced Monetary Survey, by Olivier Frécaut and Eric Sidgwick, 1998. PPAA/98/9

Working Papers, 1997

This series is designed to make Fund staff research available to a wide audience. The series began in 1991, about 180 working papers are released each year. In many cases the papers are subject to ongoing work and revision. Many will eventually be published by the Fund as articles in one of the Fund's serial publications. The series is available on a subscription basis.

Staff Country Reports

The IMF releases Staff Country Reports on about 150 member countries each year. The reports contain comprehensive background material on economic developments as part of the annual consultations that the IMF conducts with most member countries.

General Bibliography

General

Bank for International Settlements. *Annual Reports.* Basle, Switzerland, 1931 to date.

Harrod, R. F. *The Life of John Maynard Keynes,* Harcourt, Brace (Princeton and London, 1951).

Howell, Kristin. "The Role of the Bank for International Settlements in Central Bank Cooperation," *Journal of European Economic History,* Vol. 22, No. 2 (Fall 1993).

Jacobsson, Erin E. *A Life for Sound Money: Per Jacobsson; His Biography,* Clarendon Press (Oxford, 1979).

Keynes, John Maynard. *The Collected Writings of John Maynard Keynes,* Vols. 24, 25, and 26, ed. by Donald Moggridge, Macmillan (London and New York, 1982).

Odell, John S. *U.S. International Monetary Policy: Markets, Power, and Ideas as Sources of Change,* Princeton University Press (Princeton, New Jersey, 1982).

Rees, David. *Harry Dexter White: A Study in Paradox,* Coward, McCann and Geoghenan (New York, 1973).

Salda, Anne C. M. *International Monetary Fund: A Selected Bibliography,* International Organizations Series, Vol. 4, Transaction Publishers (New Brunswick, New Jersey, 1992).

Skidelsky, Robert. *John Maynard Keynes: The Economist as Saviour,* Macmillan (London, 1992).

Background of the Bretton Woods System

Bernanke, Ben, and Harold James. "The Gold Standard, Deflation, and Financial Crisis in the Great Depression: An International Comparison," in *Financial Markets and Financial Crises,* ed. by R. Glenn Hubbard, University of Chicago Press (Chicago, 1991).

Bernstein, Edward M. "The Adequacy of United States Gold Reserves," *American Economic Review* (Papers and Proceedings of the Seventy-Third Annual Meeting of the American Economic Association), Vol. 51 (1961), pp. 439-46.

Bloomfield, Arthur I. *Monetary Policy Under the Gold Standard: 1880-1914,* Federal Reserve Bank of New York (New York, 1959).

Brown, William Adams, Jr. *The International Gold Standard Reinterpreted 1914-1934,* National Bureau of Economic Research (New York, 1940).

Cassel, Gustav. *The Downfall of the Gold Standard,* Clarendon Press (Oxford, 1936).

Clarke, Stephen V. O. *The Reconstruction of the International Monetary System: The Attempts of 1922 and 1933,* Princeton Studies in International Finance No. 33, Princeton University Press (Princeton, 1973).

———. *Exchange-Rate Stabilization in the Mid—1930s: Negotiating the Tripartite Agreement,* Princeton Studies in International Finance No. 41, Princeton University Press (Princeton, 1977).

Clavin, Patricia. "The World Economic Conference 1933: The Failure of British Internationalism," *Journal of European Economic History,* Vol. 20, No. 3 (Winter, 1991).

Cooper, Richard N. *Gold Standard: Historical Fact and Future Prospects,* Brookings Papers on Economic Activity (Washington, D.C., 1982).

De Cecco, Marcello. *The Internatiional Gold Standard: Money and Empire,* St. Martin's Press (New York, 1984).

Eichengreen, Barry J. "The Gold Standard and the Great Depression," *NBER Reporter,* National Bureau of Economic Research (Spring 1991).

———. *Golden Fetters: The Gold Standard and the Great Depression, 1919-1939,* Oxford University Press (New York, 1992).

Eichengreen, Barry J., and Jeffery Sachs. "Exchange Rates and Economic Recovery in the 1930s," *Journal of Economic History,* Vol. 45 (1985).

Palyi, Melchior. *The Twilight of Gold 1914–1936: Myths and Realities,* Henry Regnery (Chicago, 1972).

Schubert, Aurel. *The Credit-Anstalt Crisis of 1931,* Cambridge University Press (Cambridge, England, 1991).

Establishing the Bretton Woods System

Argy, Victor. *The Postwar International Money Crisis: An Analysis,* Allen & Unwin (London, 1981).

Black, Stanley W. *A Levite Among the Priests: Edward M. Bernstein and the Origins of the Bretton Woods System,* Westview Press (Boulder, Colorado, 1991).

Bordo, Michael D. "The Bretton Woods System: A Historical Overview," in *A Retrospective on the Bretton Woods System: Lessons for International Monetary Reform,* ed. by Michael D. Bordo and Barry Eichengreen, University of Chicago Press (Chicago, 1993).

Bordo, Michael D., and Barry Eichengreen, eds. *A Retrospective on the Bretton Woods System: Lesson for International Monetary Reform*, University of Chicago Press (Chicago, 1993).

Bordo, Michael D., Dominique Simard, and Eugene White. "France and the Bretton Woods International Monetary System, 1960 to 1968," NBER Working Paper No. 4642, National Bureau of Economic Research (Cambridge, Massachusetts, 1994).

Dormael, Armand van. *Bretton Woods: Birth of a Monetary Order*, Holmes and Meier (New York, 1978).

Ebke, Werner F., et al., eds. *Festschrift in Honor of Sir Joseph Gold*, Verlag Recht und Wirtschaft (Heidelberg, Germany, 1990).

Feis, Herbert. "Restoring Trade After the War," *Foreign Affairs* (New York), Vol. 20 (1941-42).

Gardner, Richard N. *Sterling-Dollar Diplomacy*, Columbia University Press (New York, 1969).

Mikesell, Raymond F. "Negotiating at Bretton Woods, 1944," in *Negotiating with the Russians*, ed. by Raymond Dennett and Joseph E. Johnson, World Peace Foundation (Boston, 1951), pp. 101-16.

Mikesell, Raymond F. *The Bretton Woods Debates: A Memoir*, Essays in International Finance No. 192, Princeton University Press (Princeton, New Jersey, 1994).

Mossé, Robert. *Le système monétaire de Bretton Woods et les grands problèmes de l'après guerre*, Recueil Sirey (Paris, 1948).

Officer, Lawrence H. "Are International Monetary Fund Quotas Unfavorable to Less-Developed Countries? A Normative Historical Analysis," *Journal of International Money and Finance*, Vol. 10, No. 2 (June 1991).

Robertson, Dennis H. "The Post-War Monetary Plans," *The Economic Journal* (London), Vol. 53 (1943), pp. 352-60.

——. *Utility and All That*, Allen and Unwin (London, 1952).

Robinson, Joan. "The International Currency Plans," *The Economic Journal* (London), Vol. 53 (1943), pp. 161-75.

Southard, Frank. *The Evolution of the International Monetary Fund*, Essays in International Finance, No. 135, Princeton University Press (Princeton, New Jersey, 1979).

United Nations Monetary and Financial Conference, Bretton Woods, New Hampshire, 1944. *Proceedings and Documents*, 2 vols., U.S. Government Printing Office (Washington, D.C., 1944).

[U.S.] Board of Governors of the Federal Reserve System. *Bretton Woods Agreements: A Bibliography, April 1943-December 1945* (Washington, D.C., 1946).

[U.S.] Department of State. *Proceedings and Documents of United Nations Monetary and Financial Conference, Bretton Woods, New Hampshire, July 1-22, 1944* (Washington, D.C., 1948).

[U.S.] Treasury Department. *Questions and Answers on the International Monetary Fund* (Washington, D.C., June 1944).

Van Dormael, Armand. *Bretton Woods: Birth of a Monetary System,* Holmes and Meier (New York, 1978).

Viner, Jacob. "Two Plans for International Monetary Stabilization," *Yale Review* (New Haven), Vol. 33 (1943-44).

White, Harry D. "Post-War Currency Stabilization," *The American Economic Review,* Vol. 33 (1943), Supplement.

Williams, John. H. *Postwar Monetary Plans and Other Essays,* Wilkins (New York, 1947).

Young, John Parke. "Developing Plans for an International Monetary Fund and a World Bank," *Department of State Bulletin* (Washington, D.C.), Vol. 23 (1950).

Macroeconomic and Structural Adjustment
and Fund Conditionality

Acheson, A. L. K., J. F. Chant, and M. F. J. Prachowny, eds. *Bretton Woods Revisited: Evaluations of the International Monetary Fund and the International Bank for Reconstruction and Development,* University of Toronto Press (Toronto, 1972).

Aliber, Robert Z. *The International Money Game,* Basic Books (New York, 1987).

Bangura, Yusuf. "IMF/World Bank Conditionality and Nigeria's Structural Adjustment Programme," in *The IMF and the World Bank in Africa: Conditionality, Impact and Alternatives,* ed. by Kjell J. Havnevik, Scandinavian Institute of African Studies (Uppsala, 1987).

——. "Crisis and Adjustment: The Experience of Nigerian Workers," in *The IMF, the World Bank and African Debt,* Vol. 2, *The Social and Political Impact,* ed. by Bade Onimode, Institute for African Alternatives and Zed Books (London, 1989).

Bazdresch, Carlos, and Santiago Levy. "Populism and Economic Policy in Mexico 1970-1982," in *Macroecomics of Populism in Latin America,* ed. by Rudiger Dornbusch and Sebastian Edwards, University of Chicago Press (Chicago, 1991).

Bergsten, C. Fred. *International Adjustment and Financing: The Lessons from 1985–1991,* Institute for International Economics (Washington, D.C., 1991).

Bourguignon, François, and Cristian Morrison. *Adjustment and Equity in Developing Countries: A New Approach,* Organization of Economic Cooperation and Development (Paris, 1992).

Bruno, Michael. "Stabilization and the Macroeconomics of Transition: How Different Is Eastern Europe?" *Economics of Transition,* Vol. 1 (1993).

Callaghy, Thomas M. "Lost Between State and Market: The Politics of Economic Adjustment in Ghana, Zambia, and Nigeria," in *Economic Crisis and Policy Choice: The Politics of Adjustment in the Third World*, ed. by Joan Nelson, Princeton University Press (Princeton, New Jersey, 1990).

Campbell, Horace. *Tanzania and the IMF: The Dynamics of Liberalization*, Westview (Boulder, Colorado, 1992).

Campbell, K., and John Loxley, eds. *Structural Adjustment in Africa*, St. Martin's Press (New York, 1989).

Campos, Roberto de Oliveiro. "Inflation and Balanced Growth," in *Economic Development in Latin America: Proceedings of a Conference Held by the International Economic Association*, ed. by Howard S. Ellis, St. Martin's Press (New York, 1961).

Cline, William R., and Sidney Weintraub, eds. *Economic Stabilization in Developing Countries*, Brookings Institution (Washington, 1981).

Cornia, Andrea, Richard Jolly, and Francis Stewart, eds. *Adjustment with a Human Face*, 2 vols., Oxford University Press (Oxford, 1987).

Cotés Conde, Roberto. "Growth and Stagnation in Argentina," in *Towards a Development Strategy for Latin America: Pathways from Hirschman's Thought*, ed. by Simón Teitel, Inter-American Bank (Washington, 1992).

David, Wilfrid L. *The IMF Policy Paradigm: The Macroeconomics of Stabilization, Structural Adjustment and Economic Development*, Praeger (New York, 1985).

De Vries, Rimmer. "The Limited Role of the IMF," *World Financial Markets*, Morgan Guarantee Trust Company, Apr. 1982.

Dell, Sidney. "The Question of Cross-Conditionality," *World Development*, Vol. 16, No. 5 (May 1988).

——. *On Being Grandmotherly: The Evolution of IMF Conditionality*, Essays in International Finance, No. 144, Princeton University Press (Princeton, New Jersey, 1981).

——. "Balance of Payments Adjustment in the 1980s," *World Development*, Vol. 14, No. 8, (Aug. 1986), pp. 873-1105.

Dell, Sidney, and Roger Lawrence. *The Balance of Payments Adjustment Process in Developing Countries*, Pergamon Press (New York, 1980).

Dornbusch, Rudiger. *Structural Adjustment in Latin America*, Woodrow Wilson Center (Washington, 1991).

Edwards, Sebastian. "The International Monetary Fund and the Developing Countries: A Critical Evaluation," *Carnegie-Rochester Conference Series on Public Policy*, Vol. 31 (Fall 1989), pp. 7-68.

Feinberg, Richard E. "The Changing Relationship Between the World Bank and the International Monetary Fund," *International Organization*, Vol. 42, No. 3 (Summer 1988), pp. 545-60.

Finch, David. *The Record and the Prospect*, Essays in International Finance, No. 175, Princeton University Press (Princeton, New Jersey, 1989).

———. "Let the IMF be the IMF," *The International Economy*, Jan./Feb. 1988.

Frenkel, Jeffrey A., and Harry G. Johnson, eds. *The Monetary Approach to the Balance of Payments*, Allen and Unwin (London, 1976).

Goode, Richard B. *Economic Assistance to Developing Countries Through the IMF*, Brookings Institution (Washington, D.C., 1985).

Gwin, Catherine. "Financing India's Adjustment: The Role of the Fund," in *IMF Conditionality*, ed. by John Williamson, Institute for International Economics (Washington, D.C., 1983).

Haggard, Stephan, Richard N. Cooper, and Chung-in-Moon. "Policy Reform in Korea," in *Political and Economic Interactions in Economic Policy Reform: Evidence from Eight Countries*, ed. by Robert H. Bates and Anne O. Krueger, Basil Blackwell (Oxford, 1993).

Hawkins, Jeffrey J. "Understanding the Failure of IMF Reform: The Zambian Case," *World Development*, Vol. 19, No. 7 (July 1991).

Herbst, Jeffrey. "The Structural Adjustment of Politics in Africa," *World Development*, Vol. 18, No. 7 (July 1990).

Johnson, Harry G. "Economic Policies for Less Developed Countries," in *International Monetary Reform*, Brookings Institution (Washington, D.C., 1967), pp. 212-36.

Kenen, Peter B. *Financing, Adjustment and the International Monetary Fund*, Brookings Institution, (Washington, D.C., 1986).

Killick, Tony. "Kenya, the IMF, and the Unsuccessful Quest for Stabilization." In *IMF Conditionality*, ed. by John Wiliamson, Institute for International Economics (Washington, D.C., 1983).

———. ed. *The Quest for Economic Stabilization: The IMF and the Third World*, St. Martin's Press (Washington, D.C., 1984).

Krueger, Anne O. *Liberalization Attempts and Consequences*, Ballinger for National Bureau of Economic Research (New York, 1978).

———. *Political Economy of Policy Reform in Developing Countries*, MIT Press (Cambridge, Massachusetts, 1993).

Lancaster, Carol. *African Economic Reform: The External Dimension*, Institute for International Economics (Washington, D.C., 1991).

Leith, J. Clark, and Michael F. Lofchie. "The Political Economy of Structural Adjustment in Ghana," in *Political and Economic Inter-*

actions in Economic Policy Reform: Evidence from Eight Countries, ed. by Robert H. Bates and Anne O. Krueger, Basil Blackwell (Oxford, 1993).

Levitt, Kari. "Stabilisation and Structural Adjustment: Rhetoric and Reality," *Caribbean Affairs,* Vol. 3, No. 1 (Jan./Mar. 1990).

Loxley, John. "Structural Adjustment in Africa: Reflections on Ghana and Zambia," *Review of African Political Economy,* No. 47 (Spring 1990).

Manzetti, Luigi. *The International Monetary Fund and Economic Stabilization: The Argentine Case,* Praeger (New York, 1991).

Matin, K. M. "Structural Adjustment Under the Extended Fund Facility: The Case of Bangladesh," *World Development,* Vol. 16, No. 6 (June 1990).

Mikesell, Raymand F. "Appraising IMF Conditionality: "Too Loose, Too Tight, or Just Right," in *IMF Conditionality,* ed. by John Williamson, Institute for International Economics (Washington, D.C., 1983).

Moore, Will H., and James R. Scarritt. "IMF Conditionality and Policy Characteristics in Black Africa: An Exploratory Analysis," *Africa Today,* Vol. 37 (4th quarter, 1990).

Myers, Robert J., ed. "The Political Morality of the International Monetary Fund," *Ethics and Foreign Policy,* Vol. 3, Transaction Books (New Brunswick, New Jersey, 1987).

Ncube, P. D., M. Sakala, and M. Ndulo. "The International Monetary Fund and the Zambian Economy: A Case," in *The IMF and the World Bank in Africa: Conditionality, Impact and Alternatives,* ed. by Kjell J. Havnevik, Scandinavian Institute of African Studies (Uppsala, 1987).

Nelson, Joan M., and contributors. *Fragile Conditions: The Politics of Economic Adjustment,* Transaction Books (New Brunswick, New Jersey, 1989).

Nelson, Joan M., ed. *Economic Crisis and Policy Choice: The Politics of Adjustment in Developing Countries,* Princeton University Press (Princeton, New Jersey, 1990).

Obstfeld, Maurice, and Kenneth Rogoffs. *Foundations of International Macroecomics,* MIT Press (Cambridge, Massachusetts, 1996).

Pauly, Lewis W. *Who Elected the Bankers? Surveillance and Control in the World Economy,* Cornell University Press (Ithaca, New York, 1997).

Plumptre, A. F. W. *Three Decades of Decision: Canada and the World Monetary System, 1944-75,* McClelland and Stewart (Toronto, 1977).

Pöhl, Karl Otto. "You Can't Robotize Policymaking," *The International Economy,* Oct./Nov. 1987.

Polak, Jacques J. *The Changing Nature of IMF Conditionality*, Essays in International Finance, No. 184, Princeton University Press (Princeton, New Jersey, 1991).

Sachs, Jeffrey D. "The Current Account and Macroeconomic Adjustment in the 1970s," *Brookings Papers on Economic Activity*, Brookings Institution (Washington, D.C., 1981).

Seddon, David. "The Politics of Adjustment: Egypt and the IMF, 1987-1990," *Review of African Political Economy*, No. 47 (Spring, 1990).

Sidell, Scott R. *The IMF and Third-World Political Instability: Is There a Connection?* St. Martin's Press (New York, 1988).

Spraos, John. *IMF Conditionality: Ineffectual, Inefficient, Mistargeted*, Essays in International Finance, No. 166, Princeton University Press (Princeton, New Jersey, 1986).

Taylor, Lance. *Varieties of Stabilization Experience: Towards Sensible Macroeconomics in the Third World*, prepared for the World Institute for Development Economic Research of the United Nations University, Clarendon Press (Oxford, 1988).

Thirwell, A. P. *Growth and Development, with Special Reference to Developing Economies*, Macmillan (Basingstoke, Hampshire, England, 1989).

Williamson, John. "On Judging the Success of IMF Policy Advice," in *IMF Conditionality*, ed. by Williamson, Institute for International Economics (Washington, D.C., 1984).

———. ed. *IMF Conditionality*, Institute for International Economics (Washington, D.C., 1983).

Wohlmuth, Karl, ed. *Structural Adjustment in the World Economy and East-West-South Economic Cooperation*, Institute for World Economics and International Management, University of Bremen (Bremen, Germany, 1989).

Wulf, Jürgen. "Zambia Under the IMF Regime," *African Affairs*, Vol. 87 (Oct. 1988).

Exchange Rate Systems and Markets

Approaches to Greater Flexibility of Exchange Rates: The Bürgenstock Papers, arranged by C. Fred Bergsten, George N. Halm, Fritz Machlup, and Robert V. Roosa, and edited by George N. Halm, Princeton University Press (Princeton, New Jersey, 1970).

Artus, Jacques R., and Andrew D. Crockett. *Floating Exchange Rates and the Need for Surveillance*, Essays in International Finance, No. 127, Princeton University Press (Princeton, New Jersey, 1978).

Balassa, Bela. "The Purchasing-Power Parity Doctrine: A Reappraisal," *Journal of Political Economy*, Vol. 72 (Dec. 1964).

Balassa, Bela, and John Williamson. *Adjusting to Success: Balance of Payments Policy in the East Asian NICs*, Institute for International Economics (Washington, D.C., 1987).

Branson, William H., Jacob A. Frenkel, and Morris Goldstein, eds. *International Policy Coordination and Exchange Rate Fluctuations*, University of Chicago Press (Chicago, 1990).

Bürgenstock Papers. See *Approaches to Greater Flexibility of Exchange Rates*.

Catte, Pietro Giampaulo Gali, and Salvatore Rebecchini. "Concerted Interventions and the Dollar: An Analysis of Daily Data," in *The International Monetary System*, ed. by Peter Kenen, Cambridge University Press (Cambridge, 1994).

Cooper, Richard N., et al. *The International Monetary System Under Flexible Exchange Rates, Global, Regional, and National: Essays in Honor of Robert Triffin*, Ballinger (Cambridge, Massachusetts, 1982).

Council on [U.S.] Foreign Relations. *Smithsonian Agreement and Its Aftermath: Several Views*, The Council (New York, 1972).

De Grauwe, Paul, Hans Dewachter, and Marc Embrechts. *Exchange Rate Theory: Chaotic Models of Foreign Exchange Markets*, Basil Blackwell (Oxford, 1993).

Destler, I. M., and C. Randall Henning. *Dollar Politics: Exchange Rate Policymaking in the United States*, Institute for International Economics (Washington, D.C., 1989).

Dominguez, Kathryn, and Jeffrey A. Frankel. *Does Foreign Exchange Intervention Work?* Institute for International Economics (Washington, D.C., 1993).

Edwards, Sebastian. *Real Exchange Rates, Devaluation and Adjustment: Exchange Rate Policy in Developing Countries*, MIT Press (Cambridge, Massachusetts, 1989).

Funabashi, Yoichi. *Managing the Dollar: From the Plaza to the Louvre, 2nd ed.* Institute for International Economics (Washington, D.C., 1989).

Kenen, Peter B. *EMU After Maastricht*, Group of Thirty (Washington, D.C., 1992). *Managing Exchange Rates*, Routledge (London, 1988).

——. "The Coordination of Macroeconomic Policies," in *International Policy Coordination and Exchange Rate Fluctuations*, ed. by William Branson, Jacob A. Frenkel, and Morris Goldstein, University of Chicago Press (Chicago, 1990).

League of Nations. *International Currency Experience: Lessons of the Inter-War Period*, League of Nations (Geneva, 1944).

——. *Report on Exchange Control*, League of Nations (Geneva, 1938).

Mikesell, Raymond F. *Foreign Exchange in the Post-War World*, 20th Century (New York, 1954).

Pauls, B. Dianne. "U.S. Exchange Rate Policy: Bretton Woods to Present," *Federal Reserve Bulletin*, Board of Governors of the Federal Reserve System, Vol. 76, No. 11 (November 1990).

Ungerer, Horst. *A Concise History of European Monetary Integration: From EPU to EMU*, Quorum Books (Westport, Connecticut, 1997).

Williamson, John. *The Crawling Peg*, Essays in Internatiional Finance, No. 50, Princeton University Press (Princeton, New Jersey, 1965).

Williamson, John. *Currency Convertibility in Eastern Europe*, Institute for International Economics (Washington, D.C., 1991).

——. *The Exchange Rate System*, Institute for International Economics (Washington, D.C., 1983; 2nd ed. 1985).

Williamson, John, and Marcus H. Miller. *Targets and Iindicators: A Blueprint for International Coordination of Economic Policy*, Institute for International Economics (Washington, D.C., 1987).

International Currencies, Liquidity, and the SDR

Balogh, Thomas. *The Dollar Crisis: Causes and Cure, A Report to the Fabian Society*, Basil Blackwell (Oxford, 1949).

Bell, Geoffrey. *The Euro-Dollar Market and the International Financial System*, Wiley (New York, 1973).

Bergsten, C. Fred. *The Dilemmas of the Dollar: The Economics and Politics of United States International Monetary Policy*, New York University Press (New York, 1975).

Bernstein, Edward M. "The Dollar Is the Problem of the International Monetary System," *Quarterly Review and Investment Survey*, Model, Roland & Co. (New York, Second Quarter, 1971).

——. "Further Evolution of the International Monetary System," *Moorgate and Wall Street* (London, Summer 1965).

——. "A Practical Program for International Monetary Reserves," *Quarterly Review and Investment Survey*, Model, Roland & Co. (New York, Fourth Quarter, 1963).

——. "Statement: The Problem of International Monetary Reserves," in *International Payments Imbalances and Need for Strengthening International Financial Arrangements*, U.S. Congress, Joint Economic Committee, Hearings Before the Subcommittee on International Exchange and Payments, 87th Cong., 1st sess., May 16-June 21, 1961 (Washington, 1961).

——. "The U.S. Balance of Payments and International Liquidity" (June 18, 1965), "Changes in the International Monetary System" (Oct. 27, 1964), "Two Reports on International Liquidity" (Aug. 19, 1964), and "The Underdeveloped Countries and Monetary Reserves" (Mar. 24, 1965), in *Guidelines for International Monetary Reform*, U.S. Congress, Joint Economic Committee, Hearings Before the Subcommittee on International Exchange and Payments, 89th Cong., 1st sess., Part 2, Supplement (Washington, D.C., 1965).

Bolton, Sir George. "Background and Emergence of the Eurodollar Market," in *The Eurodollar*, ed. By Herbert V, Prochnow, Rand McNally (Chicago, 1970).

Cairncross, Alec, and Barry Eichengreen. *Sterling in Decline: The Devaluations of 1931, 1949, and 1976*, Basil Blackwell (Oxford, 1983).

Chrystal, K. Alec. *International Money and the Future of the SDR*, Essays in International Finance, No. 128, Princeton University Press (Princeton, New Jersey, 1978).

Coats, Warren L. "Enhancing the Attractiveness of the SDR," *World Development*, Vol. 18, No. 7 (July 1990).

Despres, Emile, Charles Kindleberger, and Walter S. Salant. "The Dollar and World Liquidity: A Minority View," *Economist*, Feb. 11, 1966.

Feaveryear, Sir Albert. *The Pound Sterling: A History of English Money*, 2nd ed. Oxford University Press (Oxford, 1963).

Goodhart, Charles A. E. "Monetary Policy in the United Kingdom," in *Monetary Policy in Twelve Industrial Countries*, ed. Karel Holbik, Federal Reserve Bank of Boston (Boston 1973).

Haberler, Gottfried. "How Important Is Control over International Reserves?" (1977) in *Selected Essays of Gottfried Haberler*, ed. by Anthony Y. C. Koo, MIT Press (Cambridge, Massachusetts, 1985).

Harrod, R. F. *Reforming the World's Money*, Macmillan (London, 1965).

Hirsch, Fred. *The Pound Sterling: A Polemic*, Victor Gallancz (London, 1965).

Hoffmeyer, Erik. *Dollar Shortage and the Structure of U.S. Foreign Trade*, Ejnar Munksguard (Copenhagen, 1958).

Kindelberger, Charles P. *The Dollar Shortage*, MIT Press (Cambridge, Massachusetts, 1950).

———. "The Price of Gold and the N-1 Problem," in Kindleberger, *International Money: A Collection of Essays*, Allen and Unwin (London, 1981).

———. "International Monetary Stabilization," in *Postwar Economic Problems*, ed. by S. E. Harris, McGraw-Hill (New York, 1943).

Park, Y. S. *The Link Between Special Drawing Rights and Development Finance*, Essays in International Finance, No. 100, Princeton University Press (Princeton, New Jersey, 1973).

Patel, I. G. *The Link Between the Creation of International Liquidity and the Provision of Development Finance,* United Nations Conference on Trade and Development (Geneva, 1967).

Polk, Judd. *Sterling: Its Meaning in World Finance,* Harper (New York, 1956).

Strange, Susan. *Sterling and British Policy: A Political Study of an International Currency in Decline,* Oxford University Press (Oxford, 1971).

Swoboda, Alexander K. *The Euro-Dollar Market: An Interpretation,* Essays in International Finance, No. 64, Princeton University Press (Princeton, New Jersey, 1968).

Tavlas, George S. *On the International Use of Currencies: The Case of the Deutschemark,* Essays in International Finance No. 181, Princeton University Press (Princeton, New Jersey, 1991).

Triffin, Robert. *Gold and the Dollar Crisis: The Future of Convertibility,* Yale University Press (New Haven, Connecticut, 1960).

——. *Gold and the Dollar Crisis: Yesterday and Tomorrow,* Essays in International Finance, No. 132, Princeton University Press (Princeton, New Jersey, 1961).

——. "The Return to Convertibility: 1926-1931 and 1958- ? or, Convertibility and the Morning After," *Quarterly Review,* Banca Nazionale del Lavoro (Rome), Mar. 1959.

——. "Tomorrow's Convertibility: Aims and Means of International Monetary Policy," *Quarterly Review,* Banca Nazionale del Lavoro (Rome), June 1959.

——. *The World Money Maze: National Currencies in International Payments,* Yale University Press (New Haven, Connecticut, and London, 1966).

Walters, Alan. *Sterling in Danger: The Economic Consequences of Pegged Exchange Rates,* Fontana (London, 1990).

Williams, David. "The Evolution of the Sterling System," in *Essays in Money and Banking in Honour of R.S. Sayers,* ed. by C. R. Whittlesay and J. S. G. Wilson, Clarendon Press (Oxford, 1968).

Williamson, John. *A New SDR Allocation,* Institute for International Economics (Washington, D.C., 1984).

International Trade and Payments

Bacha, Edmar Lisboa, and Carlos F. Díaz-Alejandro. "Tropical Reflections on the History and Theory of International Financial Markets," in *For Good or Evil: Economic Theory and North-South Negotiations,* ed. Gerald K. Helleiner, University Press of Toronto, (Toronto, 1982).

Bergsten, C. Fred. *America in the World Economy: A Strategy for the 1990s.* Institute for International Economics (Washington, D.C., 1988).

——. "Economic Imbalances and World Politics," *Foreign Affairs,* Vol. 65, No. 4 (Spring 1987)

Bhagwati, Jagdish N. "Export Market Disruption, Compensation and GATT Reform," in *The New International Economic Order: The North-South Debate,* ed. by Bhagwati, MIT Press (Cambridge, Massachusetts, 1977).

——. *Anatomy and Consequence of Exchange Control Regimes,* Ballinger for National Bureau for Economic Research (New York, 1978).

Bruno, Michael. "Inflation and Growth in Recent History and Policy: Applications of an Integrated Approach," in *Understanding Interdependence: The Macroeconomics of the Open Economy,* ed. by Peter Kenen, Princeton University Press (Princeton, 1995).

Bryant, Ralph C., *International Financial Intermediation,* Brookings Institution (Washington, D.C., 1987).

Bryant, Ralph C. et al., eds. *Macroeconomic Policies in an Interdepedent World,* Brookings Institution (Washington, D.C., 1989).

Coombs, Charles A. *The Arena of International Finance,* Wiley (New York, 1976).

Cooper, Richard N. et al. *Can Nations Agree? Issues in International Economic Cooperation,* Brookings Institution (Washington, D.C., 1989).

Crockett, Andrew. *International Money: Issues and Analysis,* Nelson (Sunbury-on-Thames, Surrey, England, 1977).

——. "Strengthening International Economic Cooperation: The Role of Indicators in Multilateral Surveillance," in the *The Quest for National and Global Economic Stabillity,* ed. by Wietze Eizenga, E. Frans Limburg, and Jacques J. Polak, Kluwer (Dordrecht, 1988).

Day, C. C. L. "The World's Payments System," in *International Payments Imbalances and Need for Strengthening International Financial Arrangements,* U.S. Congress, Joint Economic Committee, Hearings Before the Subcommittee on International Exchange and Payments, 87th Cong., 1st sess., May 16-June 21, 1961 (Washington, D.C., 1961).

Diaz-Alejandro, Carlos. "Some Economic Lessons of the Early 1980s," in *Power, Passion, and Purpose: Prospects for North South Negotiations,* ed. by Jagdish N. Bhagwati and John Ruggie, MIT Press (Cambridge, Massachusetts, 1984).

Dobson, Wendy. *Economic Policy Coordination: Requiem or Prologue?* Institute for International Economics (Washington, D.C., 1991).

Dornbusch, Rudiger. "Discussion," in Federal Reserve Bank of Boston, *Key Issues in International Banking,* Federal Reserve Bank of Boston (Boston 1977).

Ellis, Howard S. *Bilateralism and the Future of International Trade,* Essays in International Finance, No. 5, Princeton University Press (Princeton, New Jersey, 1945).

Feldstein, Martin, ed. *International Economic Cooperation,* Chicago University Press (Chicago, 1988).

Fellner, William, et al. *Maintaining and Restoring Balance in International Payments,* Princeton University Press (Princeton, New Jersey, 1966).

Fleming, J. Marcus. *Essays in International Economics,* Allen and Unwin (London, 1971).

Frankel, Jeffrey A., and Kathrine C. Rockett. "International Macroeconomic Policy Coordination When Policymakers Do Not Agree on the True Model," *American Economic Review,* Vol. 78 (June 1988).

Ghai, Dharam, ed. *The IMF and the South: The Social Impact of Crisis and Adjustment,* Zed Books (London, 1991).

Gilbert, Milton. *Quest for World Monetary Order: The Gold-Dollar System and Its Aftermath,* Wiley (New York, 1980).

Gwin, Catherine, and Richard E. Feinberg, eds. *Pulling Together: The International Monetary Fund in a Multipolar World,* Transaction Books (New Brunswick, New Jersey, 1989).

Hewitt, Adrian P. "Stabex and Commodity Export Compensation Schemes: Prospects for Globalization," *World Development,* Vol. 15, No. 5 (May 1987).

Hoffmeyer, Erik. *The International Monetary System: As Essay in Interpretation,* North Holland (Amsterdam, 1992).

Jacobson, Harold Karan, and Michel Oksenberg. *China's Participation in the IMF, the World Bank and GATT: Toward a Global Economic Order,* University of Michigan Press (Ann Arbor, Michigan, 1990).

Johnson, Harry G. *Money, Balance of Payments Theory, and the International Monetary Problem,* Essays in International Finance, No. 124, Princeton University Press (Princeton, New Jersey, 1977).

Karns, Margaret P., and Karen A. Mingst, eds. *The United States and Multilateral Institutions: Patterns of Changing Instrumentality and Influence,* Unwin Hyman (Boston, Massachusetts, 1990).

Kenen, Peter B. "Capital Controls, the EMS and EMU," *Economic Journal,* Vol. 105 (Jan., 1995).

Kindelberger, Charles P. *International Money: A Collection of Essays,* Allen & Unwin (London and Boston, Massachusetts, 1981).

Lim, David. *Export Instability and Compensatory Financing*, Routledge (New York, 1991).

Meade, J. E. "International Economics," in the *Collected Papers of James Meade*, Vol. IV, ed. by Susan Howson, Allen & Unwin (London, 1988).

Meier, Gerald M. *Problems of a World Monetary Order*, Oxford University Press (New York, 1982).

Mossé, Robert. *Les Problèmes monétaires internationaux*, Payot (Paris, 1967).

Mundell, Robert A., and Alexander K. Swoboda, eds., *Monetary Problems of the International Economy*, University of Chicago Press (Chicago, 1969).

Mundell, Robert. "A Theory of Optimal Currency Areas," *American Economic Review*, Vol. 51 (Sep. 1961).

Patterson, Gardner. *Discrimination in International Trade: The Policy Issues, 1945-1965*, Princeton University Press (Princeton, New Jersey, 1966).

Penrose, Edith. "The Development of Crisis," in *The Oil Crisis*, ed. by Raymond Vernon, W. W. Norton (New York, 1976).

Polak, Jacques J. *Financial Policies and Development*, Development Centre of the Organisation for Economic Co-operation and Development (Paris, 1989).

Polk, Judd, and Gardner Patterson. "The Emerging Pattern of Bilateralism," *Quarterly Journal of Economics*, Vol. 62 (1947-48).

Fried, Edward R., and Philip H. Trezise. *The Third World Debt: The Next Phase*, Brookings Institution (Washington, D.C.,1989).

Scammell, William McConnell. *The Stability of the International Monetary System*, Macmillan (Basingstoke, Hampshire, England, 1987).

Shonfield, Andrew, ed. *International Economic Relations of the Western World, 1959-1971*, 2 vols., Oxford University Press for the Royal Institute of International Affairs (London and New York, 1976).

Soloman, Robert. *The International Monetary System, 1945-1981*, Harper & Row (New York, 1982).

U.S. Commission on International Trade and Investment Policy, *United States International Economic Policy in an Interdependent World: Report to the President* (Washington, D.C., 1971).

U.S. Congress, Joint Economic Committee. "Action Now to Strengthen the U.S. Dollar," *Report of the Subcommittee on International Exchange and Payments*, 92d Cong., 1st sess., (Washington, D.C., 1971).

Van Meerhaeghe, M. A. G. *International Economic Institutions*, Longman (London, 1971).

Volker, Paul A., and Toyoo Gyohten. *Changing Fortunes: The World's Money and the Decline of American Supremacy,* Times Books (New York, 1992).

Williamson, John. *The Economic Opening of Eastern Europe,* Institute for International Economics (Washington, D.C., 1991).

[Radcliffe] Committee on the Working of the Monetary System, *Report,* Cmnd. 827, HMSO (London, 1959).

International Debt Problems

Aspe Armello, Pedro. "The Renegotiation of Mexico's External Debt," Institute of Development Studies, *IDS Bulletin,* Vol. 21, No. 2 (1990).

——. *Economic Transformation: The Mexican Way,* MIT Press (Cambridge, Massachusetts, 1993).

Aubon, Roger. *The Bank for International Settlements, 1930-1955,* Essays in International Finance No. 22, Princeton University Press (Princeton, New Jersey, 1955).

Avery, William P. "Origins of Debt Accumulation Among LDCs in the World Political Economy," *Journal of Developing Areas,* Vol. 24 (July 1990).

Bird, Graham, ed. *Third World Debt: The Search for a Solution,* E. Elgar (Aldershot, Hampshire, England, 1989).

Grown, Richard P. C. *Public Debt and Private Wealth: Debt, Capital Flight and the IMF in Sudan,* Macmillan (London, 1992).

Clark, John, and Caroline Allison. *Zambia: Debt & Poverty,* Oxfam (Oxford, 1989).

Claudon, Michael P., ed. *World Debt Crisis: International Lending on Trial,* Ballinger (Cambridge, Massachusetts, 1986).

Cline, William R. "International Debt: Analysis, Experience and Prospects," *Journal of Development Planning,* No. 16 (1985).

——. "The Baker Plan and Brady Reformulation: An Evaluation," in *Dealing with the Debt Crisis,* ed. by Ishrat Husain and Ishac Diwan, World Bank (Washington, D.C., 1989).

Cohen, Benjamin J. *Developing-Country Debt: A Middle Way,* Essays in International Finance, No. 173, Princeton University Press (Princeton, New Jersey, 1989).

Commonwealth Secretariat. *The Debt Crisis and the World Economy: Report by a Commonwealth Group of Experts,* Commonwealth Secretariat (London, 1984).

Congdon, Tim. *The Debt Threat: The Dangers of High Real Interest Rates for the World Economy,* Basil Blackwell (Oxford, 1988).

Conway, Patrick. "Baker Plan and International Indebtedness," *World Economy,* Vol. 10, No. 2 (June 1987).

Diaz-Alejandro, Carlos F. *Some Aspects of the 1982-83 Brazilian Payments Crisis*, Brookings Papers on Economic Activity, No. 2, Brookings Institution (Washington, D.C., 1983).

——. *Exchange-Rate Devaluation in a Semi-Industrialized Country: The Experience of Argentina 1955–1961*, MIT Press (Cambridge, Massachusetts, 1965).

Dornbusch, Rudiger. "Overborrowing: Three Case Studies," in *Dollars, Debts and Deficits*, by Dornbusch, MIT Press and Leuven University Press (Cambridge, Massachusetts, and Leuven, Belgium, 1986).

——. Mexico: Stabilization, Debt and Growth," *Economic Policy*, No. 7 (October 1988).

——. "The World Debt Problem: 1980-84 and Beyond," in Dornbusch, *Dollars, Debts and Deficits*, MIT Press and Leuven University Press (Cambridge, Massachusetts and Leuven, Belgium, 1986).

Felix, David. "Latin America's Debt Crisis," *World Policy Journal*, Vol. 7, No. 4 (Fall 1990).

Fried, Edward R., and Charles L. Shultze, *Higher Oil Prices and the World Economy: The Adjustment Problem*, Brookings Institution (Washington, D.C., 1975).

George, Susan. *A Fate Worse Than Debt*, Penguin Books (London, 1988).

Ghosh, Jayati. "Foreign Debt and Economic Development: The Case of Zaire," *Development and Change*, Vol. 17 (1986).

Griffith-Jones, Stephany, ed. *Managing World Debt*, Harvester-Wheatsheaf (Hemel Hempstead, Hertfordshire, England, 1988) and St. Martin's Press (New York, 1988).

Helleiner, Gerald K. "International Policy Issues Posed by Sub-Saharan African Debt," *World Economy*, Vol. 12, No. 3 (Sept. 1989).

Kenen, Peter B. "Organizing Debt Relief: The Need for a New Institution," *Jounal of Economic Perspectives*, Vol. 4 (Winter 1990).

Knox, David. *Latin American Debt: Facing Facts*, Oxford International Institute (Oxford, 1990).

Kraft, Joseph. *The Mexican Rescue, Group of Thirty* (New York, 1984).

Lancaster, Carol, and John Williamson, eds. *African Debt and Financing*, Institute for International Economics (Washington, D.C., 1986).

Lissakers, Karin. *Banks, Borrowers, and the Establishment: A Revisionist Account of the International Debt Crisis*, Basic Books (New York, 1991).

Lomax, David F. *The Developing Country Debt Crisis*, St. Martin's Press (New York, 1986).

Lustig, Nora. *Mexico, The Remaking of an Economy,* Brookings Institution (Washington, D.C., 1992).

MacDonald, Scott B., Margie Lindsay, and David Crum. *The Global Debt Crisis: Forecasting for the Future,* Pinter (London and New York, 1990).

Miller, Morris. *Coping Is Not Enough! The International Debt Crisis and the Roles of the World Bank and International Monetary Fund,* Dow Jones-Irwin (Homewood, Illinois, 1986).

Nafziger, E. Wayne. *The Debt Crisis in Africa,* Johns Hopkins University Press (Baltimore, 1993).

Onimode, Bade, ed. *The IMF, the World Bank and African Debt,* 2 vols., Zed Books (London and Atlantic Highlands, New Jersey, 1989) .

Parfitt, Trevor W., and Stephen P. Riley. *The African Debt Crisis,* Routledge (London, 1989).

Rieffel, Alexis. *The Role of the Paris Club in Managing Debt Problems,* Essays in International Finance, No. 161, Princeton University Press (Princeton, New Jersey, 1985).

Rieke, Wolfgang. "The Development of the Deutschemark as a Reserve Currency, in *Reserve Currencies in Transition,* Group of Thirty (New York, 1982).

Roll, Eric. "Behind Bretton Woods: The Climate Then and Today," in *International Capital Movements, Debt and Monetary System,* ed. by Wolfram Engels, Armin Gutowski, and Heny C. Wallich, v. Hase & Koehler (Mainz, 1984).

Sampson, Anthony. *The Money Lenders: Bankers in a Dangerous World,* Hodder & Stoughton (London, 1988).

Singer, H. W., and Soumitra Sharma, eds. *Economic Development and World Debt,* Macmillan (London, 1989).

Stiles, Kendall Wayne. *Negotiating Debt: The IMF Lending Process,* Westview Press (Boston, Massachusetts, 1991).

World Institute for Development Economics Research. *Debt Reduction: Report of a Study Group of the World Institute for Development Economics Research,* World Institute for Development Economics Research of the United Nations University, Study Group Series, No. 3 (Helsinki, 1989).

Reform of the International Monetary System

Bhagwati, Jagdish N., ed. *The New International Economic Order: The North-South Debate,* MIT Press (Cambridge, Massachusetts, 1977).

Bird, Graham. *World Finance and Adjustment: An Agenda for Reform,* Macmillan (London, 1985).

Bretton Woods Commission. "Commission Report," in *Bretton Woods: Looking to the Future,* Bretton Woods Committee (Washington, D.C., 1994).

Cline, William R. *International Monetary Reform and the Developing Countries,* Brookings Institution (Washington, D.C., 1976).

Cooper, Richard N. "A Monetary System for the Future," *Foreign Affairs,* Vol. 63, No. 1 (Fall 1984).

———. "What Future for the International Monetary System?" in *International Financial Policy: Essays in Honor of Jacques J. Polak,* ed. by Jacob A. Frenkel and Morris Goldstein, International Monetary Fund and De Nederlandsche Bank (Washington, D.C., 1991).

———. The Evolution of the International Monetary Fund Toward a World Central Bank," in *The International Monetary System: Essays in World Economics,* ed. by Cooper, MIT Presss (Cambridge, Massachusetts, 1987, originally published in 1983).

———. *The International Monetary System*: Essays in World Economics, MIT Press (Cambridge, Massachusetts, 1987).

Crockett, Andrew. "The International Monetary Fund in the 1990s," *Government and Opposition,* Vol. 27, No. 3 (1992).

Dam, Kenneth W. *The Rules of the Game: Reform and Evolution in the International Monetary System,* University of Chicago Press (Chicago, 1982).

de Grauwe, Paul. *International Money: Post-War Trends and Theories,* Clarendon Press (Oxford, 1989).

de Vries, Tom. "Jamaica, or the Non-reform of the International Monetary System," *Foreign Affairs,* Vol. 54, No. 3 (April 1976).

Dell, Sydney, ed. *The International Monetary System and Its Reform: Papers Prepared for the Group of Twenty-four by a United Nations Project directed by Sidney Dell,* North Holland (New York, 1987).

Dornbusch, Rudiger. *Economic Performance,* Vol. 1, *The International Financial System,* ed. by Jeffrey D. Sachs, University of Chicago Press (Chicago, 1989).

Edwards, Richard W. *International Monetary Collaboration,* Transnational Publishers (Dobbs Ferry, New York, 1985).

Expert Group on International Monetary Issues (UNCTAD). *International Monetary Issues and the Developing Countries,* UN document TD/B/32 and TD/B/C. 3/6 (New York, 1965).

Friedman, Irving S. *Toward World Prosperity: Reshaping the Global Money System,* Lexington Books (Lexington, Massachusetts, 1986).

German Council of Economic Experts. *Toward a New Basis for International Monetary Policy,* Princeton Essays in International Finance, No. 31, Princeton University Press (Princeton, New Jersey, 1972).

Gowa, Joanne S. "Hegemons, IOs, and Markets: The Case of the Sub-
stitution Account," *International Organization*, Vol. 38, No. 4
(Autumn 1984).
———. *Closing the Gold Window: Domestic Politics and the End of
Bretton Woods*, Cornell University Press (Ithaca, New York,
1983).
Group of Thirty. *Towards a Less Unstable International Monetary Sys-
tem: Reserve Assets and a Substitution Account*, Reserve Asset
Study Group, Group of Thirty (New York, 1980).
Grubel, George N. *Jamaica and the Par-Value System*, Essays in Inter-
national Finance, No. 20, Princeton University Press (Princeton,
New Jersey, 1977).
Grubel, Herbert G. *The International Monetary System: Efficiency and
Practical Alternatives*, Penguin Books (Harmondsworth, Greater
London, England, 1984).
———. ed. *World Monetary Reform: Plans and Issues*, Stanford Univer-
sity Press (Stanford, California, 1963).
Hamouda, Omar F., Robin Rowley, and Bernard M. Wolf, eds. *The
Future of the International Monetary System: Change, Coordina-
tion or Instability?* E. Elgar (Aldershot, Hampshire, England,
1989).
Houthakker, Hendrik S. "The Breakdown of Bretton Woods," in *Eco-
nomic Advice and Executive Policy: Recommendations from Past
Members of the Council of Economic Advisers*, ed. by Werner Si-
chel, Praeger (New York, 1978).
Independent Commission on International Development Issues. *North-
South: A Programme for Survival; A Report of the Independent
Commission on International Development Issues Under the
Chairmanship of Willy Brandt*, MIT Press (Cambridge, Massachu-
setts, 1980).
International Institute of International Finance. *Financial Crises in
Emerging Markets*, by a working goup chaired by William Cline
(Washington D.C., 1999).
Khatkhate, Deena, ed. "The Evolving International Monetary System,"
World Development, Vol. 15, No. 12 (Dec. 1987).
Machlup, Fritz. *Plans for Reform of the International Monetary Sys-
tem*, Special Papers in International Economics, No. 3, Princeton
University Press (Princeton, New Jersey, 1962 and 1964).
———. *Remaking the International Monetary System: The Rio Agree-
ment and Beyond*, Committee for Economic Development, Sup-
plementary Paper, No. 24, Johns Hopkins Press (Baltimore, 1968).
Machlup, Fritz, and Burton G. Malkiel, eds. *International Monetary
Arrangements: The Problem of Choice*, Study Group of 32
Economists (Princeton, New Jersey, 1964).

McKinnon, Ronald I. *An International Standard for Monetary Stabilization*, Institute for International Economics (Washington, D.C., 1984).

——. "The Rules of the Game: International Money in Historical Perspective," *Journal of Economic Literature*, Vol. 31 (March 1993).

Mozhin, Alexei V. "Russia's Negotiations with the IMF," in *Changing the Economic System in Russia*, ed. by Anders Åslund and Richard Layard, Pinter Publishers (London, 1993).

Mundell, Robert A., and Jacques J. Polak, eds. *The New International Monetary System*, Columbia University Press (New York, 1977).

Narasimham, M. *Bretton Woods—Forty Years On*, Forum of Free Enterprise (Bombay, 1984).

Ossola, Rinaldo. *Towards New Monetary Relationships*, Essays in International Finance, No. 87, Princeton University Press (Princeton, New Jersey, 1971).

Palyi, Melchior. *Managed Money at the Crossroads: The European Experience*, University of Notre Dame Press (Notre Dame, Indiana, 1958).

Polak, Jacques. J. *The World Bank and the International Monetary Fund: A Changing Relationship*, Brookings Institution (Washington, D.C., 1994).

Putnam, Robert D., and Nicholas Bayne. *Hanging Together: The Seven-Power Summits*, Harvard University Press (Cambridge, Massachusetts, 1984).

Rasminski, Louis. "Canadian Views," in *Bretton Woods Revisited*, ed. by A. L. K. Acheson, J. F. Chant, and M. F. J. Prachowny, University of Toronto Press (Toronto, 1972).

Roosa, Robert V. *Monetary Reform for the World Economy*, The Elihu Root Lectures, 1964-65 (New York, 1965).

Soloman, Robert. "International Monetary Reform: The Future Is Not What It Used To Be!" in *The Future of the International Monetary System: Change, Coordination or Instability*, ed. by Omar F. Hamouda, Robin Rowley, and Bernard M. Wolf, M. E. Sharpe (Armonk, New York, 1989).

Soros, George. *The Crisis of Global Capitalism*, American Public Affairs (Washington D.C., 1998).

Suzuki, Yoshio, Junichi Miyake, and Mitsuaki Okabe, eds. *The Evolution of the International Monetary System: How Can Efficiency and Stability Be Maintained?* University of Tokyo Press (Tokyo, 1990).

Tinbergen, Jan. *Reshaping the International Order: A Report to the Club of Rome*, E. P. Dutton (New York, 1976).

Triffin, Robert. "The European Monetary System: Tombstone or Cornerstone," in Federal Reserve Bank of Boston, *The International*

Monetary System: Forty Years After Bretton Woods, Conference Series, No. 28, Federal Bank of Boston (Boston, 1984).

Tsoukalis, Loukas, ed., *The Political Economy of International Money: In Search of a New Order,* Royal Institute of International Affairs, Sage Publications (London, 1985).

United Nations Conference on Trade and Development (UNCTAD). *Compendium of Selected Studies on International Monetary and Financial Issues for the Developing Countries,* United Nations (New York, 1987).

[U.S.] Federal Reserve Bank of Boston. *The International Monetary System: Forty Years After Bretton Woods.* Proceedings of a Conference Sponsored by the Federal Reserve Bank of Boston in May 1984, Conference Series, No. 28 (Boston, 1984).

Williamson, John. *The Failure of World Monetary Reform, 1971-74,* New York University Press (New York, 1977).

About the Author

Norman K. Humphreys was a member of the staff of the International Monetary Fund, holding the post of Chief Editor for 14 years before retiring in 1986. Born in the United Kingdom, he graduated from the London School of Economic and Political Science with a B.Sc. (Econ.), specializing in Banking and Currency. For many years he worked in the City of London as an economist in the Research Department of an international bank, and for two years was the resident economist for that bank in Brazil. While in Brazil, he was the Rio de Janeiro correspondent of the London *Financial Times*. He has contributed articles to a number of financial journals and newspapers. He moved to Washington, D.C., in 1963, first joining the staff of the World Bank and then the staff of the International Monetary Fund, where he had overall responsibility for the Fund's extensive publications program.